2596B: Managing Microsoft® Systems Management Server 2003

Course Number: 2596B
Part Number: X10-75758
Released: 07/2004

END-USER LICENSE AGREEMENT FOR OFFICIAL MICROSOFT LEARNING PRODUCTS – STUDENT EDITION

PLEASE READ THIS END-USER LICENSE AGREEMENT ("EULA") CAREFULLY. BY USING THE MATERIALS AND/OR USING OR INSTALLING THE SOFTWARE THAT ACCOMPANIES THIS EULA (COLLECTIVELY, THE "LICENSED CONTENT"), YOU AGREE TO THE TERMS OF THIS EULA. IF YOU DO NOT AGREE, DO NOT USE THE LICENSED CONTENT.

1.   **GENERAL.** This EULA is a legal agreement between you (either an individual or a single entity) and Microsoft Corporation ("Microsoft"). This EULA governs the Licensed Content, which includes computer software (including online and electronic documentation), training materials, and any other associated media and printed materials. This EULA applies to updates, supplements, add-on components, and Internet-based services components of the Licensed Content that Microsoft may provide or make available to you unless Microsoft provides other terms with the update, supplement, add-on component, or Internet-based services component. Microsoft reserves the right to discontinue any Internet-based services provided to you or made available to you through the use of the Licensed Content. This EULA also governs any product support services relating to the Licensed Content except as may be included in another agreement between you and Microsoft. An amendment or addendum to this EULA may accompany the Licensed Content.

2.   **GENERAL GRANT OF LICENSE.** Microsoft grants you the following rights, conditioned on your compliance with all the terms and conditions of this EULA. Microsoft grants you a limited, non-exclusive, royalty-free license to install and use the Licensed Content solely in conjunction with your participation as a student in an Authorized Training Session (as defined below). You may install and use one copy of the software on a single computer, device, workstation, terminal, or other digital electronic or analog device ("Device"). You may make a second copy of the software and install it on a portable Device for the exclusive use of the person who is the primary user of the first copy of the software. A license for the software may not be shared for use by multiple end users. An "Authorized Training Session" means a training session conducted at a Microsoft Certified Technical Education Center, an IT Academy, via a Microsoft Certified Partner, or such other entity as Microsoft may designate from time to time in writing, by a Microsoft Certified Trainer (for more information on these entities, please visit www.microsoft.com). WITHOUT LIMITING THE FOREGOING, COPYING OR REPRODUCTION OF THE LICENSED CONTENT TO ANY SERVER OR LOCATION FOR FURTHER REPRODUCTION OR REDISTRIBUTION IS EXPRESSLY PROHIBITED.

3.   **DESCRIPTION OF OTHER RIGHTS AND LICENSE LIMITATIONS**

    3.1   *Use of Documentation and Printed Training Materials.*

        3.1.1   The documents and related graphics included in the Licensed Content may include technical inaccuracies or typographical errors. Changes are periodically made to the content. Microsoft may make improvements and/or changes in any of the components of the Licensed Content at any time without notice. The names of companies, products, people, characters and/or data mentioned in the Licensed Content may be fictitious and are in no way intended to represent any real individual, company, product or event, unless otherwise noted.

        3.1.2   Microsoft grants you the right to reproduce portions of documents (such as student workbooks, white papers, press releases, datasheets and FAQs) (the "Documents") provided with the Licensed Content. You may not print any book (either electronic or print version) in its entirety. If you choose to reproduce Documents, you agree that: (a) use of such printed Documents will be solely in conjunction with your personal training use; (b) the Documents will not republished or posted on any network computer or broadcast in any media; (c) any reproduction will include either the Document's original copyright notice or a copyright notice to Microsoft's benefit substantially in the format provided below; and (d) to comply with all terms and conditions of this EULA. In addition, no modifications may made to any Document.

        Form of Notice:

        Copyright undefined.

        © 2004. Reprinted with permission by Microsoft Corporation. All rights reserved.

        Microsoft and Windows are either registered trademarks or trademarks of Microsoft Corporation in the US and/or other countries. Other product and company names mentioned herein may be the trademarks of their respective owners.

    3.2   *Use of Media Elements.* The Licensed Content may include certain photographs, clip art, animations, sounds, music, and video clips (together "Media Elements"). You may not modify these Media Elements.

    3.3   *Use of Sample Code.* In the event that the Licensed Content include sample source code ("Sample Code"), Microsoft grants you a limited, non-exclusive, royalty-free license to use, copy and modify the Sample Code; if you elect to exercise the foregoing rights, you agree to comply with all other terms and conditions of this EULA, including without limitation Sections 3.4, 3.5, and 6.

    3.4   *Permitted Modifications.* In the event that you exercise any rights provided under this EULA to create modifications of the Licensed Content, you agree that any such modifications: (a) will not be used for providing training where a fee is charged in public or private classes; (b) indemnify, hold harmless, and defend Microsoft from and against any claims or lawsuits, including attorneys' fees, which arise from or result from your use of any modified version of the Licensed Content; and (c) not to transfer or assign any rights to any modified version of the Licensed Content to any third party without the express written permission of Microsoft.

3.5 *Reproduction/Redistribution Licensed Content.* Except as expressly provided in this EULA, you may not reproduce or distribute the Licensed Content or any portion thereof (including any permitted modifications) to any third parties without the express written permission of Microsoft.

4. **RESERVATION OF RIGHTS AND OWNERSHIP.** Microsoft reserves all rights not expressly granted to you in this EULA. The Licensed Content is protected by copyright and other intellectual property laws and treaties. Microsoft or its suppliers own the title, copyright, and other intellectual property rights in the Licensed Content. You may not remove or obscure any copyright, trademark or patent notices that appear on the Licensed Content, or any components thereof, as delivered to you. **The Licensed Content is licensed, not sold.**

5. **LIMITATIONS ON REVERSE ENGINEERING, DECOMPILATION, AND DISASSEMBLY.** You may not reverse engineer, decompile, or disassemble the Software or Media Elements, except and only to the extent that such activity is expressly permitted by applicable law notwithstanding this limitation.

6. **LIMITATIONS ON SALE, RENTAL, ETC. AND CERTAIN ASSIGNMENTS.** You may not provide commercial hosting services with, sell, rent, lease, lend, sublicense, or assign copies of the Licensed Content, or any portion thereof (including any permitted modifications thereof) on a stand-alone basis or as part of any collection, product or service.

7. **CONSENT TO USE OF DATA.** You agree that Microsoft and its affiliates may collect and use technical information gathered as part of the product support services provided to you, if any, related to the Licensed Content. Microsoft may use this information solely to improve our products or to provide customized services or technologies to you and will not disclose this information in a form that personally identifies you.

8. **LINKS TO THIRD PARTY SITES.** You may link to third party sites through the use of the Licensed Content. The third party sites are not under the control of Microsoft, and Microsoft is not responsible for the contents of any third party sites, any links contained in third party sites, or any changes or updates to third party sites. Microsoft is not responsible for webcasting or any other form of transmission received from any third party sites. Microsoft is providing these links to third party sites to you only as a convenience, and the inclusion of any link does not imply an endorsement by Microsoft of the third party site.

9. **ADDITIONAL LICENSED CONTENT/SERVICES.** This EULA applies to updates, supplements, add-on components, or Internet-based services components, of the Licensed Content that Microsoft may provide to you or make available to you after the date you obtain your initial copy of the Licensed Content, unless we provide other terms along with the update, supplement, add-on component, or Internet-based services component. Microsoft reserves the right to discontinue any Internet-based services provided to you or made available to you through the use of the Licensed Content.

10. **U.S. GOVERNMENT LICENSE RIGHTS**. All software provided to the U.S. Government pursuant to solicitations issued on or after December 1, 1995 is provided with the commercial license rights and restrictions described elsewhere herein. All software provided to the U.S. Government pursuant to solicitations issued prior to December 1, 1995 is provided with "Restricted Rights" as provided for in FAR, 48 CFR 52.227-14 (JUNE 1987) or DFAR, 48 CFR 252.227-7013 (OCT 1988), as applicable.

11. **EXPORT RESTRICTIONS.** You acknowledge that the Licensed Content is subject to U.S. export jurisdiction. You agree to comply with all applicable international and national laws that apply to the Licensed Content, including the U.S. Export Administration Regulations, as well as end-user, end-use, and destination restrictions issued by U.S. and other governments. For additional information see <http://www.microsoft.com/exporting/>.

12. **TRANSFER.** The initial user of the Licensed Content may make a one-time permanent transfer of this EULA and Licensed Content to another end user, provided the initial user retains no copies of the Licensed Content. The transfer may not be an indirect transfer, such as a consignment. Prior to the transfer, the end user receiving the Licensed Content must agree to all the EULA terms.

13. **"NOT FOR RESALE" LICENSED CONTENT.** Licensed Content identified as "Not For Resale" or "NFR," may not be sold or otherwise transferred for value, or used for any purpose other than demonstration, test or evaluation.

14. **TERMINATION.** Without prejudice to any other rights, Microsoft may terminate this EULA if you fail to comply with the terms and conditions of this EULA. In such event, you must destroy all copies of the Licensed Content and all of its component parts.

15. <u>**DISCLAIMER OF WARRANTIES.**</u> **TO THE MAXIMUM EXTENT PERMITTED BY APPLICABLE LAW, MICROSOFT AND ITS SUPPLIERS PROVIDE THE LICENSED CONTENT AND SUPPORT SERVICES (IF ANY)** *AS IS AND WITH ALL FAULTS,* **AND MICROSOFT AND ITS SUPPLIERS HEREBY DISCLAIM ALL OTHER WARRANTIES AND CONDITIONS, WHETHER EXPRESS, IMPLIED OR STATUTORY, INCLUDING, BUT NOT LIMITED TO, ANY (IF ANY) IMPLIED WARRANTIES, DUTIES OR CONDITIONS OF MERCHANTABILITY, OF FITNESS FOR A PARTICULAR PURPOSE, OF RELIABILITY OR AVAILABILITY, OF ACCURACY OR COMPLETENESS OF RESPONSES, OF RESULTS, OF WORKMANLIKE EFFORT, OF LACK OF VIRUSES, AND OF LACK OF NEGLIGENCE, ALL WITH REGARD TO THE LICENSED CONTENT, AND THE PROVISION OF OR FAILURE TO PROVIDE SUPPORT OR OTHER SERVICES, INFORMATION, SOFTWARE, AND RELATED CONTENT THROUGH THE LICENSED CONTENT, OR OTHERWISE ARISING OUT OF THE USE OF THE LICENSED CONTENT. ALSO, THERE IS NO WARRANTY OR CONDITION OF TITLE, QUIET ENJOYMENT, QUIET POSSESSION, CORRESPONDENCE TO DESCRIPTION OR NON-INFRINGEMENT WITH REGARD TO THE LICENSED CONTENT. THE ENTIRE RISK AS TO THE QUALITY, OR ARISING OUT OF THE USE OR PERFORMANCE OF THE LICENSED CONTENT, AND ANY SUPPORT SERVICES, REMAINS WITH YOU.**

16. <u>**EXCLUSION OF INCIDENTAL, CONSEQUENTIAL AND CERTAIN OTHER DAMAGES.**</u> **TO THE MAXIMUM EXTENT PERMITTED BY APPLICABLE LAW, IN NO EVENT SHALL MICROSOFT OR ITS SUPPLIERS BE LIABLE FOR ANY SPECIAL, INCIDENTAL, PUNITIVE, INDIRECT, OR CONSEQUENTIAL DAMAGES WHATSOEVER (INCLUDING, BUT NOT**

LIMITED TO, DAMAGES FOR LOSS OF PROFITS OR CONFIDENTIAL OR OTHER INFORMATION, FOR BUSINESS INTERRUPTION, FOR PERSONAL INJURY, FOR LOSS OF PRIVACY, FOR FAILURE TO MEET ANY DUTY INCLUDING OF GOOD FAITH OR OF REASONABLE CARE, FOR NEGLIGENCE, AND FOR ANY OTHER PECUNIARY OR OTHER LOSS WHATSOEVER) ARISING OUT OF OR IN ANY WAY RELATED TO THE USE OF OR INABILITY TO USE THE LICENSED CONTENT, THE PROVISION OF OR FAILURE TO PROVIDE SUPPORT OR OTHER SERVICES, INFORMATION, SOFTWARE, AND RELATED CONTENT THROUGH THE LICENSED CONTENT, OR OTHERWISE ARISING OUT OF THE USE OF THE LICENSED CONTENT, OR OTHERWISE UNDER OR IN CONNECTION WITH ANY PROVISION OF THIS EULA, EVEN IN THE EVENT OF THE FAULT, TORT (INCLUDING NEGLIGENCE), MISREPRESENTATION, STRICT LIABILITY, BREACH OF CONTRACT OR BREACH OF WARRANTY OF MICROSOFT OR ANY SUPPLIER, AND EVEN IF MICROSOFT OR ANY SUPPLIER HAS BEEN ADVISED OF THE POSSIBILITY OF SUCH DAMAGES. BECAUSE SOME STATES/JURISDICTIONS DO NOT ALLOW THE EXCLUSION OR LIMITATION OF LIABILITY FOR CONSEQUENTIAL OR INCIDENTAL DAMAGES, THE ABOVE LIMITATION MAY NOT APPLY TO YOU.

17.   **LIMITATION OF LIABILITY AND REMEDIES.** NOTWITHSTANDING ANY DAMAGES THAT YOU MIGHT INCUR FOR ANY REASON WHATSOEVER (INCLUDING, WITHOUT LIMITATION, ALL DAMAGES REFERENCED HEREIN AND ALL DIRECT OR GENERAL DAMAGES IN CONTRACT OR ANYTHING ELSE), THE ENTIRE LIABILITY OF MICROSOFT AND ANY OF ITS SUPPLIERS UNDER ANY PROVISION OF THIS EULA AND YOUR EXCLUSIVE REMEDY HEREUNDER SHALL BE LIMITED TO THE GREATER OF THE ACTUAL DAMAGES YOU INCUR IN REASONABLE RELIANCE ON THE LICENSED CONTENT UP TO THE AMOUNT ACTUALLY PAID BY YOU FOR THE LICENSED CONTENT OR US$5.00. THE FOREGOING LIMITATIONS, EXCLUSIONS AND DISCLAIMERS SHALL APPLY TO THE MAXIMUM EXTENT PERMITTED BY APPLICABLE LAW, EVEN IF ANY REMEDY FAILS ITS ESSENTIAL PURPOSE.

18.   **APPLICABLE LAW.** If you acquired this Licensed Content in the United States, this EULA is governed by the laws of the State of Washington. If you acquired this Licensed Content in Canada, unless expressly prohibited by local law, this EULA is governed by the laws in force in the Province of Ontario, Canada; and, in respect of any dispute which may arise hereunder, you consent to the jurisdiction of the federal and provincial courts sitting in Toronto, Ontario. If you acquired this Licensed Content in the European Union, Iceland, Norway, or Switzerland, then local law applies. If you acquired this Licensed Content in any other country, then local law may apply.

19.   **ENTIRE AGREEMENT; SEVERABILITY.** This EULA (including any addendum or amendment to this EULA which is included with the Licensed Content) are the entire agreement between you and Microsoft relating to the Licensed Content and the support services (if any) and they supersede all prior or contemporaneous oral or written communications, proposals and representations with respect to the Licensed Content or any other subject matter covered by this EULA. To the extent the terms of any Microsoft policies or programs for support services conflict with the terms of this EULA, the terms of this EULA shall control. If any provision of this EULA is held to be void, invalid, unenforceable or illegal, the other provisions shall continue in full force and effect.

Should you have any questions concerning this EULA, or if you desire to contact Microsoft for any reason, please use the address information enclosed in this Licensed Content to contact the Microsoft subsidiary serving your country or visit Microsoft on the World Wide Web at http://www.microsoft.com.

Si vous avez acquis votre Contenu Sous Licence Microsoft au CANADA :

DÉNI DE GARANTIES. Dans la mesure maximale permise par les lois applicables, le Contenu Sous Licence et les services de soutien technique (le cas échéant) sont fournis *TELS QUELS ET AVEC TOUS LES DÉFAUTS* par Microsoft et ses fournisseurs, lesquels par les présentes dénient toutes autres garanties et conditions expresses, implicites ou en vertu de la loi, notamment, mais sans limitation, (le cas échéant) les garanties, devoirs ou conditions implicites de qualité marchande, d'adaptation à une fin usage particulière, de fiabilité ou de disponibilité, d'exactitude ou d'exhaustivité des réponses, des résultats, des efforts déployés selon les règles de l'art, d'absence de virus et d'absence de négligence, le tout à l'égard du Contenu Sous Licence et de la prestation des services de soutien technique ou de l'omission de la 'une telle prestation des services de soutien technique ou à l'égard de la fourniture ou de l'omission de la fourniture de tous autres services, renseignements, Contenus Sous Licence, et contenu qui s'y rapporte grâce au Contenu Sous Licence ou provenant autrement de l'utilisation du Contenu Sous Licence. PAR AILLEURS, IL N'Y A AUCUNE GARANTIE OU CONDITION QUANT AU TITRE DE PROPRIÉTÉ, À LA JOUISSANCE OU LA POSSESSION PAISIBLE, À LA CONCORDANCE À UNE DESCRIPTION NI QUANT À UNE ABSENCE DE CONTREFAÇON CONCERNANT LE CONTENU SOUS LICENCE.

EXCLUSION DES DOMMAGES ACCESSOIRES, INDIRECTS ET DE CERTAINS AUTRES DOMMAGES. DANS LA MESURE MAXIMALE PERMISE PAR LES LOIS APPLICABLES, EN AUCUN CAS MICROSOFT OU SES FOURNISSEURS NE SERONT RESPONSABLES DES DOMMAGES SPÉCIAUX, CONSÉCUTIFS, ACCESSOIRES OU INDIRECTS DE QUELQUE NATURE QUE CE SOIT (NOTAMMENT, LES DOMMAGES À L'ÉGARD DU MANQUE À GAGNER OU DE LA DIVULGATION DE RENSEIGNEMENTS CONFIDENTIELS OU AUTRES, DE LA PERTE D'EXPLOITATION, DE BLESSURES CORPORELLES, DE LA VIOLATION DE LA VIE PRIVÉE, DE L'OMISSION DE REMPLIR TOUT DEVOIR, Y COMPRIS D'AGIR DE BONNE FOI OU D'EXERCER UN SOIN RAISONNABLE, DE LA NÉGLIGENCE ET DE TOUTE AUTRE PERTE PÉCUNIAIRE OU AUTRE PERTE

DE QUELQUE NATURE QUE CE SOIT) SE RAPPORTANT DE QUELQUE MANIÈRE QUE CE SOIT À L'UTILISATION DU CONTENU SOUS LICENCE OU À L'INCAPACITÉ DE S'EN SERVIR, À LA PRESTATION OU À L'OMISSION DE LA 'UNE TELLE PRESTATION DE SERVICES DE SOUTIEN TECHNIQUE OU À LA FOURNITURE OU À L'OMISSION DE LA FOURNITURE DE TOUS AUTRES SERVICES, RENSEIGNEMENTS, CONTENUS SOUS LICENCE, ET CONTENU QUI S'Y RAPPORTE GRÂCE AU CONTENU SOUS LICENCE OU PROVENANT AUTREMENT DE L'UTILISATION DU CONTENU SOUS LICENCE OU AUTREMENT AUX TERMES DE TOUTE DISPOSITION DE LA U PRÉSENTE CONVENTION EULA OU RELATIVEMENT À UNE TELLE DISPOSITION, MÊME EN CAS DE FAUTE, DE DÉLIT CIVIL (Y COMPRIS LA NÉGLIGENCE), DE RESPONSABILITÉ STRICTE, DE VIOLATION DE CONTRAT OU DE VIOLATION DE GARANTIE DE MICROSOFT OU DE TOUT FOURNISSEUR ET MÊME SI MICROSOFT OU TOUT FOURNISSEUR A ÉTÉ AVISÉ DE LA POSSIBILITÉ DE TELS DOMMAGES.

LIMITATION DE RESPONSABILITÉ ET RECOURS. MALGRÉ LES DOMMAGES QUE VOUS PUISSIEZ SUBIR POUR QUELQUE MOTIF QUE CE SOIT (NOTAMMENT, MAIS SANS LIMITATION, TOUS LES DOMMAGES SUSMENTIONNÉS ET TOUS LES DOMMAGES DIRECTS OU GÉNÉRAUX OU AUTRES), LA SEULE RESPONSABILITÉ 'OBLIGATION INTÉGRALE DE MICROSOFT ET DE L'UN OU L'AUTRE DE SES FOURNISSEURS AUX TERMES DE TOUTE DISPOSITION DEU LA PRÉSENTE CONVENTION EULA ET VOTRE RECOURS EXCLUSIF À L'ÉGARD DE TOUT CE QUI PRÉCÈDE SE LIMITE AU PLUS ÉLEVÉ ENTRE LES MONTANTS SUIVANTS : LE MONTANT QUE VOUS AVEZ RÉELLEMENT PAYÉ POUR LE CONTENU SOUS LICENCE OU 5,00 $US. LES LIMITES, EXCLUSIONS ET DÉNIS QUI PRÉCÈDENT (Y COMPRIS LES CLAUSES CI-DESSUS), S'APPLIQUENT DANS LA MESURE MAXIMALE PERMISE PAR LES LOIS APPLICABLES, MÊME SI TOUT RECOURS N'ATTEINT PAS SON BUT ESSENTIEL.

À moins que cela ne soit prohibé par le droit local applicable, la présente Convention est régie par les lois de la province d'Ontario, Canada. Vous consentez Chacune des parties à la présente reconnaît irrévocablement à la compétence des tribunaux fédéraux et provinciaux siégeant à Toronto, dans de la province d'Ontario et consent à instituer tout litige qui pourrait découler de la présente auprès des tribunaux situés dans le district judiciaire de York, province d'Ontario.

Au cas où vous auriez des questions concernant cette licence ou que vous désiriez vous mettre en rapport avec Microsoft pour quelque raison que ce soit, veuillez utiliser l'information contenue dans le Contenu Sous Licence pour contacter la filiale de succursale Microsoft desservant votre pays, dont l'adresse est fournie dans ce produit, ou visitez écrivez à : Microsoft sur le World Wide Web à http://www.microsoft.com

Contents

About This Course

This section provides you with a brief description of the course, audience, suggested prerequisites, and course objectives.

Description

The goal of this course is to provide system administrators with the knowledge and skills to manage a Microsoft® Systems Management Server (SMS) 2003 environment successfully. In this five-day instructor-led course, students will learn how to deploy SMS components and how to manage the ongoing operations of an SMS infrastructure in a medium-sized or large enterprise organization.

Audience

This course is designed for system administrators who have experience in management technologies and who will be responsible for configuring and managing one or more SMS 2003 sites and all supporting systems. The audience is expected to have one to three years of experience supporting multiple-desktop and server computers running Microsoft Windows® 2000 in medium-sized to large enterprise organizations.

Student prerequisites

This course requires that students meet the following prerequisites:

- Completion of Course 2277, *Implementing, Managing, and Maintaining a Microsoft Windows Server™ 2003 Network Infrastructure: Network Services*, or equivalent knowledge

- Completion of Course 2272, *Implementing and Supporting Microsoft Windows XP Professional*, or equivalent knowledge

- Have system administrator–level working knowledge of the following topics:

  - Transmission Control Protocol/Internet Protocol (TCP/IP) networking

  - Deployment and configuration of Microsoft Windows–based personal computers

  - The Active Directory® directory service

  - Supporting/troubleshooting personal computers

  - Microsoft SQL Server™

Experience with SMS 2.0 is not a requirement for this course.

Course objectives   After completing this course, the student will be able to:

- Describe the features and infrastructure of SMS 2003.
- Describe the SMS site architecture.
- Prepare for the deployment of SMS clients.
- Deploy SMS clients.
- Collect inventory and deploy software metering.
- Create, run, and view queries and reports.
- Describe and configure software distribution.
- Manage software distribution.
- Implement the software update tools and manage update deployment.
- Use SMS Remote Tools.
- Work with an SMS site hierarchy.
- Perform maintenance, backup, and recovery tasks for an SMS site.

Student Materials Compact Disc Contents

The Student Materials compact disc contains the following files and folders:

- *Autorun.inf.* When the compact disc is inserted into the compact disc drive, this file opens **StartCD.exe**.

- *Default.htm.* This file opens the Student Materials Web page. It provides you with resources pertaining to this course, including additional reading, review and lab answers, lab files, multimedia presentations, and course-related Web sites.

- *Readme.txt.* This file explains how to install the software for viewing the Student Materials compact disc and its contents and how to open the Student Materials Web page.

- *StartCD.exe.* When the compact disc is inserted into the compact disc drive, or when you double-click the **StartCD.exe** file, this file opens the compact disc and allows you to browse the Student Materials compact disc.

- *StartCD.ini.* This file contains instructions to launch **StartCD.exe**.

- *Addread.* This folder contains additional reading pertaining to this course.

- *Appendix.* This folder contains appendix files for this course.

- *Flash.* This folder contains the installer for the Macromedia Flash 6.0 browser plug-in.

- *Fonts.* This folder contains fonts that may be required to view the Microsoft Word documents that are included with this course.

- *Media.* This folder contains files that are used in multimedia presentations for this course.

- *Mplayer.* This folder contains the setup file to install Microsoft Windows Media® Player.

- *Webfiles.* This folder contains the files that are required to view the course Web page. To open the Web page, open Windows Explorer, and in the root directory of the compact disc, double-click **StartCD.exe**.

- *Wordview.* This folder contains the Word Viewer that is used to view any Word document (.doc) files that are included on the compact disc.

Document Conventions

The following conventions are used in course materials to distinguish elements of the text.

Convention	Use
Bold	Represents commands, command options, and syntax that must be typed exactly as shown. It also indicates commands on menus and buttons, dialog box titles and options, and icon and menu names.
Italic	In syntax statements or descriptive text, indicates argument names or placeholders for variable information. Italic is also used for introducing new terms, for book titles, and for emphasis in the text.
Title Capitals	Indicate domain names, user names, computer names, directory names, and folder and file names, except when specifically referring to case-sensitive names. Unless otherwise indicated, you can use lowercase letters when you type a directory name or file name in a dialog box or at a command prompt.
ALL CAPITALS	Indicate the names of keys, key sequences, and key combinations—for example, ALT+SPACEBAR.
`monospace`	Represents code samples or examples of screen text.
[ ]	In syntax statements, enclose optional items. For example, [*filename*] in command syntax indicates that you can choose to type a file name with the command. Type only the information within the brackets, not the brackets themselves.
{ }	In syntax statements, enclose required items. Type only the information within the braces, not the braces themselves.
|	In syntax statements, separates an either/or choice.
▶	Indicates a procedure with sequential steps in a demonstration, practice, or lab.
...	In syntax statements, specifies that the preceding item may be repeated.
. . .	Represents an omitted portion of a code sample.

Introduction

Contents

Introduction

- Name
- Company affiliation
- Title/function
- Job responsibility
- Networking experience
- Microsoft Systems Management Server experience
- Expectations for the course

Your instructor will ask you to introduce yourself and provide a brief overview of your background, addressing the bulleted items on the slide as appropriate.

Course Materials

- **Name card**
- **Student workbook**
- **Student Materials compact disc**
- **Course evaluation**

The following materials are included with your kit:

- *Name card.* Write your name on both sides of the name card.

- *Student workbook.* The student workbook contains the material covered in class, in addition to the hands-on lab exercises.

- *Student Materials compact disc.* The Student Materials compact disc contains the Web page that provides you with links to resources pertaining to this course, including additional readings, review and lab answers, lab files, multimedia presentations, and course-related Web sites.

    Note   To open the Web page, insert the Student Materials compact disc into the CD-ROM drive and then, in the root directory of the compact disc, double-click **StartCD.exe**.

- *Course evaluation.* To provide feedback on the course, training facility, and instructor, you will have the opportunity to complete an online evaluation near the end of the course.

    To provide additional comments or feedback on the course, send e-mail to support@mscourseware.com. To inquire about the Microsoft Certified Professional program, send e-mail to mcphelp@microsoft.com.

Prerequisites

- Completion of Course 2277, *Implementing, Managing, and Maintaining a Microsoft Windows Server 2003 Network Infrastructure: Network Services*, or have equivalent knowledge

- Completion of Course 2272, *Implementing and Supporting Microsoft Windows XP Professional*, or have equivalent knowledge

- System administrator-level working knowledge of:
  - Deployment, configuration, and troubleshooting for Windows-based personal computers
  - TCP/IP networking
  - SQL Server
  - Active Directory directory service

This course requires that you meet the following prerequisites:

- Completion of Course 2277, *Implementing, Managing, and Maintaining a Microsoft® Windows Server™ 2003 Network Infrastructure: Network Services*, or equivalent knowledge

- Completion of Course 2272, *Implementing and Supporting Microsoft Windows® XP Professional*, or equivalent knowledge.

- Have system administrator–level working knowledge of:
  - Deployment, configuration, and troubleshooting for Windows-based personal computers
  - TCP/IP networking
  - Microsoft SQL Server™
  - Microsoft Active Directory® directory service

Course Framework

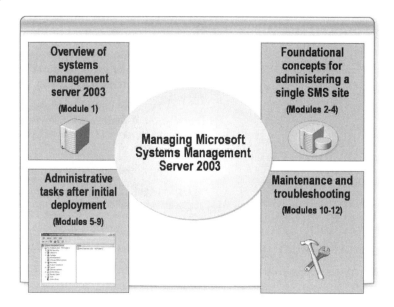

This course is comprised of four sections:

- *Overview of Microsoft Systems Management Server*. Module 1, "Overview of Systems Management Server 2003," introduces the key features of SMS 2003, explains differences between SMS 2.0 and SMS 2003, and describes the primary components of the SMS 2003 infrastructure.

- *Foundational concepts for administering a single SMS site*. Modules 2 through 4 start the course by establishing the foundational concepts required for administering a single SMS site. These concepts are then used by the student to create a single SMS site server and several clients in a simulated environment. Microsoft Virtual PC technology provides the student with a hands-on environment to practice key SMS skills:

  - Module 2, "Exploring SMS Site Architecture," explains the components of an SMS site server, as well as how to use and install the SMS Administrator console and other tools supporting administration and implementation. This module also explains the role of technologies that SMS uses, such as Active Directory directory service, Background Intelligent Transfer Service (BITS), Microsoft Windows Management Instrumentation (WMI), and Microsoft Windows Installer (MSI).

  - Module 3, "Preparing to Deploy the SMS Clients," explains the process of preparing for SMS Client deployment. This module explains resource discovery, guidelines for deployment, and the configuration of site systems that support clients.

  - Module 4, "Deploying SMS Clients," explains how to deploy the SMS Advanced Client and Legacy Client. This module also explains how to isolate problems that might be encountered during client installation.

- *Administrative tasks after initial deployment.* Modules 5 through 9 present a logical flow of tasks that an administrator would typically do after initial deployment of an SMS site and clients:

  - Module 5, "Collecting Inventory and Software Metering," explains how to use SMS hardware and software inventory collection features to collect a wide variety of information about client computers and files in an SMS hierarchy. This module also explains how to use software metering to identify which applications are being used in your company.

  - Module 6, "Querying and Reporting Data," explains how to create, run, and view queries, reports, and dashboards. This module also explains how to deploy the reporting point site system.

  - Module 7, "Preparing an SMS Site for Distribution," explains the SMS software distribution process, including the flow of software distribution and the roles played by the site, the SMS objects that distribute software, and the SMS client. This module also explains how to prepare a site for software distribution by allocating distribution points and configuring the SMS client.

  - Module 8, "Managing Software Distribution," explains how to distribute software to SMS clients by creating a package and then advertising a program from the package to a collection of clients.

  - Module 9, "Implementing SMS Software Update Tools and Managing Update Deployment" explains the SMS software update process. This module also explains how to install and use software update scanning tools, perform software update inventory, and deploy software updates.

- *Maintenance and troubleshooting.* Modules 10 though 12 teach change and configuration management and topics involved in maintaining an SMS organization:

  - Module 10, "Using Remote Tools for Client Support," explains how to configure and use remote tools to provide troubleshooting support to clients.

  - Module 11, "Working with SMS Hierarchies," explains the SMS site hierarchy architecture. This module also explains how to configure communication between sites, install an SMS secondary site server, and manage roaming clients in the hierarchy.

  - Module 12, "Performing Site Maintenance, Backup, and Recovery Tasks," explains how to perform SMS site maintenance tasks and prepare for backup and recovery operations.

Setup

Setup information	Description
Virtual machines	• *Glasgow* is the **domain controller** for your Windows Server 2003 domain in the NWTraders forest • *Dublin* is running Windows Server 2003 Advanced Server and SMS 2003. This is the **SMS primary site** • *Paris* is running Windows Server 2003 Advanced Server and SMS 2003. This will be the **SMS secondary site** • *Bonn* is running Windows XP SP1. This is an **SMS Advanced Client** • *Perth* is running Windows NT4. This is an **SMS Legacy Client**
Course files	• Demonstrations, practice, and lab files are in the C:\Program Files\Microsoft Learning\2596\Labfiles\Lab*XX* folder on the appropriate virtual machine
Classroom setup	• This course uses the virtual machine program that hosts an entire network of servers on a single computer

Virtual machines

The following table shows the virtual machines used in this course and their roles.

Virtual machine	Role
WS03_Base	Base image for differencing drives
2596_1-Glasgow_DC	Domain Controller
2596_2-Dublin_SMSsite1	SMS Primary Site
2596_3-Paris_SMSsite2	SMS Secondary Site
2596_4-Bonn_WinXPclient	SMS Advanced Client
2596_5-Perth_NT4client	SMS Legacy Client

Course files

There are files associated with the practices, demonstrations, and labs in this course. The lab files are located in the folder C:\2596 on the virtual machines. When you reach a point at which you need a file to complete a demonstration, practice, or lab file, you will be provided with the appropriate virtual machine and file path.

Classroom setup

This course uses Microsoft Virtual PC 2004 to allow you to host an entire network of servers on a single computer. Each computer in the classroom will have the same group of virtual machines configured in the same way.

Demonstration: How to Use Virtual PC

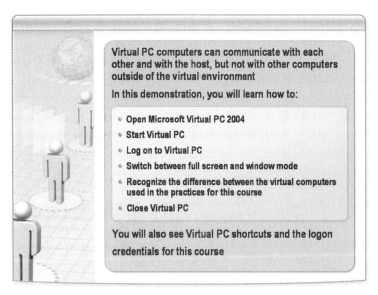

Virtual computers can communicate with each other and with the host, but they cannot communicate with other computers that are outside of the virtual environment. (For example, no Internet access is available from the virtual environment.) In this demonstration, your instructor will help familiarize you with the Virtual PC 2004 environment that you will work in to complete the practices in this course. You will learn:

- How to open Virtual PC

- How to start Virtual PC

- How to log on to Virtual PC

- How to switch between full screen and window mode

- How to tell the difference between the virtual computers that are used in the practices for this course

- How to close Virtual PC

Your instructor will also show you some Virtual PC shortcuts and the logon credentials for this course.

Note For more information about Virtual PC, see Virtual PC Help.

Virtual PC keyboard shortcuts

While working in the virtual machine environment, you may find it useful to use keyboard shortcuts. All virtual machine shortcuts include a key that is referred to as the HOST key. By default, the HOST key is the ALT key on the right side of your keyboard.

Some useful shortcuts are included in this table.

Action	Keyboard shortcut
Log on to virtual machine	RIGHT ALT+DELETE
Switch between full screen mode and window mode	RIGHT ALT+ENTER
Display the next virtual machine	RIGHT ALT+RIGHT ARROW
Shut down the virtual machine	RIGHT ALT+F4

Important   When shutting down a virtual machine, you must click **Action** in the upper left corner, click **Close**, and then select **Save state and save changes**.

Logon credentials for this course

Use this table to find the correct logon credentials for each virtual machine.

Password for all accounts: P@ssw0rd

Active Directory account	Group membership	Account
Administrator	Active Directory\Domain Admins	Domain Administrator
JaePa (Jae Pak)	Active Directory\Domain User Dublin\Administrators	Dublin Local Administrator
DonHa (Don Hall)	Active Directory\Domain User Paris\Administrators	Paris Local Administrator
SMartinez (Sandra Martinez)	Active Directory\Domain User Bonn\Administrators	Bonn Local Administrator
JudyLe (Judy Lew)	Active Directory\Domain User Perth\Administrators	Perth Local Administrator

Practice: Starting and Logging Onto Virtual PC 2004

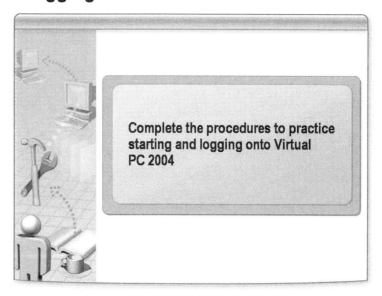

Complete the procedures to practice starting and logging onto Virtual PC 2004

Instructions

Complete the procedures to practice starting and logging onto Virtual PC 2004.

In this practice, use the following values.

Variable	Value
Virtual machine—SMS Site 1	Dublin
Dublin Administrator	JaePa (Jae Pak)
Virtual machine—domain controller	Glasgow
Domain administrator	Administrator

Procedures

▶ **To start Virtual PC 2004**

1. On your local (or host) computer, click **Start**, point to **All Programs**, and then click **Microsoft Virtual PC**.

2. In the **Virtual PC Console**, click **Glasgow**, and then click **Start**.

Caution Classroom computers have 1 GB of memory. With this amount of memory, you can run up to three virtual computers at a time, but starting more than three virtual machines will cause performance problems.

---

3. In the **Virtual PC Console**, click **Dublin**, and then click **Start**.

Note It will take about two or three minutes for each virtual machine to start.

▶ **To Log onto Virtual PC 2004**

1. On the Glasgow virtual machine, press right ALT+DELETE.

Note The ALT key on the right side of the keyboard is referred to as both the right ALT key and the HOST key in Virtual PC Help and menus.

---

2. In the **Log On to Windows** dialog box, in the **User name** box, type **Administrator**. In the **Password** box, type **P@ssw0rd**. In the **Log onto** box, verify or select **NWTraders**.

3. Minimize the Glasgow virtual machine.

4. Repeat steps 1–3 for the Dublin virtual machine.

5. Leave the Glasgow and Dublin virtual machines running.

Introduction to Northwind Traders

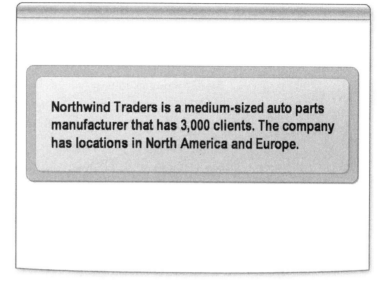

When you perform activities in this course, you will be working for a fictitious company called Northwind Traders. These activities will help you develop the technical and administrative skills necessary to manage SMS 2003 and will also help you learn about typical business drivers associated with SMS 2003, such as security policies and customer service.

This topic provides a company overview and important components of the corporate policy.

Company overview

Northwind Traders is a medium-sized auto parts manufacturer consisting of 3,000 clients. The company has locations in Europe in the cities of Glasgow, Dublin, Paris, and Bonn, as well as a site in Perth, which is located in southwestern Australia.

Northwind Traders recently deployed SMS 2003 in order to better control their Desktop Management environment. As an SMS administrator, you will be responsible for deploying SMS Advanced and Legacy clients, collecting hardware and software inventories, managing software metering, software distribution and update deployment, supporting local and remote clients using remote tools, configuring the site hierarchy, and performing site maintenance, backup, and recovery tasks.

There are other SMS administrators working at the primary SMS site in Dublin, Ireland, as well as at the secondary SMS site in Paris, France.

Northwind Traders policy specifications

The corporate policy for Northwind Traders includes the following specifications of interest:

- **Change Management Process:** You will need to establish a Change Management process if your business doesn't already have one. This is needed to control any changes that accrue within your SMS environment. Note: This will not be taught within this course.

- **SMS administrator**. The SMS administrator has certain System Administrator permissions. For example the SMS administrator will have:
  - A domain user account
  - Administrator privileges of the primary SMS site
  - System Administrator privileges on the secondary SMS site
  - System Administrator privileges in the SQL database
- **Domain controller administrator**. The domain controller administrator (but *not* the SMS administrator) will have:
  - Domain Administrator rights
  - Schema Administrator rights
- **Local Administrators on client computers**. Client users have local administrator rights on their computers. The client computer base consists of Windows Server™ 2003, Windows XP, Windows 2000, Windows NT® 4.0, and Legacy Windows 98 operating systems.
- **Desktop configuration**. The Northwind Traders policy states that there is a Standard Desktop configuration that includes a:
  - Common hardware configuration.
  - Common suite of software applications. This will aid them in managing desktop images, which will in the long run reduce operational costs.
- **Hardware and Software Inventory policy**. Northwind Traders uses the following inventory guidelines:
  - Hardware inventory
    - Run on a weekly basis.
    - The company is only interested in tracking hardware for Asset Management and budget planning in order to replace desktops approaching their *end of life*.
  - Software inventory
    - Run on a monthly basis.
    - Ensures that employees have not installed rogue software. For example: unlicensed software control, reduces operational costs of non-standard applications.
    - Data is only collected on .exe files.
  - Software metering
    - Software metering is only used for gathering usage on the CAD/CAM systems that are used by a small group of manufacturing engineers.
- **Reporting**. Northwind Traders does not have specific reporting guidelines; however, reports are typically generated based on specific requests to provide management reports, or for SMS administrator system verification purposes.

Additional Reading from Microsoft Learning

Microsoft Windows Server 2003 books from Microsoft Learning can help you do your job—from the planning and evaluation stages through deployment and ongoing support—with solid technical information to help you get the most out of the Windows Server 2003 key features and enhancements. The following titles supplement the skills taught in this course.

Title	ISBN
Microsoft® Systems Management Server 2003 Administrator's Companion	0-7356-1888-7
Migrating from Microsoft® Windows NT® Server 4.0 to Windows Server™ 2003	0-7356-1940-9
Microsoft® Windows Server™ 2003 Deployment Kit	0-7356-1486-5
Microsoft® Windows Server™ 2003 Security Administrator's Companion	0-7356-1574-8
Microsoft® Windows Server™ 2003 Administrator's Pocket Consultant	0-7356-1354-0
Active Directory® for Microsoft® Windows Server™ 2003 Technical Reference	0-7356-1577-2
Microsoft® Windows Server™ 2003 Administrator's Companion	0-7356-1367-2

Microsoft Learning Recommended Courses

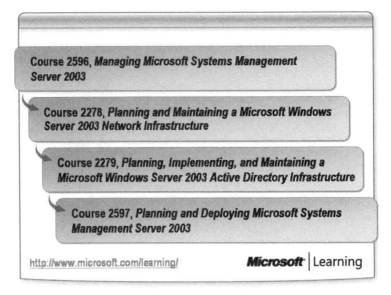

| Introduction | Microsoft Learning develops Official Microsoft Learning Products for computer professionals who design, develop, support, implement, or manage solutions by using Microsoft products and technologies. These learning products provide comprehensive skills-based training in instructor-led and online formats. |

Introduction

Microsoft Learning develops Official Microsoft Learning Products for computer professionals who design, develop, support, implement, or manage solutions by using Microsoft products and technologies. These learning products provide comprehensive skills-based training in instructor-led and online formats.

Recommended courses

Each course relates in some way to another course. A related course may be a prerequisite, a follow-up course in a recommended series, or a course that offers additional training.

It is recommended that you take the following courses in this order:

- 2596: *Managing Microsoft Systems Management Server 2003*
- 2278: *Planning and Maintaining a Microsoft Windows Server 2003 Network Infrastructure*
- 2279: *Planning, Implementing, and Maintaining a Microsoft Windows Server 2003 Active Directory Infrastructure*
- 2597: *Planning and Deploying Microsoft Systems Management Server 2003*

Other related courses may become available in the future, so for up-to-date information about recommended courses, visit the Microsoft Learning Web site.

Microsoft Learning information

For more information, visit the Microsoft Learning Web site at http://www.microsoft.com/learning/.

Microsoft Certified Professional Program

Microsoft Learning offers a variety of certification credentials for IT professionals. The Microsoft Certified Professional program is the leading certification program for validating your experience and skills, keeping you competitive in today's changing business environment.

MCP certifications

The Microsoft Certified Professional program includes these and other certifications:

- MCSA on Microsoft Windows Server 2003

  The Microsoft Certified Systems Administrator (MCSA) certification is designed for professionals who implement, manage, and troubleshoot existing network and system environments based on Microsoft Windows 2000 platforms, including the Windows Server 2003 family. Implementation responsibilities include installing and configuring parts of the systems. Management responsibilities include administering and supporting the systems.

- MCSE on Microsoft Windows Server 2003

  The Microsoft Certified Systems Engineer (MCSE) credential is the premier certification for professionals who analyze the business requirements and design and implement the infrastructure for business solutions based on the Windows 2000 platform and Microsoft server software, including the Windows Server 2003 family. Implementation responsibilities include installing, configuring, and troubleshooting network systems.

- MCP

  The Microsoft Certified Professional (MCP) credential is for individuals who have the skills to successfully implement a Microsoft product or technology as part of a business solution in an organization. Hands-on experience with the product is necessary to successfully achieve certification.

- MCT

  Microsoft Certified Trainers (MCTs) demonstrate the instructional and technical skills that qualify them to deliver Official Microsoft Learning Products through Microsoft Certified Partners for Learning Solutions (CPLS).

Certification requirements

The certification requirements differ for each certification category and are specific to the products and job functions addressed by the certification. To become a Microsoft Certified Professional, you must pass rigorous certification exams that provide a valid and reliable measure of technical proficiency and expertise.

For More Information   See the Microsoft Learning Web site at http://www.microsoft.com/learning/.

You can also send e-mail to mcphelp@microsoft.com if you have specific certification questions.

Acquiring the skills tested by an MCP exam

Official Microsoft Learning Products can help you develop the skills that you need to do your job. They also complement the experience that you gain while working with Microsoft products and technologies. However, no one-to-one correlation exists between Official Microsoft Learning Products and MCP exams. Microsoft does not expect or intend for the courses to be the sole preparation method for passing MCP exams. Practical product knowledge and experience is also necessary to pass the MCP exams.

To help prepare for the MCP exams, use the preparation guides that are available for each exam. Each Exam Preparation Guide contains exam-specific information such as a list of the topics on which you will be tested. These guides are available on the Microsoft Learning Web site at http://www.microsoft.com/learning/.

Facilities

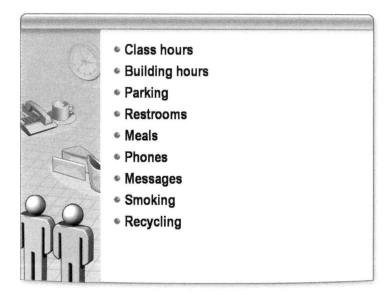

Module 1: Overview of Systems Management Server 2003

Contents

Overview

- Where SMS Fits in the Windows Server System
- Describing How SMS 2003 Features Provide Change and Configuration Management
- Explaining SMS Hierarchies
- Explaining SMS Site-to-Site Communication
- Explaining SMS Site and Roaming Boundaries

Introduction

Microsoft® Systems Management Server (SMS) 2003 provides powerful desktop administration tools for managing hardware inventory, software inventory, software distribution, and remote client troubleshooting. As an SMS administrator, you will need to know how to configure and manage these tools. This module introduces the key features of SMS 2003, explains differences between SMS 2.0 and SMS 2003, and describes the primary components of the SMS 2003 infrastructure.

Objectives

After completing this module, you will be able to:

- Describe the position of SMS in the Microsoft Windows Server System™.
- Describe the features of SMS 2003 and how they provide change and configuration management.
- Describe SMS site hierarchies.
- Describe SMS site-to-site communication.
- Describe the role of SMS site boundaries and roaming boundaries.

Lesson: Where SMS Fits in the Windows Server System

* The Operations Infrastructure Technologies of the Windows Server System
* Issues that SMS Helps Administrators Address

Introduction

The Windows Server System is integrated server infrastructure software designed to provide administrators with the tools to develop, deploy, and operate IT infrastructures more efficiently. The Windows Server System was designed to support end-to-end solutions built on Microsoft Windows Server™ 2003. The software that is part of the Windows Server System is designed to work together and interact with other data and applications across your IT environment to help reduce the costs of ongoing operations, deliver a highly reliable and secure IT infrastructure, and drive valuable new capabilities the future growth of your business.

This lesson introduces Microsoft's operations infrastructure technologies and describes the role of Microsoft Systems Management Server (SMS) 2003 in the Windows Server System.

Lesson objectives

After completing this lesson, you will be able to:

- Describe the operating system solutions and products that comprise the Operations Infrastructure technologies.

- Describe the key issues that SMS 2003 helps you manage in a Microsoft Windows®-based enterprise environment.

The Operations Infrastructure Technologies of the Windows Server System

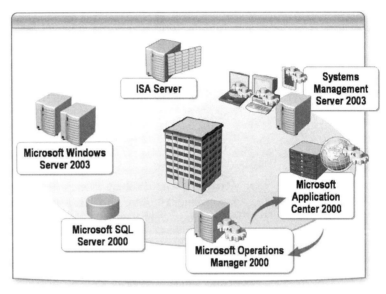

The foundation for Windows Server System is the Windows Server 2003 operating system, which delivers the core infrastructure and common services across each of these categories. The server platform provides:

- The underlying security model, directory services, and operations and management services to support the Operations Infrastructure.

- The core application definition and programming model as the foundation for the Application Infrastructure.

- The core data and collaboration services that support the Information Worker Infrastructure.

The Windows Server 2003 server platform is designed to deliver simplicity, automation, and flexibility in the data center and across the IT environment by focusing on server consolidation, increased server usage, and the automation of core management tasks. The Windows Server System security and management servers build on the Windows Server 2003 server platform to deliver an integrated operations infrastructure that promotes operational efficiencies through simplified deployment, management, and security, in addition to reduced IT infrastructure costs.

Operations infrastructure technologies

The operations infrastructure technologies and products include:

- Microsoft Internet Security and Acceleration (ISA) Server, which is an extensible, multilayer enterprise firewall and Web cache that helps provide secure, fast, and manageable Internet connectivity. ISA Server also provides a high-performance Web proxy and cache that improves performance and delivers cost savings by effectively managing network bandwidth.

- Microsoft Systems Management Server, which delivers cost-effective, scalable change and configuration management for desktops and servers based on Microsoft Windows and helps administrators to distribute security updates for all Microsoft products throughout the enterprise. Built on industry-standard management protocols, Systems Management Server is compatible with complementary management tools from Microsoft and other companies.

- Microsoft Application Center, which is the Microsoft deployment and management tool for high-availability Web applications, built on Windows. Application Center makes managing groups of servers as simple as managing a single computer. Application Center empowers developers and Web site administrators to deploy applications quickly and easily while minimizing the in-depth application knowledge requirements. In turn, this reduces the complexity and cost of operating scalable, highly available applications.

- Microsoft Operations Manager, which delivers enterprise-class operations management by providing comprehensive event management, proactive monitoring and alerting, reporting, and trend analysis. It is also crucial in helping reduce the day-to-day support costs associated with running applications and services in a Windows-based IT environment.

- Microsoft SQL Server™ 2000 supports the rapid development of enterprise-class business applications. Benchmarked for scalability, speed, and performance, SQL Server 2000 is a fully enterprise-class database product, providing core support for Extensible Markup Language (XML) and Internet queries.

In addition, Microsoft provides the Microsoft Solutions for Management (MSM) Solution Accelerators, patterns and practices that provide proven technical guidance that can help you successfully plan, develop, and implement your organization's projects. These are lab-tested, customer-approved Microsoft best practices that are intended to be used by Microsoft Consulting Services (MCS) and Microsoft partners to help customers achieve optimal solutions.

Note For additional information about the technologies in the Windows Server System, see the Microsoft Web site at http://www.microsoft.com/windowsserversystem.

Issues that SMS Helps Administrators Address

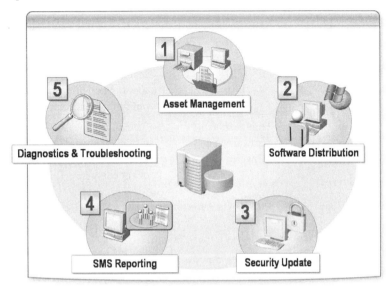

As a key component of the Windows Server System, SMS 2003 provides a comprehensive solution for controlling and managing your enterprise by using centralized management tools.

SMS 2003 can help you address the following key issues in managing a Windows-based enterprise environment.

Issue	SMS Capabilities
Asset management	Track what applications are installed and application usage. Monitor what users are running applications, for how long, and how many instances concurrently. Use this information to: • Collect information about the hardware and software configuration of computers in your network. • Collect information about hardware assets. • Plan software procurement and licensing. • Save money on potential new application purchases. • Stay compliant on existing products. • Effectively phase out unused applications.
Software distribution	Target software distribution for every computer in your network, whether server or desktop, based on administrator-defined properties, such as network or hardware configuration. Distribute the software, analyze the status of the distribution, and configure the distributed software.
Security updates	Manage security on computers running Windows operating systems by automatically identifying security vulnerabilities and suitable updates, and then test and reliably deploy these updates throughout the environment. Configure the distribution software without user intervention.

(continued)

Issue	SMS Capabilities
SMS Reports	SMS reporting can ensure that the rich inventory and usage tracking information collected is easily accessible and organized in a way that is relevant to your business. SMS 2003 includes a robust, highly flexible and fully extensible Web reporting engine with more than 120 pre-built reports available out of the box. Reports can be customized or created.
Troubleshooting hardware and software	Several troubleshooting utilities are included with SMS to provide software, hardware, and network diagnostic information. You can also use these utilities to troubleshoot client computers from a remote location.

Practice: Identifying Products in the Windows Server System

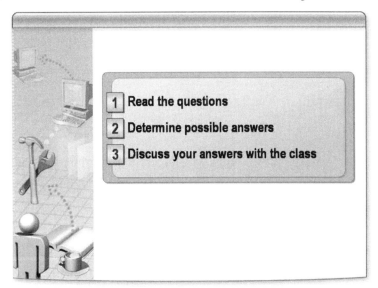

Instructions

Read the following questions, determine answers, and then discuss your answers with the rest of the class.

Scenario

Clair Hector is the director of IT department for Northwind Traders. Jae Pak is the systems administrator in charge of managing the day-to-day operations of the network and server environment. To better understand what is needed to develop the server environment prior to SMS 2003 implementation, Clair has asked Jae to gather what SMS 2003 does and how it fits into the Windows Server system.

Discussion questions

1. What are the products in the Operations Infrastructure of the Windows Server System?

_____

_____

_____

_____

2. How do these products complement each other and work together to create a complete infrastructure for managing your Windows-based enterprise environment?

    _____

    _____

    _____

    _____

3. How will you use SMS in your environment?

    _____

    _____

    _____

    _____

Lesson: Describing How SMS 2003 Features Provide Change and Configuration Management

* The Primary Features of SMS
* Administrative Support Features of SMS
* Mixed-Version Hierarchy Considerations

Introduction

This lesson describes the key features of SMS 2003 and the differences between SMS 2003 and SMS 2.0.

The features and managements tools of SMS 2003 provide business value to help organizations:

- Collect information about hardware and software installed on clients on the network.
- Distribute software to clients on the network.
- Track software usage.
- Manage critical software updates
- Allow remote administration of client computers.
- Create queries and reports.

Lesson objectives

After completing this lesson, you will be able to:

- Describe the primary features in SMS 2003.
- Describe the administrative support features in SMS 2003.
- Compare and contrast SMS 2.0 with SMS 2003.

The Primary Features of SMS

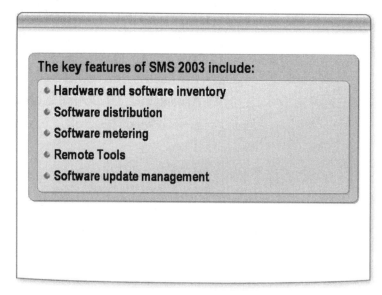

The key features of SMS 2003 include hardware and software inventory, software distribution, software metering, remote tools, and security update management.

Hardware and software inventory

SMS performs hardware and software inventories on SMS client computers. You can run a wide variety of reports against the resulting data, so you can plan upgrades, track hardware and software assets, or check software license compliance.

Software distribution

SMS significantly reduces the time and complexity of maintaining and upgrading software for organizations with distributed networks by allowing you to:

- Upgrade and configure each computer from a central location or from multiple locations.

- Schedule individual software files or software programs for distribution to specific computers.

- Initiate unattended software installations to selected computers.

Software metering

The software metering feature allows you to monitor program usage on client computers. By using software metering, you can:

- Collect data about software usage in your organization.

- Summarize data to produce useful reports that can help you monitor licensing compliance and plan software purchases in your organization.

- Collect detailed information about the programs that you want to monitor, such as usage, program users, the program start time, and the length of time the program is used.

Remote Tools

SMS Remote Tools is a suite of tools that you can use to provide help desk assistance and troubleshooting support to clients in an SMS hierarchy. With Remote Tools, it is not necessary to physically be at the client's location to provide assistance. Remote Tools give you full control over a client computer and allows you to perform any operation as if you were physically at the client's location.

Note For security purposes, do not use Remote Tools for clients running Windows XP, Windows 2000 Server, or Windows 2003. Use Remote Desktop or Remote Assistance instead.

Software update management

Software update management is the process of keeping computers and servers that are running Windows operating systems updated with security and Microsoft Office updates. Software update management includes:

- Performing an inventory of the installed and applicable updates on managed computers and pulling updates from the www.microsoft.com servers.

- Evaluating and testing available updates.

- Authorizing and distributing the updates.

- Tracking software update compliance.

SMS 2003 provides new tools for software update management. You can use these tools to take advantage of the critical software updates that Microsoft provides for Windows operating systems, Microsoft Office, SQL Server, Exchange Server, Internet Information Services (IIS), and other system software.

Administrative Support Features of SMS

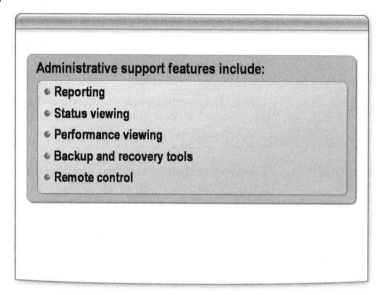

Administrative support features of SMS 2003 include several tools that simplify the processes of gathering information about the site, such as reporting and troubleshooting tools. SMS 2003 also provides comprehensive backup and recovery tools, which are designed to ensure that this information is continuously available and secure.

Reporting

SMS 2003 provides a comprehensive set of predefined, secure reports containing information about the client computers across the enterprise and the current state of managed systems across an organization. You can provide management and other SMS users with reports that can be viewed using Microsoft Internet Explorer. Reports include a wide range of information, including:

- Hardware and software inventory.

- Computer configuration details and status.

- Software deployment, deployment errors, and usage status.

- Software update compliance.

SMS reports are customizable, so you can generate custom reports that are useful to your organization. You can import and export existing reports. You can also view multiple reports at one time, in a single window, using an SMS tool called Report Viewer. All reports are based on Structured Query Language (SQL).

Status viewing

SMS generates status messages to report the activity of components on site systems and clients. A status message is a text string that describes a specific activity performed by a component. Each status message contains the following information:

- The name of the component.
- The time that the message was generated.
- The severity of the message.

Status messages are sent from clients and site systems to the site server and are stored in the SMS site database. You can then view status messages in the SMS Administrator console. Viewing status messages in the SMS Administrator console helps you monitor the activity of the various components, determine the health of SMS, and identify issues that might require your attention.

Tip SMS2003StatusMessages.xls is a downloadable troubleshooting tool that lists all status messages generated by SMS 2003. You can filter messages by message ID, by message type (such as error messages, warning messages), or by the component that generates the message. The link to this spreadsheet is included on the Internet links pages of the Student Materials compact disc.

Performance viewing

SMS includes a tool that allows you to monitor the performance of your network. The network maintenance and monitoring tool helps you monitor, capture, and interpret network data. By using this tool, you can diagnose network problems, monitor and analyze patterns of network activity to avoid network problems, and identify optimization opportunities.

Backup and recovery tools

SMS provides functionality that you can use to back up and recover a site. You can back up the site's data on a regular basis and then use recovery and repair tools to restore that backup and to recover the site to its original state. The backup and recovery feature ensures that the site loses a minimum amount of data and that the site continues to operate properly after it is recovered.

SMS includes the following two critical SMS backup and recovery tools:

- *Recovery Expert*. The SMS Site Recovery Expert collects information about a site failure scenario and produces a list of tasks to be performed for site recovery.
- *Repair Wizard*. You can perform complicated recovery tasks by using the SMS Site Repair Wizard, which is integrated with the SMS Site Recovery Expert. The Recovery Expert instructs you when to use the SMS Site Repair Wizard.

Note Check the Product Documentation page on the SMS 2003 Web site for the latest information regarding backup and recovery tools. The link to this page is included on the Internet links page of the Student Materials compact disc.

Remote control

SMS Remote Tools provide help desk assistance and troubleshooting support to computers in your network. Remote Tools gives you full control over the computers and allows you to perform any operation if you were physically at the computer's location. In addition to SMS Remote Tools, SMS 2003 allows you to use Windows Remote Assistance and Remote Desktop to assist supported clients.

Mixed-Version Hierarchy Considerations

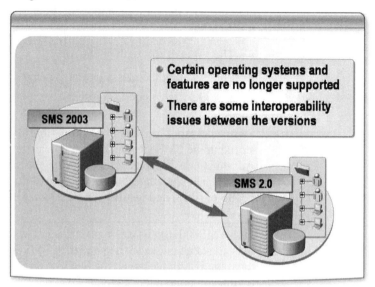

Before you introduce SMS 2003 into your organization, it is important to recognize the differences between SMS 2003 and SMS 2.0. Not all the operating systems or features supported by SMS 2.0 are supported by SMS 2003.

Operating systems and features that are no longer supported

The following table outlines operating systems and features that are not supported in SMS 2003.

Item	Description
Client operating system	Windows 3.1, Windows 3.11, Windows 95, Microsoft Windows NT® 4.0 SP5 (or earlier), Windows Me, Windows XP Home Edition, Windows CE, Novell NetWare
SQL Server	SQL Server 7.0 SP2 and earlier, Intel IA64-based computers running SQL Server
Other	Microsoft Small Business Server, Alpha-based systems

Interoperability issues between SMS 2.0 and SMS 2003

Considerations for using a mixed-version hierarchy are as follows:

- *Client discovery and installation*. SMS 2003 sites cannot use SMS 2.0 logon points. However, server locator points can be supported in SMS 2.0 sites as long as there is interoperability between SMS 2003 and SMS 2.0 and the SLP is high enough in the hierarchy.

- *Collections and queries*. Collections or groups of resources that are defined in SMS 2003 sites propagate down to SMS 2.0 sites in the same manner that they propagate down to lower-level SMS 2003 sites. However, there are interoperability issues with collections and queries in a mixed-version hierarchy. For example, queries that run against SMS 2.0 classes that do not exist in SMS 2003 return only the classes that exist in SMS 2003.

■ *Hardware inventory*. In a mixed-version hierarchy, it is recommended that all sites use a standardized SMS_def.mof file. Differences between the SMS_def.mof files at different sites in the hierarchy can result in conflicting hardware inventory data. Conflicting hardware inventory data in the SMS site database can result in multiple tables for the same class.

■ *Software Distribution*. SMS 2.0 16-bit clients that are identified by user accounts or user groups in collections do not receive programs sent to them by using the software distribution feature from SMS 2003 sites. Only 32-bit clients can receive software distribution programs that are based on user accounts or user groups. Settings on the **Advanced Client** tab and the **Suppress program notifications** check box are ignored when the program reaches SMS 2.0 sites.

■ *Reporting*. SMS 2003 does not use Crystal Reports. Instead, it uses a Web-based reporting solution.

■ *Software metering*. SMS 2003 software metering does not interoperate with SMS 2.0 software metering. Software metering rules from SMS 2003 sites do not propagate to SMS 2.0 sites, and software metering data from SMS 2.0 sites does not propagate up to SMS 2003 sites.

Note For a complete list of unsupported operating systems and features, and detailed information about interoperability of SMS 2.0 features with SMS 2003 features, see the *Concepts, Planning, and Deployment Guide* on the Additional Reading page of your Student Materials compact disc. This book gives you valuable information about planning to deploy SMS 2003 in your organization, important SMS concepts, and directions to install SMS 2003.

In a single-version hierarchy, you can centrally manage the entire hierarchy. However, with the changes introduced in SMS 2003, some incompatibilities between the versions are unavoidable. In a mixed-version hierarchy, you can continue to manage the entire hierarchy centrally, but some issues exist.

Practice: Describing the Features of SMS

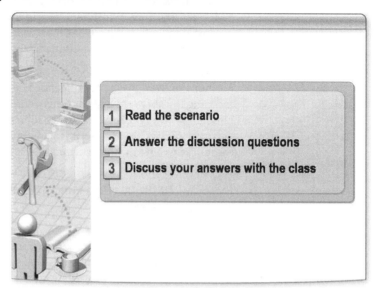

Instructions

In this exercise, you will pair with the student beside you and create a presentation based on the scenario below. After you talk about the scenario with your partner, use the lines below to answer the discussion questions. Your instructor will then ask your team to discuss your answers.

Scenario

Clair Hector is the director of IT and Jae Pak is the systems administrator for Northwind Traders. Clair oversees all the IT and IS departments. Jae is in charge of managing the day-to-day operations of the network and server environment.

Discussion questions

1. Jae Pak wants to know if his organization has enough software licenses for their computers. Which SMS feature should he use to determine how many software licenses he needs?

   Software Inventory.

   Metering

   _____

   _____

2. Jae Pak reports to Clair Hector that their organization needs 100 licenses for a particular software product. Clair is trying to trim the budget in their department. She wants to determine if all 100 licenses are absolutely necessary to perform their work. What SMS feature can Jae use to determine usage levels for the software product? What kind of data does this SMS feature provide?

_____

_____

_____

_____

Lesson: Explaining SMS Hierarchies

- **What Is an SMS Site?**
- **What Is the SMS Hierarchy?**
- **The Key Components of an SMS Site**
- **Services that Site Systems Provide**
- **The Role of an SMS Client**
- **What Are Collections?**

Introduction

Administering an SMS enterprise requires an in-depth understanding of how an SMS *site*, the fundamental organizational unit of SMS 2003, is organized and connected to create an SMS hierarchy. This lesson describes an SMS site and the roles performed by each of the SMS site components, site servers, site systems, and clients, in this site.

In this lesson, you will also learn how SMS categorizes *resources*. Resources are objects, such as computers or user groups, that can be managed by SMS. This lesson describes how SMS organizes resources into collections to perform important administrative tasks.

Lesson objectives

After completing this lesson, you will be able to:

- Define the differences between primary and secondary sites.
- Describe the characteristics of a hierarchy.
- Describe the main components of an SMS site.
- Describe site systems used by SMS.
- Describe the role of the SMS client and how the features of SMS are delivered by means of client agents.
- Describe the purpose of SMS collections.

What Is an SMS Site?

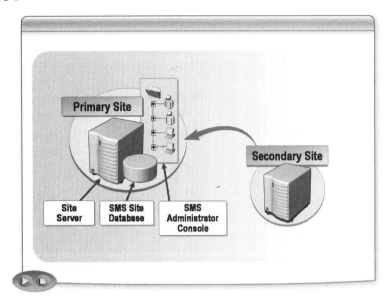

When you first install SMS, you install a single SMS site. This is the fundamental administrative unit in SMS. It defines the computers, users, groups, and other resources that are managed by SMS. Each SMS site is identified by a three-character alphanumeric code. The site code must be unique in your organization. The purpose of the site code is to identify the site to which clients are assigned and to identify site objects.

SMS provides two types of sites: primary sites and secondary sites.

Primary site

The first SMS site you install is a primary site. A primary site stores SMS data for itself and all the sites beneath it in a SQL Server database. This is called the *SMS site database*. An SMS site database stores information about the enterprise, such as client data, client configuration, and status information. Every primary site in the SMS hierarchy contains an SMS site database and requires an SMS site database server.

Primary sites have administrative tools, such as the *SMS Administrator console*, that enable the SMS administrator to manage the site directly. The SMS Administrator console is the user interface for configuring and administering the site.

SMS Setup creates each primary site as a stand-alone site. Primary sites can have multiple secondary sites, which send data to the primary site.

Secondary site

A secondary site has no SMS site database. It is attached to and reports to a primary site. The secondary site is managed by an SMS administrator running an SMS Administrator console that is connected to the primary site. A secondary site itself cannot have child sites.

The secondary site forwards the information it gathers from SMS clients, such as computer inventory data and SMS system status information, to its parent site. The primary site then stores the data of both the primary and secondary sites in the SMS site database.

What Is the SMS Hierarchy?

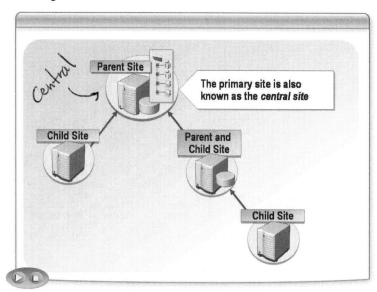

The parent site that has no sites above it in the hierarchy is called the central site. After you install your first SMS site, you can add sites above and beneath it. When you attach a site to another site, you create a parent-child relationship. This is called an SMS hierarchy.

An SMS hierarchy defines the relationship of all the SMS sites in an organization that report to one central site. The central site is the highest site in the hierarchy and will contain all client data from all other sites below it. You can attach primary sites to the central site and attach secondary sites to the primary sites. Secondary sites report to primary sites.

Parent and child relationships in the SMS hierarchy

A *parent site* is a primary site that has at least one site attached below it in the hierarchy. Only a primary site can have child sites. A secondary site can only be a child site. A parent site contains pertinent information about its lower-level sites, such as computer inventory data and SMS system status information, and controls many operations at the child sites.

A *child site* is a site that is attached to a site above it in the hierarchy. The site it reports to is its parent site. SMS copies all the data that is collected at a child site to its parent site. A child site is either a primary site or a secondary site, but a secondary site can only be a child site.

When do you create an SMS hierarchy?

It is not always necessary to create an SMS hierarchy. For example, in a simple LAN environment, it is possible to manage your entire organization with one SMS site. However, if your organization has a large number of clients or your networks are connected by slow links, SMS effectiveness will improve if you spread the workload across multiple SMS sites.

Note   For more information about creating multiple sites, see the next lesson, "Explaining SMS Site-to-Site Communication."

The Key Components of an SMS Site

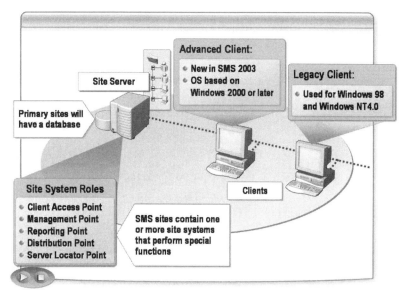

Each SMS site always contains a site server, one or more site systems, and clients. If the SMS site is a primary site, it will also contain an SMS site database.

Site servers

A *site server* is a computer that manages the SMS site and all its components and services.

When SMS is installed on a computer, that computer is automatically assigned the site server role. By default, the SMS Administrator console is installed on a primary site server during SMS Setup.

Site systems and site system roles

A *site system* is a server in an SMS site that provides some special functionality to the site. There are several types of site systems, each of which is responsible for performing a particular role. Examples of site systems include servers that perform the function of server locator points, or client access points, or management points.

To simplify identification, site systems are often referred to by their *site system role* name. For example, a server that performs the functions of a distribution point role is often called a *distribution point*.

The SMS administrator can assign site system roles to the primary site server or distribute them among several site systems. It is also possible for multiple servers to be assigned the same site role where necessary. Some site system roles are assigned during installation. Other site system roles are assigned through the SMS Administrator console.

Clients

Any computer running an SMS 2003–supported operating system that has a connection to your organization's network can potentially become an SMS 2003 client. A computer becomes an SMS client after the SMS client software is installed on that computer.

SMS 2003 provides two types of clients: Advanced Clients and Legacy Clients.

- Advanced Client
  - New client type introduced in SMS 2003
  - Operating systems based on Windows 2000 or later
- Legacy Client
  - Required for Windows 98 and Windows NT 4.0 Service Pack 6
  - Managed by the Client Access Point server role

Both client types can be deployed on desktop computers, mobile computers, and remote computers; however, the Advanced Client is the recommended client type to deploy on all computers running Windows 2000 or later. The Advanced Client is especially recommended for mobile and remote computers because the Advanced Client has features that are specifically designed to support those types of computers.

Services that Site Systems Provide

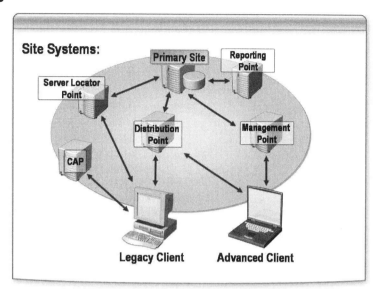

As described in the previous topic, a site system is one of the key components of an SMS site. Unlike a site server, which performs core data processing tasks for the site, a site system provides additional services for the SMS site.

When a server provides a site system role (the functionality that the server provides within SMS) that server is referred to by its site system role name. The following table describes some of the main services provided by site systems.

Service	Description
Client access point (CAP)	The *client access point* is the point of contact between *Legacy Clients* and the SMS site. The CAP passes all Legacy Client data to the site server. Legacy Client computers contact the CAP for management information from the SMS site server. A CAP serves only one SMS site and is installed by default on the site server. Even if your SMS site uses only Advanced Clients, one CAP is still required in the SMS site.
Server locator point	The server locator point locates CAPs for Legacy Clients and provides assigned site details for Advanced Clients. The server locator point is used primarily for installation of logon scripts (capinst) and Advanced Clients for automatic discovery of the assigned site code.

(*continued*)

Service	Description
Reporting point	A reporting point is a server that hosts the code for Report Viewer and any supplemental reports. A reporting point communicates directly with its SMS site database server.
Management point	The *management point* is the primary point of contact between *Advanced Clients* and the SMS site server. An SMS site has only one default management point, although you can provide network load balancing between multiple management points using Windows Network Load Balancing. In a relationship similar to the relationship between CAPs and Legacy Clients, a management point provides specific client configuration details (also known as *Advanced Client policy*) for the Advanced Client after client installation, serves as the location where Advanced Client computers check for advertisements, locates distribution points for Advanced Clients, and receives data from Advanced Clients and forwards it to the SMS site server.
Distribution point	The distribution point stores SMS package source files that SMS clients use when installing software programs.

The Role of an SMS Client

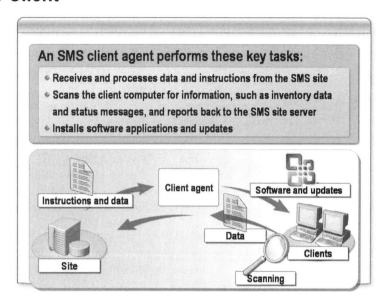

An SMS client agent performs these key tasks:
- Receives and processes data and instructions from the SMS site
- Scans the client computer for information, such as inventory data and status messages, and reports back to the SMS site server
- Installs software applications and updates

When you install SMS client software on a computer and assign that client to a site to be managed, the computer becomes an SMS client. SMS clients contain special software called *client agents*. Client agents support SMS primary features, such as software distribution and inventory. To support SMS primary features, SMS client agents perform the following key tasks:

- Receive and process data and instructions from the SMS site.

- Scan the client computer for information, such as inventory data and status messages to report back to the SMS site server.

- Install software applications and updates.

Key differences between Advanced and Legacy Clients

For many administrative and end-user purposes, the two client types appear to be identical. For that reason, you can often administer SMS with little consideration about which client type is deployed on individual computers. Both client types support the primary features of SMS, such as software distribution and inventory collection, with only minor differences.

However, because the Legacy Client is based on the earlier technology of the SMS 2.0 client, it relies heavily on domain accounts to carry out key tasks on the SMS client computer, such as installing software in an administrative context when the logged-on user account does not have the appropriate security credentials. The Advanced Client, however, uses the local system security context and the computer account to carry out these same key tasks. This makes managing the Advanced Client much more secure.

The following table outlines additional differences between Advanced Clients and Legacy Clients.

Issue	Description
Support for mobile and remote computers	Advanced Clients are recommended for mobile and remote computers because the architecture is designed to support those types of computers.
Communication with site systems	Advanced Clients use management points to send and receive data from the site server. The Legacy Client uses a client access point to communicate with the site server.
Operating system and version support	You must deploy the Legacy Client when the client computer is running Windows 98 or Windows NT 4.0 Service Pack 6. If you are running Windows 2000 or later, Microsoft recommends that you install or upgrade clients to the Advanced Client as soon as possible.

Communicating with the SMS site systems and domain controllers

SMS clients use domain controllers to authenticate domain accounts and to access logon scripts. SMS clients can find server locator points by using Microsoft Active Directory® directory service domain controllers. Advanced Clients can use Active Directory domain controllers to find distribution points at the local site.

What Are Collections?

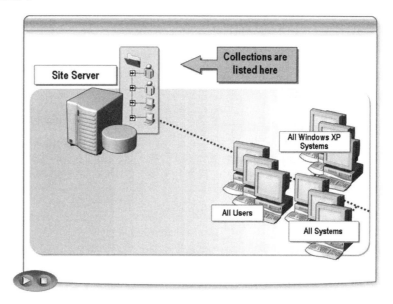

SMS manages resources in groups called *collections*. Collections are logical groups of SMS resources that satisfy criteria defined by the administrator. Data about collections and their attributes is stored in the site's database. Collections are used to distribute software, view the inventories of clients, and access clients for remote control sessions.

Why do we need collections?

Collections are designed to gather resources into useful groups that you can manage within your site hierarchy. Some SMS features can operate on clients only if they are members of a collection. For example, to distribute software to clients in the hierarchy, you must first create a collection that includes all the clients that need to receive the distributed software.

Practice: Identifying SMS Site Roles

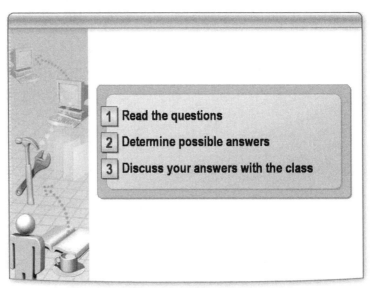

Instructions

Read the following questions, determine answers, and then discuss your answers with the rest of the class.

Tip   You can also create an example hierarchy to illustrate the different roles in an SMS hierarchy.

Scenario

Clair Hector is the director of the IT department for Northwind Traders. Jae Pak is the systems administrator in charge of managing the day-to-day operations of the network and server environment. Jae's next task is to work with his team and to examine the SMS hierarchy to determine what roles the sites will play.

Discussion questions

1. What are the differences between the primary and secondary SMS sites?

_____

_____

_____

_____

_____

2. What is a central site? What are parent and child sites?

_____

_____

_____

_____

_____

3. What are the new developments with SMS 2003 Advanced Client?

_____

_____

_____

_____

_____

4. What are site systems? Name two site systems. What do they do?

_____

_____

_____

_____

_____

Lesson: Explaining SMS Site-to-Site Communication

- Considerations for Creating Multiple Sites
- How Information Flows From Site to Site
- SMS Support for Multiple-Language Organizations

Introduction

In your role as SMS administrator, you might be responsible for administering only one SMS site, or you might be responsible for administering multiple sites. This lesson describes considerations in creating multiple sites and explains how SMS handles communication between sites.

Lesson objectives

After completing this lesson, you will be able to:

- Describe considerations in designing an SMS hierarchy.

- Describe the flow of site and client information and administration control within a hierarchy.

- Describe how different language environments can be implemented.

Considerations for Creating Multiple Sites

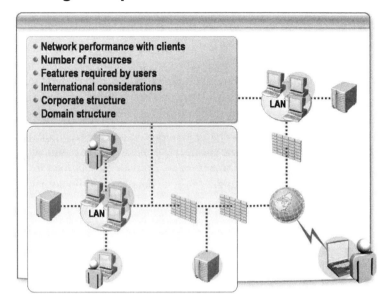

Single SMS sites are the easiest to configure and manage. Within a single site, SMS uses existing LAN connections for communication between site systems. You may need special account configuration for sending data between site servers and site systems.

However, there are circumstances in which it is advantageous to set up multiple sites in an SMS hierarchy. Because SMS works by summarizing and compressing significant amounts of data and transferring this data through network lines, SMS efficiency might improve dramatically if you spread the workload across multiple SMS sites.

Two key factors to consider when planning an SMS hierarchy are client support and organizational needs.

Client support

Client support considerations include:

- *Network performance with clients*. Slow network connectivity between the site systems and some clients might indicate a need to set up and manage those clients in their own site if the group of clients is well-connected.

- *Number of resources*. If there are more resources than can be supported by a single site using the SMS features you have chosen, consider creating additional sites.

- *Features required by users*. Because all clients in a single SMS site use the same set of client features (agents), if you want different sets of features for different sets of clients, you will need multiple SMS sites.

Organizational needs   The needs of your organization might include:

- *International considerations*. You might need to install an international version of SMS in the same hierarchy that contains an English or other localized version of SMS.

- *Corporate structure*. Your organization's policies can play a role in how the sites are defined. For example, there might be multiple system administration groups within an organization that require administration of their own resources.

- *Domain structure*. Your existing domain model might dictate how the SMS site locates resources, or you might choose to organize or reorganize your domain model to more closely map to your SMS architecture (although single sites can handle multiple domains).

How Information Flows from Site to Site

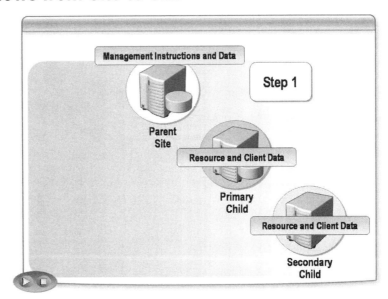

Although it is possible to organize your computers into one large SMS site, or into an assembly of unconnected sites, most SMS environments are based on a carefully planned hierarchy of interconnected sites.

What types of information flow from site to site?

In general, management and configuration data moves down the hierarchy from higher-level sites. Resource and client data move up the hierarchy from lower-level sites.

For example, a parent site sends management instructions and data intended for client distribution down to its child sites. Child sites report their status up to their parent sites. This status includes the information the site gathers from SMS clients, such as computer inventory data and SMS system status information.

The process

In an SMS environment based on a hierarchy of interconnected sites, information flows like this:

1. The parent site sends management instructions to child sites.
2. Child sites send client data to parent sites.

SMS Support for Multiple-Language Organizations

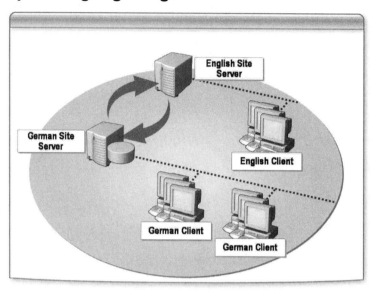

International organizations might need to implement a multiple-language hierarchy. The SMS client language that is installed must be compatible with the language of the site server to which the client reports.

SMS supports:

- Multiple language versions of the SMS Administrator console.
- Multiple language versions of the SMS client.
- Double-byte and single-byte character sets for both servers and clients.

Supported site server languages

The following table lists the seven languages that SMS site servers support. The first column lists the languages into which SMS servers are localized or enabled. However, with SMS 2003 Service Pack 1, an English version of SMS can be installed on any localized Operating System. The second column lists the corresponding client languages supported by each of the server language packages. Any site server language version listed in the table can be the child site or the parent site of any other listed localized server. Except for the French server, all localized servers support U.S. English clients.

Site server language	Supported client language
English	English and all Windows 2000 Professional and Windows XP Professional languages
French	French
German	German, English
Japanese	Japanese, English
Korean	Korean, English
Simplified Chinese	Simplified Chinese, English
Traditional Chinese	Traditional Chinese, English

Note The English-language server is available in both English and International English. The contents of the SMS product compact disc for these two versions are identical and can be used interchangeably; however, their license agreements are different.

Supported client languages

An SMS client is available in the following localized languages:

- Czech
- Danish
- Dutch
- Finnish
- French
- German
- Greek
- Hungarian
- Italian
- Japanese
- Korean

- Norwegian
- Polish
- Portuguese
- Portuguese-Brazilian
- Russian
- Simplified Chinese
- Spanish
- Swedish
- Traditional Chinese
- Turkish

Note For detailed information about using SMS in an international organization, see Appendix D of the *Microsoft Systems Management Server 2003 Operations Guide*, which you can access on the "Additional Reading" page of your Student Materials compact disc.

Practice: Identifying Considerations for Creating Multiple Sites

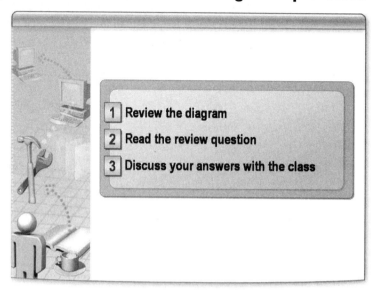

Instructions

Review the diagram below and then read the two scenarios that follow. Talk about possible site-to-site communication considerations with a partner. When you and your partner have identified at least three considerations, discuss your ideas with the rest of the class.

Scenario

Clair Hector is the director of the IT department for Northwind Traders. Jae Pak is the systems administrator in charge of managing the day-to-day operations of the network and server environment. At the end of the previous practice, Jae and his team had identified SMS site roles. Now they need to identify considerations for managing clients in remote offices by adding sites to the SMS hierarchy. Northwind Traders has offices in New York, Chicago, and Tokyo. A primary site exists in New York. Clair and Jae need to identify considerations for creating sites to manage clients in Chicago and Tokyo and adding those sites to the hierarchy.

Diagram

Diagram 1. Identifying Site-to-Site Communication Considerations

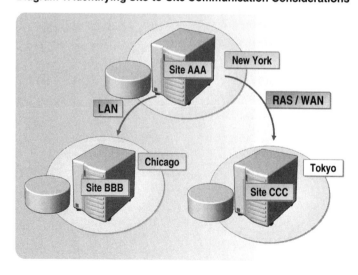

Questions

Scenario 1: Creating a Site in the Chicago Office and Adding It to the Hierarchy:

The connection between New York and Chicago is a high-speed WAN connection, and it is generally considered a good connection. However, the connection receives a lot of traffic, particularly between the hours of 8 A.M. and 5 P.M. What are the main considerations for implementing a primary site (BBB) in Chicago to manage clients there?

after hours

Scenario 2: Creating a Site in the Tokyo Office and Adding It to the Hierarchy:

The connection between New York and Tokyo is a long-distance RAS connection. What are the main considerations for implementing a primary site (CCC) in Tokyo to manage clients there?

courier

Lesson: Explaining SMS Site and Roaming Boundaries

* What Are SMS Site Boundaries?
* How Legacy and Advanced Clients Use Site Boundaries
* What Are Roaming Boundaries?

Introduction

This lesson describes the SMS site and roaming boundaries. Boundaries are a key element during the design and setup of the site to enable you to deploy SMS clients successfully in an organization. Without boundaries, the SMS site will not know where to look to discover resources.

Lesson objectives

After completing this lesson, you will be able to:

- Describe the purpose of SMS site boundaries.
- Describe how Legacy Clients and Advanced Clients use site boundaries.
- Describe roaming boundaries.

What Are SMS Site Boundaries?

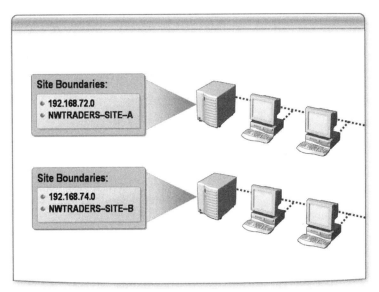

SMS sites are defined by site boundaries. You would use *site boundaries* to assign clients to a site. Site boundaries are defined by IP subnets, Active Directory site names, or both.

Site boundaries are defined at the planning stage of your SMS deployment. Planning site boundaries involves deciding which resources and subnets to include in each site. Each SMS 2003 client is assigned to a single SMS site.

How Legacy and Advanced Clients Use Site Boundaries

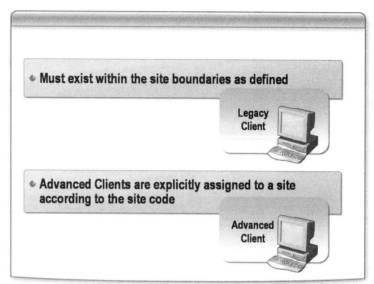

Legacy Clients and Advanced Clients use site boundaries differently:

- Legacy Clients must exist within the site boundaries as defined. If this condition is not met, the Legacy Client software will not be installed, or it might be removed from client computers if already installed. Legacy Clients are included in an SMS site if their IP address or Active Directory site name is within the site boundaries that the SMS administrator has configured for the SMS site.

- Advanced Clients are explicitly assigned to a site according to the site code. Advanced Client installation may be configured to proceed only if the client is within site boundaries.

Network bandwidth considerations

The subnets included in your site boundaries should be connected with reliable links so that all resources in the site have a fast connection to all other site resources.

Therefore, if two subnets are separated by a slow link, you should create a separate SMS site at each physical location. If the physical location contains many users, contains users with varying needs, or has more than one group managing the computers, you might consider splitting a single physical location into more than one SMS site.

What Are Roaming Boundaries?

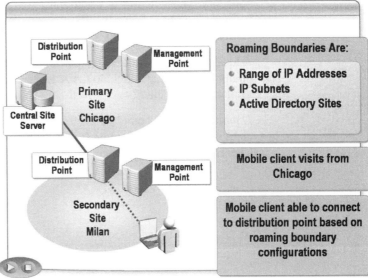

In SMS 2003, Advanced Clients are able to move, or *roam*, from one location to another in the organization and still be managed by SMS. Legacy Clients, however, are designed to be bound to a specific site boundary.

Roaming is the ability to move a computer running the SMS Advanced Client from one IP subnet or Active Directory site to another. Roaming always involves an IP address change on the client.

Although Advanced Clients are assigned only to primary sites, they can roam to both primary and secondary sites. Legacy Clients can be assigned to both primary and secondary sites, but not at the same time.

Roaming boundaries are the list of IP subnets, IP address ranges, and Active Directory sites that determine which roaming Advanced Clients are able to access the site's distribution points. By using roaming boundaries, an SMS Advanced Client computer can move from one location to another in the organization and still be managed by SMS.

Roaming boundaries enable SMS to provide software distribution to Advanced Clients. Roaming boundaries are also used to configure protected distribution points. Access to a protected distribution point is restricted to Advanced Clients that are within a specified set of boundaries configured by the SMS administrator for that distribution point.

Roaming boundaries are used by Advanced Clients when they perform an automated discovery of the assigned site's site code. This can occur during client installation or be initiated manually at the client computer.

When configuring roaming boundaries, the SMS administrator specifies whether a roaming boundary is a local roaming boundary or a remote roaming boundary. This determines whether the Advanced Client treats distribution points in the site as being locally available for each roaming boundary that is configured.

A local roaming boundary is a roaming boundary in which the site distribution points are locally available to the Advanced Client and software packages are available to that client over a well-connected link.

A remote roaming boundary is a roaming boundary in which the site distribution points are remote (that is, is not well-connected) to the Advanced Client, and software packages are not available locally to that client.

Practice: Identifying SMS Site Boundaries

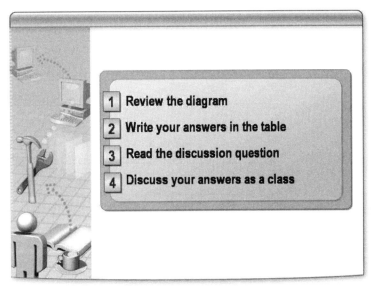

Instructions	Review the diagram below, and then choose which site, if any, to which the client will be assigned. Write the correct site code in the column on the right. When you are finished, discuss your answers with the class.
Scenario	Clair Hector is the director of IT department of Northwind Traders. Jae Pak is the systems administrator in charge of managing the day-to-day operations of the network and server environment. Jae Pak and his team have identified site boundaries for sites in the hierarchy. They need to ensure that clients throughout the organization can be assigned to sites based on the boundaries that have been configured.
Diagram	

Diagram 2. Identifying SMS Site Boundaries

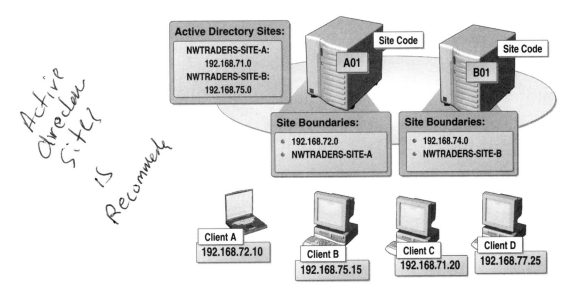

Discussion question

For each client, discuss why you assigned it to a particular site, if any.

Client A:

_____

_____

_____

Client B:

_____

_____

_____

Client C:

_____

_____

_____

Client D:

_____

_____

_____

Discussion: Overview of Systems Management Server 2003

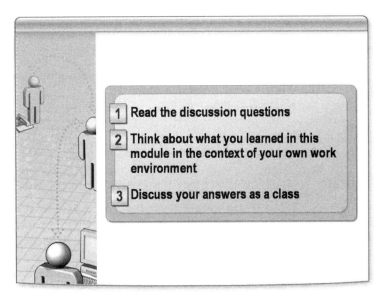

1. Which of the products in the Microsoft Management Family does your organization use or anticipate using?

   _____

   _____

   _____

   _____

2. How do you anticipate your organization will use the features provided by SMS 2003?

   _____

   _____

   _____

3. What type of SMS hierarchy do you have or do you anticipate having?

_____

_____

_____

4. Which network and communication considerations are relevant to your organization's site structure?

_____

_____

_____

5. Do you anticipate that your organization will implement IP subnet, or Active Directory site boundaries, or both? Does your organization have many mobile clients? What kind of boundaries will you use to support them?

_____

_____

_____

Module 2: Exploring SMS Site Architecture

Contents

Overview

- Introduction to the SMS Site Server
- Exploring the SMS Administrator Console and the SMS 2003 Toolkit 1
- Explaining the Role of Active Directory in SMS 2003
- Explaining How SMS Uses Dependent Technologies

Introduction

In this module, you will learn how Microsoft® Systems Management Server (SMS) 2003 is implemented in a site. You will explore the properties of the principal site system—the SMS site server. You will learn how to install and use the SMS Administrator console and other tools that allow administration and support of an SMS implementation. You will also learn about the new role of the Active Directory® directory service in SMS and how SMS uses related technologies such as Background Intelligent Transfer Service (BITS), Microsoft Windows® Management Instrumentation (WMI), and the Windows Installer (MSI).

Objectives

After completing this module, you will be able to:

- Describe the SMS site server and its components.
- Use the SMS Administrator console and the SMS 2003 Toolkit 1.
- Describe how SMS uses Active Directory.
- Describe how SMS uses dependent technologies such as Microsoft Internet Information Services (IIS), BITS, WMI, and MSI.

Lesson: Introduction to the SMS Site Server

* Components of a Site Server
* SMS Security Modes
* The Role of the SMS Service Account
* The Purpose of Extending the Active Directory Schema
* Tasks You Can Perform During SMS Setup

Introduction

In this lesson, you will learn about the components of an SMS site server.

Lesson objectives

After completing this lesson, you will be able to:

- Describe the SMS site server components.
- Describe the SMS security modes.
- Describe the role of the SMS service account.
- Describe the benefit of extending the Active Directory schema for SMS.
- Describe what tasks you can perform during SMS setup.

Components of a Site Server

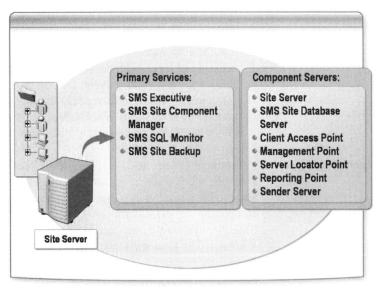

SMS is installed on the *SMS site server*, which is a server that manages the SMS site and all its components and services. The SMS site server is the primary point of access between SMS clients and the SMS site database, which is a Microsoft SQL Server™ database that stores information, such as client data that is discovered and inventoried by SMS and configuration and status information.

The site server hosts the SMS components that are necessary to monitor and manage an SMS site. When SMS is installed on a computer, that computer is automatically assigned the site server role. The site server can perform additional roles, such as serving as a client access point (CAP), management point, or distribution point. By default, the SMS Administrator console is installed on a primary site server during SMS setup. By default, a site server is configured to be a distribution point and a CAP.

Primary services

The site server runs the following primary services:

- *SMS Executive*. This is the main SMS service. It contains many SMS threads that carry out specific SMS functions. These threads include the processes that control software distribution and manage site-to-site communication.

- *SMS Site Component Manager*. This service ensures that the component server processes are running properly. It performs the initial installation of components and performs regular checks to ensure that they are running properly. This service installs and monitors four of the site systems (client access point, reporting point, management point, and server locator point) and the site database server and sender server. SMS Site Component Manager also installs the SQL Monitor and monitors the communication between the site and SQL Server. It also reinstalls the SMS services on the SMS site server during a site reset.

■ *SMS SQL Monitor*. This service manages the SMS database operations and runs maintenance tasks. This service runs on the computer designated as the SMS site database server, which may be the site server or another SMS site system.

■ *SMS Site Backup*. This service runs on the site server to accomplish the backup task operation. At its scheduled time, the SMS_SITE_BACKUP service starts a backup cycle. During the backup cycle, the service performs some initial steps and then backs up data from the site server. It then backs up data from the SMS site database server and from the provider server, if either is set up on a computer other than the site server.

Component servers

Component servers host one or more SMS components that support the site. For example, when a sender is installed on a server, or when the CAP role is assigned to a site system, that site system is automatically assigned the role of component server. A component server is a site system role that is filled by any SMS site system running an SMS component installed by SMS Site Component Manager. The only site system that is not a component server is the distribution point.

The following table describes the component servers.

Component Server	Description
Site server	Site servers are computers that manage the SMS site and all its components and services. The SMS site server is the primary point of access between you and the SMS site database.
SMS site database server	SMS uses Windows Management Instrumentation (WMI) as the interface to the site database. See Explaining How SMS Uses Dependent Technologies, in this module, for an explanation of how SMS uses WMI.
Client access point (CAP)	The client access point role is the point of contact between *Legacy Clients* and the SMS site server. The CAP passes all Legacy Client data to the site server.
Management point	The management point is the primary point of contact between Advanced Clients and the SMS site server. A management point provides specific client configuration details for the Advanced Client after client installation, serves as the location where Advanced Client computers check for advertisements, locates distribution points for Advanced Clients, and receives data from Advanced Clients and forwards it to the SMS site server.
Server locator point (SLP)	The server locator point locates CAPs for Legacy Clients and provides assigned site details for Advanced Clients. The server locator point is primarily used in client installation; however, it can also be used for automatic discovery of the assigned site code for advanced clients.

(continued)

Component Server	Description
Reporting point	A reporting point is a server that hosts the code for Report Viewer and any supplemental reports. A reporting point communicates only with its SMS site database server.
Sender server	A sender is a server that uses existing connectivity to transmit instructions and data from one site to another site in the hierarchy. Senders do not provide a physical connection to another site. They use existing network connectivity to manage connections, ensure integrity of transferred data, recover from errors, and close connections when they are no longer necessary.

SMS Security Modes

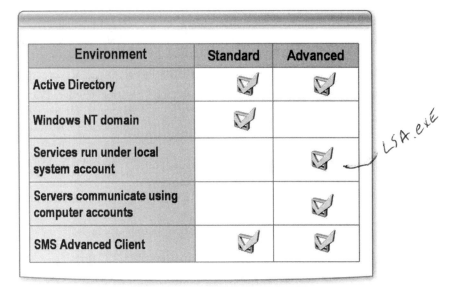

SMS uses security modes to control how SMS client computers are managed and how SMS sites communicate with other SMS sites and site systems. SMS runs in either standard security mode or advanced security mode. The security mode that you enable affects the type and number of accounts used for SMS security. Each security mode has its advantages, so you must choose the mode that is appropriate for your SMS sites.

Standard security mode   This security mode allows SMS 2003 to function like SMS 2.0 for organizations that have not yet implemented Active Directory. Standard security mode sites do not require their SMS servers to be in Active Directory. SMS 2003 standard security relies on user accounts to run services, to make changes to computers, and to connect between computers.

If you upgrade your SMS 2.0 site to SMS 2003, you will run SMS 2003 in standard security mode by default. You can migrate from standard security to advanced security once your site is ready to run in advanced security.

Advanced security mode   SMS 2003 advanced security uses the local system account on SMS servers to run SMS services and make changes on the servers. Advanced security uses computer accounts (rather than user accounts) to connect to other computers and to make changes on other computers. Computer accounts can be used only by services running in the local system account context, and only local administrators can configure services.

The local system account and computer accounts have several advantages over user accounts:

- The local system account is local to the computer itself, so the jurisdiction of the account is limited. However, computers can be configured to allow remote connections from other computer accounts.

- Only the operating system has access to the password for a computer account, so network users cannot use computer accounts to access network resources.

- The local system account does not have a password or require one. Local system and computer accounts do not require any manual maintenance, even in organizations that require that all passwords be changed on a regular basis because the computer regularly and automatically changes computer account passwords.

- The local system account does not need to be a member of the Domain Administrators user group.

Important   Advanced security is the recommended security mode. However, you must use standard security if your site does not meet the requirements for installing advanced security. In addition, you will use standard security if you are upgrading directly from an existing SMS 2.0 site. You can then migrate to advanced security.

The Role of the SMS Service Account

The SMS Service Account:

* Provides the security context in which the SMS Executive service and other SMS services on the site server run

* Creates operating system objects on the site server and the other servers on which it is used

* Accesses SQL Server, if SQL Server is accessed by means of Windows Authentication

* Accesses domain controllers when enumerating users, groups, containers, or systems for the discovery methods

The SMS Service Account is used:

- To provide the security context in which the SMS Executive service and other SMS services on the site server run.

- To create operating system objects (such as directories, files, and services) on the site server and the other servers on which it is used.

- To access SQL Server, if SQL Server is accessed by means of Windows Authentication.

- To access domain controllers when enumerating users, groups, containers, or systems (computer accounts) for the discovery methods (which are procedures that detect and acquire information about resources on the network).

SMS allows the administrator to specify accounts to use for communication between sites and site systems. If the site uses advanced security, you can use the site server's computer account for site-to-site system communication.

The SMS Service Account must have the **Log on as a service** right on the SMS site server. This right can be provided by a Group Policy setting on the organizational unit that the site server is in, or during the installation of the site server when running SMS Setup. If the site server is moved to another organizational unit, a policy in that organizational unit must be set to give the SMS Service Account the **Log on as a service** right.

When the SMS Service Account is used to enumerate users, groups, containers, or systems in domains other than the domain the site server is in, the SMS Service Account must have user rights on those domains. (The account must at least be a member of the Domain Users group for the domains.)

The local system account serves as the SMS Service Account role on an advanced security site server. When accessing network resources, the advanced security site server uses the computer account for this role.

The Purpose of Extending the Active Directory Schema

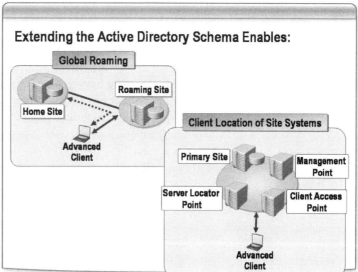

To improve client location of site systems and roaming, extend the Active Directory schema to allow SMS-specific classes and attributes to be created. If you do not want to extend the Active Directory schema, you can use Windows Internet Naming Service (WINS) instead. However, WINS is only used for regional roaming; to enable global roaming, you must extend the Active Directory schema.

Why extend the Active Directory schema?

You extend the Active Directory schema to publish SMS objects in Active Directory. If you do not extend the schema, SMS cannot publish objects, and the following features are not available for Advanced Clients in SMS:

- Global roaming.

- Automatic site assignment in which the server locator point is not specified in WINS.

When to extend the Active Directory schema

Although SMS 2003 Setup prompts you to extend the schema, you can extend the schema before, during, or after you run Setup.

If you choose to extend the Active Directory schema during setup, perform this task only once per Active Directory forest. The logged-on user who is running SMS Setup must have Schema Administrator credentials.

Important Before you enable any Active Directory schema changes in a Windows 2000 domain, the option to allow the schema to be extended has to be enabled. This does not apply to Microsoft Windows Server™ 2003 domains.

The schema is extended once per forest, but each domain will have its own System Management container that SMS needs proper rights to publish its data. The System Management container needs to be created for every domain containing site systems, and the containers permissions need to be set appropriately.

More information

For additional information about extending the Active Directory schema, see following documents on the Additional Reading page of your Student Materials compact disc.

- Chapter 15, "Deploying and Configuring Sites," in the *Microsoft Systems Management Server 2003 Concepts, Planning, and Deployment Guide*.

- The white paper "Active Directory Schema Modification and Publishing for Systems Management Server 2003." This white paper is also available on the Download Center page of the Microsoft Web site. The link to this paper is included on the Internet links page of the Student Materials compact disc.

Tasks You Can Perform During SMS Setup

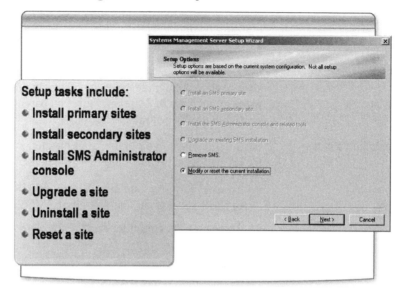

Before and after the actual installation of SMS, you can perform a number of tasks using the SMS Setup Wizard.

Installing a primary site

The first SMS site you install is a primary site. A primary site stores SMS data for itself and all the sites in the same hierarchy in a SQL Server database. This is called the *SMS site database*. Primary sites have administrative tools, such as the SMS Administrator console, that enable the SMS administrator to directly manage the site.

SMS Setup creates each primary site as a stand-alone site. Primary sites can have multiple child sites, which send data to the primary site.

Installing a secondary site

A secondary site has no SMS site database. It is attached to and reports to a primary site. The secondary site is managed by an SMS administrator running an SMS Administrator console that is connected to the primary site or any other primary site above the parent site in the SMS hierarchy.

The secondary site forwards the information it gathers from SMS clients, such as computer inventory data and SMS system status information, to its parent site. The primary site then stores the data of both the primary and secondary sites in the SMS site database.

Installing the SMS Administrator console

The SMS Administrator console is the primary interface that you use to access, configure, and run SMS features and tools, and to accomplish daily tasks that are required to administer an SMS system. The SMS Administrator console supports SMS site configuration, site database maintenance, and SMS hierarchy status monitoring.

The SMS Administrator console is installed automatically on all primary sites. To distribute administrative tasks among various personnel in your organization, you might choose to install the SMS Administrator console on other computers.

Upgrading a site

SMS Setup allows you to upgrade a primary site from SMS 2.0 to SMS 2003. The upgrade process converts only the components that were installed in the SMS 2.0 site. After the upgrade process is complete, you must modify the site to install components that are new to SMS 2003 or that were not installed on the SMS 2.0 site you upgraded.

Because SMS 2003 can only report to other SMS 2003 sites and not to SMS 2.0 sites, you must upgrade your site hierarchy in a top-down manner. In other words, you upgrade a site only after its parent site has already been upgraded, starting with the central site.

Uninstalling a site

SMS Setup allows you to uninstall the site. Following are examples of reasons for taking this action:

- To remove a previous installation of SMS—whether a corrupted installation of SMS 2003, or an installation of SMS 2.0 or earlier.

- To change the computer name after SMS is installed.

- To repurpose a server.

If you choose to remove SMS and your SMS hierarchy consists of several SMS sites, you must remove SMS from every site. It is recommended that you begin with the lowest level sites in the hierarchy and end with the central site.

For more information about upgrading a site, see Chapter 14, "Upgrading to SMS 2003," in the *Microsoft Systems Management Server 2003 Concepts, Planning, and Deployment Guide* on the Additional Reading page of your Student Materials compact disc.

Resetting a site

Site reset is the process of running the SMS Setup Wizard and selecting the **Modify or reset the current installation** option to initiate configuration changes in an SMS site. SMS site reset stops the core SMS site services, removes them, and then reinstalls them. By using SMS site reset, you can:

- Repair a damaged site server.

- Make account or password changes effective.

- Force the site to use a different SQL Server database name or a server running SQL Server, or a different SQL Server security mode.

If there has been a change to the accounts used by the SMS components, site reset ensures the account details used by the SMS components are correct.

During site reset, changes specified while running the SMS Setup Wizard are written to the master site control file. SMS components and threads are removed from site servers and site systems, and are then reinstalled.

Reviewing the results

After you install a primary or secondary site, or upgrade or reset a site, you can review the setup results in SMSSetup.log. The SMS Setup process writes the settings to this log file, which is located at the root of your system drive.

Practice: Reviewing the SMS Site Server Installation Log and Verifying Installed Services

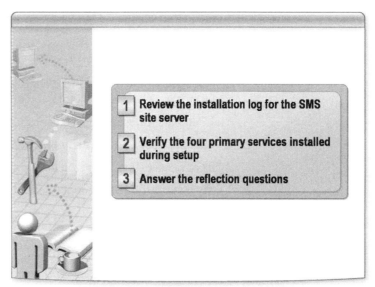

Instructions

Complete the procedures to practice reviewing the installation log for the SMS site server and verifying the four primary services installed during setup. Then, answer the reflection questions that follow.

In this practice, use the following values.

Variable	Value
Virtual machine—MS Site 1	Dublin
Dublin\Administrator	JaePa (Jae Pak)
Virtual machine—Domain controller	Glasgow
Domain Administrator	Administrator

Procedures

▶ **To review the installation log for the SMS site server**

1. Verify that the Glasgow virtual machine is running. If Glasgow is not running, log it on to the NWTRADERS domain with a user name of **Administrator** and a password of **P@ssw0rd**.

   After the Glasgow virtual machine opens, you can minimize it.

2. Log Administrator off the Dublin virtual Machine.

3. Log the Dublin virtual machine on to the NWTRADERS domain with a user name of **JaePa** and a password of **P@ssw0rd**.

4. On the Dublin virtual machine, click **Start**, point to **All Program**s, point to **Accessories**, and then click **Windows Explorer**.

5. Browse to drive C and then open the SMSSetup.log.

6. Review the log, and attempt to:

   - Verify the creation of the site database and database objects.

   - Identify the installed files and components.

7. Close the SMSSetup.log, and then close Windows Explorer.

▶ **To verify the four primary services installed during setup**

1. On the Dublin virtual machine, click **Start**, point to **Administrative Tools**, and then click **Computer Management**.

   The Computer Management console opens.

2. Expand **Services and Applications**, and then click **Services**.

   A list of services appears in the details pane.

3. Verify that the following services have been installed:

   - SMS_EXECUTIVE

   - SMS_SITE_COMPONENT_MANAGER

   - SMS_SQL_MONITOR

   - SMS_SITE_BACKUP

Note You can perform several actions for any service. For example, you can stop, start, pause, and resume the service. You can also modify properties for any service; however, it is not recommended to modify the properties for any SMS service by using Computer Management. Instead, use the SMS Administrator console.

---

4. On the **File** menu, click **Exit** to close the Microsoft Management Console.

5. Leave the Glasgow and Dublin virtual machines running because they will be used in subsequent practices.

Reflection questions

Jae Pak is the systems administrator at Northwind Traders and is responsible for managing the day-to-day operations of the SMS 2003 primary site. This morning, Jae received an e-mail from Jane Clayton, a systems administrator at a partner company. In her e-mail, Jane seeks advice about SMS 2003. She just installed SMS on the SMS site server and now she wants to know which primary services to verify are running in the installation log, why these services are so important to an SMS site. Her enterprise contains only Advanced Clients.

1. What services should he tell her to look for and why are they important?

   _____

   _____

   _____

   _____

2. Jane also asks you which type of security mode she should employ at her enterprise?

   _____

   _____

   _____

   _____

Lesson: Exploring the SMS Administrator Console and the SMS 2003 Toolkit 1

- How to Use the SMS Administrator Console to Explore a Site
- Demonstration: How to View Site Properties and Connect to Other SMS Sites
- How to Locate and View SMS Site Server Folders
- The Tools in the SMS 2003 Toolkit 1

Introduction

In this lesson, you will use the SMS Administrator console to view site properties and objects. You will learn how to use it to administer an SMS implementation. You will explore the principal nodes used for administration in the SMS Administrator console. You will investigate the core components of a site server, including folders, shares, permissions, components, and registry keys. You will also become familiar with some of the tools in the SMS 2003 Toolkit 1.

Lesson objectives

After completing this lesson, you will be able to:

- Use the SMS Administrator console to explore a site.
- View site properties and connect to other SMS sites.
- Locate and view site folders and files by using Windows Explorer.
- Describe the use of SMS 2003 Toolkit 1.

How to Use the SMS Administrator Console to Explore a Site

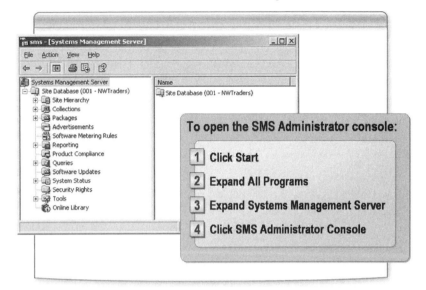

What is the SMS Administrator console?

In SMS 2003, the SMS Administrator console is the primary interface you use to access, configure, and run SMS features and tools. As an administrator, you install and use the SMS Administrator console to accomplish the day-to-day tasks required to administer an SMS system. The SMS Administrator console provides items you can use to configure your SMS sites, maintain your SMS site database, and monitor the status of your SMS hierarchy.

Procedure

To access the SMS Administrator console:

1. Click **Start**.
2. Point to **All Programs**.
3. Point to **Systems Management Server**.
4. Click **SMS Administrator Console**.

Using the SMS Administrator console

There are two panes in the SMS Administrator console: the console tree on the left and the details pane on the right. The details pane displays the contents of an item in the console tree. For example, when you click a specific collection in the console tree, the contents of that collection are displayed in the details pane.

If you are administering several sites, you can use the SMS Administrator console to connect to and manage multiple SMS sites in a single SMS Administrator console window.

Although software and hardware inventory, software distribution, Remote Tools, and software metering are the primary SMS features, most of the primary SMS features do not appear in the console tree. Each console item (such as Site Hierarchy, Collections, and Queries) provides access to the specific tasks that you use to achieve management operations as categorized by the SMS features. You can use a specific SMS feature by using a combination of console tree items. For example, you can perform software distribution by using the Packages and Advertisements console tree items.

Demonstration: How to View Site Properties and Connect to Other SMS Sites

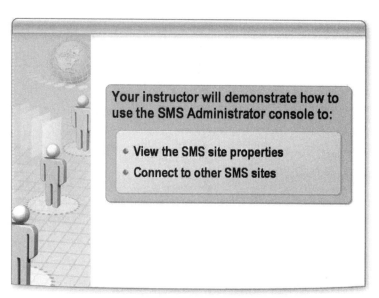

In this demonstration, your instructor will open the SMS Administrator console to demonstrate how the console enables you to view the SMS site hierarchy nodes and site objects and to connect to another primary site.

Your instructor will use the following values in this demonstration.

Variable	Value
Virtual machine—SMS Site 1	Dublin
Dublin\Administrator	JaePa (Jae Pak)
Virtual machine—Domain controller	Glasgow
Domain Administrator	Administrator

Important   These steps are included for your information. Do not attempt to do them in the classroom. If you perform these steps in the classroom environment, you may leave your computer in an incorrect state for upcoming practices.

Demonstration steps performed by instructor only

▶ **To view the SMS site properties**

1. Log the Glasgow virtual machine on to the NWTRADERS domain with a user name of **Administrator** and a password of **P@ssw0rd**.

   After the Glasgow virtual machine opens, you can minimize it.

2. Log the Dublin virtual machine on to the NWTRADERS domain with a user name of **JaePa** and a password of **P@ssw0rd**.

3. On the Dublin virtual machine, click **Start**, point to **All Programs**, point to **Systems Management Server**, and then click **SMS Administrator Console**.

4. In the console tree of the SMS Administrator console, expand **Site Database (001 – NWTraders)**.

   A list of site functions appears in the tree.

5. Expand the **Site Hierarchy** node.

6. Right-click the **001 – NWTraders** site node, and then click **Properties**.

   The **Site Properties** dialog box appears. This dialog box contains six tabs:

   - **General**. Provides general site information and enables you to set a parent site if necessary.

   - **Accounts**. Provides the account or accounts to be used as your SMS Service and SQL Server accounts.

   - **Site Boundaries**. Enables you to set the boundary type (IP subnet or Active Directory site), and boundary ID, such as IP subnet or Active Directory site name.

   - **Roaming Boundaries**. Enables to you to determine which Advanced Clients will be able to access the site's distribution points. You can set the boundary type (IP subnet, Active Directory site, or IP Address Range), and boundary ID (IP subnet, Active Directory site name, or IP address range).

   - **Advanced**. Enables you to specify settings that affect the publishing of data to Active Directory and the security of data transfer between this site and its child site. To use these features, they must be enabled. By default, SMS is configured to publish data to Active Directory. If you do not extend the Active Directory schema, you should disable publishing data to Active Directory.

   - **Security**. Enables you to view and specify security rights that users have on this object class or instance. NT AUTHORITY and the user who installed SMS are the default security accounts created during setup.

7. Close the **001-NWTraders Site Properties** dialog box, but leave the SMS Administrator console open.

▶ **To connect to a different SMS site**

1. On the Dublin virtual machine, in the console tree of the SMS Administrator console, right-click **Systems Management Server**, point to **All Tasks**, and then click **Connect to Site Database**.

   The Database Connection Wizard appears.

2. On the **Welcome to the Site Database Connection Wizard** page, click **Next**.

3. On the **Locate Site Database** page, click **Connect to the site database for this server**, type **DUBLIN** in the text box, click **Load all console tree items (typical)**, and then click **Next**.

4. On the **Completing the Site Database Connection Wizard** page, the wizard displays the list of tree items that will be accessible from your site console. Click **Finish**.

5. **Site Databas**e now appears on the console tree.

   You can browse through the tree to view the various items.

6. Close the SMS Administrator console.

7. Leave the Glasgow and Dublin virtual machines running because they will be used in subsequent practices.

How to Locate and View SMS Site Server Folders

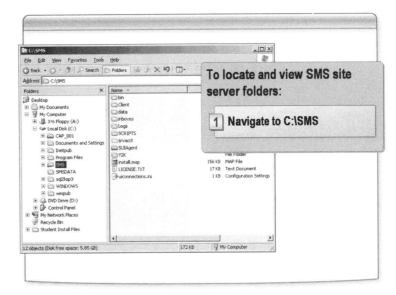

The installation process creates the SMS folder in the location specified during the setup process.

Procedure

To access the SMS folder to view site server folders, files, shares, and permissions, navigate to C:\SMS.

Primary subfolders in the SMS folder

Assuming SMS is installed on drive C, the primary subfolders are:

- C:\SMS\bin\i386. This folder contains the files that run the SMS site server. Two notable files in this folder are smsexec.exe, which runs the SMS_EXECUTIVE service, and sms.msc, which runs the SMS Administrator console.

- C:\SMS\Client. This folder contains a subfolder with client installation files.

- C:\SMS\inboxes. This folder contains subfolders in which SMS stores and processes site and object configuration data and client data.

- C:\SMS\Logs. This folder contains all the SMS site server log files used for troubleshooting.

The SMS folder is shared as SMS_*sitecode*.

The Tools in the SMS 2003 Toolkit 1

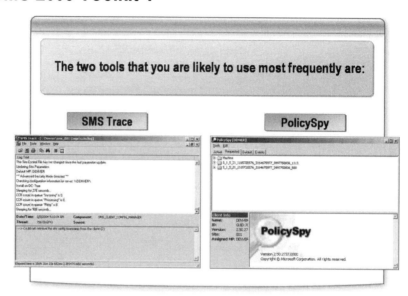

The SMS 2003 Toolkit 1 contains tools to help you with client deployment, software distribution management, health reporting, site maintenance, and problem troubleshooting.

Important   To accommodate the need to update tools and expand the toolkit on an as-needed basis, the SMS 2003 Toolkit 1 is not included on the SMS2003 compact disc. Instead, the toolkit is available for download from the Microsoft Windows Server System™ page of the Microsoft Web site at http://www.microsoft.com/smserver/downloads/2003/tools/toolkit.asp. Visit this site periodically to check for new releases.

Of the fourteen tools currently available in the SMS 2003 Toolkit 1, the two that you are likely to use most frequently are SMS Trace and Policy Spy.

SMS Trace   You can use SMS Trace (Trace32.exe) to view and monitor log files, including:

- Legacy Client and Advanced Client log files.

- Plain American Standard Code for Information Interchange (ASCII) or Unicode text files, such as Windows Installer logs.

- SMS site server log files.

The tool also helps simplify the analysis of log files, including highlighting, filtering, and error lookup.

The major components of the SMS Trace tool are:

■ The Log pane. The Log pane displays lines from log files.

  • Items with errors are displayed with a red background and yellow text color. In Advanced Client logs, log entries have an explicit type value that indicates whether the entry is an error. For other log formats, SMS Trace performs a case-insensitive search in each entry for the text string matching *error*.

  • Items with warnings are displayed with a yellow background. In Advanced Client logs, log entries have an explicit type value that indicates whether the entry is a warning. For other log formats, SMS Trace performs a case-insensitive search in each entry for the text string matching *warn*.

■ The Info pane. The Info pane displays details about the currently selected log entry. These details include:

  • The date and time that the log entry occurred.

  • The component that generated the log entry.

  • The thread on which the log entry was generated.

  • For Advanced Client logs, the source file and line that generated the log entry.

  When a large file is first opened, the Info pane is replaced by a progress bar indicating how much of the existing file contents have been loaded. When this indicator reaches 100 percent, the progress bar is removed and replaced with the Info pane. This provides feedback to you when you load large files, providing an indication of how long the load might take.

■ The Status bar. For SMS server and client log files, the status bar displays the elapsed time for the selected log entries. If a single entry is selected, the tool displays the time from the first log entry to the selected entry. If multiple entries are selected, the time is calculated from the topmost selected entry to the bottommost selected entry.

Policy Spy

Policy Spy (PolicySpy.exe) is a tool for viewing and troubleshooting the policy system on SMS Advanced Clients. Although Policy Spy is primarily intended for use through its user interface, it does provide limited command-line options to support automation and batch processing.

Other tools

The other tools and their specific purposes are listed in a table on the toolkit Web page mentioned in the Important note at the beginning of this topic. The two tools that have security implications are:

■ IIS Lockdown 2.1 Template. This tool secures Internet Information Server (IIS) 5.0 running on Windows 2000 Server–based computers that host SMS site systems (including distribution points, management points, reporting points, and server locator points) from attacks.

■ URLScan 2.5 Template. This tool secures IIS 6.0 running on Windows Server 2003–based computers that host SMS site systems (including distribution points, management points, reporting points, and server locator points) from attacks.

Practice: Exploring the SMS Administrator Console and the SMS 2003 Toolkit 1

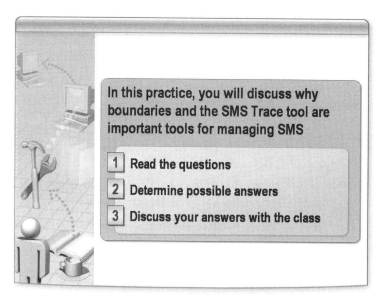

In this practice, you will discuss why boundaries and the SMS Trace tool are important tools for managing SMS.

Discussion questions

1. What are some of the advantages to managing a site by using boundaries?

   _____

   _____

   _____

   _____

   _____

2. Are there any potential issues associated with using site and roaming boundaries to manage a site?

    Active Directory

    _____

    _____

    _____

    _____

3. The SMS Trace utility has two primary areas in which you work: the log pane and the info pane. How do these two panes work in SMS trace?

    _____

    _____

    _____

    _____

    _____

4. SMS Trace provides two indicator bars that can assist you in your work. What purposes do the progress bar and the status bar serve in SMS Trace?

    _____

    _____

    _____

    _____

    _____

Lesson: Explaining the Role of Active Directory in SMS 2003

- **Advantages of Extending the Active Directory Schema**
- **How Active Directory Is Used for Locating Sites and Site Systems**
- **What Is the System Management Container?**
- **The Active Directory Discovery Methods**
- **Demonstration: How to View the System Management Container and the Objects Created by the SMS Site**

Introduction

In this lesson, you will learn how SMS integrates with Active Directory to provide features for discovery and boundaries. You will also learn how the Active Directory schema can be extended so that site systems can be registered.

Lesson objectives

After completing this lesson, you will be able to:

- Describe the advantages of extending the Active Directory schema.
- Describe how Active Directory is used for locating sites and site systems.
- Describe the System Management container.
- Describe the Active Directory discovery methods.
- View the System Management container and the objects created by the SMS site.

Advantages of Extending the Active Directory Schema

> - ◈ Advanced Clients can perform global roaming
> - ◈ Using SMS data published in Active Directory:
>   - ◈ Advanced Clients can discover their assigned site code
>   - ◈ Advanced Clients can identify a site's default management point
>   - ◈ Server locator points can be located
> - ◈ Secure key exchange can occur automatically between SMS sites

Active Directory integration makes it possible for you to identify users and computers to which you want to distribute software, based on organizational units. SMS site boundaries can be defined as Active Directory sites rather than being strictly limited to IP subnets. This allows easier configuration of SMS site boundaries and allows for more granular control over your IP subnets.

Active Directory support is accomplished by using LDAP (Lightweight Directory Access Protocol) to import some directory objects into the SMS 2003 database as records of Active Directory resources (such as users and computers). You can customize directory synchronization by choosing various schedules and which directory tree objects are to be scanned.

Note   LDAP is a standard protocol for accessing information in Active Directory.

Advantages of extending Active Directory

Extending the Active Directory schema results in the following advantages:

- Advanced Clients can perform global roaming, which is the ability to roam to a different portion of the SMS hierarchy outside your assigned site's hierarchy, such as to a parent or sibling site.

- Advanced clients can automatically discover their assigned site code from SMS data published in Active Directory.

- Advanced clients can identify the default management point for a site through SMS data published to Active Directory.

- Server locator points can be located from SMS data published in Active Directory.

■ Secure key exchange can occur automatically between SMS sites.

SMS 2003 signs all data sent to SMS 2003 and SMS 2.0 Service Pack 5 sites by using private/public encryption key pairs. The keys are generated at each site when the sites are set up. The value of the private key is only available to the operating system of the site server. The keys change when the SMS Service Account is changed for the site. The site automatically transfers the new public key to its parent site and all its direct child sites.

Sites can exchange keys securely by receiving the intersite key exchange files during the establishment of a parent/child site relationship and then verifying their validity by reading the public keys from Active Directory. The ability to write public keys to Active Directory requires significant rights, so this ensures that the site is not a rogue site. This method of key exchange happens automatically, but it requires Active Directory and that the account being used to set up the sites has sufficient rights to write to the Active Directory objects. This method does not work across forests.

How Active Directory Is Used for Locating Sites and Site Systems

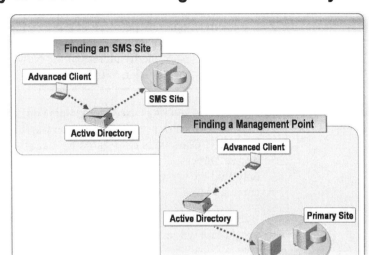

SMS clients can use Active Directory to locate some SMS resources. Before SMS clients can query Active Directory for these resources, the Active Directory schema must be extended and the SMS resource information must be published to Active Directory. When you extend the Active Directory schema, you add several classes and attributes that any SMS 2003 site in the SMS hierarchy can use later. These attributes are added to the global catalog and allow the clients to locate the information quickly.

How Advanced Clients find SMS sites

Advanced Clients that are configured for automatic assignment attempt to locate an SMS site from roaming boundaries that are stored in the Active Directory global catalog. If the Advanced Client cannot find a site by using the Active Directory data, it attempts to find a server locator point that can find a site for the client. Server locator points are found from Active Directory or from WINS. If the Advanced Client cannot find a site with roaming boundaries that it is currently within, it checks the next time the SMS Agent Host service is restarted.

How Advanced Clients find management points

In an Active Directory environment, the client queries Active Directory for the default management point. It does this by searching the Active Directory global catalog for a site code, which has been registered (by a site server) with a matching IP subnet, Active Directory site name, or IP address range roaming boundary. If the client does not find a suitable management point, or if it reverts to the assigned site because the required content is not available at the local site, the client uses the site code of its assigned site. In both cases, the client needs to query Active Directory again to find the appropriate management point for that site code.

If there is a single management point at the site, the client gets the name of that management point from Active Directory. If there are multiple management points behind a Windows Network Load Balancing cluster, the client gets the IP address of the Windows Network Load Balancing cluster.

Note In a WINS environment, without Active Directory, the client must query the management point of the assigned site. The client locates the IP address of a management point by performing a WINS lookup that is based on the site code. If there are multiple management points behind a Windows Network Load Balancing cluster, the IP address of the Network Load Balancing cluster must be manually registered in WINS.

How clients find server locator points

If the /SLP= switch is used, computers configured for Legacy Client installation find server locator points by using the Capinst.exe command, not Active Directory. Computers configured for Legacy Client installation that are not Active Directory–enabled (Windows 98 and Microsoft Windows NT® 4.0 SP6) only find the server locator point for use with Capinst through the /SLP command line switch.

If the /SLP= switch is not used, computers configured for Legacy Client installation will attempt to find server locator points by using Active Directory.

How clients find distribution points

In an Active Directory environment, SMS queries Active Directory to determine in which site's roaming boundaries the Advanced Client is located. Active Directory returns the site code of the client's assigned site or of another site in the hierarchy. If the returned site code indicates that the client is roaming to another site, SMS queries Active Directory for the management point in that site. SMS then queries the returned management point for distribution points with the necessary package source files within that site. If none of the returned distribution points have the necessary package source files, the client reverts to its assigned site. To find distribution points within the client's assigned site, SMS queries Active Directory for the management point in the assigned site, and then queries the returned management point for distribution points that have the necessary package source files.

Note In a WINS environment, the only site code that is available is the site code of the Advanced Client's assigned site. SMS queries WINS to find the management point for that site. SMS then queries the returned management point for a distribution point with the necessary package source files.

What Is the System Management Container?

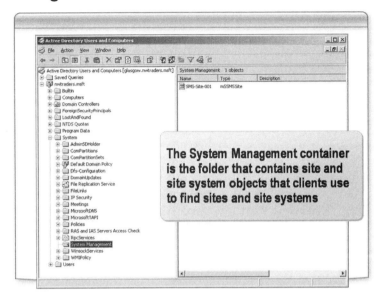

The System Management container is the folder that contains site and site system objects that clients use to find sites and site systems.

To ensure that SMS clients can query Active Directory for all necessary SMS information, you must extend the Active Directory schema and grant permissions to SMS to publish to the System Management container. Failure to properly extend and publish might result in clients being unable to use various SMS features and will generate error messages in the status message viewer.

SMS does not automatically create the System Management container when it extends the schema. The schema is extended once per forest, but each domain needs to have its own System Management container.

You can either manually create the container or allow SMS to attempt to create it the first time a site tries to publish to Active Directory. SMS can only create the System Management container if the SMS service account has full control permission on the System container and all child objects. Although it is possible to grant those permissions on System and later change them so SMS only has full control on the newly created System Management container, it is more secure to create the System Management container manually by using ADSIEdit and grant full control to the System Management container and all child objects. ADSIEdit is included with the Windows support tools on both the Windows 2000 Server and Windows Server 2003 CDs, but it is not installed by default.

Note   For more information about extending the Active Directory schema, see the white paper "Active Directory Schema Modification and Publishing for Systems Management Server 2003" on the Additional Reading page of your Student Materials compact disc. This white paper is also available on the Download Center page of the Microsoft Web site. The link to this paper is included on the Internet links page of the Student Materials compact disc.

The Active Directory Discovery Methods

This method	Discovers
Active Directory User Discovery	• Users and User Groups • Containers and Sub-containers
Active Directory System Discovery	• Computers
Active Directory System Group Discovery	• Organizational Units • Global Groups • Universal Groups • Nested Groups • Other Non-Security Groups _— distribution groups_

With the Active Directory discovery methods, SMS polls Active Directory to discover computers, users, or system groups in the containers specified. This process can generate significant network traffic, so you should plan to schedule it accordingly.

You specify the containers that you want polled (such as specific domains, organizational units, or user groups), and SMS polls the specified containers (and, optionally, their child containers) for users and their user groups, for systems, or for system groups, depending on the discovery method you are using. You can also adjust the schedule of the polling.

SMS provides three Active Directory discovery methods.

- The *Active Directory User Discovery* method polls an Active Directory domain controller to discover users and the user groups of which they are members. Active Directory User Discovery can poll specified Active Directory containers and sub-containers.

- The *Active Directory System Discovery* method polls the specified Active Directory containers, such as domains and sites in an Active Directory domain controller, to discover computers. Active Directory System Discovery can also poll the specified Active Directory containers recursively. Active Directory System Discovery connects to each discovered computer to retrieve details about the computer.

The Active Directory System Discovery method gathers discovery information such as:

- Computer name.

- Active Directory container name.

- IP address.

- Active Directory site.

■ The *Active Directory System Group Discovery* method polls an Active Directory domain controller to discover system groups for computer systems that are discovered by other discovery methods and assigned to the SMS site and any secondary sites. In this way, Active Directory System Group Discovery enhances the discovery data of other discovery methods. If a resource is not assigned to an SMS site, Active Directory System Group Discovery does not discover system group information for that resource.

The Active Directory System Group Discovery method gathers discovery information about:

- Organizational units.
- Global groups.
- Universal groups.
- Nested groups.
- Other non-security groups, such as Windows distribution groups.

Demonstration: How to View the System Management Container and the Objects Created by the SMS Site

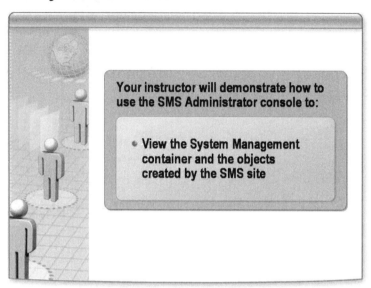

In this demonstration, your instructor will use the Active Directory Service Interface (ADSI) Edit console to view the System Management container and the objects created by the SMS site after the Active Directory schema was extended.

Your instructor will use the following values in this demonstration.

Variable	Value
Virtual machine—Domain controller	Glasgow
Domain Administrator	Administrator

Important These steps are included for your information. Do not attempt to do them in the classroom. If you perform these steps in the classroom environment, you may leave your computer in an incorrect state for upcoming practices.

Demonstration steps performed by instructor only

▶ **To identify the new containers created when Active Directory is extended during setup**

1. Verify that Glasgow virtual machine is running and screen is maximized.

Note It is not recommended that you use the domain controller to perform Active Directory tasks. You should perform them by using the Active Directory administrative tools included with Windows Server 2003; however, the configuration of the virtual machines in this course necessitates that this practice be completed by using the domain controller.

---

2. On Glasgow virtual machine, click **Start**, click **Run**, type **ADSIEDIT.MSC** and then click **OK**.

3. Expand **Domain [Glasgow.nwtraders.msft]**, expand **DC=nwtraders,DC=msft**, expand **CN=System** node, and then click **CN=System Management**.

   The list of new objects that SMS creates after setup appears in the details pane. The one object you will see is CN=SMS-Site-001.

4. In the details pane, double-click **CN=SMS-Site-001**.

   The container's properties dialog box appears. From here you can view an object's attributes, in addition to its security and permission settings.

5. Scroll through the **Attribute list** to find the following attributes:

   - mSSMSAssignmentSiteCode
   - mSSMSRoamingBoundaries
   - mSSMSSiteBoundaries
   - mSSMSSiteCode

   These are important attributes because they identify the site code, site boundaries, and roaming boundaries. If the site is a secondary site, the mSSMSAssignmentSiteCode attribute identifies its primary site.

6. On the **CN=SMS-Site-001 Properties** dialog box, click **OK**.

7. Close **ADSI Edit**.

8. Leave the Glasgow virtual machine running.

Practice: Exploring the System Management Container

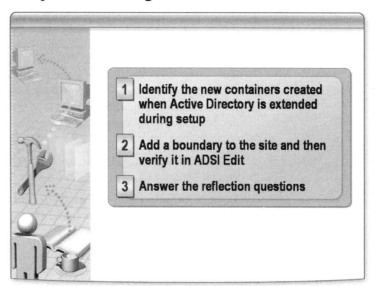

Instructions

Complete the procedures to practice identifying the new containers created when Active Directory is extended during setup and adding a boundary to the site and then verifying it in ADSI Edit. Then complete the reflection questions that follow.

In this practice, use the following values.

Variable	Value
Virtual machine—SMS Site 1	Dublin
Dublin\Administrator	JaePa (Jae Pak)
Virtual machine—Domain controller	Glasgow
Domain Administrator	Administrator

Procedures

▶ **To identify the new containers created when Active Directory is extended during setup**

1. Verify that both the Glasgow and Dublin virtual machines are running.

2. On the Glasgow virtual machine, click **Start**, click **Run**, in the **Open** box, type **ADSIEDIT.MSC** and then click **OK**.

Note It is not recommended that you use the domain controller to perform Active Directory tasks. You should perform them by using the Active Directory administrative tools included with Windows Server 2003; however, the configuration of the virtual machines in this course necessitates that this practice be completed by using the domain controller.

3. Expand **Domain [Glasgow.nwtraders.msft]**, expand **DC=nwtraders,DC=msft**, expand the **CN=System** node, and then click **CN=System Management**.

   The list of new objects that SMS creates after setup appears in the details pane. The one object you will see is CN=SMS-Site-001.

4. Double-click **CN=SMS-Site-001**. The container's properties dialog box appears. From here you can view an object's attributes in addition to its security and permission settings.

5. Scroll through the **Attribute list** to find the following attributes:

   - mSSMSAssignmentSiteCode
   - mSSMSRoamingBoundaries
   - mSSMSSiteBoundaries
   - mSSMSSiteCode

   These are important attributes because they identify the site code, site boundaries, and roaming boundaries. Also, if the site is a secondary site, the mSSMSAssignmentSiteCode attribute identifies its primary site.

6. Click **OK**.

7. On the **File** menu, click **Exit**.

▶ **To add a boundary to the site and then verify it in ADSI Edit**

1. Verify that the Dublin virtual machine is running.

2. On the Dublin virtual machine, click **Start**, point **All Programs**, point to **Systems Management Server**, and then click **SMS Administrator console**.

3. Expand the **Site Database (001 – NWTraders)** node.

   A list of site functions appears in the tree.

4. Expand the **Site Hierarchy** node.

5. Right-click the **001 – NWTraders** site node, and then click **Properties**.

   The **001 – NWTraders Site Properties** dialog box appears.

6. On the **Site Boundaries** tab, click the **New** [icon] icon.

7. In the **New Site Boundary** dialog box, in the **Boundary type** box select **Active Directory site**, type **NWTRADERS-SITE-A** in the **Site name** text box, and then click **OK**.

Note This Active Directory site does not exist in the VPC domain in the classroom environment; it is included in this step only for purposes of this practice.

---

8. On the **001 – NWTraders Site Properties** dialog box, click **OK**.

9. Switch to the Glasgow virtual machine.

10. On the Glasgow virtual machine, click **Start**, click **Run**, in the **Open** box, type **ADSIEDIT.MSC** and then click **OK**. ADSI Edit appears.

11. In the console tree, expand **Domain [Glasgow.nwtraders.msft]**, expand **DC=nwtraders,DC=msft**, expand **CN=System** node, and then click **CN=System Management**.

    The list of new objects that SMS creates after setup appears in the details pane. At this stage of site configuration, CN=SMS-Site-001 is the only object that exists.

12. Double-click **CN=SMS-Site-001**.

The container's properties dialog box appears.

13. Scroll through the **Attribute list**, select **mSSMSSiteBoundaries**, and then click **Edit**.

The **Multi-valued String Editor** dialog box displays.

14. In the **Multi-valued String Editor** dialog box, verify that the value **NWTRADERS-Site-A** now displays in the values field.

You successfully added a new site boundary to your site.

15. In the **Multi-valued String Editor** dialog box, click **OK**.

16. In the **CN=SMS-Site-001 Properties** dialog box, click **OK**.

17. On the Glasgow Virtual Machine, close **ADSI EDIT**.

18. Leave the Glasgow and Dublin virtual machines running because they will be used in subsequent practices.

Reflection questions

Clair Hector, the IT director at Northwind Traders, is preparing a presentation about SMS to the senior management team. She sends Jae Pak an e-mail in which she inquires about the purpose of containers in SMS and why it is so important that the System Administrators understand how to manage them. She also wants to know about the permissions necessary for a site to manage the Systems Management container in Active Directory.

1. What information should Jae include in his reply to the IT director?

_____

_____

_____

_____

_____

2. You learned how to add a new site boundary and then verify it by using ADSI Edit. Why might this be important when you manage your SMS site?

_____

_____

_____

_____

Lesson: Explaining How SMS Uses Dependent Technologies

- **What SMS Uses Internet Information Services For**
- **What SMS Uses Background Intelligent Transfer Service For**
- **What SMS Uses Windows Management Instrumentation For**
- **What SMS Uses Windows Installer For**

Introduction

In this lesson, you will learn how SMS uses dependent technologies to deliver its change and configuration management functionality. Internet Information Services (IIS) and Background Intelligent Transfer Service (BITS) assist with the delivery of SMS site system functionality. BITS also enables Advanced Client computers to have more control of how they handle software installations. Windows Management Instrumentation (WMI) underpins a large part of the SMS feature set and also facilitates SMS integration with Active Directory. SMS uses Windows Installer files to deploy software packages consistently across every client computer.

Lesson objectives

After completing this lesson, you will be able to:

- Describe what SMS uses IIS for.
- Describe what SMS uses BITS for.
- Describe what SMS uses WMI for.
- Describe what SMS uses Windows Installer (MSI) for.

What SMS Uses Internet Information Services For

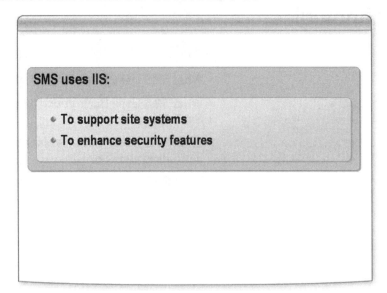

SMS uses IIS:

- • To support site systems
- • To enhance security features

How SMS uses IIS

SMS 2003 relies on Internet Information Services (IIS) to support the management point, server locator point, BITS-enabled distribution point (which is described in the next topic), and reporting point site systems. Each of these site systems must have IIS installed and enabled to communicate over HTTP.

In addition, SMS 2003 incorporates IIS security features to ensure the integrity of these SMS site systems. IIS security is especially important if IIS is installed on SMS site servers when the site is running in SMS advanced security mode because:

- ■ The site server's computer account has administrative privileges on other computers. IIS runs by using the local system account, which is the only account with the right to use the computer account. This typically is the case only on site servers.

- ■ When using advanced security, the SMS site server manages its local files and registry entries by using the local system account. Software running in the local system account context of IIS has equal access to those files and registry entries.

Recommendations for securing IIS

Recommendations for securing IIS include:

- ■ Use the latest version of IIS that is available. Usually this means using the latest operating system available.

- ■ Apply service packs and security-related hotfixes as they become available.

- ■ Disable IIS functions that you do not require.

- ■ Put IIS on servers that are separate from other applications, or on servers with few other functions.

- ■ Use IIS security lockdown and other IIS security tools, as described in the IIS documentation. The SMS 2003 Toolkit 1 supplies an SMS 2003–specific IIS Lockdown template for IIS 5.0 and the URLScan.ini file for IIS 6.0.

What SMS Uses Background Intelligent Transfer Service For

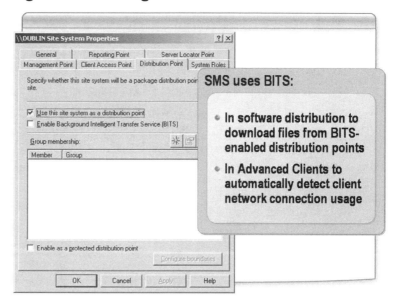

What is BITS?

The Background Intelligent Transfer Service (BITS) is a Windows component that performs background file transfers and queue management.

What SMS uses BITS for

Software distribution uses BITS to download files from distribution points that are BITS-enabled. Advanced Clients use BITS technology to automatically detect if other applications or processes are using the network connection.

The Benefits of BITS

BITS provides the following benefits:

- Package downloads from distribution points use checkpoint restarts, so that if the download process is interrupted, the download resumes without completely restarting the download. If the package is downloaded by using BITS, and the client resumes the download from the same distribution point, the download resumes at the beginning of the last network packet that was being transferred. Otherwise, the download is resumed at the beginning of the last file being downloaded.

- If the user needs to use the network connection for other purposes, such as reading e-mail, BITS makes the connection available to the user. BITS uses the connection when the user is not using it.

- BITS uses HTTP so that the Advanced Client can send and receive files in any situation in which an HTTP link can be established.

- BITS can send and receive information by using a virtual private network (VPN), with or without a firewall that does not do network address translation (NAT). Use of the Advanced Client with NAT is not supported.

- A download request is not completed if the version of the package changes. The download is restarted with the new version. If the Advanced Client changes locations during file download, it can continue the download by using a local server if a local server is available.

What SMS Uses Windows Management Instrumentation For

Because SMS uses WMI, you can:

- Script SMS operations
- Increase or decrease the details that SMS collects as part of the hardware inventory
- Build tools to manage SM
- Directly connect to client computers, if they are accessible on your network
- Report, query, and build collections
- Secure your SMS Administrator console

What is WMI?

Windows Management Instrumentation (WMI) is a management infrastructure in Windows that supports monitoring and controlling system resources through a common set of interfaces and provides a logically organized, consistent model of Windows operation, configuration, and status.

WMI is the Microsoft implementation of the Web-based Enterprise Management (WBEM) standard. WBEM builds on a series of industrywide initiatives to standardize computer management.

WMI architecture

WMI is designed to function as a middle layer by serving as a standard interface between management applications and the systems that they manage.

The Common Information Model (CIM) Object Manager is implemented in the WMI service in Microsoft Windows NT 4.0, Windows 2000, Windows XP, and operating systems in the Windows Server 2003 family.

Using WMI Control, which is accessible through the Computer Management console, you can back up the repository, control logging, and configure elements of WMI.

The CIM Repository is a database for static WMI data and object definitions. Very little client data is stored in the CIM Repository; it primarily contains Advanced Client settings. Most of the data is retrieved dynamically and is therefore only accurate at the time that you ask for it. The classes that are defined to use providers specify which provider to use and supply sufficient details for the provider to get the data. When WMI receives a request for data, it checks the class definition for the details and then queries the relevant provider to get the data from the system.

Note For more information on WMI architecture and the WMI object model, see Appendix B, "Windows Management Instrumentation," in the *Microsoft Systems Management Server 2003 Operations Guide* on the Additional Reading page of your Student Materials compact disc.

What SMS uses WMI for

SMS uses WMI on clients for hardware inventory collection, to notify the Software Metering Agent on SMS clients that a process has started, on site servers as an interface to the SMS site database, and on SMS Administrator consoles as an interface to the SMS site database. You can also use WMI to set configuration details on your computer and to detect and respond to changes in the configuration of your computer.

Because SMS uses WMI, you can:

- Script SMS operations to ease your SMS administration tasks.
- Increase or decrease the details that SMS collects as part of the hardware inventory.
- Build tools to manage SMS.
- Directly connect to client computers, if they are accessible on your network, to verify in real time any details that you see in Resource Explorer.
- Report, query, and build collections based on any configuration details that are available from client computers.
- Configure an SMS Administrator console to allow the console user to have access only to features of the SMS site that the user needs.

Note For more information on SMS integration on WMI, see Appendix B, "Windows Management Instrumentation," in the *Microsoft Systems Management Server 2003 Operations Guide* on the Additional Reading page of your Student Materials compact disc.

What is Wbemtest?

Wbemtest (Wbemtest.exe) is a GUI-based tool you can use to view and modify data stored in WMI. You can use Wbemtest to view data for any application, such as SMS, that stores data in WMI. Wbemtest is located on all server and client operating systems that SMS 2003 supports.

For more information about using Wbemtest, see Windows help.

What SMS Uses Windows Installer For

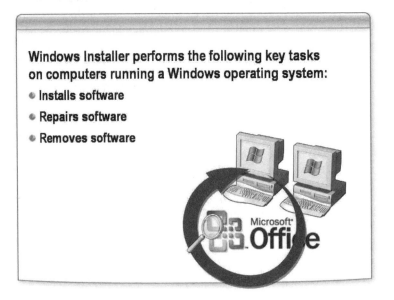

What is Windows Installer?

Windows Installer is a service that runs on computers running a Windows operating system. Windows Installer installs, repairs, or removes software according to instructions contained in .msi files provided with applications. SMS uses Windows Installer in software distribution to provide source path management and to take advantage of MSI per-user elevated rights.

Managing application installations

Prior to Windows Installer, software applications used various setup technologies, each of which contained unique installation rules for each application. At times, the applications did the wrong things at setup time. For instance, an earlier version of a particular file might be installed over a newer version of that same file. Some setup technologies made it difficult to maintain accurate reference counts on shared components for the many applications installed on a computer. As a result, installing or removing certain applications might break other applications.

When you use Windows Installer, the operating system implements all the proper installation rules. To adhere to those rules and to avoid the problems described in the preceding paragraph, an application needs only to describe itself in a Windows Installer package. Windows Installer then performs the installation tasks for each application, which can help to prevent or minimize common installation problems.

Consistent and reliable version rules

Traditionally, software manufacturers delivered a unique Setup program for each application. When an application was added, modified, upgraded, or removed from a system, the Setup program enforced its own rules, such as providing version-control directives. Because each Setup program provided its own rules, interactions among two or more applications sometimes caused conflicting results.

Windows Installer provides consistent and reliable installation for all applications, which prevents newer files from being overwritten by older files.

System-wide management of shared resources

Inter-application conflicts can occur when uninstalling one application removes files shared by other applications on the computer.

Windows Installer maintains and manages all setup and installation information about each product it installs. When you uninstall a product, Windows Installer does not remove any component that has other applications in its client list.

Restoring the pre-installation state of a computer

Windows Installer keeps track of all the changes it makes to a computer. Therefore, if you attempt to add, modify, or remove an application and the action fails, Windows Installer restores the computer to its previous state. The restoration procedure is known as a *rollback*.

With earlier setup technologies, if an upgraded version of an application failed, neither version remained in a functional state. With Windows Installer, if an application upgrade fails, the system restores the computer and its contents to its previous state.

Application customization methods

Windows Installer enables you to customize a broad set of applications in standard ways by using:

- Command-line properties. These properties are variables that Windows Installer uses during an installation. A subset of these properties, called public properties, can be set on the command line.

- Transforms. A *transform* is a collection of changes you can apply to a base .msi file. You can customize applications by using Windows Installer transform (.mst) files. You configure transforms to modify a Windows Installer package to dynamically affect installation behavior according to your requirements.

Note For more information about the Windows Installer, see "Windows Installer Service Overview" on the Windows 2000 page of the Microsoft Web site. The link to this document is included on the Internet links page of the Student Materials compact disc.

Practice: Verifying SMS Settings in WMI

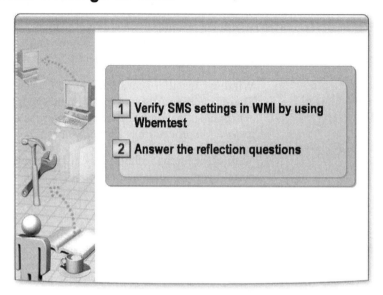

Instructions

Complete the following procedures to practice verifying SMS settings in WMI by using Wbemtest. Then answer the reflection questions that follow.

In this practice, use the following values.

Variable	Value
Virtual machine—SMS Site 1	Dublin
Dublin\Administrator	JaePa (Jae Pak)
Virtual machine—Domain controller	Glasgow
Domain Administrator	Administrator

Procedures

▶ **To verify SMS settings in WMI by using Wbemtest**

1. Verify that the Glasgow and Dublin virtual machines are running.

2. On the Dublin virtual machine, click **Start**, click **Run**, in the **Open** box, type **Wbemtest.exe** and then click **OK**.

   The **Windows Management Instrumentation Tester** dialog box appears.

   Note   The IWbemServices features are unavailable until you connect to an appropriate namespace.
   ---

3. In the **Windows Management Instrumentation Tester** dialog box, click **Connect**.

4. In the **Connect** dialog box, in the **Namespace** text box, type **root\sms\site_001** and then click **Connect**.

   The IWbemServices features are now enabled.

5. In the **Windows Management Instrumentation Tester** dialog box, click **Enum Classes**.

6. In the **Superclass Info** dialog box, click **Recursive**, and then click **OK**.

> **Caution** Be sure to leave the **Enter superclass name** box blank.

7. In the **Query Result** dialog box, scroll down to view the SMS top-level classes, and then click **Close**.

8. In the **Windows Management Instrumentation Tester** dialog box, click **Exit**.

9. Close the **SMS Administrators Console**.

10. Leave the Glasgow and Dublin virtual machines running because they will be used in subsequent practices.

Reflection questions

1. What are the implications of how SMS Advanced Clients use BITS technology?

   _____

   _____

   _____

   _____

2. Why is it important to understand the SMS settings in WMI?

   _____

   _____

   _____

   _____

Discussion: Exploring SMS Site Architecture

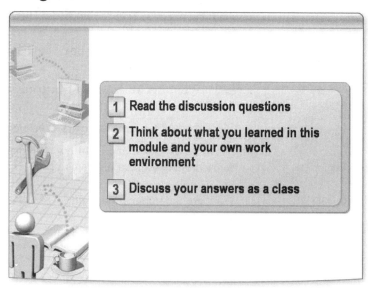

1. What are the principal services that run on the SMS site server?

   _____

   _____

   _____

   _____

2. How do the SMS Administrator Console and other tools allow administration and support of an SMS implementation?

   _____

   _____

   _____

   _____

3. What are the advantages of Windows Management Instrumentation (WMI) in an SMS site?

    _____

    _____

    _____

    _____

Module 3: Preparing to Deploy the SMS Clients

Contents

Overview

- Introduction to SMS Clients
- Discovering Resources
- Managing the Site Systems That Support Client Installation and Client/Server Communication

Introduction

In this module, you will learn how to prepare for Microsoft® Systems Management Server (SMS) client deployment. This process involves configuring and deploying the site systems required to support clients and using discovery methods to identify resources.

Objectives

After completing this module, you will be able to:

- Describe the clients that are assigned to an SMS site.

- Describe resource discovery methods that are included in SMS 2003.

- Explain the guidelines to configure, manage, and troubleshoot the site systems used by SMS to support clients.

Lesson: Introduction to the SMS Clients

- What Is the SMS Advanced Client?
- What Is the SMS Legacy Client?
- Considerations for Determining Which Client to Use
- What Is Client Assignment?

Introduction

SMS 2003 supports two client types: the Advanced Client and the Legacy Client. The Advanced Client is a new client type introduced in SMS 2003. The Legacy Client is based on the SMS 2.0 client. You can deploy both client types on desktop computers, mobile computers, and remote computers.

In this lesson, you will learn about the different SMS clients and how to determine which client to use.

Lesson objectives

After completing this lesson, you will be able to:

- Describe the Advanced Client.
- Describe the Legacy Client.
- Determine which client to use in various situations.
- Describe client assignment.

What Is the SMS Advanced Client?

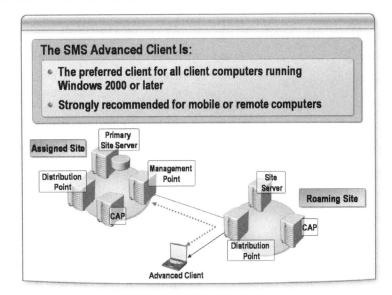

The Advanced Client is the client recommended for computers running Microsoft Windows® 2000 or later. It is strongly recommended for mobile and remote computers, because it has features specifically designed to support those types of computers.

Advanced Clients use management points to send and receive data from the site server. To receive configuration and advertised program details, Advanced Clients use policies, which are downloaded from management points. The Advanced Client policies are unique to SMS and are not related to policies associated with Active Directory® directory service.

Advantages of the Advanced Client

Advanced Clients have several advantages over Legacy Clients, including:

- Advanced Clients can roam to other sites to download applications that the SMS administrator has configured for software distribution. This includes access to distribution points at SMS 2.0 secondary sites whose parent sites are SMS 2003 sites. This makes Advanced Clients effective for mobile computers.

- Highly scriptable Advanced Client functions allow for the automation of Advanced Client configuration and operations.

- Advanced Clients use Windows Management Instrumentation (WMI), which allows access to Advanced Client configuration data for troubleshooting purposes.

- Advanced Clients are more scalable. You can have more Advanced Clients accessing a management point than you can Legacy Clients accessing a CAP.

- The Windows Installer package that installs the Advanced Client contains not only core SMS client components, but also client agents, such as the Hardware Inventory Client Agent. Installing all agents during SMS Advanced Client installation ensures that the agents are always available to the client.

- Advanced Clients have the ability to install the Advanced Client software during operating system image creation deployment without assigning the client to any site.

- Better support for clients connecting to the SMS site through remote connections, such as RAS or wireless.

- Better security as the Advanced Client does not use SMS specific user accounts, but the Local System context for the SMS services and the computer account for network access.

- Use of BITS for data uploads and policy downloads. This provides checkpoint restarts of interrupted transfers. The use of BITS is optional for software distribution package source file downloads.

- If a client has multiple network cards (possibly a LAN network card and a dial-up modem) and multiple Internet Protocol (IP) addresses, the network card that is bound first is used for evaluating Advanced Client site assignment.

What Is the SMS Legacy Client?

The SMS Legacy Client is a client based on the earlier technology of the SMS 2.0 client

The SMS Legacy Client:

- Provides support to assist with upgrades
- Offers no support for roaming
- Can be upgraded to an Advanced Client if the operating system requirements are met
- Is automatically upgraded when site is upgraded

The Legacy Client is a client based on the earlier technology of the SMS 2.0 client. Therefore, it relies heavily on domain and local user accounts to carry out key tasks on the SMS client computer; tasks such as installing software in an administrative context when the logged-on user account does not have the appropriate security credentials. The Legacy Client offers no support for roaming (mobile clients).

What to do when upgrading from SMS 2.0 to SMS 2003

When you upgrade the SMS 2.0 site to SMS 2003, the Legacy Client is automatically installed on the SMS 2.0 client computers by default. It is strongly recommended that you install the Advanced Client as soon as possible after the upgrade to take advantage of the enhanced security and the other benefits it provides.

What to do when upgrading from Legacy Client to Advanced Client

The SMS 2003 status message system is designed to periodically notify you if there are Legacy Clients installed on computers running Microsoft Windows® 2000 or later within your SMS site. The message reminds you that these clients should be upgraded to the Advanced Client. Additionally, you can run the report or query named "Computers recommended for Advanced Client upgrade," which lists these computers. These features are explained in more detail in Module 6, "Querying and Reporting Data."

Important SMS 2003 Service Pack 1 will discontinue support for the SMS Legacy Client on computers running Windows 2000 or later operating system platforms. Current information on Service Pack 1 is available on the Systems Management Server Web site at http://www.microsoft.com/smserver.

Considerations for Determining Which Client to Use

Factors for consideration	Advanced	Legacy
Support for clients running Windows 98 (with Internet Explorer 5.0 installed) or later, Windows NT 4.0 SP6		☑
Roaming to other sites	☑	
Administrator controlled SMS client version upgrades	☑	☑
Better security	☑	
Can download software distribution programs before running them	☑	
Allowances for slow, inconsistent, or short connections to SMS site	☑	

Initially, you will determine the operating systems that are used within your organization. This will dictate whether to install the Legacy or Advanced Client software. In addition to installing SMS on a server computer, you must install the SMS client software on every computer in your organization that you wish to manage. After the SMS software is installed, the computers become SMS clients. To use SMS to manage computer change and configuration throughout your organization, all your computers must be SMS clients.

After you install and configure an SMS 2003 site server and the necessary site systems, you can deploy the computers in your organization as SMS 2003 clients. Computers must be SMS clients before you can distribute software, collect hardware and software inventory, use software metering, or use remote tools.

The main differences between the Advanced Client and the Legacy Client are summarized on the slide above. Other factors to consider include:

- Although Advanced Clients may be installed in a secondary site, they can only be assigned to the parent primary site. Therefore, the Advanced Client will use the configuration settings and advertisements from the primary site they are installed to, but can still use the local distribution points at the secondary site.

- You can change the site assignment of an Advanced Client to a different primary site. To change the site assignment, use the client's System Management Control Panel, or run an appropriate script on the client.

- When the Legacy Client detects that it is no longer assigned to an SMS site, it will automatically deinstall. Advanced Clients will not deinstall even if they are removed from site or roaming boundaries.

Note   For additional information on scripts, see Appendix C of the *Microsoft Systems Management Server 2003 Operations Guide* on the Additional Reading page of your Student Materials compact disc.

- We recommend you install the Advanced Client when the client platform supports it.

Which client type should you deploy?

For many administrative and end-user purposes, the two client types appear similar. Both client types support the primary features of SMS, such as software distribution and inventory collection, with only minor differences.

Security is one of the deciding factors for choosing which client to deploy because the client type will dictate the site's security mode. Legacy Clients require standard security mode.

It is recommended that you deploy the Advanced Client so that you can take advantage of the advanced security mode features.

Minimum software and hardware requirements

The software requirements for installing clients can be found in the SMS help menu under the **Contents** tab. Expand the **Part 1: Introduction** node, expand the **Getting Started** node, and then expand the **Requirements for SMS Clients** node. From here you can explore the following topics:

- Requirements for SMS Clients
- Unsupported Operating Systems and Features

To view the minimum hardware requirements for server components and client installations, see the Internet links page of the Student Materials compact disc.

What Is Client Assignment?

Client assignment is the process that determines which SMS site will manage a client computer

Client assignment involves:

- Managing each site according to the clients assigned to that site
- Assigning the client to an SMS site either automatically or manually

In order for an SMS client computer to be managed, each SMS client must belong to an SMS site. *Client assignment* is the process that determines which SMS site will manage a client computer.

What client assignment allows you to do

Client assignment allows you to manage clients at each site differently from clients at other sites. For example, you might set the software distribution client agent at your headquarters site to check for new advertisements once every hour, but you might set the software distribution client agent to check daily for new advertisements at remote locations.

When you configure an SMS site, you specify the site boundaries and roaming boundaries of that site. During deployment, the installed clients may use those settings to determine site assignment.

How Advanced Client assignment happens

Advanced Clients can be manually or automatically assigned to a primary site during the client installation phase or at a later point. During installation, Advanced Clients can be configured to be assigned to a specific site, or they can be configured with automatic assignment and automatically determine a site to which they can be assigned.

If the Advanced Client is not assigned to any site during the client installation phase or is assigned a site code that does not exist yet, the client installation phase completes but the client is dormant. An Advanced Client is considered dormant when it is installed or when it is waiting to find its assigned site for the first time. Because it is not assigned to any site, it is not functional as an SMS client.

Constraints of automatic assignment

Advanced Clients that are configured with automatic assignment attempt to locate an SMS site from roaming boundaries stored in the Active Directory global catalog. If the Advanced Client cannot find a site by using the Active Directory data, it attempts to find a server locator point to discover the assigned site for the client.

Server locator points are determined from Active Directory or from Windows Internet Name Service (WINS). If the Advanced Client cannot find a site with roaming boundaries that it is currently in, it checks the next time the SMS Agent Host service is restarted.

You can only assign Advanced Clients automatically to a site if they are not currently assigned to any site, or if the **Discover** button is used after the client is installed. After the Advanced Client is assigned to a site, the client remains assigned to that site even if it roams to another site. Only an administrator can manually assign the client to another site or remove the client assignment.

SMS 2003 Legacy clients must be within the site boundaries to be installed as a Legacy client. If the Legacy client is already installed, and the client no longer is assigned to any SMS 2003 site, the Legacy client will be automatically deinstalled. The SMS 2003 Advanced Client does not exhibit this behavior, so is recommended for roaming scenarios.

Practice: Determining Which Clients to Deploy

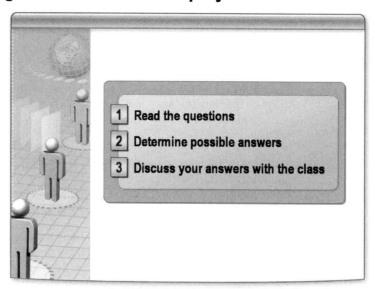

Instructions

Read the following questions and discuss your answers with the rest of the class.

Discussion questions

1. What types of clients will you be deploying in your organization?

_____

_____

_____

2. What is one security implication of deploying the Legacy client?

_____

_____

_____

3. What impact does Active Directory have on client assignment?

_____

_____

_____

Lesson: Discovering Resources

- **What is Resource Discovery?**
- **SMS Resource Discovery Methods**
- **When to Use Each Discovery Method**
- **Network Discovery Options**
- **Multimedia: Introduction to SMS Discovery**
- **Demonstration: How to Configure and Enable Discovery Methods**
- **Guidelines for Enabling and Configuring Active Directory User, System, and System Group Discovery**
- **Guidelines for Enabling and Configuring Heartbeat Discovery**

Introduction

SMS 2003 discovery methods are used individually or in combination to identify resources in your organization. Although all SMS discovery methods generate discovery data, the different methods discover different types of resources and serve different purposes. You will learn about the value of each discovery method, when to use each method, and guidelines for using the most common methods.

Lesson objectives

After completing this lesson, you will be able to:

- Describe resource discovery.
- Describe the resource discovery methods used by SMS.
- Describe when to use each discovery method.
- Describe the three Network Discovery options.
- Describe SMS Discovery after participating in a multimedia activity.
- Configure and enable discovery methods.
- Describe the guidelines to enable and configure Active Directory User, System, and System Group Discovery.
- Describe the guidelines to enable and configure Heartbeat Discovery.

What Is Resource Discovery?

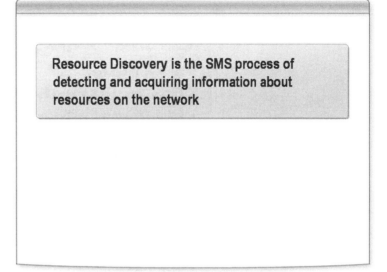

Resource Discovery is the SMS process of detecting and acquiring information about resources on the network

Discovering resources is the first phase of the client deployment process. During this initial phase, SMS gathers information about resources in your organization's network and then stores that information in the SMS site database as discovery data records (DDRs). A *resource* is defined as any object found by SMS. The default list of resources could consist of computers (including mainframes and UNIX workstations), routers, printers, or user and group accounts.

Note You can add additional resource types by using details included in Appendix C, "Scripting SMS Operations," in the *Microsoft Systems Management Server 2003 Operations Guide* on the Additional Reading page of your Student Materials compact disc.

Information gathered during discovery is limited compared to data that the inventory feature can gather. Discovery information includes data such as the name of a discovered resource, including its Active Directory site membership, operating system and IP address. Administrators can query the SMS site database for discovery data, include discovery data in reports, and enter discovered resources in collections.

It is important to note that you cannot use any primary features of SMS, such as inventory or software distribution, on discovered resources that do not have the SMS client installed. Also, although child sites can forward discovery data to parent sites, one SMS site cannot directly use other SMS sites to discover resources.

SMS Resource Discovery Methods

Resource Discovery Methods

- Network Discovery
- Active Directory System Discovery
- Active Directory User Discovery
- Active Directory System Group Discovery
- Windows User Account Discovery
- Windows User Group Discovery
- Heartbeat Discovery
- Site System Discovery

SMS 2003 includes several discovery methods that you can enable and configure from the SMS Administrator console. The discovery method that you choose will depend primarily on the types of resources that exist in your organization. The following table outlines each discovery method.

Resource discovery method	Description
Network Discovery	The Network Discovery method gathers discovery information about your network topology, potential clients, and their operating systems. Network Discovery is unique because it not only finds computers; it also finds network devices such as printers, routers, and bridges.
Active Directory System Discovery	Active Directory System Discovery polls an Active Directory domain controller to discover computer systems. This method gathers discovery information such as computer name, Active Directory container name, IP address, Active Directory site, and operating system.
Active Directory User Discovery	Active Directory User Discovery polls an Active Directory domain controller to discover computer users. The Active Directory User Discovery method gathers discovery information such as user name, unique user name (includes domain name), domain, Active Directory container names, and security group and other group names.

(continued)

Resource discovery method	Description
Active Directory System Group Discovery	Active Directory System Group Discovery polls an Active Directory domain controller to discover computer system groups for assigned system resources in the local primary site as well as its secondary sites. The Active Directory System Group Discovery method gathers discovery information about an organizational unit, global groups, universal groups, nested groups, and other non-security groups, such as Windows distribution groups.
Windows User Account Discovery	Windows User Account Discovery finds Windows domain user accounts in the domains that you specify. This method creates a DDR for each user account.
Windows User Group Discovery	The Windows User Group Discovery finds Windows domain user groups in the domains you specify. This method creates a DDR for each group.
Heartbeat Discovery	Heartbeat Discovery is a method used to refresh SMS client computer discovery data in the SMS site database. Heartbeat Discovery is useful for maintaining up-to-date discovery data on clients that are not normally affected by one of the other discovery methods,.
Site System Discovery	Site System Discovery automatically discovers SMS site servers and site systems. Because this discovery method is fully automated, you cannot configure it, you cannot disable it, and you do not see it in the SMS Administrator console.

Note   For additional information on discovery methods, see Chapter 4 and Chapter 17 of the *Microsoft Systems Management Server 2003 Concepts, Planning, and Deployment Guide* on the Additional Reading page of your Student Materials compact disc.

When to Use Each Discovery Method

Use the appropriate discovery method, depending on the type of data you want

Discovery method	Discovery data the method will provide
Network	Devices on your network that have an IP address
Active Directory User	Active Directory user account resources on the domain
Active Directory System	Active Directory enabled computers on the domain
Active Directory System Group	More detailed Active Directory data for systems
Windows User Account	Domain user accounts in particular domains
Windows User Group	Groups of users in domains
Heartbeat	Maintains current discovery data on all SMS clients

The discovery method that you choose depends on whether you have Active Directory and which resource types you want to find. The table above can help you determine which discovery method is best suited to your organization.

When to use Network Discovery

Use the Network Discovery method to find any device on your network that has an IP address. Use Network Discovery to search specific subnets, domains, Simple Network Management Protocol (SNMP) devices, and Microsoft Windows NT® or Windows 2000–based Dynamic Host Configuration Protocol (DHCP) servers for resources. Network Discovery can also use SNMP to discover resources that are recognized by routers.

You can use Network Discovery to collect resource discovery data so that SMS can perform Client Push Installation.

When to use Active Directory User Discovery

Use the Active Directory User Discovery method to poll the domain for user account resources. This discovery method works on primary and secondary sites.

When to use Active Directory System Discovery

Use the Active Directory System Discovery method to discover Active Directory enabled computers on the domain.

When to use Active Directory System Group Discovery

Use the Active Directory System Group Discovery method when you require more detailed discovery data. This is because the Active Directory System Group Discovery method serves as an enhancement of the discovery data of other discovery methods. You can run this discovery method only on primary sites. If you must discover users or groups in domains that only a secondary site is in, configure the secondary site's parent primary site to discover those domains. Use this discovery method when you need information about:

- An organizational unit.
- Global groups.
- Universal groups.
- Nested groups.
- Other non-security groups, such as Windows distribution groups.

When to use Windows User Account Discovery

The Windows-based discovery methods should be used when Active Directory is not available. Use the Windows User Account Discovery method if you want to find domain user accounts in particular domains. In Windows NT 4.0 domains, this discovery method should only be used to ensure efficiency.

When to use Windows User Group Discovery

Use the Windows User Group Discovery method for creating group-based collections for software distribution. For example, if you want to distribute software based on groups of users, you can use this discovery method to determine which groups are in your domains. If your organization has an Accountants user group, you can discover that group and then advertise software to a collection containing that group.

When to use Heartbeat Discovery

Use the Heartbeat Discovery method for maintaining current discovery data on all SMS clients. By default, this discovery method is enabled.

Network Discovery Options

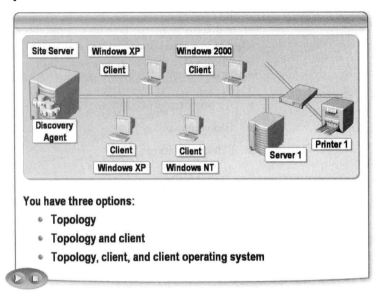

You have three options:
- Topology
- Topology and client
- Topology, client, and client operating system

You can use Network Discovery to search specific subnets, domains, SNMP devices, and Microsoft DHCP servers for resources. Network Discovery creates a DDR for a resource only if it discovers either the resource's IP subnet (it needs the subnet mask) or its Active Directory site membership.

You can configure discovery methods to set discovery type, discovery schedule, and other elements that apply to each discovery method. Use the same dialog box in the SMS Administrator console to both enable and configure discovery methods.

Before you enable Network Discovery, configure discovery type and discovery scope in the **Network Discovery Properties** dialog box in the Discovery Methods item in the SMS Administrator console.

Network discovery options

There are three Network Discovery options: topology; topology and client; and topology, client, and client operating system. As their names suggest, each network discovery type gathers more information than the preceding type. You can configure the selected network discovery type by using the **Subnets**, **DHCP** (available only in standard security mode), **SNMP**, and **SNMP Devices** tabs in the **Network Discovery Properties** dialog box.

- **Topology**. You can discover subnets and network devices that have an SNMP agent and detect how they are connected by selecting the **Topology** option in the **Network Discovery Properties** dialog box.

- **Topology and client**. You can discover other IP devices within the subnets and domains that you specify by selecting the **Topology and client** option in the **Network Discovery Properties** dialog box. When the device is displayed under Collections in the SMS Administrator console, the IP address appears in the Name column.

- **Topology, client, and client operating system**. The topology, client, and client operating system type of network discovery is the most robust and comprehensive of the three network discovery types. You can discover subnets, IP devices, and client computer operating systems within the subnets and domains you specify by selecting this option in the **Network Discovery Properties** dialog box.

Tabs in the Network Discovery Properties dialog box

You can specify the discovery scope, and enable and configure a combination of discovery options by using the **Subnets**, **Domains**, **SNMP**, **SNMP Devices**, **DHCP**, and **Schedule** tabs in the **Network Discovery Properties** dialog box.

Important   When setting schedules you should give special consideration to network bandwidth and time constraints. Performing a search on a local subnet might only require 2 hours. However, if you're performing a search of an enterprise network across several router hops with several thousand resources, you might need more time so that Network Discovery has a chance to complete its search.

Note   For additional information on the Network Discovery tabs, see Chapter 17 of the *Microsoft Systems Management Server 2003 Concepts, Planning, and Deployment Guide* on the Additional Reading page of your Student Materials compact disc.

Multimedia: Introduction to SMS Discovery

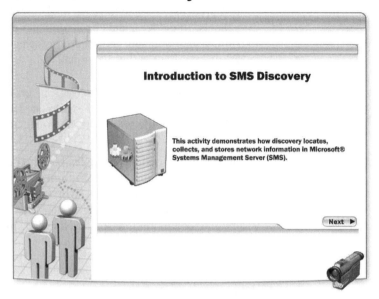

This activity illustrates SMS discovery methods. The animation demonstrates how SMS discovery locates, collects, and stores information about resources on the network. After you complete the activity, you will reinforce your understanding of the discovery methods by discussing them with the class.

Instructions

1. Open the Web page on the Student Materials compact disc, click **Multimedia**, and then click **Introduction to SMS Discovery** to open the activity.

2. Follow your instructor's directions for completing this activity.

Note You can view this animation from beginning to end and then complete the assessment, or you can pause the animation and answer questions as you go.

Demonstration: How to Configure and Enable Discovery Methods

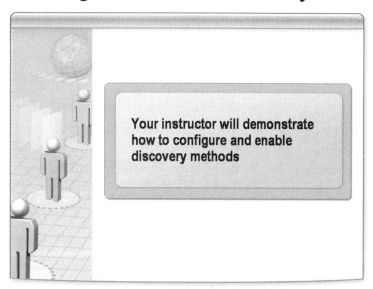

In this demonstration, your instructor will show you how to configure and enable discovery methods.

Your instructor will use the following values in this demonstration.

Variable	Value
Virtual machine—SMS Site 1	Dublin
Dublin Administrator	JaePa (Jae Pak)
Virtual machine—Domain controller	Glasgow
Domain Administrator	Administrator

Important   These steps are included for your information. Do not attempt to perform them in the classroom. If you perform these steps in the classroom environment, you might leave your computer in an incorrect state for upcoming practices.

Demonstration steps performed by instructor only

▶ **To enable and configure discovery methods**

1. Verify that the Glasgow virtual machine is running. If Glasgow is not running, log it on to the NWTRADERS domain with a user name of **Administrator** and a password of **P@ssw0rd**.

   After the Glasgow virtual machine opens, you can minimize it.

2. Verify that the Dublin virtual machine is running. If Dublin is not running, log it on to the NWTRADERS domain with a user name of **JaePa** and a password of **P@ssw0rd**.

3. On the Dublin virtual machine, click **Start**, point to **All Programs**, point to **Systems Management Server**, and then click **SMS Administrator Console**.

4. Expand **Site Database (001 – NWTraders)**, expand **Site Hierarchy**, expand **001 - NWTraders**, expand **Site Settings**, and then click **Discovery Methods**.

5. Double-click **Active Directory User Discovery**.

6. On the **Active Directory User Discovery Properties** dialog box, select the **Enable Active Directory User Discovery** check box.

7. Click on the **New** ⁜ button, select **Local domain**, and then click **OK**.

8. In the **Select New Container** dialog box, expand **nwtraders**, click **Users**, and then click **OK**.

9. In the **Active Directory User Discovery Properties** dialog box, on the **Polling Schedule** tab, select the **Run discovery as soon a possible** check box, and then click **OK**.

▶ **To enable and configure the Active Directory System Discovery**

1. On the Dublin virtual machine, in the details pane of the SMS Administrator console, in the **Discovery Methods** list, double-click **Active Directory System Discovery**.

2. In the **Active Directory System Discovery Properties** dialog box, select the **Enable Active Directory System Discovery** check box.

3. Click on the **New** ⁜ button, select **Local domain**, and then click **OK**.

4. In the **Select New Container** dialog box, verify that **nwtraders** is selected and then click **OK**.

5. In the **Active Directory System Discovery Properties** dialog box on the **Polling Schedule** tab, select the **Run discovery as soon a possible** check box.

6. Click **OK**.

▶ **To enable and configure the Active Directory System Group Discovery**

1. On the Dublin virtual machine, in the details pane of the SMS Administrator console, in the **Discovery Methods** list, double-click **Active Directory System Group Discovery**.

2. In the **Active Directory System Group Discovery Properties** dialog box, select the **Enable Active Directory System Group Discovery** check box.

3. Click on the **New** ⁜ button, select **Local domain**, and then click **OK**.

4. In the **Select New Container** dialog box, verify that **nwtraders** is selected and then click **OK**.

5. In the **Active Directory System Group Discovery Properties** dialog box on the **Polling Schedule** tab, select the **Run discovery as soon a possible** check box, and then click **OK**.

6. On the SMS Administrator console, expand **Collections**, and then click **All Systems**.

7. In the details pane, double-click **Dublin**.

8. In the **Dublin** Properties dialog box, under the **General** tab, under the **Property** and **Value** columns, verify the following values:

    *   AgentName[1] SMS_AD_SYSTEM_DISCOVERY_AGENT

    *   AgentName[2] SMS_AD_SYSTEM_GROUP_DISCOVERY_AGENT

9. Click **Close**.

▶ **To verify that SMS discovered user resources**

1. On the Dublin virtual machine, in the console tree of the SMS Administrator console, verify that **Collections** is expanded, and then click **All Users**.

2. In the console tree, right-click **All Users**, point to **All Tasks**, and then click **Update Collection Membership**.

3. In the **All Users** dialog box, click **OK**.

4. Note that an hourglass appears and then quickly changes to a smaller hour glass. Press F5 to complete the collection update.

5. Double-click **NWTRADERS\Administrator (Administrator)** which opens the **NWTRADERS\Administrator (Administrator) Properties** dialog box.

6. On the **General** tab, under **Property** and **Value** columns, verify the instances of the **User Group Name** property.

7. Click **Close**.

8. Close the SMS Administrator console.

9. Leave both Glasgow and Dublin virtual machines running because they will be used in subsequent practices.

Guidelines for Enabling and Configuring Active Directory User, System, and System Group Discovery

Guidelines:

• Specify at least one Active Directory container for each Active Directory discovery method you enable

• After you specify which Active Directory containers to scan, specify whether to scan recursively

You can configure the three types of Active Directory discovery in the **Active Directory User Discovery Properties**, **Active Directory System Discovery Properties**, and **Active Directory System Group Discovery Properties** dialog boxes in the Discovery Methods item in the SMS Administrator console.

Guidelines

Follow these guidelines to enable and configure user, system, and system group Active Directory discovery:

- **Specify at least one Active Directory container for each Active Directory discovery method you enable.** You specify the schedule for discovery to run on the **Polling Schedule** tab. The schedule that you create specifies when the Active Directory discovery method polls an Active Directory resource to discover systems, users, or system groups in the container that you specify. If you do not select **Run discovery as soon as possible** on the **Polling Schedule** tab for each discovery method, no resources are discovered until the next scheduled discovery.

- **After you specify which Active Directory containers to scan, specify whether to scan recursively.** Recursive scanning finds objects that are stored in the Active Directory containers that you specify, and it finds any sub containers. By default, all containers are scanned recursively. You can turn the recursive scanning of containers on or off by selecting the container and clicking the **Recursive** button.

Note   Active Directory discovery methods require that the SMS Service account or computer account of the site server (if using advanced security) has read access to the containers designated.

Dialog Box	Purpose
Active Directory User Discovery	Discovers user name, unique user name (including domain name), domain, Active Directory container name, and group membership.
Active Directory System Discovery	Retrieves details about the computer, such as computer name, Active Directory container name, IP address, and Active Directory site. It generates a DDR for each valid computer it discovers in Active Directory.
Active Directory System Group Discovery	Works only for systems that are already discovered and assigned to the local primary site and any direct child secondary sites. Active Directory System Group Discovery is not available for secondary sites. If a resource has been discovered and is assigned to the SMS site, Active Directory System Group Discovery extends other discovery methods by retrieving details such as organizational unit, global groups, universal groups, and nested groups.

How to ensure use of a particular domain controller

To ensure that the Active Directory discovery methods use a particular domain controller, specify the Active Directory container by using a query with the following syntax:

LDAP://server/DC=domain,DC=third-tier DNS name,DC=second-tier DNS name,DC=first-tier DNS name

To ensure that the Active Directory discovery methods use the Active Directory global catalog, specify the Active Directory container by using a query with the following syntax:

GC://DC=domain,DC=third-tier DNS name,DC=second-tier DNS name,DC=first-tier DNS name

Guidelines for Enabling and Configuring Heartbeat Discovery

Guidelines for Heartbeat Discovery:

* **Keep it enabled**
* **Avoid scheduling it to run frequently in large SMS sites**
* **Schedule it to run weekly**
* **Lengthen the heartbeat period to cut down on network traffic, once a site has been established and is stable**

What is Heartbeat Discovery?

Heartbeat Discovery is a method used to refresh SMS client computer discovery data in the SMS site database. If Heartbeat Discovery remains enabled, the discovery data is refreshed on a schedule you determine. The data is refreshed by means of the client creating the DDR and sending it to the SMS site. If you disable Heartbeat Discovery, the discovery data is refreshed only when another discovery method is invoked or run on a schedule. By default, this discovery method is always enabled.

Guidelines

To keep existing SMS clients updated so that they are not deleted from the SMS site database, you should keep Heartbeat Discovery enabled. You configure the schedule for SMS to generate updated DDRs in the **Heartbeat Discovery Properties** dialog box in the Discovery Methods item in the SMS Administrator console.

Note   Be aware that SMS runs an automated task to clean out resources that have not been updated for the past 90 days (default).

You can configure the discovery schedule on the **General** tab. You should avoid scheduling Heartbeat Discovery to run frequently in large SMS sites or on many sites at the same time. It is recommended that you schedule Heartbeat Discovery to run weekly. The volume of network traffic produced for each client is minimal, so Heartbeat Discovery should remain enabled at all SMS sites.

For Legacy Clients, if you configure Heartbeat Discovery to a frequency that is less than the frequency at which the client refresh cycle runs (every 25 hours), the SMS site receives Heartbeat Discovery DDRs only at the frequency at which the client refresh cycle runs. For Advanced Clients, a DDR is sent according to the Heartbeat Discovery schedule only.

Remember that when you enable, disable, or configure the Heartbeat Discovery schedule, these settings are applied on a site-wide basis.

Practice: Discovering Resources

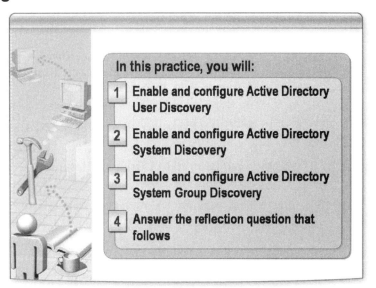

In this practice, you will:

1. Enable and configure Active Directory User Discovery

2. Enable and configure Active Directory System Discovery

3. Enable and configure Active Directory System Group Discovery

4. Answer the reflection question that follows

Instructions

Complete the procedures to practice enabling the Active Directory discovery methods and exploring the differences between them. Then answer the reflection question that follows.

In this practice, use the following values.

Variable	Value
Virtual machine—SMS Site 1	Dublin
Dublin Administrator	JaePa (Jae Pak)
Virtual machine—Domain controller	Glasgow
Domain Administrator	Administrator

Procedures

▶ **To enable and configure Active Directory User Discovery**

1. Verify that Glasgow virtual machine is running. If Glasgow is not running, log it on to the NWTRADERS domain with a user name of **Administrator** and a password of **P@ssw0rd**. After the Glasgow virtual machine opens, you can minimize it.

2. Verify that Dublin virtual machine is running. If Dublin is not running, log it on to the NWTRADERS domain with a user name of **JaePa** and a password of **P@ssw0rd**.

3. On the Dublin virtual machine, click **Start**, point to **All Programs**, point to **Systems Management Server**, and then click **SMS Administrator Console**.

4. Expand **Site Database (001 – NWTraders)**, expand **Site Hierarchy**, expand **001 - NWTraders**, expand **Site Settings**, and then click **Discovery Methods**.

5. Double-click **Active Directory User Discovery**.

6. On the **Active Directory User Discovery Properties** dialog box, select the **Enable Active Directory User Discovery** check box.

7. Click on the New ⬦ button, select **Local domain**, and then click **OK**.

8. In the **Select New Container** dialog box, expand **nwtraders**, click **Users**, and then click **OK**.

9. In the **Active Directory User Discovery Properties** dialog box, on the **Polling Schedule** tab, select the **Run discovery as soon a possible** check box, and then click **OK**.

▶ **To enable and configure the Active Directory System Discovery**

1. On the Dublin virtual machine, in the details pane of the SMS Administrator console, in the **Discovery Methods** list, double-click **Active Directory System Discovery**.

2. In the **Active Directory System Discovery Properties** dialog box, select the **Enable Active Directory System Discovery** check box.

3. Click on the New ⬦ button, select **Local domain**, and then click **OK**.

4. In the **Select New Container** dialog box, verify that **nwtraders** is selected and then click **OK**.

5. In the **Active Directory System Discovery Properties** dialog box on the **Polling Schedule** tab, select the **Run discovery as soon a possible** check box.

6. Click **OK**.

▶ **To enable and configure the Active Directory System Group Discovery**

1. On the Dublin virtual machine, in the details pane of the SMS Administrator console, in the **Discovery Methods** list, double-click **Active Directory System Group Discovery**.

2. In the **Active Directory System Group Discovery Properties** dialog box, select the **Enable Active Directory System Group Discovery** check box.

3. Click on the New ⬦ button, select **Local domain**, and then click **OK**.

4. In the **Select New Container** dialog box, verify that **nwtraders** is selected and then click **OK**.

5. In the **Active Directory System Group Discovery Properties** dialog box on the **Polling Schedule** tab, select the **Run discovery as soon a possible** check box, and then click **OK**.

6. On the SMS Administrator console, expand **Collections**, and then click **All Systems**.

7. In the details pane, double-click **Dublin**.

8. In the **Dublin** Properties dialog box, under the **General** tab, under the **Property** and **Value** columns, verify the following values:

   • Agent Name[1] SMS_AD_SYSTEM_DISCOVERY_AGENT

   • Agent Name[2] SMS_AD_SYSTEM_GROUP_DISCOVERY_AGENT

9. Click **Close**.

▶ **To verify that SMS discovered user resources**

1. On the Dublin virtual machine, in the console tree of the SMS Administrator console, verify that **Collections** is expanded, and then click **All Users**.

2. In the console tree, right-click **All Users**, point to **All Tasks**, and then click **Update Collection Membership**.

3. In the **All Users** dialog box, click **OK**.

Note Notice that an hourglass icon appears and then quickly changes to a smaller hourglass icon.

---

4. Press F5 to refresh the system and complete the collection update.

5. Double-click **NWTRADERS\JaePa (Jae Pak)** which opens the **NWTRADERS\JaePa (Jae Pak)** properties dialog box.

6. On the **General** tab, under **Property** and **Value** columns, verify the instances of the **User Group Name** property.

7. Click **Close**.

8. Close the SMS Administrator console.

9. Leave both Glasgow and Dublin virtual machines running because they will be used in subsequent practices.

Reflection question   If your network did not have Active Directory enabled, which resource discovery method would you use to discover your users?

Bonn, Paris, Glasgow

Lesson: Managing the Site Systems That Support Client Installation and Client/Server Communication

* The Site Systems Used to Support SMS Clients
* Guidelines for Configuring and Deploying a Server Locator Point
* Guidelines for Configuring and Deploying a Client Access Point
* Guidelines for Configuring and Deploying a Management Point
* How to Create an SMS Site System Diagram Using Network Trace
* Demonstration: Deploying the Site Systems That Support Client Installation

Introduction

In this lesson, you will learn about the site systems needed to support SMS clients. You will learn how to configure and deploy each site system and how to investigate the components and communication methods involved.

Lesson objectives

After completing this lesson, you will be able to:

- Describe the site systems used to support SMS clients.
- Describe the guidelines to configure and deploy a server locator point.
- Describe the guidelines to configure and deploy a client access point server.
- Describe the guidelines to configure and deploy a management point server.
- Explain how to create an SMS Site System diagram using Network Trace.

The Site Systems Used to Support SMS Clients

To reduce the workload on your site server, to support a larger number of clients in a site, and for improved reliability, you can add site systems to your SMS site and assign roles to those systems. A site system role is a particular function that a site system performs during SMS operation. For example, the SMS site server (the computer on which you installed SMS) is assigned the site server role, and the computer with the Microsoft SQL Server™ database for the site is assigned the site database server role. By adding site systems to the site and assigning appropriate site system roles, you can distribute the load on servers and improve system performance as well as support larger numbers of clients.

Three site systems are relevant to the deployment of SMS clients: client access points (CAPs), server locator points (SLPs), and management points. The three site systems are explained in the following descriptions.

Server locator point (SLP)

A server locator point is an SMS site system that locates client access points for Legacy Clients. An SLP is a site code for Advanced Clients, directing the client there to complete installation.

An SLP is used primarily in client installation and is generally implemented in the SMS central site because the central site has information about the SMS hierarchy and the structure of the SMS sites in that hierarchy. Server locator points can also be used by Advanced Clients to discover the assigned site code when performing automatic site code discovery.

Client access point (CAP)

The client access point role provides a communication point between the SMS site and Legacy Client computers.

Legacy Client computers contact CAPs to install and update SMS client software. After SMS client software has been installed, Legacy Client computers contact a CAP for updated information from the SMS site server, including any applicable advertised programs. To reduce the load on the site server, assign the CAP role to one or more site systems, other than the site server. Legacy Client computers also deliver collected files, inventory information, discovery data records, software metering, and status information to CAPs.

Management point

The management point serves as the primary point of contact between Advanced Clients and the SMS site server.

The Advanced Client communicates with SMS sites by using management points. Like CAPs and Legacy Clients, management points provide Advanced Clients with configuration details and advertisements. They also receive discovery, inventory, software metering, and status information from the clients.

Unlike a CAP, however, management points contact the SMS site database directly to retrieve client settings, advertisements, and available distribution points instead of relying on file replication as do CAPs.

Guidelines for Configuring and Deploying a Server Locator Point

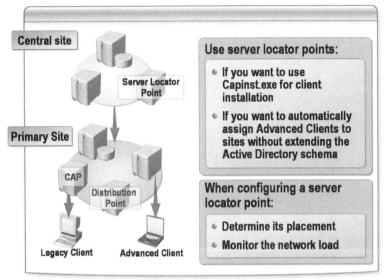

To complete SMS client installation, the client computer can use a server locator point to find CAPs or SMS site codes. The SLP replaces the SMS 2.0 logon point and eliminates most traffic between SMS and domain controllers. It also eliminates the need to install SMS component servers on domain controllers. SLPs can be used for installation of both Legacy Clients and Advanced Clients.

Guidelines

Use a server locator point in your SMS hierarchy when you want to automatically assign Advanced Clients to sites without extending the Active Directory schema for SMS and when you want to install SMS 2003 clients using Capinst.exe.

Follow these guidelines to configure and deploy a server locator point:

- *Determine the placement of SLPs*. The server locator point requires minimal planning. Server locator points are supported only in primary sites, not secondary sites, and they are used for both Advanced Clients and Legacy Clients. Generally, you need only one server locator point in your SMS hierarchy. You might choose to install additional SLPs on remote sites to reduce WAN traffic. However, the additional SLP might not be necessary if the WAN links are adequate.

  You usually install the server locator point at the central site. If the server locator point creates too much load at the SMS site database, you have the option to use a replicated SQL Server database for that site. If there are excessive client requests causing excessive traffic on a single server locator point, you can set up multiple server locator points at the central site.

  Remember that the server locator point also requires Internet Information Services (IIS).

- *Monitor the network load.* If you have created a logon script–based installation method, the Legacy Client accesses a server locator point at client logon time and produces minimal network traffic. Similarly, the Advanced Client accesses the server locator point at client logon time for auto-assignment at its initial logon time and generates the same amount of traffic as the Legacy Client. There is also network traffic between the client and the domain controller when the client runs the logon script. For Advanced Clients, you can reduce the load on the server locator points by installing the SMS client software throughout your organization in phases.

Server locator points also rely on accessing the SMS site database to obtain information about CAPs and site boundaries. Therefore, it is necessary to monitor the network traffic generated between a server locator point and the site database server. You can reduce the load on the SMS site database server by implementing an additional computer running SQL Server to replicate the SMS site database.

The role of the SLP

Client computers can use the SLP to install the Advanced Client or the Legacy Client. Advanced Clients can also use the SLP for site assignment. The SLP directly queries the database of the associated site for the site boundaries that the site supports. The queries are small, and the SLP caches the requested information locally. If the client computer is configured to install the Legacy Client, the SLP returns the available assigned site's CAP or CAPs to complete the client installation. If the client computer is configured to install the Advanced Client, the SLP returns a site for the client to complete the client installation from. After it is installed, the Advanced Client can use the SLP for automatic site assignment.

Server locator points have no role during regular client operations. Advanced Clients find server locator points by using Active Directory, WINS, or the /SLP switch when using Capinst. Legacy clients can find an SLP through Active Directory or the /SLP switch when using Capinst.

Why clients must use server locator points during client deployment

You don't have to use an SLP unless you want to use Capinst.exe. Clients can use an SLP during client deployment for the following reasons:

- Client computers configured to install the Advanced Client use an SLP to get information about the assigned site from which they can install the client.

- When the logged on user does not have administrative privileges, computers configured for Advanced Client installation use a server locator point to get information about a management point to which they can send a client configuration request (CCR).

- Client computers configured to install the Legacy Client use an SLP to get information about CAPs that they can use to install the client.

- Client computers configured to install the Advanced Client can use server locator points for automatic site assignment if Active Directory has not been extended.

Guidelines for Configuring and Deploying a Client Access Point

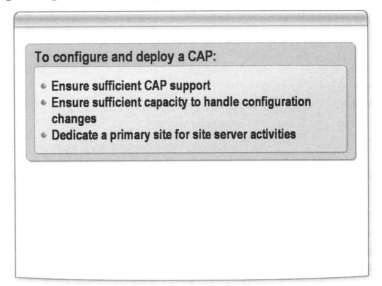

To configure and deploy a CAP:

- Ensure sufficient CAP support
- Ensure sufficient capacity to handle configuration changes
- Dedicate a primary site for site server activities

A client access point (CAP) is primarily responsible for relaying the majority of the objects sent from Legacy Clients to the site server. It provides clients with the SMS client components during Legacy Client installation. Both CAPs and management points function as the primary communication points for SMS clients.

Guidelines

When you deploy CAPs, you must plan carefully to ensure that your CAPs can support varied numbers of distributed Legacy Clients efficiently and with enough capacity to perform all required operations.

Follow these guidelines to configure and deploy a CAP:

- *Ensure sufficient CAP support.* Plan to have at least one CAP for every 2,000 client computers. If the SMS site contains only Advanced Clients, you do not need to have multiple CAPs, because without Legacy Clients, the CAP is used only by SMS site server components.

  Your goal is to keep the number of CAPs deployed to a minimum. Because SMS site server processes replicate serially and must cycle through each CAP, this process takes longer if you have many CAPs. This is an important consideration because all client configuration files are replicated to each CAP.

- *Ensure sufficient capacity to handle configuration changes.* When you make configuration changes to an SMS site, all the Legacy Clients contact the CAPs at their next client refresh cycle and update the client from the CAPs based on these changes. An example of a configuration change is the installation of an SMS service pack. It is also important to remember that CAPs receive data, such as inventory and status messages, from clients.

- *Dedicate a primary site for site server activities.* The SMS site server is automatically installed as a CAP. If you want to dedicate a primary site to performing only SMS server activities, you can remove the CAP role from the site server after you have created another CAP in the site and then assign the CAP site system role to another server.

How CAPs and Legacy Clients communicate

The CAP passes all Legacy Client data to the site server. Legacy Client computers contact the CAP for management information from the SMS site server. A CAP serves only one SMS site and is installed by default on the site server. The CAP also:

- Provides specific configuration instructions and files for the Legacy Client during client installation and when changes are made after client installation.

- Serves as the location where Legacy Client computers check for advertisements.

- Receives data from Legacy Clients, which it forwards to the SMS site server. For example, when a client completes either hardware or software inventory and has created an inventory data file, it sends this data to the CAP. Any discovery, inventory, and software metering data, in addition to status messages originating from the client, are sent to the CAP.

The site server replicates a set of files down to the CAP. The client then reads those files and copies them from the CAP, and then processes them. If the CAP is offline, the site server cannot update the CAP, so the clients that access that CAP might be out of date.

CAPs do not require IIS; they perform file transfers by means of server message blocks (SMBs).

Guidelines for Configuring and Deploying a Management Point

To configure and deploy a management point:

- Ensure that each site has one logical management point (the default management point)
- Configure multiple management points with Windows Network Load Balancing service to provide failover
- Reduce the load on the management point, if necessary

The management point is the primary point of contact between Advanced Clients and the SMS site. It is used to allow Advanced Clients to receive and send information to SMS sites. Management points require IIS, Background Intelligent Transfer Service (BITS), and access to the SMS site database.

Guidelines

Follow these guidelines to configure and deploy a management point:

- *Ensure that each site has one logical management point (the default management point)*. Management points require access to the SMS site database.

- *Configure multiple management points with Windows Network Load Balancing service to provide failover.* Using a Network Load Balancing cluster, you can implement multiple management points in one primary site to meet the failover and capacity needs of your organization.

Note For additional information about Network Load Balancing, see Chapter 10 of the *Microsoft Systems Management Server 2003 Concepts, Planning, and Deployment Guide* on the Additional Reading page of your Student Materials compact disc.

- *Reduce the load on the management point, if necessary.* Be aware that there are many factors that affect the load on a management point. One sizing consideration is the performance of SQL Server. If performance is slow, plan to implement an additional computer running SQL Server for replication purposes.

  As with the CAP, the main performance objects to track for sizing and capacity are those related to CPU usage and queue lengths, followed closely by disk and memory usage.

> **Note** For more information about management point capacity and performance, see Chapter 8 of the *Microsoft Systems Management Server 2003 Concepts, Planning, and Deployment Guide.*

- **Note the following system requirements and troubleshooting information**.

  - Management point site systems require Windows 2000 Server SP3 or later.

  - Management point site systems require IIS and BITS Server Extensions to be manually installed on Microsoft Windows Server™ 2003 (automatically installed on Windows 2000 Server).

  - The World Wide Publishing service (installed as part of IIS) must be running.

  - The Distributed Transaction Coordinator (DTC) and Task Scheduler services need to be started before the management point can be successfully installed.

  - Verify that the management point computer has been added to the SMS_SiteSystemToSQLConnection_*sitecode* and SMS_SiteSystemToSiteServerConnection_*sitecode* groups.

  - The site server computer account (or the SMS Service Account) requires administrative rights to the management point computer.

The role of the management point

Although CAPs and management points have similar roles, they operate in quite different ways. The following table helps to differentiate between CAPs and management points.

Management points	Client access points
Supports the Advanced Client	**Supports the Legacy Client**
Supports 25,000 users	Supports 2,000 users
Requires IIS to be installed and enabled	Does *not* require IIS
Uses more processing time than CAPs	Uses more disk space than management points
No static SMS files (uses SQL)	Static SMS configuration files
Causes more memory issues because management points cache Advanced Client policy	

A management point has a similar role to the relationship between CAPs and Legacy Clients in that it:

- Provides specific client configuration details (also known as *Advanced Client policy*) for the Advanced Client after client installation.

  - Serves as the location where Advanced Client computers check for advertisements.

- Locates distribution points for Advanced Clients.

- Receives discovery, inventory, software metering, and status information from Advanced Clients and forwards it to the SMS site server.

How to Create an SMS Site System Diagram Using Network Trace

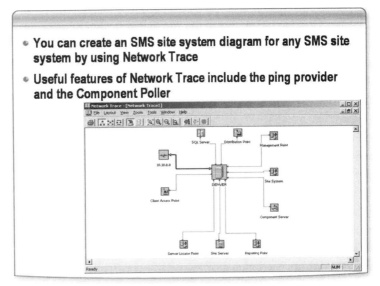

You can use Network Trace to create an SMS site system diagram to view the health of any SMS site system. The network diagram that you create displays network connectivity from the perspective of the site system that you have selected, not from the perspective of the computer from which you are running Network Trace. You can use Network Trace to display the IP network connections of a remote site system. Also, you can use Network Trace to display the site system roles performed by the selected site system and by all the servers connected to that site system.

You can create network diagrams that display the following information:

- All servers connected to the selected site system
- Site system roles performed by each server
- Network devices such as routers
- IP subnets

A network diagram displays information in either a trace view or a site view. In trace view, only the site systems within the site database appear. In site view, all known subnets and routers also appear, along with the site systems within the site database.

Network Trace creates network diagrams that are based upon information in the SMS site database. SMS gathers this information during the server and network discovery processes. SMS site system discovery runs immediately after SMS installation and periodically thereafter to discover servers that you have configured as site systems. After Site System Discovery runs, Network Trace can diagram the communication links between other servers and the site system you select.

Network Discovery is not enabled by default. Also, you must schedule and configure Network Discovery to discover devices such as routers. To diagram devices outside your local subnet, you must run Network Discovery on all subnets in the site that you want to diagram. If you do not do this, the network diagrams created by Network Trace will display the local subnet only.

Procedure

To create a network diagram using Network Trace:

1. In the console tree of the SMS Administrator console, expand **Systems Management Server**, expand **Site Database (001 – NWTraders)**, expand **Site Hierarchy**, expand **001 - NWTraders**, expand **Site Settings**, and then click **Site Systems**.

2. Right-click **\\DUBLIN**, point to **All Tasks**, and then click **Start Network Trace**.

   The Network Trace window opens and displays a diagram of the IP communication links between the site system you selected and other servers and network devices that are connected to the selected site system.

Additional features of Network Trace

Other features of Network Trace include the ping provider and the Component Poller. You can use the ping provider to transmit an Internet Control Message Protocol echo, which is more commonly known as a *ping*. You can send a ping to all devices displayed in the network diagram, or to only the devices that you select, to confirm the IP communication link. Pings are sent from the site server, not from the computer you are logged on to.

You can use the Component Poller to query the status of SMS components installed on the selected site server. You can use it to determine if a component is running, paused, or stopped, the last time the component was polled, and the component type. Like the ping provider, the Component Poller runs from the site server.

Demonstration: Deploying the Site Systems That Support Client Installation

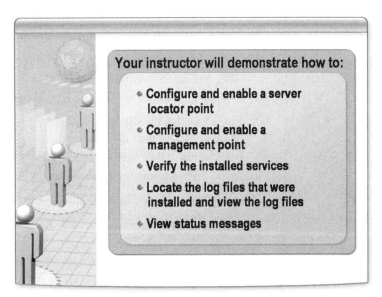

In this demonstration, your instructor will show you how to configure and enable a server locator point and a management point, verify the installed services, locate and view the log files, and then view the status messages.

Your instructor will use the following values in this demonstration.

Variable	Value
Virtual machine—SMS Site 1	Dublin
Dublin Administrator	JaePa (Jae Pak)
Virtual machine—Domain controller	Glasgow
Domain Administrator	Administrator

Important These steps are included for your information. Do not attempt to do them in the classroom. If you perform these steps in the classroom environment, you may leave your computer in an incorrect state for upcoming practices.

Demonstration steps performed by instructor only

▶ **To configure and enable a server locator point**

1. Verify that the Glasgow and Dublin virtual machines are running.

2. On Dublin virtual machine, click **Start**, point to **All Programs**, point to **Systems Management Server**, and the click **SMS Administrator Console**.

3. In the console tree of the SMS Administrator console, expand **Site Database (001- NWTraders)**, expand **Site Hierarchy**, expand **001-NWTraders**, then expand **Site Settings**, and then click **Site Systems**.

4. In the details pane, right-click **\\DUBLIN**, and then click **Properties**.

5. In the **\\DUBLIN Site System Properties** dialog box, on the **Server Locator Point** tab, select the **Use this site system as a server locator point** check box.

6. In the **Database** list, verify that **Use the site database** is selected, and then click **OK**.

7. Leave the SMS Administrator console open.

▶ **To configure and enable the management point**

1. On the Dublin virtual machine, verify the SMS Administrator console is open and the **Site Systems** list appears in the details pane.

2. Right-click **\\DUBLIN**, and then click **Properties**.

3. In the **\\DUBLIN Site System Properties** dialog box, click the **Management Point** tab, and then select the **Use this site system as a management point** check box.

4. In the **SMS Management Point** dialog box, click **OK**.

5. In the **Database** field, verify that **Use the site database** is selected, and then click **OK**.

6. In the **\\DUBLIN Site System** dialog box, click **Yes**.

   This will make the new management point the default management point.

7. Close the SMS Administrator console.

Note   Be sure to wait about five minutes for SMS to enable the server locator point and management point before you move on to the next procedure.

▶ **To verify the installed services**

1. On the Dublin virtual machine, click **Start**, point to **Control Panel**, point to **Administrative Tools**, and then click **Computer Management**.

2. In Computer Management, in the console tree, expand **Services and Applications**, and then click **Services**.

   The services display in the details pane.

3. Click the **Standard** tab.

4. Locate the **SMS Agent Host** service.

   This was installed when the Management Point was enabled.

5. Locate the **SMS_SERVER_LOCATOR_POINT** service.

   This was installed when the Server Locator Point was enabled.

6. Close Computer Management.

▶ **To locate the log files that were installed and view the log files**

1. On Dublin virtual machine, click **Start**, point to **All Programs**, point to **SMS 2003 Toolkit 1**, and then click **SMS Trace**.

2. In the **SMS Trace** message box, click **Yes** to ensure that SMS Trace is the default viewer.

3. On the **File** menu, click **Open**.

4. In the **Open** dialog box, double-click **sitecomp.log**.

5. In the **SMS Trace** dialog box, on the **Tools** menu, click **Find**.

6. In the **Find** dialog box, type **Installing component SMS_SERVER_LOCATOR_POINT** and then click **Find**.

7. Scroll down and verify that **Installation successful.** appears.

8. On the **Tools** menu, click **Find**.

9. In the **Find** dialog box, type **Installing component SMS_MP_CONTROL_MANAGER** and then click **Find**.

10. Scroll down and verify that **Installation successful.** appears.

11. Close SMS Trace.

▶ **To view status messages**

1. On Dublin virtual machine, click **Start**, point to **All Programs**, point to **Systems Management Server**, and then click **SMS Administrator Console**.

2. Expand **Site Database (001- NWTRADERS)**, expand **System Status**, expand **Site Status**, and then click **Status Message Queries**.

   The status messages display in the details pane.

3. Right-click **All Status Messages** and then click **Show Messages**.

4. In the **All Status Messages** dialog box, in the **Prompted value** field, select **Time**.

5. Under value, click **Select date and time**, select **1 hour ago**, and then click **OK**.

   The messages in your selected range populate in the **SMS Status Message Viewer**.

Tip   To automatically resize all the columns to fit their contents exactly, click anywhere on the active window, and then press Ctrl + on the number pad of your keyboard.

---

6. Right-click anywhere in the window, and then click **Filter**.

7. In the **Message ID** box, type **1015** and then click **OK**.

8. Verify that the **SMS_SERVER_LOCATOR_POINT** and **SMS_MP_CONTROL_MANAGER** display the following description:

   SMS Site Component Manager successfully installed this component on this site system!

9. Close the SMS Status Message viewer and the SMS Administrator console.

10. Leave both Glasgow and Dublin virtual machines running.

Practice: Deploying the Site Systems That Support Client Installation

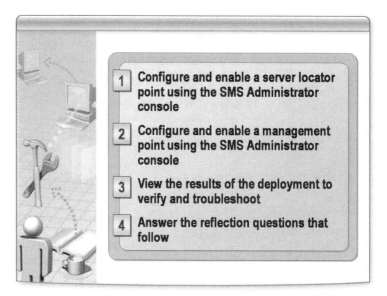

1. Configure and enable a server locator point using the SMS Administrator console

2. Configure and enable a management point using the SMS Administrator console

3. View the results of the deployment to verify and troubleshoot

4. Answer the reflection questions that follow

Instructions

Complete the procedures to practice configuring and deploying a server locator point and a management point, and then verifying a successful installation. After you are finished, complete the reflection questions that follow.

Warning You must successfully complete this practice so that later practices in Course 2596, Module 4, "Installing the Advanced Client," will work.

In this practice, use the following values.

Variable	Value
Virtual machine—SMS Site 1	Dublin
Dublin Administrator	JaePa (Jae Pak)
Virtual machine—Domain controller	Glasgow
Domain Administrator	Administrator

Procedures

▶ **To configure and enable a server locator point**

1. Verify that the Glasgow and Dublin virtual machines are running.

2. On Dublin virtual machine, click **Start**, point to **All Programs**, point to **Systems Management Server**, and then click **SMS Administrator Console**.

3. In the console tree of the SMS Administrator console, expand **Site Database (001- NWTraders)**, expand **Site Hierarchy**, expand **001-NWTraders**, then expand **Site Settings**, and then click **Site Systems**.

4. In the details pane, right-click **\\DUBLIN**, and then click **Properties**.

5. In the **\\DUBLIN Site System Properties** dialog box, on the **Server Locator Point** tab, select the **Use this site system as a server locator point** check box.

6. In the **Database** list, verify that **Use the site database** is selected, and then click **OK**.

7. Leave the SMS Administrator console open.

▶ **To configure and enable the management point**

1. On the Dublin virtual machine, verify that the **SMS Administrator Console** is open and the **Site Systems** list appears in the details pane.

2. Right-click **\\DUBLIN**, and then click **Properties**.

3. In the **\\DUBLIN Site System Properties** dialog box, on the **Management Point** tab, select the **Use this site system as a management point** check box.

4. In the **SMS Management Point** message box, click **OK**.

5. In the **Database** list, verify that **Use the site database** is selected, and then click **OK**.

6. In the **\\DUBLIN Site System** message box, click **Yes**.

    This will make the new management point the default management point.

7. Close the SMS Administrator console.

Note Be sure to wait about five minutes for SMS to enable the server locator point and management point before you move on to the next procedure.

▶ **To verify the installed services**

1. On Dublin virtual machine, click **Start**, point to **Control Panel**, point to **Administrative Tools**, and then click **Computer Management**.

2. In Computer Management, in the console tree, expand **Services and Applications**, and then click **Services**.

    The services display in the details pane.

3. Click the **Standard** tab.

4. Locate the **SMS Agent Host** service.

    This was installed when the Management Point was enabled.

5. Locate the **SMS_SERVER_LOCATOR_POINT** service.

    This was installed when the Server Locator Point was enabled.

6. Close Computer Management.

▶ **To locate the log files that were installed and view the log files**

1. On Dublin virtual machine, click **Start**, point to **All Programs**, point to **SMS 2003 Toolkit 1**, and then click **SMS Trace**.

2. In the **SMS Trace** message box, click **Yes** to ensure that SMS Trace is the default viewer.

3. On the **File** menu, click **Open**.

4. In the **Open** dialog box, double-click **sitecomp.log**.

5. In the **SMS Trace** dialog box, on the **Tools** menu, click **Find**.

6. In the **Find** dialog box, type **Installing component SMS_SERVER_LOCATOR_POINT** and then click **Find**.

7. Scroll down and verify that **Installation successful.** appears.

8. On the **Tools** menu, click **Find**.

9. In the **Find** dialog box, type **Installing component SMS_MP_CONTROL_MANAGER**, and then click **Find**.

10. Scroll down and then verify that **Installation successful.** appears.

11. Close SMS Trace.

▶ **To view status messages**

1. On the Dublin virtual machine, click **Start**, point to **All Programs**, point to **Systems Management Server**, and then click **SMS Administrator Console**.

2. In the console tree of the SMS Administrator console, expand **Site Database (001- NWTRADERS)**, expand **System Status**, and then click **Status Message Queries**.

   The status messages display in the details pane.

3. Right-click **All Status Messages** and then click **Show Messages**.

4. In the **All Status Messages** dialog box, in the **Prompted value** list, select **Time**.

5. Under value, click **Select date and time**, select **1 hour ago**, and then click **OK**.

   The messages in your selected range populate in the **SMS Status Message Viewer**.

Tip To automatically resize all the columns to fit the data cells exactly, click anywhere on the active window, and then press Ctrl + on the number pad of your keyboard.

---

6. Right-click anywhere in the window, and then click **Filter**.

7. In the **Message ID** box, type **1015**, and then click **OK**.

8. Verify that the **SMS_SERVER_LOCATOR_POINT** and **SMS_MP_CONTROL_MANAGER** display the following description, **SMS Site Component Manager successfully installed this component on this site system!**

9. Close the SMS Status Message viewer and the SMS Administrator console.

10. Leave the Glasgow and Dublin virtual machines running.

Warning You must successfully complete this practice so that later practices in Course 2596, Module 4, "Installing the Advanced Client," will work.

Reflection Questions

Why is it important that management points have access to information stored in the site database?

_____

_____

_____

Does SMS 2003 require permissions to the DCs, or have the AD schema extended, to implement logon script client installation?

_____

_____

_____

Why is it important not to install more CAPs that you need?

_____

_____

_____

Discussion: Preparing to Deploy the SMS Clients

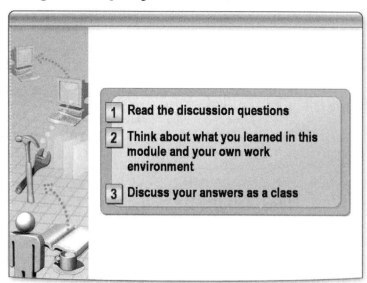

1. What are the key issues you will face when preparing to deploy the SMS client in your organization's environment?

_____

_____

_____

_____

_____

2. What is the difference between Network Discovery and Heartbeat Discovery? In what situations would you use Network Discovery for your organization?

_____

_____

_____

_____

_____

3. What is a Management Point (MP)? What is its purpose?

_____

_____

_____

_____

_____

4. What is a Server Locator Point (SLP)? What is its purpose?

_____

_____

_____

_____

_____

Microsoft

Module 4: Deploying SMS Clients

Contents

Overview

- Deploying the Advanced Client
- Deploying the Legacy Client
- Troubleshooting Problems When Installing SMS Clients

Introduction

In this module, you will learn to deploy the Microsoft® Systems Management Server (SMS) Advanced Client and the SMS Legacy Client. You will learn about available installation methods and their benefits. You will also learn how to isolate problems that you might encounter during Advanced Client installation.

Objectives

After completing this module, you will be able to:

- Deploy the SMS Advanced Client.

- Deploy the SMS Legacy Client.

- Troubleshoot problems that you might encounter during Advanced Client installation.

Lesson: Deploying the Advanced Client

- **What Are the Advanced Client Installation Files?**
- **Installation Methods for the Advanced Client**
- **What is the Client Push Installation Method?**
- **What is the Logon Script-initiated Client Installation Method?**
- **How the Manual Installation Method Works**
- **How the Advanced Client Installation Is Configured**
- **How Successful Installation Is Confirmed**
- **Demonstration: How to Install the Advanced Client**

Introduction

In this lesson, you will learn how to deploy the Advanced Client. Deployment of the Advanced Client is usually a two-part process. First, there are several configurations that you may choose to make, such as boundaries and network access accounts. Second, there are numerous installation properties that an administrator can configure to modify client installation behavior.

Lesson objectives

After completing this lesson, you will be able to:

- Describe the Advanced Client installation files.
- Describe installation methods for the Advanced Client.
- Describe the Client Push Installation method.
- Describe the requirements for the Logon Script–initiated client installation method.
- Describe the manual installation method.
- Describe the process for configuring a site for Advanced Client installation.
- Confirm successful installation.

What Are the Advanced Client Installation Files?

File name	Installation
Ccmsetup.exe	Advanced Client Installer
Client.msi	Windows Installer Package
Capinst.exe	Uses SLP and creates CCR

The Advanced Client installation files are the three main files on which the installation of the Advanced Client depends. Without these files, the installation cannot take place. These three files contain all the necessary components to install the Advanced Client. The three installation files are Ccmsetup.exe, Client.msi, and Capinst.exe. It is important to know that Ccmsetup.exe needs Client.msi to carry out the Advanced Client installation, while Capinst.exe needs both Ccmsetup.exe and Client.msi to perform the Advanced Client installation.

Ccmsetup.exe

Ccmsetup.exe is referred to as the Advanced Client Installer. Ccmsetup.exe is in the Client\i386 folder of the SMSClient share on the management point. It is also available on the SMS 2003 product compact disc. Ccmsetup.exe is a program that manages the downloading and installation of Client.msi Windows Installer file.

You can use the Advanced Client Installer to initiate Advanced Client installation manually or from a logon script. When started by a client, Ccmsetup.exe installs a small bootstrap on the client that downloads Client.msi to perform the installation. Client.msi is a Windows Installer file that contains all the components required for a full Advanced Client installation.

The Advanced Client Installer works in the background in all Advanced Client installations, except for Group Policy–based installations or directly invoking Client.msi.

The Advanced Client Installer offers the following advantages:

- It uses Active Directory® to assign to a site and find management points.

- It copies installation files to the client computer so, if the network connection is interrupted, the download can resume when the connection is reestablished.

- Applies correct localization transform to Client.msi if an International Client Pack is applied to the SMS site.

Client.msi

Client.msi is the Windows Installer package that contains the Advanced Client software. The Advanced Client Installer passes the installation properties that were specified by the administrator to client.msi. Client.msi uses those properties to configure the Advanced Client installation. Administrators need to make sure to have Client.msi in the shared folder, as well as Ccmsetup.exe and Capinst.exe, so that installation can take place.

Note   Client.msi is available on the destination computer's hard disk, which makes repair of the installations easy and allows for more efficient and complete application of updates to the Advanced Client software.

Capinst.exe

The Capinst.exe file is used with the Logon Script–initiated installation method. Capinst.exe uses the Server Locator Point to find a site for the client to download Client.msi. It also creates the Client Configuration Request (CCR) on computers for which the logged-on user does not have administrative privileges.

Installation Methods for the Advanced Client

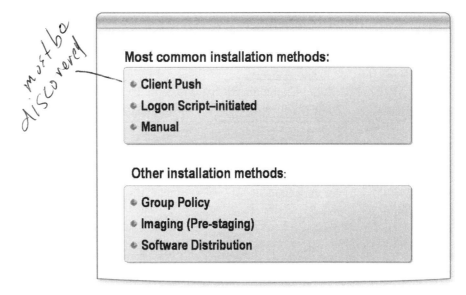

most be discovered

Most common installation methods:
- Client Push
- Logon Script–initiated
- Manual

Other installation methods:
- Group Policy
- Imaging (Pre-staging)
- Software Distribution

There are several methods for installing the Advanced Client. These methods include both automatic and manual techniques. All the methods use the Advanced Client Installer during installation.

Three of the most common methods of installing the Advanced Client are:

- Client Push installation

  Using the Client Push Installation Wizard, the SMS administrator remotely installs Advanced Clients on designated computers on the network. SMS sends the client software to the computers and installs it without user intervention. However, if you so choose, you can automate a Client Push installation.

- Logon Script–initiated installation

  The SMS administrator creates a script with commands to install the Advanced Client. A domain administrator copies the script file to domain controllers and configures users to run the script when they log on to the network. When a user logs on, the client computer automatically runs the script to install the Advanced Client without user intervention.

- Manual installation

  Manually run the Advanced Client Installer to install the Advanced Client. For example, the user types in a command line to install the Advanced Client.

These three methods will be discussed in more detail later in this lesson. There are other methods of installing the Advanced Client, such as:

■   Group Policy

■   Client imaging

Note   Upgrading SMS 2.0 to SMS 2003 Advanced or SMS 2003 Legacy to Advanced can also be considered a type of installation method.

These methods are beyond the scope of this module, but for more information, refer to the *Microsoft Systems Management Server 2003 Concepts, Planning, and Deployment Guide*, which you can access on the Additional Reading page of your Student Materials compact disc.

What Is the Client Push Installation Method?

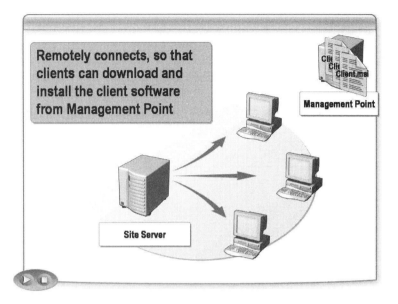

What is the Client Push Installation Method?

The Client Push installation method finds newly discovered and assigned computers and attempts to remotely connect to them. If the connection is successful, the client will pull Client.msi from the management point, after which, Client Push installation installs the specified client type without user intervention on the installed computers. This method installs client software on computers running Microsoft Windows® 2000, Windows XP, or operating systems in the Microsoft Windows Server™ 2003 family.

Note   The Client Push method can also be used to push client software to Microsoft Windows NT® 4.0 Service Pack 6 computers. However, NT 4.0 Service Pack 6 computers can only support Legacy Clients.

By default, Client Push installation does not install clients on domain controllers and on site systems. Site systems are discovered automatically by SMS. Also by default, when a site system is discovered, SMS does not trigger Client Push installation to install a client on the site system, even if Client Push installation is enabled. However, you can configure Client Push installation to install the SMS client on site systems.

Important   You can use Client Push installation to replace a Legacy Client with an Advanced Client, but you cannot use Client Push installation to replace an Advanced Client with a Legacy Client. You can also force the upgrade of an SMS 2.0 or SMS 2003 Legacy Client to the SMS 2003 Advanced Client with the Client Push Installation Wizard.

**Client push
requirements**

You can enable and configure the Client Push installation method in the SMS Administrator console. The requirements for using this method include:

- You must give administrative credentials on all chosen client computers to either the SMS Service account (if the site is running in standard security mode) or Client Push Installation accounts. If the SMS 2003 site is running in advanced security, you are required to create a Client Push Installation account if you want to push client installations to target systems.

- The Server service must be started on the client computers, file sharing must be enabled, and the ADMIN$ share must exist.

- There must be a management point installed and available.

What Is the Logon Script–Initiated Client Installation Method?

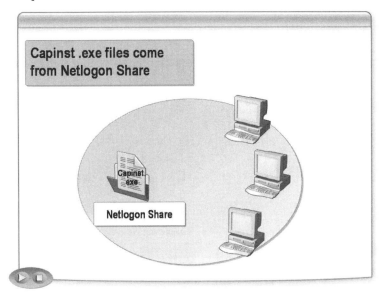

Although SMS 2003 does not provide the same logon installation features available in SMS 2.0, you can use logon scripts to launch Capinst.exe for SMS 2003 client deployment. You can use command-line switches to customize your deployment. The Capinst.exe application is strongly recommended because of the enhanced options it provides.

Logon script requirements

The requirements for using this method include:

- You must create your own logon scripts and place them in the Netlogon share.

- User accounts should be configured to use the logon script.

- The appropriate command-line switches for Capinst.exe must be included in the logon script. For example, use the /Advcli switch to install an Advanced Client.

- In an environment that is not based on non–Active Directory directory service, the Capinst.exe command-line option must include the /SLP switch to specify the Server Locator Point that should be accessed by Capinst.exe.

- By default, client installation initiated using Capinst.exe does not install SMS client software on domain controllers.

- For Advanced Client installation, Capinst.exe and Ccmsetup.exe must reside in the Netlogon share of each domain controller. For Legacy Client installation, you must have Smsman.exe in the Netlogon share.

Note If you try to run Capinst.exe with nonadministrative rights for an Advanced Client installation, it will create a CCR and send it to the site. The site then initiates installation by using the Client Push installation method.

How the Manual Installation Method Works

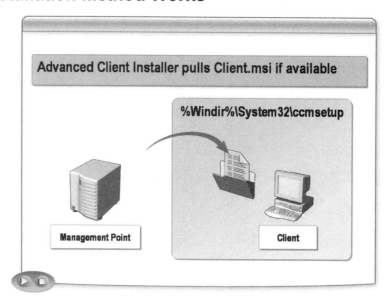

The process of manual installation

When you start the Advanced Client Installer, it installs the Advanced Client by intelligently pulling Client.msi and a language-specific transform from the SMSClient share on the management point, if available, down to the computer. The files are downloaded and then stored in the %Windir%\System32\ccmsetup folder.

After the download is complete, the Advanced Client Installer installs the client components on the computer. The download process stops while the user is logged off or while the computer is in a power standby state unless Ccmsetup.exe is installed as a service.

Advanced Client Installer can install itself as a temporary service, in which case it continues to install the SMS client even if the user logs off. If the computer restarts, the service automatically starts. When the user logs on, the installation runs. When the service completes the installation, it removes itself as a service.

The requirements for using the manual installation method are that the user has administrative privileges on the computer to which the user is installing the Advanced Client, a management point has to be installed and available, and the user must have access to Ccmsetup.exe. Administrators will configure a script that includes Ccmsetup for users with administrative privileges. Those without administrative privileges will use Capinst.exe to install the Advanced Client, which will be placed in a shared location by administrators.

Those who do not have administrative rights on the computer where the Advanced Client is to be installed will use Capinst.exe for the installation.

The three ways to perform this method

You can perform manual installation three ways:

- Using Ccmsetup command-line options

  Command-line options, also referred to as switches, for Ccmsetup.exe are identified by a forward slash (/).The switches are used alone or in combination, following Ccmsetup.exe on the command line. These options specify Advanced Client Installer behavior. For example, the command line \\Dublin\SMSClient\i386\Ccmsetup.exe   /source:\\Dublin\SMSClient\i386 /mp:DUBLIN, specifies that Ccmsetup will use the Client.msi in the SMSClient share and reference the DUBLIN management point.

  Note   When installing the Advanced Client by using Ccmsetup.exe, bear in mind that the user initiating the installation must be an administrator for the initial installation to succeed.

- Using Capinst.exe

  If you have low-rights users in your environment and they might initiate installation of the Advanced Client, we recommend that you use Capinst.exe. If a user without administrative rights to the computer launches Capinst.exe, a CCR will be created and the site server will attempt to push the Advanced Client onto the computer.

- Performing client imaging

  Client imaging is another manual method for installing the Advanced Client. You can install the Advanced Client on a client computer master image by installing core SMS client components without specifying an SMS site code for assignment. When you deploy the master image to computers, the Advanced Client is preinstalled on those computers and remains dormant until you assign the client to an SMS site.

For more information concerning client imaging, see Chapter 17, "Discovering Resources and Deploying Clients," in the *Microsoft Systems Management Server 2003 Concepts, Planning, and Deployment Guide*, which you can access on the Additional Reading page of your Student Materials compact disc.

How the Advanced Client Installation Is Configured

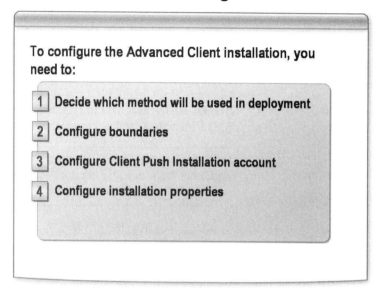

To configure the Advanced Client installation, you need to:

1. Decide which method will be used in deployment

2. Configure boundaries

3. Configure Client Push Installation account

4. Configure installation properties

Before installing the Advanced Client, you can configure the installation. The process of configuring the installation involves four parts:

1. Decide which method will be used in deployment.

   After determining the method, you will configure the installation properties that are most relevant to the type of deployment that best fits your needs.

2. Configure boundaries.

   By default, site boundaries are roaming boundaries, so site boundaries need to be configured. However, sometimes there may be clients who are not well-connected. In these cases, roaming boundaries will need to be configured as well.

3. Configure the Client Push Installation account.

   You use the Client Push Installation account to install software on clients running the Windows NT 4.0, Windows 2000, Windows XP, or Windows Server 2003 family operating systems when the user who is running the installation method does not have local administrative rights.

   You can create multiple Client Push Installation accounts. If you have clients that are not members of domains and therefore cannot authenticate domain accounts, you can use accounts that are local to the clients themselves.

4. Configure installation properties.

There are several optional installation properties to consider when deploying SMS. These properties include:

- Advanced Client file storage.

- Requiring a reboot to complete the Advanced Client installation for Windows XP without the Service Pack 1.

- Logging properties.

- Cache size.

- End-user capabilities. For example, you can configure installation properties such that users cannot use the systems management control panel to change the assigned site.

Note You can also configure the Advanced Client Network Access Account. This is necessary when the environment you are in is not using Active Directory and if the user at the client computer is not logged on.

Configure the Advanced Client Network Access Account to ensure that the site server can push Ccmsetup.exe and Client.msi from a management point.

Where to specify installation properties

The installation properties are what modify Client.msi behavior. It is possible to specify the installation properties on the **Advanced Client** tab in the **Client Push Installation Properties** dialog box.

Command line options

There are also four command-line options available when using the Advanced Client Installer. The four options are:

- /source—Provides a local or remote location where Ccmsetup.exe locates Client.msi and any language specific files or folders, such as Client.mst.

- /mp—Provides a management point as an installation source.

- /useronly—Forces Ccmsetup.exe to run in the logged-on user's security context.

- /service—Forces Ccmsetup.exe to run in the local system account context.

How Successful Installation Is Confirmed

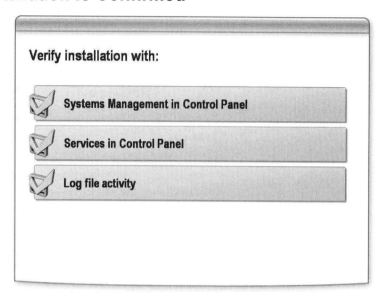

There are times when it may be helpful to verify that the Advanced Client has been successfully installed. For example, you might be testing a deployment technique or troubleshooting a problem that seems to affect only a specific client system.

To confirm successful installation, check any of the following locations on the client. These locations do not need to be checked in any particular order.

- Systems Management in Control Panel.

    a. Verify that the icon is installed, and then open it and look at the **Components** tab.

    b. Verify that the expected components are installed and enabled.

    c. Click the **Advanced** tab to verify the current SMS Site assignment.

- Client component files—located in the %Windir%\System32\CCM folder.

- Service in Control Panel—here you can verify that the SMS Agent Host service has been installed and that it is running.

- Log files—here you can check for log-file activity relating to the client installation.

    Log files are updated on both the client and the site server. These are documented in the practices that accompany this module.

- From the SMS Administrator console, you can view status messages that will indicate success or failure of the installation.

Demonstration: How to Install the Advanced Client

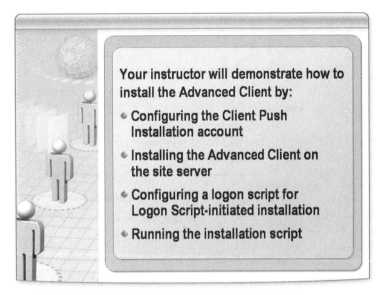

In this demonstration, your instructor will show you how to install the Advanced Client by using both the Client Push installation method and the Login Script-initiated client installation method.

Your instructor will use the following values in this demonstration.

Variable	Value
Virtual machine—SMS Site 1	Dublin
Dublin\Administrator	JaePa (Jae Pak)
Virtual machine—domain controller	Glasgow
Domain Administrator	Administrator
Login Script–initiated installation virtual machine	Bonn
Bonn\Administrator	SMartinez (Sandra Martinez)

Important   These steps are included for your information. Do not attempt to perform them in the classroom. If you perform these steps in the classroom environment, you might leave your computer in an incorrect state for upcoming practices.

Demonstration steps performed by instructor only

▶ **To configure a Client Push Installation account**

1. If you have not already done so, log the Glasgow virtual machine on to the NWTRADERS domain with a user name of **Administrator** and a password of **P@ssw0rd**.

2. Log the Dublin virtual machine on to the NWTRADERS domain with a user name of **JaePa** and a password of **P@ssw0rd**.

3. Log the Bonn virtual machine on to the NWTRADERS domain with a user name of **SMartinez** and a password of **P@ssw0rd**.

4. On the Dublin virtual machine, click **Start**, point to **All Programs**, point to **Systems Management Server**, and then click **SMS Administrator Console**.

5. Expand **Site Database (001 – NWTraders)**, expand **Site Hierarchy**, expand **001 – NWTraders**, expand **Site Settings**, and then select **Client Installation Methods**.

6. Right-click **Client Push Installation**, and then click **Properties**.

Caution   In the next step, Client Push check boxes must *not* be selected; doing so will leave your computer in an incorrect state and cause later demonstrations not to function.

---

7. On the **General** tab, perform the following steps:

   a. Verify that the **Enable Client Push Installation to site systems** check box is **cleared** by default.

   b. Under **Client types**, click **Advanced Client**.

   c. Verify that the **Enable Client Push Installation to assigned resources** check box is also **cleared** by default.

Note   The Client Push account has already been created and is part of the VPC environment. It is a member of Domain Admins.

---

8. Click the **Accounts** tab, and then perform the following steps:

   a. Click the **New** ⁙ icon.

   b. In the **Windows User Account** dialog box, in the **User name** box, type **NWTraders\SMS_Client_Push**.

   c. In the **Password** box and the **Confirm password** box, type **P@ssw0rd**, and then click **OK**.

9. Click the **Advanced Client** tab, and then perform the following steps:

   a. Verify the following property value appears in the **Installation Properties** field:

   ```
   SMSSITECODE=AUTO
   ```

   b. Enter the following property values in the **Installation Properties** field after **SMSSITECODE=AUTO**, as shown:

   ```
   SMSSITECODE=AUTO CCMENABLELOGGING=TRUE
   CCMLOGMAXSIZE=1000000 CCMLOGLEVEL=0
   ```

10. Click **OK**.

▶ **To install the Advanced Client on the site server by using the Client Push installation method**

1. On the Dublin virtual machine, in the console tree of the SMS Administrator console, expand **Collections**, and then click **All Systems**.

2. Right-click **Dublin**, point to **All Tasks**, and then click **Install Client**.

   The Client Push Installation Wizard opens.

3. On the **Welcome to the Client Push Installation Wizard** page, click **Next**.

4. On the **Installation options** page, verify that **Install the SMS client** is selected, click **Advanced Client**, and then click **Next**.

5. On the **Client Installation Options** page, verify that the **Include only clients assigned to this site** check box is selected, and then click **Next**.

6. Review the installation details, and then click **Finish**.

   The site server will begin installing the client on Dublin.

Note Because this installation will take a few minutes, you will skip to configuring a logon script for Logon Script–initiated installation. You will come back and verify successful Advanced Client installation for the Dublin virtual machine.

▶ **To configure a logon script for Logon Script–initiated installation for installing the Advanced Client**

1. On the Glasgow virtual machine, click **Start**, point to **All Programs**, point to **Accessories**, and then click **Notepad**.

2. In the new text document, type the following lines of script:

```
ECHO ON
\\Glasgow\netlogon\CAPINST.EXE  /ADVCLI  /SLP=Dublin
  /ADVCLICMD SMSSITECODE=AUTO CCMENABLELOGGING=TRUE
CCMLOGMAXSIZE=1000000 CCMLOGLEVEL=0
```

Note Starting with **\\Glasgow...** make sure you enter the entire script all on one line; do *not* enter any carriage returns until after **CCMLOGLEVEL=0**.

---

3. On the **File** menu, click **Save As**.

4. Browse to **C:\WINDOWS\sysvol\sysvol\nwtraders.msft\scripts**.

5. In the **File name** box, type **smsinstall.bat** and then click **Save**.

6. Click **Start**, point to **Administrative Tools**, and then click **Active Directory Users and Computers**.

7. If needed, expand the **nwtraders.msft** folder and click the **Users** folder.

8. Double-click **Sandra Martinez**.

   The **Properties** dialog box opens.

9. On the **Profile** tab, type **smsinstall.bat** in the **Logon script** box.

10. Click **OK**.

11. Close any open windows.

▶ **To verify successful Advanced Client installation on Dublin**

1. On the Dublin virtual machine, click **Start**, point to **Control Panel**, and then click **Systems Management**.

    Note If the System Management icon does not appear in the Control Panel list, then the Client installation has not yet completed.

2. On the **Components** tab, verify that the status of the following components is shown as **Installed**:

    • **CCM Framework**

    • **CCM Policy Agent**

    • **CCM Status and Eventing Agent**

    • **SMS Client Core Components**

    • **SMS Client Shared Components**

    Note Until all these components are displayed, installation is not complete.

3. On the **Actions** tab, verify that the following actions are displayed:

    • **Discovery Data Collection Cycle**

    • **Machine Policy Retrieval & Evaluation Cycle**

    • **User Policy Retrieval & Evaluation Cycle**

    • **Windows Installer Source List Update Cycle**

    Note Until all these actions are displayed, installation is not complete.

4. On the **Advanced** tab, verify that the SMS Site is currently assigned to the site code 001. If the SMS site is not assigned to this site code, type **001** in the text box, and then click **Apply**.

5. Click **OK**.

6. Close any open windows.

    Note You are now continuing the procedures for Logon Script–initiated installation. You will return to the Glasgow virtual machine.

▶ **To place Capinst.exe and Ccmsetup.exe into the Netlogon shared folder**

1. On the Glasgow virtual machine, click **Start**, click **Run**.

2. In the **Open** field, type **\\DUBLIN\SMSCLIENT\I386** and then click **OK**.

   Windows Explorer opens the I386 folder.

3. In the Windows Explorer details pane, copy the Capinst.exe and Ccmsetup.exe files.

4. Click **Start**, and then click **Run**.

5. In the **Open** box type **C:\WINDOWS\SYSVOL\sysvol\ nwtraders.msft\scripts**, and then click **OK**.

   This is the Netlogon shared folder.

6. In the Netlogon shared folder, paste the copied files.

7. Close any open windows.

▶ **To run the installation script**

1. On the Bonn virtual machine, click **Start**, click **Shut down**, select **Log off SMartinez**, and then click **OK**.

2. Press <Right>Alt+Delete to log on to Bonn.

3. Log in with a user name of **SMartinez** and a password of **P@ssw0rd**.

   After you log on, the script initiates the client installation script.

Note   If the script does not initiate automatically, wait two minutes, then log off and log on again.

▶ **To verify successful installation**

1. On the Bonn virtual machine, click **Start**, click **Run**, type **Cmd** and then click **OK**.

2. In the **Command Prompt** line, type **notepad %temp%\capinst.log** and then press ENTER.

   By typing **notepad** in the command above, the Capinst log opens in Notepad, not in SMS Trace. This log file confirms that the client successfully started to download the client installation files.

3. Click **Start**, point to **All Programs**, point to **Accessories**, and then click **Windows Explorer**.

4. Browse to **C:\Windows\System32\ccmsetup**.

   This folder contains the logs for the Advanced Client components.

5. Double-click **ccmsetup.log**.

Note   Depending on your file extension settings in Windows Explorer, you will see either Ccmsetup.log or Ccmsetup.

---

6. Review the log file. Near the end of the file you should find the phrase **Installation succeeded**.

   If you see this entry, the installation was successfully completed. If this entry does not appear, the installation may still be running; close the Ccmsetup.log file and reopen it to see if the **Installation succeeded** message has finally appeared.

   Note   The installation could take up to eight minutes. Also, before shutting down Bonn, verify that Bonn has become a client by looking in the SMS Administrator console.

   ---

7. Close the log file, Windows Explorer, and any open windows.

8. On the Bonn virtual machine, on the **Action** menu, click **Close**.

9. Verify that **Save state and save changes** is selected in the drop-down list, and then click **OK**.

   The Bonn virtual machine begins to shut down.

10. Leave Glasgow and Dublin virtual machines running; they will be used in subsequent practices.

Practice: Installing the Advanced Client

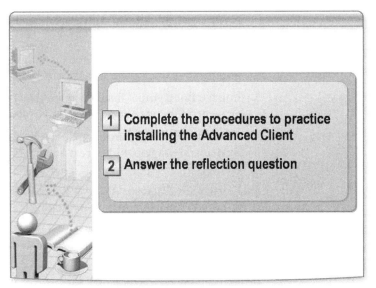

Instructions

Complete the procedures to practice installing the Advanced Client by using both the Client Push installation method, and the Login Script–initiated client installation method.

First you will configure a Client Push installation and use the Client Push Installation Wizard to install the Advanced Client on the Site Server virtual machine. Then you will configure a logon script for Logon Script–initiated installation and use this method to install the client on the Bonn virtual machine. When you complete the procedures, answer the reflection question that follows and discuss any questions that you have with the class.

In this practice, use the following values.

Variable	Value
Virtual machine—SMS Site 1	Dublin
Dublin\Administrator	JaePa (Jae Pak)
Virtual machine—domain controller	Glasgow
Domain Administrator	Administrator
Login Script–initiated installation virtual machine	Bonn
Bonn\Administrator	SMartinez (Sandra Martinez)

Procedures

▶ **To configure Client Push Installation**

1. If you have not already done so, log the Glasgow virtual machine on to the NWTRADERS domain with a user name of **Administrator** and a password of **P@ssw0rd**.

2. Log the Dublin virtual machine on to the NWTRADERS domain with a user name of **JaePa** and a password of **P@ssw0rd**.

3. Log the Bonn virtual machine on to the NWTRADERS domain with a user name of **SMartinez** and a password of **P@ssw0rd**.

4. On the Dublin virtual machine, click **Start**, point to **All Programs**, point to **Systems Management Server**, and then click **SMS Administrator Console**.

5. Expand Site Database (001 – NWTraders), expand Site Hierarchy, expand 001 – NWTraders, expand Site Settings, and then select Client Installation Methods.

6. Right-click **Client Push Installation**, and then click **Properties**.

Caution   In the next step, Client Push check boxes must *not* be selected; doing so will leave your computer in an incorrect state and cause later practices to not function at all.

---

7. On the **General** tab, perform the following steps:

   a. Verify that the **Enable Client Push Installation to site systems** check box is cleared by default.

   b. Under **Client types**, select the **Advanced Client** option.

   c. Verify that the **Enable Client Push Installation to assigned resources** check box is also cleared by default.

8. Click the **Advanced Client** tab, and then perform the following steps:

   a. Verify the following property value appears in the **Installation Properties** field:

   ```
   SMSSITECODE=AUTO
   ```

   b. Enter the following property values in the **Installation Properties** field after **SMSSITECODE=AUTO**, as shown:

   ```
   SMSSITECODE=AUTO CCMENABLELOGGING=TRUE
   CCMLOGMAXSIZE=1000000 CCMLOGLEVEL=0
   ```

9. Click **OK**.

▶ **To install the Advanced Client on the site server by using the Client Push installation method**

1. On the Dublin virtual machine, in the console tree of **SMS Administrator console**, expand **Collections**, and then click **All Systems**.

2. Right-click **Dublin**, point to **All Tasks**, and then click **Install Client**.

   The Client Push Installation Wizard opens.

3. On the **Welcome to the Client Push Installation Wizard** page, click **Next**.

4. On the **Installation options** page, verify that the **Install the SMS client** is selected, click **Advanced Client**, and then click **Next**.

5. On the **Client Installation Options** page, verify that the **Include only clients assigned to this site** check box is selected, and then click **Next**.

6. Review the installation details and then click **Finish**.

▶ **To verify that the Client Push Installation started**

1. On the Dublin virtual machine, click **Start**, point to **All Programs**, point to **Accessories**, and then click **Windows Explorer**.

2. In Windows Explorer, browse to **C:\SMS\Logs**.

3. Double-click **ccm.log**.

4. Review the log file.

Caution   Notice the error message near the end of the log file (*Warning: no remote client installation or SMS service account found*). This is the expected result of this procedure.

---

5. Close **ccm.log**.

6. Resolve the error in the log file by performing the next procedure, **To specify a Client Push Installation Account**.

▶ **To specify a Client Push Installation Account**

- This procedure does not list detailed steps; instead, you will attempt to identify why the Advanced Client installation could not start successfully. Then use the SMS Administrator console on the Dublin virtual machine to fix the problem.

  To complete this procedure, you will need to use the following values.

Variable	Value
Client Push account	NWTRADERS\SMS_Client_Push
Client Push account password	P@ssw0rd

Note   For a comprehensive set of steps to complete this procedure, refer to Appendix A, "Course 2596B, *Managing Microsoft Systems Management Server 2003* – Troubleshooting Practices Answer Key" on your Student Materials compact disc. Also, you must fix this problem before proceeding.

▶ **To retry installing the Advanced Client on the site server by using the Client Push Installation method**

1. On the Dublin virtual machine, in the console tree of **SMS Administrator console**, expand **Site Database (001 – NWTraders)**, expand **Collections**, and then click **All Systems**.

2. Right-click **Dublin**, point to **All Tasks**, and then click **Install Client**.

   The Client Push Installation Wizard opens.

3. On the **Welcome to the Client Push Installation Wizard** page, click **Next**.

4. On the **Installation options** page, verify that the **Install the SMS client** is selected, click **Advanced Client**, and then click **Next**.

5. On the **Client Installation Options** page, verify that the **Include only clients assigned to this site** check box is selected, and then click **Next**.

6. Review the installation details and then click **Finish**

▶ **To verify that the Client Push Installation successfully started**

1. On the Dublin virtual machine, in Windows Explorer, verify that C:\SMS\Logs is the current folder.

2. Double-click **ccm.log**.

3. Review the log file.

   If there no new error messages in the log file, the account was successfully configured.

4. Close all open windows.

5. Leave the virtual machines running.

▶ **To configure a logon script for Logon Script–initiated installation for installing the Advanced Client**

1. On the Glasgow virtual machine, click **Start**, point to **All Programs**, point to **Accessories**, and then click **Notepad**.

2. In the new text document, type the following lines of script:

```
ECHO ON
\\Glasgow\netlogon\CAPINST.EXE  /ADVCLI  /SLP=Dublin
  /ADVCLICMD SMSSITECODE=AUTO CCMENABLELOGGING=TRUE
CCMLOGMAXSIZE=1000000 CCMLOGLEVEL=0
```

Note   Starting with **\\Glasgow...** make sure you enter the entire script all on one line; do *not* enter any carriage returns until after **CCMLOGLEVEL=0**.

3. On the **File** menu, click **Save As**.

4. Browse to C:\WINDOWS\sysvol\sysvol\nwtraders.msft\scripts.

5. In the **File name** box, type **smsinstall.bat** and then click **Save**.

6. Click **Start**, point to **Administrative Tools**, and then click **Active Directory Users and Computers**.

7. If needed, in the console tree, expand **nwtraders.msft** and then click **Users**.

8. In the details pane, double-click **Sandra Martinez**.

   The **Sandra Martinez Properties** dialog box opens.

9. On the **Profile** tab, in the **Logon script** box, type **smsinstall.bat** and then click **OK**.

10. Close any open windows.

▶ **To verify successful Advanced Client installation on Dublin**

1. On the Dublin virtual machine, click **Start**, point to **Control Panel**, and then click **Systems Management**.

   Note If the System Management icon does not appear in the Control Panel list, then the Client installation has not yet completed.
   ---

2. On the **Components** tab, verify that the status of the following components is shown as **Installed**:

   - **CCM Framework**
   - **CCM Policy Agent**
   - **CCM Status and Eventing Agent**
   - **SMS Client Core Components**
   - **SMS Client Shared Components**

   Note Until all these components are displayed, installation is not complete.
   ---

3. On the **Actions** tab, verify the following actions are displayed:

   - **Discovery Data Collection Cycle**
   - **Machine Policy Retrieval & Evaluation Cycle**
   - **User Policy Retrieval & Evaluation Cycle**
   - **Windows Installer Source List Update Cycle**

   Note Until all these actions are displayed, installation is not complete.
   ---

4. On the **Advanced** tab, verify that the SMS Site is currently assigned to the site code 001. If the SMS site is not assigned to this site code, type **001** in the text box, and then click **Apply**.

5. Click **OK**.

6. Close any open windows.

Note You are now continuing the procedures for Logon Script–initiated installation. You will return to the Glasgow virtual machine.

▶ **To place Capinst.exe and Ccmsetup.exe into the Netlogon shared folder**

1. On the Glasgow virtual machine, click **Start**, click **Run**.

2. In the **Open** box, type **\\DUBLIN\SMSCLIENT\I386** and then click **OK**.

   Windows Explorer opens the I386 folder.

3. In the Windows Explorer details pane, copy the Capinst.exe and Ccmsetup.exe files.

4. Click **Start**, and then click **Run**.

5. In the **Open** box type **C:\WINDOWS\SYSVOL\sysvol\ nwtraders.msft\scripts** and then click **OK**.

   This is the Netlogon shared folder.

6. In the Netlogon shared folder, paste the copied files.

7. Close any open windows.

▶ **To run the installation script**

Note   To initiate the installation script, you must log off the client and then log on.

---

1. On the Bonn virtual machine, click **Start**, click **Shut down**, select **Log off SMartinez**, and then click **OK**.

2. Press <Right>Alt+Delete to log on to Bonn.

3. Log on to NWTraders domain with a user name of **SMartinez** and a password of **P@ssw0rd**.

   After you log on, the script initiates the client installation script. If the script does not initiate automatically, wait two minutes, then log off and log on again.

▶ **To verify successful installation**

1. On the Bonn virtual machine, click **Start**, click **Run**, type **Cmd** and then click **OK**. A command prompt opens.

2. In the **command prompt** line, type **notepad %temp%\capinst.log**, and then press ENTER.

   By typing **notepad** in the command above, the Capinst log opens in Notepad, not in SMS Trace. This log file confirms that the client successfully started to download the client installation files.

3. Click **Start**, point to **All Programs**, point to **Accessories**, and then click **Windows Explorer**.

4. Browse to C:\Windows\System32\ccmsetup.

   This folder contains the logs for the Advanced Client components.

5. Double-click **ccmsetup.log**.

Note   Depending on your file extension settings in Windows Explorer, you will see either Ccmsetup.log or Ccmsetup.

---

6. Review the log file. Near the end of the file you should find the phrase **Installation succeeded**.

   If you see this entry, the installation was successfully completed. If this entry does not appear, the installation may still be running; close the Ccmsetup.log file and reopen it to see if the **Installation succeeded** message has finally appeared.

   Note   The installation could take up to eight minutes.

7. Close the log file, Windows Explorer, and any open windows.

   Note   Be sure to wait at least two minutes after installation is complete before moving on to step 8. Also, you should verify that Bonn has now become a client by looking in the SMS Administrator console before shutting down Bonn.

8. On the Bonn virtual machine, on the **Action** menu, click **Close**.

9. Verify that **Save State and save changes** is selected in the drop-down list, and then click **OK**.

   The Bonn virtual machine begins to shut down.

10. Leave Glasgow and Dublin virtual machines running; they will be used in subsequent practices.

Reflection question

In your organization, which client type will you standardize on if you have a mix of mobile and desktop devices running Windows 98/Windows NT 4.0/ Windows 2000/Windows XP?

_____

_____

_____

_____

Practice: Explaining the Differences Between the Installation Methods and When To Use Each Method

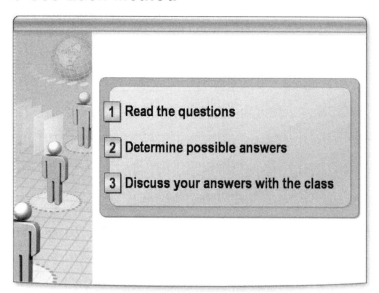

Instructions

Read the following three questions, determine possible answers, and discuss your answers with the class. Before you move on to the next lesson, make sure that you understand the differences between the installation methods and the various scenarios in which to use each of them.

Discussion questions

1. What are the main differences between the Client Push Installation Wizard installation and the Logon Script–initiated client installation method?

    _____

    _____

    _____

    _____

2. In what situations would you use the Client Push Installation Wizard?

_____

_____

_____

_____

3. In what situations would you use the Logon Script–initiated installation?

_____

_____

_____

_____

Lesson: Deploying the Legacy Client

- Installation Methods for the Legacy Client
- Considerations for Automatic Installation of the Legacy Client Using the SMS Administrator Console (Client Push Installation Method)
- Guidelines for Installing the Legacy Client by Initiating a Program File at the Client Computer
- Configuration Tasks to Perform Before Installing the Legacy Client
- How to Install Legacy Clients
- Demonstration: How to Install the Legacy Client
- Log Files that Confirm Legacy Client Installation

Introduction

In this lesson, you will learn about installation options available for the Legacy Client and where to use them.

Lesson objectives

After completing this lesson, you will be able to:

- Describe available installation methods for the Legacy Client.
- Automatically install the Legacy Client by using the SMS Administrator console.
- Describe guidelines for manual installation of Legacy Clients.
- Describe configuration tasks needed before installing Legacy Clients.
- Install the Legacy Client.
- Confirm successful installation through log files.

Installation Methods for the Legacy Client

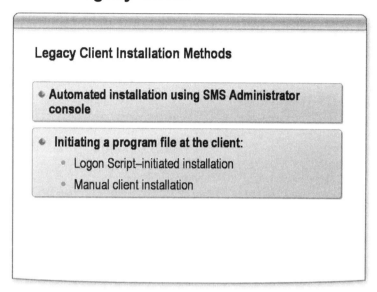

There are two methods for installing the Legacy Client:

- Automated installation using the SMS Administrator console
- Initiating a program file at the client, which includes:
  - Logon Script–initiated client installation
  - Manual client installation

The following topics describe how to deploy the Legacy Client using these methods.

Considerations for Automatic Installation of the Legacy Client Using the SMS Administrator Console (Client Push Installation Method)

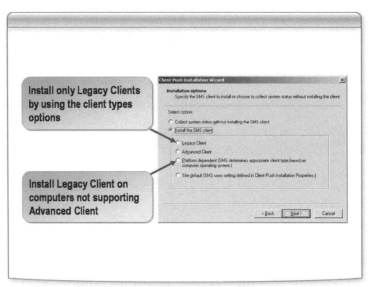

Configure Client Push installation to install only Legacy Clients by selecting the **Legacy Client** radio button on the **Installation options** screen of the Client Push Installation Wizard. If you want to install the Legacy Client on computers that cannot support the Advanced Client, such as computers running Windows NT Workstation 4.0, select **Platform dependent**. The Platform dependent option would be used if you are doing an installation to a collection with mixed operating systems. This option will ensure that the proper client is installed on the correctly supported operating system.

Important   You will need a client access point (CAP) available in each SMS site on which you want to install the Legacy Client and an SMS Client Connection account. If either the CAP or SMS Client Connection accounts is missing, the installation will fail.

Note   There is no Client Push installation method for Windows 98.

Guidelines for Installing the Legacy Client by Initiating a Program File at the Client Computer

Guidelines for initiating a program file:

- Use Capinst.exe command in the logon script if your organization uses Active Directory

- If your organization does not use Active Directory, you still use Capinst.exe, but be sure to add /SLP to the end of the command

- You might be able to use /AutoDetect=script to install a Legacy Client, depending on the value returned by the script you run

- If Smsman.exe is not run from a CAP using a UNC path, you must specify the CAP by using the SMSman.exe command-line switches

The two methods for installing the Legacy Client by initiating a program file at the client computer are:

- Logon Script–initiated client installation

    Using Logon Script–initiated client installation (Capinst.exe) to discover and install Legacy Clients when users log on is similar to using Logon Script–initiated client installation to install Advanced Clients. Capinst.exe works with Server Locator Points and CAPs to install the Legacy Client. You cannot pass any parameters to Smsman.exe from the Capinst.exe command.

- Manual client installation

    Use manual client installation (Smsman.exe) to install Legacy Clients manually. Manual client installation installs the Legacy Client directly from a CAP. You run Smsman.exe from the CAP by using a Universal Naming Convention (UNC) path.

Note   When you use Logon Script–initiated client installation or manual client installation to install an SMS Legacy Client ensure that you specify a valid client connection account in SMS. You must set up the client connection account manually if you are running in advanced security mode.

Guidelines

Follow these guidelines for installing the Legacy Client by initiating a program file at the client computer:

- You can use Capinst.exe or Smsman.exe commands in the logon script if you want to deploy the Legacy Client software by using Logon Script–initiated Client Installation. However, it is recommended that Capinst.exe be used for this type of installation. Capinst.exe checks with the Server Locator Points returned from the Active Directory global catalog. It uses the first Server Locator Point it locates that is associated with the site boundaries that the client computer is in. All CAPs will be returned by the Server Locator Point for the site, but the client randomly selects a CAP for client installation.

- If your organization does not use Active Directory, be sure to type /**SLP** at the end of the Capinst.exe command.

- You might be able to use /**AutoDetect**=*script* to install a Legacy Client, depending on the value returned by the script you point to. The Legacy Client is installed if the return value is 0.

- You run Smsman.exe from the CAP using a Universal Naming Convention. If Smsman.exe is not run from a CAP using a UNC path, you must specify the CAP either by using the SmsMan.exe command-line switches, or by using the wizard started by running Smsman.exe. SMSman.exe is found in the Client\i386 folder of the SMS_*site code* shared folder on your SMS site server. It is also available on the SMS 2003 compact disc in the SMSSetup\Client\i386 folder. If you want users to run it from other locations, such as domain controllers, you must copy it to those locations. However, if you install a future version of SMS, such as a service pack, that includes an updated version of Smsman.exe, you must update the copies of the Smsman.exe file that you put in these other locations.

  If you run Smsman.exe without any switches, the Systems Management Installation Wizard appears. This wizard guides you through the process of manual client installation.

Configuration Tasks To Perform Before Installing the Legacy Client

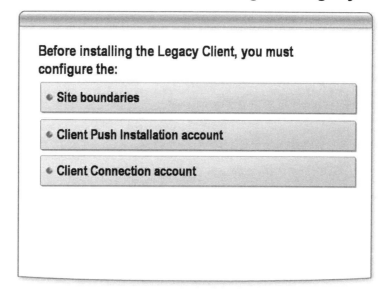

Before installing the Legacy Client, you must configure the:

- Site boundaries
- Client Push Installation account
- Client Connection account

You must configure the following three things, in no particular order, before you install the Legacy Client:

1. Configure site boundaries.

   Without site boundaries configured, installation cannot take place.

2. Configure the Client Push Installation account.

   The Client Push Installation account must be configured so that the site server can push the Legacy client installation down to clients when the logged on user does not have administrative rights. If your site uses standard security and no Client Push Installation account has been specified, SMS can use the SMS Service account if it has administrator privileges on client computers.

   Note You only need to configure the Client Push Installation account if either you plan to use Client Push Installation, or you plan to use Logon Script–initiated Client Installation on computers where the logged-on user does not have administrative privileges. The account is not required for manual installations performed by a user with administrative privileges on the client.

3. Configure the Client Connection account.

   The Client Connection account must be configured so that the client can connect to the CAP. The CAP contains the necessary components that must be downloaded so that the installation can be completed.

How to Install Legacy Clients

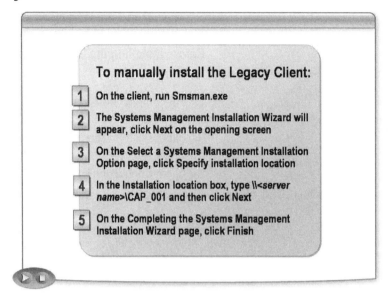

There are two methods for installing legacy clients: the manual method in which you run Smsman.exe on the client, and the Logon Script–initiated method in which you write a logon script and save it onto the domain controller.

Procedure to manually install the Legacy Client

To manually install the legacy client:

1. On the client, run Smsman.exe.

   The Smsman.exe file is located on the SMS site server in the *local_disc*\SMS\Client\i386 folder.

2. On the **Welcome to the Systems Management Installation Wizard** page, click **Next**.

3. On the **Select a Systems Management Installation Option** page, click **Specify installation location**.

4. In the **Installation location** box, type \\<*server name*>**CAP_001** and then click **Next**.

5. On the **Completing the Systems Management Installation Wizard** page, click **Finish**.

Procedure to install the Legacy Client using a logon script

To install the Legacy Client using a logon-script:

1. On the SMS site server, configure the Client Connection account.

2. Open a text editor such as Notepad.

3. Write the logon script and save it as a .bat file to the Netlogon shared folder on the domain controller.

4. Copy the Smsman.exe and Capinst.exe from the SMS site server, and save it to the Netlogon shared folder on the domain controller.

5. Modify the user profile to enable to user to run the logon script.

6. On the client, run the installation script by logging off the computer and then logging on.

7. Verify a successful installation by reviewing the log files and verifying that the SMS Client Service service is running.

Demonstration: How to Install the Legacy Client

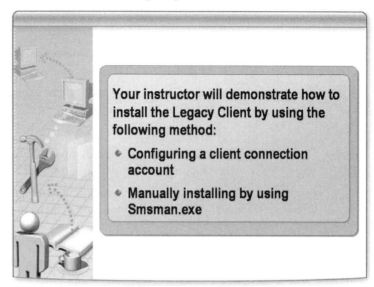

Your instructor will demonstrate how to install the Legacy Client by using the following method:

* Configuring a client connection account
* Manually installing by using Smsman.exe

In this demonstration, your instructor will demonstrate how to configure a client connection account and install the Legacy Client by using the manual installation method.

Your instructor will use the following values in this demonstration.

Variable	Value
Virtual machine—SMS Site 1	Dublin
Dublin\Administrator	JaePa (Jae Pak)
Virtual machine—domain controller	Glasgow
Domain Administrator	Administrator
Virtual machine—Legacy Client	Perth
Perth\Administrator	JudyLe (Judy Lew)

Important These steps are included for your information. Do not attempt to perform them in the classroom. If you perform these steps in the classroom environment, you might leave your computer in an incorrect state for upcoming practices.

Demonstration steps to be performed by the instructor only

Note You must have Modify permissions for the site security object class or instance to perform this procedure.

▶ **To configure a client connection account**

1. Verify that Glasgow and Dublin virtual machines are running.

2. Log the Perth virtual machine on to the NWTRADERS domain with a user name of **JudyLe** and a password of **P@ssw0rd**.

3. On the Dublin virtual machine, click **Start**, point to **All Programs**, point to **Systems Management Server**, and then click **SMS Administrator Console**.

4. From the SMS Administrator Console, expand **Site Database (001 – NWTraders)**, expand **Site Hierarchy**, expand **001 – NWTraders**, expand **Site Settings**, expand **Connection Accounts**, and then click the **Client** folder.

5. On the **Action** menu, point to **New**, and then click **Windows User Account**.

6. In the **Connection Account Properties** dialog box, click **Set**.

7. In the **Windows User Account** dialog box, in the **User name** box, type **NWTRADERS\SMS_Cli_Connect**

8. In the **Password** and **Confirm Password** boxes, type **P@ssw0rd**

9. Click **OK** twice.

10. Close the SMS Administrator Console.

▶ **To install the Legacy Client by using the manual method**

1. On the Perth virtual machine, click **Start**, click **Run**, type **cmd** and then click **OK**.

2. At the command prompt, type **\\dublin\sms_001\client\ i386\smsman.exe** and then press ENTER.

3. On the **Welcome to the Systems Management Installation Wizard** page, click **Next**.

4. On the **Select a Systems Management Installation Option** page, click **Specify installation location**, in the **Installation location** box, type **\\DUBLIN\CAP_001** and then click **Next**.

5. On the **Completing the Systems Management Installation Wizard** page, click **Finish**.

6. After the message "Systems Management components have been successfully installed on your computer" appears, click **OK**, and then close any open windows.

Note   Be sure to wait at least two minutes to make sure installation is complete before moving on to step 7. During this delay, you could verify that the SMS Client Service has started.

---

7. On the Perth virtual machine, on the **Action** menu, click **Close**.

8. Verify that **Save State and save changes** is selected in the list, and then click **OK**.

   The Perth virtual machine begins to shut down.

9. Leave Glasgow and Dublin virtual machines running; they will be used in subsequent practices.

Log Files that Confirm Legacy Client Installation

Log files that confirm installation:

- wnmanual.log—Found in %Windir%\MS\SMS\Logs

- Capinst.log—Found in %Temp%

- CCIM32.log—Found in %Windir%\MS\SMS\Logs

After installation of the Legacy Client has taken place, verify that the installation was successful.

How log files confirm installation

To verify that installation was successful first look at the Wnmanual.log, which is found in C:\%Windir%\MS\SMS\Logs. This log file will verify that the client was installed and that the SMS Client Service was installed and started.

If you used Logon Script-initiated Client installation and the installation did not start, then you should look at the Capinst.log, which is found in %Temp%. The Capinst.log will help you track why the installation did not start. The Capinst.log can also verify that Capinst found the SLP and the CAP and started installation. You can also look at Ccim32.log in %Windir%\MS\SMS\Logs to determine if the client was able to connect to the CAP to complete the installation of Legacy Client components.

Alternatives for confirming installation

Use Computer Management to verify that the SMS Client Service is installed and running or use Systems Management Control Panel to verify that client components were installed.

Practice: Installing the Legacy Client Using a Logon Script

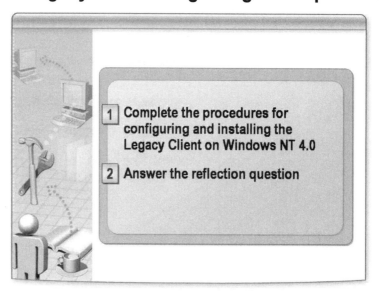

1. Complete the procedures for configuring and installing the Legacy Client on Windows NT 4.0

2. Answer the reflection question

Instructions

Complete the procedures to practice configuring the Legacy Client installation options for a logon script and installing the Legacy Client on the Perth virtual machine, which is running Windows NT 4.0. When you complete the procedures, answer the reflection question that follows.

In this practice, use the following values.

Variable	Value
Virtual machine—SMS Site 1	Dublin
Dublin\Administrator	JaePa (Jae Pak)
Virtual machine—domain controller	Glasgow
Domain Administrator	Administrator
Client push installation virtual machine	Perth
Perth\Administrator	JudyLe (Judy Lew)

Procedures

▶ **To configure the client connection account**

1. Verify that Glasgow and Dublin virtual machines are running.

2. Log the Perth virtual machine on to the NWTRADERS domain with a user name of **JudyLe** and a password of **P@ssw0rd**.

3. On the Dublin virtual machine, click **Start**, point to **All Programs**, point to **Systems Management Server**, and then click **SMS Administrator Console**.

4. From the SMS Administrator console, expand **Site Database (001 – NWTraders)**, expand **Site Hierarchy**, expand **001 – NWTraders**, expand **Site Settings**, expand **Connection Accounts**, and then click **Client**.

5. On the **Action** menu, point to **New**, and then click **Windows User Account**.

6. In the **Connection Account Properties** dialog box, click **Set**.

7. In the **Windows User Account** dialog box, in the **User name** box, type **NWTRADERS\SMS_Cli_Connect**

8. In the **Password** and the **Confirm Password** boxes, type **P@ssw0rd** and then click **OK**.

9. In the **Connection Account Properties** dialog box, click **OK**.

10. Close the SMS Administrator console.

▶ **To write and save the logon script to the domain controller**

Note   It is not recommended that you use the domain controller to perform SMS administrative tasks. You should perform them by using the Active Directory administrative tools included with Windows Server 2003; however, the configuration of the virtual machines in this course necessitates that several of these procedures in this practice be completed by using the domain controller.

---

1. On the Glasgow virtual machine, click **Start**, point to **All Programs**, point to **Accessories**, and then click **Notepad**.

2. In Notepad, type **\\GLASGOW\NETLOGON\CAPINST.EXE /SLP=DUBLIN**

3. On the **File** menu, click **Save As**.

4. Browse to C:\WINDOWS\sysvol\sysvol\nwtraders.msft\scripts.

   This is the Netlogon shared folder.

5. In the **File name** box, type **"PERTH_logon_script.bat"**

Important   Be sure to enclose the file name in quotation marks and save the file as a .bat file.

---

6. Click **Save**.

7. Close any open windows.

▶ **To copy Smsman.exe into the Netlogon shared folder on the domain controller**

1. On the Glasgow virtual machine, click **Start**, and then click **Run**.

2. In the **Open** box, type **\\DUBLIN\SMSCLIENT\I386** and then click **OK**.

   Windows Explorer opens the I386 folder.

3. In the Windows Explorer details pane, copy the Smsman.exe file.

4. Click **Start**, and then click **Run**.

5. In the **Open** box, type **C:\WINDOWS\SYSVOL\sysvol\ nwtraders.msft\scripts** and then click **OK**.

6. In the Netlogon shared folder, paste the SMSman.exe file.

7. Verify the Capinst.exe, Perth_logon_script.bat, and SMSman.exe files appear in the NetLogon folder.

   This indicates that you have all the necessary files to complete the Legacy Client installation.

8. Close any open windows.

► **To modify a user profile**

1. On the Glasgow virtual machine, click **Start**, point to **All Programs**, point to **Administrative Tools**, and then click **Active Directory Users and Computers**.

2. If needed, expand the **nwtraders.msft** folder and click the **Users** folder.

3. In the detail pane, right-click **Judy Lew**, and then click **Properties**.

4. On the **Profile** tab, in the **Logon Script** box, type **PERTH_logon_script.bat** and then click **OK**.

5. Close any open windows.

► **To run the installation script**

Note To initiate the installation script, you must log off the client and then log on.

---

1. On the Perth virtual machine, click **Start**, and then click **Shutdown**.

2. Click **Close all programs and log on as a different user?**, and then click **Yes**.

3. Press <Right>Alt+Delete to log on to Perth.

4. Log on to NWTraders domain with a user name of **JudyLe** and a password of **P@ssw0rd**.

   After you log on, the script initiates the client installation script.

Note The installation could take up to eight minutes.

▶ **To verify a successful installation**

1. On the Perth virtual machine, click **Start**, and then click **Run**.

2. In the **Open** box, type **%temp%\capinst.log**

   Capinst.log opens in Notepad. This file verifies that the logon script was able to get to the client, find the SLP and CAP, and start the installation.

3. Click **Start**, point to **Programs**, and then click **Windows NT Explorer**.

4. In Windows NT Explorer, browse to **C:\Winnt\MS\SMS\Logs**.

5. Double-click **Wnmanual.log**.

   This file verifies that the client was able to start installing client files from the CAP and install SMS Client Service.

6. In Windows NT Explorer, double-click **Ccim32.log**.

   This file verifies that a discovery data record was sent to the CAP after SMS Client Service was installed and started. If client agents are enabled, which they will not be in this practice, this is where you would verify agent installation.

7. Close any open windows.

   Note   You should verify that Perth has become a client by looking in the SMS Administrator console.

   ---

8. On the Perth virtual machine, on the **Action** menu, click **Close**.

9. Verify that **Save state and save changes** is selected in the drop-down list, and then click **OK**.

   The Perth virtual machine begins to shut down.

10. Leave Glasgow and Dublin virtual machines running.

Reflection question

Why do you have to specify the configuration for the SMS client connection account when installing the Legacy Client but not for the Advanced Client?

Before installing the Legacy Client, you must specify a configuration option that you do not need to specify when installing the Advanced Client. Which setting is this?

Practice: Describing the Characteristics of the Legacy Client Installation Methods

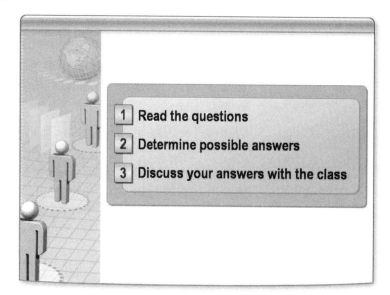

Instructions

Read the following questions, determine answers, and discuss your answers with the class. Before you move on to the next lesson, make sure that you understand the differences between the client deployment and installation methods.

Reflection question

1. What are the various Legacy Client installation methods?

   _____

   _____

   _____

2. If you were going to install the Legacy Client in your work environment, which Legacy Client installation method would you use and why?

   _____

   _____

   _____

Lesson: Troubleshooting Problems When Installing SMS Clients

- **What Are Status Messages?**
- **Where Are Status Messages Located?**
- **Log Files That Help Isolate Installation Problems**
- **Common Causes of Advanced Client Installation Problems**

Introduction

In this lesson, you will learn how to use troubleshooting techniques to help solve common problems associated with Advanced Client installations.

Use the SMS Administrator console Status System node and component log files to separate client and server issues. SMS status system errors usually specify components and recommend a solution or additional troubleshooting steps.

Lesson objectives

After completing this lesson, you will be able to:

- Define a status message.
- Identify where status messages are located and how they help isolate installation problems.
- Identify where log files are located and how to view them.
- Identify common causes of installation problems.

What Are Status Messages?

A status message is a text string, generated by a component, describing a specific activity performed by the component

Status messages contain the following information:

- Which component generated message
- Exact time message was generated
- The severity of the message

SMS generates status messages to report the activity of components on site systems and clients. A status message is a text string, generated by a component, describing a specific activity performed by the component. In addition, each status message contains important information such as which component generated the message, the exact time that the message was generated, and the severity of the message.

Status messages are sent from clients and site systems to the site server and are stored in the SMS site database. You can then view status messages in the SMS Administrator console. Viewing status messages in the SMS Administrator console helps you monitor the activity of the various components, determine the health of SMS, and identify issues that might require your attention.

Where Are Status Messages Located?

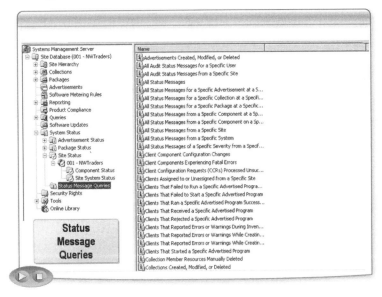

In the SMS Administrator console, navigate to System Status. Under this node are Advertisement Status, Package Status, Site Status, and Status Message Queries. Advertisement Status and Package Status are discussed in Module 8.

- Status Message Queries: Message Queries can assist you in both monitoring and troubleshooting your SMS sites. For example, you can run the Clients Assigned to or Unassigned from a Specific Site query to determine which client computers are assigned to SMS sites in your hierarchy.

  To find Status Message Queries from the SMS Administrator console expand **Site Database** *<site code – site name>*, **System Status**, and then click **Status Message Queries**.

- Site Status: The Site Status item in the SMS Administrator console contains the Component Status and Site System Status summaries for the current site and all the sites below it in the hierarchy.

  In the SMS Administrator console, use Component Status, under Site Status and the specific site, to view status information for site server components. For example, Client Configuration Manager is the component that pushes client software to computers for the Client Push installation method. You can use Component Status to view status messages for SMS_CLIENT_CONFIG_MANAGER to verify the behavior and troubleshoot that component.

  In the SMS Administrator console, use Site System Status, under Site Status and the specific site, to view status information for site systems. For example, you can view status information for a server locator point by viewing status messages for the SMS Server Locator Point site system.

  To find Site Status in the SMS Administrator console, expand **Site Database** (site code – site name), **System Status**, **Site Status**, **site code – site name**, **Component Status** or **Site System Status**.

Log Files that Help Isolate Installation Problems

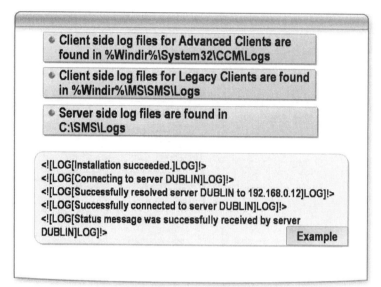

- • Client side log files for Advanced Clients are found in %Windir%\System32\CCM\Logs
- • Client side log files for Legacy Clients are found in %Windir%\MS\SMS\Logs
- • Server side log files are found in C:\SMS\Logs

<![LOG[Installation succeeded.]LOG]!>
<![LOG[Connecting to server DUBLIN]LOG]!>
<![LOG[Successfully resolved server DUBLIN to 192.168.0.12]LOG]!>
<![LOG[Successfully connected to server DUBLIN]LOG]!>
<![LOG[Status message was successfully received by server DUBLIN]LOG]!>

Example

During an SMS Advanced Client installation, log files are generated. You can use these files to help isolate installation problems.

Viewing log files

To use log files, view them to check for any errors that may have occurred during installation.

You can use the SMS Trace tool—one of the tools in SMS 2003 Toolkit 1—to view and monitor log files, including log files in SMS or Advanced Client format. It also works with plain ASCII or Unicode text files, such as Windows Installer logs. The tool includes highlighting, filtering, and error lookup.

Note You can view SMS log files using any utility that can display text files. Also, in this topic, it is assumed that site server is being installed on the C drive. It is possible to have the site server installed on other drives.

Location of log files

On the client side, these log files can be found in %Windir%\System32\CCM\ Logs. On the server side, these log files can be found in C:\SMS\Logs. SMS has tools that can assist you in managing these log files.

Example of log file contents

There are some common messages in the Advanced Client logs that will display whether the installation was successful or if it failed.

```
<![LOG[Installation succeeded.]LOG]!>
<![LOG[Connecting to server DUBLIN]LOG]!>
<![LOG[Successfully resolved server DUBLIN to
192.168.0.12]LOG]!>
<![LOG[Successfully connected to server DUBLIN]LOG]!>
<![LOG[Status message was successfully received by server
DUBLIN]LOG]!>
```

In the log entry, the Advanced Client installation succeeded. The log verifies that the Advanced Client Installer (Ccmsetup.exe) connected to management point DUBLIN to send a status message verifying the successful Advanced Client installation.

Common Causes of Advanced Client Installation Problems

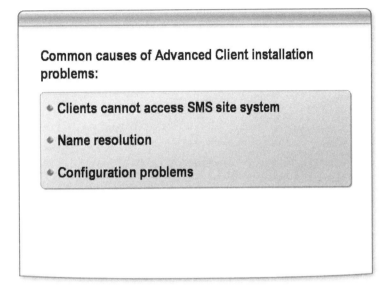

Common causes of Advanced Client installation problems:

* Clients cannot access SMS site system

* Name resolution

* Configuration problems

The most common causes of installation problems for the Advanced Client include:

- Clients cannot access SMS site systems

  Advanced Clients require access to the default management point. It must be installed and running successfully. (Verify that the SMS Agent Host service is running.) The advanced client must also be assigned to a site, so you need to verify that the client has either manually been assigned to a site, or has successfully completed an automated site discovery process.

- Name resolution

  If the SMS site cannot resolve the name of the client, or if the client cannot resolve the name of the site system to which it's trying to connect, there may be a WINS issue. To resolve this problem, troubleshoot the name resolution problems in the WINS or DNS servers. For information about WINS and DNS, refer to Windows documentation.

- Configuration problems—The SMS site may not have been correctly configured. Possible problems include:

  - The Advanced Client command line was not correctly entered

  - The Network Access (if it was used) or Client Push Installation accounts were incorrectly specified, or accounts had insufficient permissions

  - The logon script was not correctly configured

  - The user profile was not modified to run the logon script

  - The roaming boundaries were not correct

  - SMS had a problem with updating boundary and site system information in Active Directory

  - Site systems (management point, SLP) were not correctly configured

For more information concerning Configuration problems, refer to Chapter 17, "Discovering Resources and Deploying Clients," in the *Microsoft Systems Management Server Concepts, Planning, and Deployment Guide*, which you can access on the Additional Reading page of your Student Materials compact disc.

Practice: Identifying the Common Causes of Installation Problems

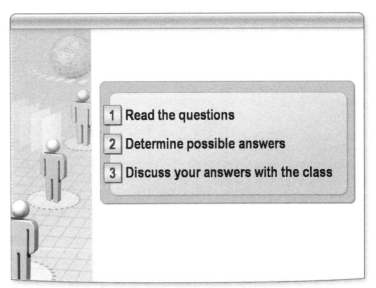

Instructions

Read the following two questions, determine possible answers, and discuss your answers with the class. Before you move on to the next lesson, make sure that you are able to identify the common causes of installation problems.

Discussion questions

1. You suspect that clients are not able to access SMS site systems. What are the possible problems that are causing this?

_____

_____

_____

_____

2. What is the difference between log files and status messages? What type of information does each of these show?

_____

_____

_____

_____

Practice: Using Troubleshooting Techniques to Solve Common Installation Problems

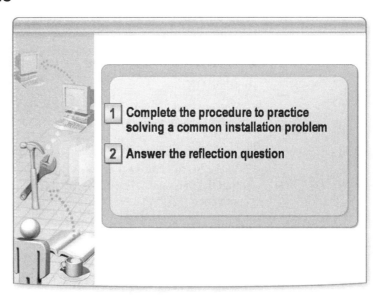

Instructions

Complete the procedures to practice solving a common installation problem. When you complete the procedures, answer the reflection question that follows.

Before moving on, make sure that you understand how to identify log files and status messages that help isolate installation problems, which allow you to use troubleshooting techniques to solve common problems associated with client installs. Be sure to refer to the information about log files presented earlier in this lesson.

In this practice, use the following values.

Variable	Value
Virtual machine—SMS Site 1	Dublin
Dublin\Administrator	JaePa (Jae Pak)
Virtual machine—domain controller	Glasgow
Domain Administrator	Administrator

Procedure

▶ **To view status messages from a client computer**

1. Verify that the Glasgow and Dublin virtual machines are running.

2. On the Dublin virtual machine, click **Start**, point to **All Programs**, point to **Systems Management Server**, and then click **SMS Administrator Console**.

3. In the console tree of the SMS Administrator console, expand **Site Database (001 – NWTraders)**, expand **System Status**, and then click **Status Message Queries**.

   All status message queries appear in the details pane.

4. Right-click **All Status Messages from a Specific System**, and then click **Show Messages**.

5. In the **All Status Messages from a Specific System** dialog box, click **Specify**.

6. In the **Specify** box, type **Bonn**

7. In the **Prompted value** section, click **Time**.

8. Click **Select date and time**.

9. In the **Select date and Time** list box, select **1 day ago**.

10. Click **OK**.

The status messages for Bonn appear in the SMS Status Message Viewer for <001> < NWTraders > window.

11. Under the **Type** column, double-click the first **Milestone** message.

12. In the **Status Message Details** dialog box, in the **Description** area, verify that the message, "The SMS Advanced Client was reassigned. The previous site code was." "The new site code is "001" " appears, and then click **Next**.

13. In the next **Status Message Details** dialog box, in the **Description** area, verify that the message, "The SMS Advanced Client was installed. The current version is 2.50.2726.0018." appears, and then click **OK**.

Note   You can click the **Severity** column to sort messages according to status message severity. There are three types of status: red icons indicate error messages, yellow icons indicate warning messages, and blue icons indicate information messages. You should always review any error messages first.

---

14. Close the SMS Status Message Viewer for <001> < NWTraders > window and the SMS Administrator console.

15. Leave Glasgow and Dublin virtual machines running; they will be used in subsequent practices.

Reflection question

What would be an alternative to running a status message query if you suspected that there was an installation problem?

_____

_____

_____

Discussion: Deploying SMS Clients

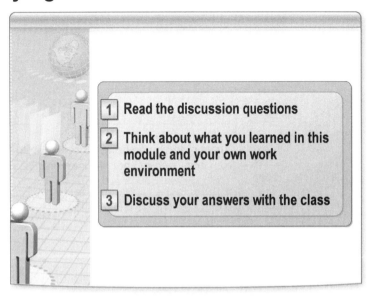

This discussion is designed to review the methods of deploying clients and how to recognize and isolate installation problems.

1. What are the factors that commonly cause installation problems?

   _____

   _____

   _____

   _____

2. What are the methods for troubleshooting the most common installation problems?

   _____

   _____

   _____

   _____

3. What installation problems do you foresee possibly arising in your work
    environment?

    _____

    _____

    _____

    _____

4. What could you do before installation to help prevent installation problems
    from occurring in your work environment?

    _____

    _____

    _____

    _____

Microsoft®

Module 5: Collecting Inventory and Software Metering

Contents

Overview

- Introduction to Inventory Collection
- Collecting Inventory Information
- Extending Inventory Collection
- Configuring Software Metering

Introduction

In this module, you will learn to use Microsoft® Systems Management Server (SMS) hardware and software inventory collection features to collect a wide variety of information about client computers and files in an SMS hierarchy. By collecting hardware and software inventory data with SMS 2003, you can build a rich database of details about the computers in your company. You will also learn to use software metering to identify which applications are being used in your company.

Objectives

After completing this module, you will be able to:

- Describe the inventory collection process.
- Collect hardware and software inventory information.
- Extend inventory collection.
- Configure software metering.

Lesson: Introduction to Inventory Collection

* What Is Inventory Collection?
* Uses of Hardware and Software Inventory
* The Key Components of Inventory Collection
* The Inventory Collection Process

Introduction

One of the key features of SMS 2003 is inventory collection. This lesson defines inventory collection and the benefits that inventory collection can bring to your organization. This lesson also identifies each of the key components in inventory collection, and describes how these components work together to collect inventory from client computers in the SMS hierarchy.

Objectives

After completing this lesson, you will be able to:

■ Explain what inventory collection is.

■ Describe the uses of hardware and software inventory.

■ Describe the key components in SMS inventory collection.

■ Explain the inventory collection process.

What Is Inventory Collection?

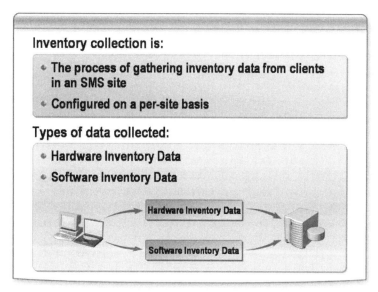

Inventory collection is:
- The process of gathering inventory data from clients in an SMS site
- Configured on a per-site basis

Types of data collected:
- Hardware Inventory Data
- Software Inventory Data

Hardware Inventory Data

Software Inventory Data

Inventory is the hardware and software data that is collected from clients assigned to an SMS site. Inventory refers to both the hardware and software inventory features. *Inventory collection* is the process of gathering information about the hardware and software inventory included in your SMS hierarchy.

The SMS hardware inventory feature collects detailed information about the hardware characteristics of SMS clients, such as memory, operating system, peripherals, services, and processes that are running on client computers. Hardware inventory also maintains a history of hardware inventories for each client, which allows you to identify changes to your clients' inventories over time.

The SMS software inventory feature collects detailed information about software installed on SMS sites, such as file size, file date, file path, and the name of the product of which a file is a part.

Uses of Hardware and Software Inventory Information

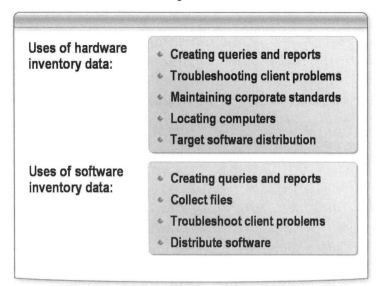

Uses of hardware inventory information

You can use hardware inventory information to:

- *Create queries and reports*. You can run queries to search for specific hardware inventory data, or run a predefined report to display hardware inventory data in an organized report format.

- *Troubleshoot client problems*. You can view recent changes to a client's hardware to identify potential issues.

- *Maintain corporate standards*. For example, if your organization has a processor speed standard, you can use hardware inventory to collect information about the processors of clients and identify the clients that are not complying with that standard.

- *Locate computers*. You can use hardware inventory data such as IP addresses, subnets, and domain names to track the physical location of every computer in the organization. This can be important if, for example, computers are leased and must be located and returned on a certain date.

- *Target software distribution*. Use inventory data to identify clients that can support the installation of a specific application, such as Microsoft Office System 2003.

Uses of software inventory information

You can use software inventory information to:

- *Create queries and reports*. You can run queries to retrieve selected software inventory data, such as information from a narrow set of files or information from a single file or files with specific file extensions. You can run reports to display software inventory data from the entire organization in an organized report format.

- *Collect files*. SMS software inventory can collect files, not just details about the files, from SMS client computers. With file collection, you specify a set of files to be copied from clients to the SMS site server to which the clients are assigned.

- *Troubleshoot client problems*. You can collect files, selected by file or by product, from client computers to help you troubleshoot problems. Collected files can help troubleshoot client problems. For example, if a client is experiencing problems, you can open at your desktop a copy of the client's recent log files that were previously collected. You can find out how many computers in your organization have the latest antivirus program installed.

- *Maintain corporate standards*. For example, if your organization has a standard set of client applications, including application updates and service packs, you can use software inventory to collect information about the applications installed on clients and identify the clients that are not complying with that standard.

- *Distribute software*. The software inventory feature is useful for software distribution. Software inventory data can be used to create collections that are based on file or product data. You can then distribute software to these collections. For example, you might want to distribute an antivirus program only to clients that do not have the program installed.

The Key Components of Inventory Collection

Component	Description
Client	• Contains client inventory agent components that collect data from clients
Site Server	• Stores and passes inventory settings to CAPs and Management Points through SQL Server • Processes inventory data and sends it to site database
Management Point	• Passes Advanced Client policies to Advanced Clients • Collects and passes inventory data from Advanced Clients to site server
CAP	• Passes inventory settings to Legacy Clients • Collects and passes inventory data from Legacy Clients to site server
Site Database	• Stores inventory data

The following components of SMS 2003 are involved in collecting hardware and software inventory:

- *Clients*. Clients contain client inventory agent components that are responsible for collecting data from the client computers and performing other inventory-related tasks on clients. SMS installs the inventory agent components on all Legacy Clients and Advanced Clients in the site after the hardware and software inventory features are enabled. On Advanced Clients, the agent is installed automatically and only requires the policy to be enabled.

- *Site server*. The site server stores settings for software and hardware inventory, and it passes these settings to client access points (CAPs) and management points through Microsoft SQL Server™. The site server processes collected inventory data and sends it to the site database.

  If the site server is not the central site server, it sends the inventory data to its parent site. The site also sends inventory data that it received from any lower-level sites on which inventory is enabled. This step is repeated until the inventory data reaches the central site.

- *Management point*. The management point passes the Advanced Client policies to Advanced Clients. It also collects inventory data files from Advanced Clients and passes this data to the site server.

- *CAP*. The client access point passes inventory settings to Legacy Clients. CAP also collects inventory data files from Legacy Clients and passes this data to the site server.

- *Site database.* The site database stores the following important inventory data:

  - An Advanced Client policy, which is created from the SMS_def.mof file and describes the hardware attributes that are collected by SMS.

  - Inventory rules that define what software inventory data needs to be collected.

  - Advanced Client policies, which contain site configuration information, inventory information, and other information that Advanced Clients need.

  - Client agent configuration settings.

  - Collected inventory data.

The Inventory Collection Process

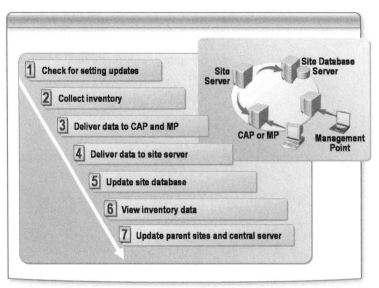

As an SMS administrator, you must determine what hardware and software inventory you will collect and how often you want the inventory collection process to take place. By default, hardware and software inventory runs once every seven days. You can modify this schedule to meet your organization's needs.

According to the specified schedule, SMS will automatically perform the inventory collection process. This process consists of the following key phases.

Phase	Description
1. Check for setting updates	If the hardware and software settings have been updated since the last inventory collection, clients will retrieve the updates from CAPs and management points and use them to configure the appropriate inventory agents.
2. Collect inventory	SMS inventory agents create inventory data files that list the collected data.
3. Deliver data to CAP (client access point) or management point	Clients send the inventory data files to CAPs or managements points.
4. Deliver data to site server	CAPs and management points (MPs) send inventory data files to the site server. MPs convert the data to SMS format before moving the data to the site server. Primary site servers add the inventory data to the SMS site database.

(continued)

Phase	Description
5. Update site database	SMS updates the database. The site database maintains a hardware inventory history for each client, but it does not maintain a software inventory history. SMS only keeps the current software inventory data for each client.
6. View inventory data in SMS Administrator console	You can view hardware and software inventory data in the SMS Administrator console and use it to create queries, collections, and reports. When viewing hardware inventory, you can view the history of each previous hardware inventory collection. When viewing software inventory, you can only view the current state.
7. Update parent sites and central site server	If the primary site server is not the central site server, the site server sends the inventory data to its parent site. The site also sends inventory data that it received from any lower-level sites. This step is repeated until the inventory data reaches the central site.

Practice: Explaining How Your Organization Can Use Inventory Collection

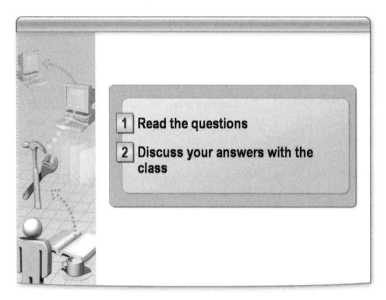

Instructions   Read the following questions and discuss your ideas with the rest of the class.

Discussion questions What role does hardware and software inventory play in software distribution?

_____

_____

_____

A user in your organization is having trouble connecting to an intranet Web page. How can you use hardware and software inventory to troubleshoot the problem?

_____

_____

_____

You have an Advanced Client assigned to a client site of your central site. How does inventory data pass from the client to the central site?

_____

_____

_____

Lesson: Collecting Inventory Information

- How to Enable the Hardware and Software Inventory Client Agents
- How to Force Inventory Collection
- How to View the Results of Inventory Collection Using the Resource Explorer
- How to Configure Software Inventory Rules
- How to Configure File Collection
- Demonstration: How to Collect Hardware Inventory Information

Introduction

This lesson describes how to configure the Hardware and Software Inventory Client Agents, how to force inventory collection to occur immediately, and how to use the Resource Explorer to examine the results of inventory collection.

Lesson objectives

After completing this lesson, you will be able to:

- Enable the Hardware and Software Inventory Client Agents.
- Force inventory collection.
- View the results of inventory collection by using the Resource Explorer.
- Configure software inventory rules.
- Configure file collection rules.
- Collect software data.
- Collect hardware inventory information.

How to Enable the Hardware and Software Inventory Client Agents

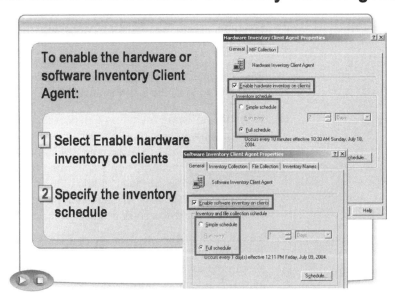

To use the hardware or software inventory feature, you must enable the appropriate inventory client agent.

Procedure

To enable the Hardware Inventory Client Agent:

1. In the SMS Administrator console, navigate to Hardware Inventory Client Agent. To do this, expand the following nodes in order: **Systems Management Server**, **Site Database (*site code – site name*), Site Hierarchy (*site code – site name*), Site Settings, Client Agents**.

2. In the details pane, right-click **Hardware Inventory Client Agent**, click **Properties**, and then select the **Enable hardware inventory on clients** check box.

   By default, SMS runs hardware inventory once every seven days. To change the schedule, enter the time of day or frequency that best suits your requirements. You can either select an interval, or you can specify a start date and time and a recurring schedule.

Procedure

To enable the Software Inventory Client Agent:

1. In the SMS Administrator console, navigate to Software Inventory Client Agent. To do this, expand the following nodes in order: **Systems Management Server**, **Site Database (*site code – site name*) Site Hierarchy (*site code – site name*), Site Settings, Client Agents**.

2. In the details pane, right-click **Software Inventory Client Agent**, click **Properties**, and then select the **Enable software inventory on clients** check box.

When is inventory collected?

When the Hardware Inventory Client Agent is installed and enabled on Legacy Clients, hardware inventory is collected after 10 minutes and then according to the hardware inventory schedule that you specify in the agent. When the SMS Inventory Agent is enabled on Advanced Clients, hardware inventory runs according to the hardware inventory schedule you specify if you set the schedule to the future. The default configuration is set to the current date and time, so when the agent is enabled, the inventory schedule is in the past and started as soon as the agent is enabled.

When the Software Inventory Client Agent is installed and enabled on Legacy Clients, software inventory is collected after 20 minutes and then according to the inventory schedule. When the SMS Inventory Agent is enabled on Advanced Clients, it runs only according to the software inventory schedule you specify if you set the schedule to the future. The default configuration is set to the current date and time, so when the agent is enabled, the inventory schedule is started as soon as the agent is enabled.

Tip   You might want to run Simple Schedule if your organization is concerned about excessive network traffic. This is because Simple Schedule runs the hardware inventory at a single, specific interval. Although it allows less flexibility in scheduling, this method usually causes less network traffic because the time each client's inventory data file is sent is based on that client's installation time. When you choose full schedule, all your clients are configured to run inventory at exactly the same time.

How to Force Inventory Collection

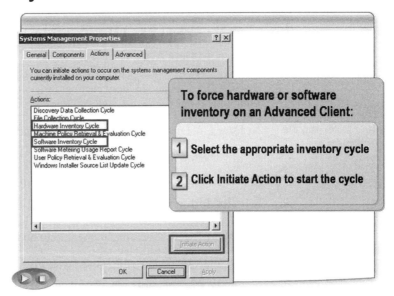

By default, hardware and software inventory run once every seven days. As described in the previous topic, you can change the inventory schedule at any time by setting the time of day or frequency that best suits your requirements. You can also force hardware and software inventory to run immediately on a single client.

Procedure to force hardware inventory on an Advanced Client

To run a hardware inventory immediately on a single Advanced Client:

1. In Control Panel, double-click **Systems Management**.

2. On the **Actions** tab, click **Hardware Inventory Cycle**.

3. Click **Initiate Action**.

Procedure to force hardware inventory on a Legacy Client

To run a hardware inventory immediately on a single Legacy Client:

1. In Control Panel, double-click **Systems Management**.

2. On the **Components** tab, click **Hardware Inventory Agent**.

3. Click **Start Component**.

Note Forcing hardware inventory does not disrupt the normal hardware inventory cycle if it is set to run on a full schedule (at a specific time and day, for example). In that case, the regularly scheduled hardware inventory still runs at the time scheduled in the Hardware Inventory Client Agent. However, if inventory is set to run on a simple schedule of once per day, for example, then the next inventory cycle is run 24 hours from the time the inventory is forced and every 24 hours thereafter.

Procedure to force software inventory on an Advanced Client

To run a software inventory immediately on a single Advanced Client:

1. In Control Panel, double-click **Systems Management**.

2. On the **Actions** tab, click **Software Inventory Cycle**.

3. Click **Initiate Action**.

Forcing the Advanced Client software inventory cycle does not enable the file collection cycle for an Advanced Client.

Procedure to force a file collection cycle

To force a file collection cycle on an Advanced Client:

1. In Control Panel, double-click **Systems Management**.

2. On the **Actions** tab, click **File Collection Cycle**.

3. Click **Initiate Action**.

Procedure to force software inventory on a Legacy Client

To run a software inventory immediately on a single Legacy Client:

1. In Control Panel, double-click **Systems Management**.

2. On the **Components** tab, click **Software Inventory Agent**.

3. Click **Start Component**.

Note   Forcing software inventory does not disrupt the normal software inventory cycle. The regularly scheduled software inventory still runs at the time scheduled in the Software Inventory Client Agent.

How to View the Results of Inventory Collection Using the Resource Explorer

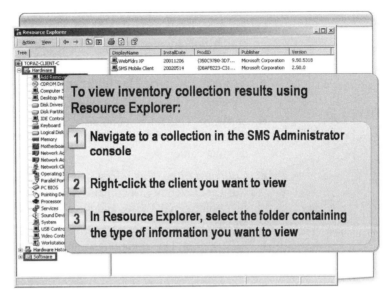

Procedure

The Resource Explorer is a tool in the SMS Administrator console that you can use to view the inventory data that was collected.

The high-level steps to view hardware and software inventory with Resource Explorer are as follows:

1. In the SMS Administrator console, navigate to a collection containing the client.

2. In the details pane, right-click the client whose information you want to view, point to **All Tasks**, and then click **Start Resource Explorer**. A new window for Resource Explorer opens and displays information about the selected client.

3. In Resource Explorer, select the folder that contains the type of information you want to view.

Detailed steps are included in the demonstration that follows this topic.

Hardware and software inventory data collected

You can find the hardware and software inventory information collected for each client in the following folders in Resource Explorer:

- *Hardware*. This folder contains a wealth of information, ranging from specifics about the manufacturer and type of hardware internals to the free space available on each disk. You can use this information to determine which computers to distribute software to, for example, or when performing remote troubleshooting.

- *Hardware History*. This folder contains hardware inventory data that has changed from previous inventory cycles.

- *Software*. This folder contains information collected by software inventory about each type of program file, such as the file name, file description, and product name.

- *Collected Files*. This folder is available if file collection is configured in software inventory. It contains a list of collected files. You can right-click a file, point to **All Tasks**, and then click **View File** to view the file in Notepad.

- *File Details*. This folder contains information about files without complete product details.

- *Product Details*. This folder contains the information about the client's software products that you specified when you configured the Software Inventory Client Agent.

How to Configure Software Inventory Rules

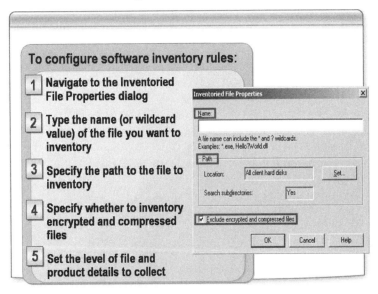

To configure software inventory rules:

1. Navigate to the Inventoried File Properties dialog

2. Type the name (or wildcard value) of the file you want to inventory

3. Specify the path to the file to inventory

4. Specify whether to inventory encrypted and compressed files

5. Set the level of file and product details to collect

Software inventory is configured to collect comprehensive information about files on your client computers. The software inventory agent on clients scans hard disks to inventory files. By default, the software inventory client agent inventories all .exe files on all SMS client hard disks. If you need to, you can specify other file types or folder trees for software inventory.

Procedure

To configure software inventory rules:

1. In the SMS Administrator console, click the **Inventory Collection** tab in the **Software Inventory Client Agent Properties** dialog box.

2. Click the **New** icon, and then type the name of a file you want to inventory.

   You can type exact file names (such as Autoexec.bat), or you can use wildcard characters. For example, you can inventory all zip files by typing ***.zip**. Any valid use of wildcard characters for the DIR command is valid in this dialog box.

3. By default, all hard disks on the SMS client are inventoried. If you want to inventory a folder or folder tree, click the **Set** button. In the **Path Properties** dialog box, click **Variable or path name**, and then specify a folder or folder tree.

   A variable is an environment variable, such as %*Windir*%. You can also specify whether subfolders should be searched by setting Search subdirectories. Wildcard characters can also be used in the last part of the path, for example, %*ProgramFiles*%\Microsoft Visual*.

4. Set **Exclude encrypted and compressed files** if you do not need to inventory encrypted and compressed files. By default, this option is enabled. This setting is particularly important if you are collecting product details during software inventory. Product details are contained within the files, so encrypted and compressed files must be decrypted and decompressed, which can use considerable computer resources on the SMS clients. If the local system account (or a group that contains the local system account) is not given administrative rights to the encrypted files, SMS cannot decrypt them.

5. Repeat steps 2 through 4 for all the inventory rules you require. Additional rules impose additional workload on the clients and might create additional network traffic or workload on the SMS servers. You should carefully consider the need for each additional rule. There is a maximum of 64 rules on the Inventory Collection tab.

6. Set the level of reporting details you want to collect by means of software inventory by setting **File details** and **Product details**.

How to Configure File Collection

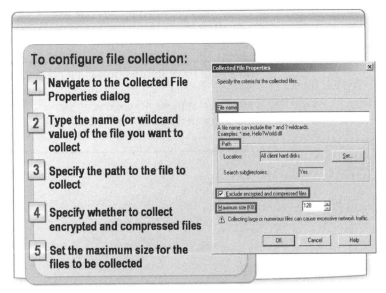

To configure file collection:

1. Navigate to the Collected File Properties dialog

2. Type the name (or wildcard value) of the file you want to collect

3. Specify the path to the file to collect

4. Specify whether to collect encrypted and compressed files

5. Set the maximum size for the files to be collected

What is file collection?

File collection is a feature provided by SMS software inventory that collects copies of files from SMS clients and stores them on the client's site server. You must specify the files that you want to collect. SMS will collect the files that you specify the next time the software inventory runs, and it will continue to collect the files during inventory collections when the files have changed.

No default rules are defined for file collection. Enabling rules that collect too many files or too large a file may generate excessive bandwidth. The maximum number of file collection rules is 64 rules, with each rule collecting up to 20 megabytes (MB).

Procedure

The steps that you perform to configure file collection are similar to the steps that you perform to configure inventory collection. Refer to the steps in the previous procedure for detailed instructions.

The high-level steps are as follows:

1. In the SMS Administrator console, click the **File Collection** tab in the **Software Inventory Client Agent Properties** dialog box.

2. Click the **New** icon, and then type the name of a file you want to inventory.

3. By default, all hard disks on the SMS client are scanned for files to collect. If you want to inventory a folder or folder tree, click the **Set** button. In the **Path Properties** dialog box, click **Variable or path name**, and then specify a folder or folder tree.

4. Set **Exclude encrypted and compressed files** if you do not need to collect encrypted and compressed files. By default, this option is enabled.

Note   Encrypted files can only be accessed by the originator.

---

5. Set the **Maximum size (KB)** for the files to be collected. This is the maximum size of the file or files collected for this rule. If the total size of the files collected by this rule exceeds this value, none of the files is collected.

Note   For more information about configuring software inventory rules and file collection, see Chapter 2, "Collecting Hardware and Software Inventory," in the *Microsoft Systems Management Server 2003 Operations Guide*. You can find this guide in the Additional Reading section of the Student Materials compact disc.

Demonstration: How to Collect Hardware Inventory Information

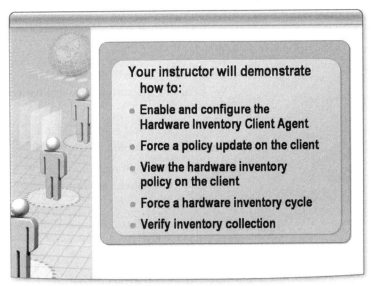

In this demonstration, your instructor will collect hardware inventory information by configuring the Hardware Inventory Client Agent and tracking its deployment across site systems to an SMS client.

Your instructor will use the following values in this demonstration.

Variable	Value
Virtual machine—SMS Site 1	Dublin
Dublin administrator	JaePa (Jae Pak)
Virtual machine—domain controller	Glasgow
Domain administrator	Administrator
Virtual machine—SMS Advanced Client	Bonn
Bonn administrator	SMartinez (Sandra Martinez)

Important   The following steps are included for your information. Do not attempt to perform them in the classroom. If you perform these steps in the classroom environment, you might leave your computer in an incorrect state for upcoming practices.

Demonstration steps performed by instructor only

▶ **To enable and configure the Hardware Inventory Client Agent**

1. If you have not already done so, log the Glasgow virtual machine on to the NWTRADERS domain with a user name of **Administrator** and a password of **P@ssw0rd**. After the Glasgow virtual machine opens, you can minimize its display.

2. If you have not already done so, log the Dublin virtual machine on to the NWTRADERS domain with a user name of **JaePa** and a password of **P@ssw0rd**.

3. Log the Bonn virtual machine on to the NWTRADERS domain with a user name of **SMartinez** and a password of **P@ssw0rd**.

4. On the Dublin virtual machine, click **Start**, point to **All Programs**, point to **Systems Management Server**, and then click **SMS Administrator Console**.

5. Expand **Site Database (001 – NWTraders)**, expand **Site Hierarchy**, expand **001 – NWTraders**, expand **Site Settings**, and then click **Client Agents**.

6. Double-click **Hardware Inventory Client Agent**.

7. On the **General** tab, select the **Enable hardware inventory on clients** check box.

8. Click **Full schedule**.

9. Click **Schedule**.

10. Verify that the **Start** date is the same as, or prior to, today's date.

11. Verify that the Recurrence pattern is set to **Interval**.

12. Set **Recur every** to **1 days**, and then click **OK**.

13. Click **Apply** to save the changes, and then click **OK**.

14. Close the SMS Administrator console.

▶ **To force a policy update on the client**

1. On the Bonn virtual machine, click **Start**, and then click **Control Panel**.

2. Click **Performance and Maintenance**, and then click **Systems Management**.

3. On the **Actions** tab, click **Machine Policy Retrieval & Evaluation Cycle**, and then click **Initiate Action**.

4. On the **Machine Policy Retrieval & Evaluation Cycle** message box, click **OK**.

Note Be sure to wait about two minutes for the policy update to complete before moving on to the next step.

5. Click the **Components** tab, and verify that **SMS Inventory Agent** appears in the **Component** column and is enabled.

6. In the **Systems Management Properties** dialog box, click **OK**.

7. Close the Control Panel.

▶ **To view the hardware inventory policy on the client**

Note The SMS 2003 Toolkit 1 is not included as part of the default SMS 2003 installation. However, for the purposes of this course, the SMS 2003 Toolkit 1 has been installed.

If you want to install the toolkit, you can download the Systems Management Server Toolkit 1 from the Microsoft Download Center.

1. On the Bonn virtual machine, click **Start**, point to **All Programs**, point to **SMS 2003 Toolkit 1**, and then click **Policy Spy**.

2. Click the **Actual** tab, expand the **Machine** folder, and then expand **InventoryAction**.

3. Click **InventoryActionID="{...001}"**.

   The policy appears in the lower pane.

4. Review the policy details.

   Note You have already updated the policy. However, you can also force the policy to update by using Policy Spy by performing the following steps:

   a. On the **Tools** menu, click **Request Machine Assignments**.

   b. On the **Tools** menu, click **Evaluate Machine Policy**.

   c. Review the updated policy details.

   Although these steps will expedite the updating process, it might take several minutes for the policy details to be refreshed.

5. Close Policy Spy.

▶ **To force a hardware inventory cycle**

Note A typical hardware inventory update on a Legacy Client takes place 10 minutes after the Hardware Inventory Client Agent is started. This is when the first complete inventory is collected from the client. However, for you to see a collected inventory in this practice, you will force the hardware inventory cycle.

1. On the Bonn virtual machine, click **Start**, and then click **Control Panel**.

2. Click **Performance and Maintenance**, and then click **Systems Management**.

3. In the **Systems Management Properties** dialog box, on the **Actions** tab, click **Hardware Inventory Cycle**, and then click **Initiate Action**.

4. In the **Hardware Inventory Cycle** message box, click **OK**.

5. In the **Systems Management Properties** dialog box, click **OK**.

6. Close the Control Panel.

► **To verify inventory collection**

1. On the Dublin virtual machine, click **Start**, point to **All Programs**, point to **Systems Management Server**, and then click **SMS Administrator Console**.

2. On the console tree, expand **Site Database (001 – NWTraders)**, expand **Collections**, and then click **All Systems**.

3. In the details pane, right-click **Bonn**, point to **All Tasks**, and then click **Start Resource Explorer**.

4. In the Resource Explorer console tree, expand **Hardware**, and then click **SMS Advanced Client State**.

5. View the components and version numbers.

6. Close Resource Explorer and the SMS Administrator console.

7. Leave Glasgow, Dublin and Bonn running.

Reflection question

In this demonstration, the instructor selected the Full Schedule option. Under what circumstances might you choose to run the hardware inventory using the Simple Schedule option?

_____

_____

_____

_____

_____

Practice: Collecting Software Inventory Information

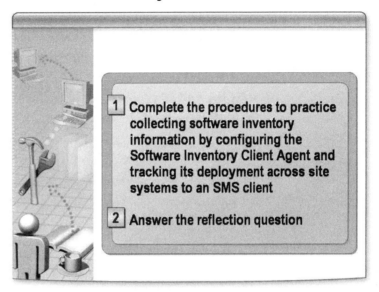

Instructions

Complete the procedures to practice collecting software inventory information by configuring the Software Inventory Client Agent and tracking its deployment across site systems to an SMS client. Then answer the reflection question that follows.

In this practice, use the following values.

Variable	Value
Virtual machine—SMS Site 1	Dublin
Dublin administrator	JaePa (Jae Pak)
Virtual machine—domain controller	Glasgow
Domain administrator	Administrator
Virtual machine—SMS Advanced Client	Bonn
Bonn administrator	SMartinez (Sandra Martinez)

Procedures

▶ **To enable and configure the Software Inventory Agent**

1. If you have not already done so, log the Glasgow virtual machine on to the NWTRADERS domain with a user name of **Administrator** and a password of **P@ssw0rd**. After the Glasgow virtual machine opens, you can minimize its display.

2. If you have not already done so, log the Dublin virtual machine on to the NWTRADERS domain with a user name of **JaePa** and a password of **P@ssw0rd**.

3. Log the Bonn virtual machine on to the NWTRADERS domain with a user name of **SMartinez** and a password of **P@ssw0rd**.

4. On the Dublin virtual machine, click **Start**, point to **All Programs**, point to **Systems Management Server**, and then select the **SMS Administrator Console**.

5. In the console tree of the SMS Administrator console, expand **Site Database (001 – NWTraders)**, expand **Site Hierarchy**, expand **001 – NWTraders**, expand **Site Settings**, and then click **Client Agents**.

6. Double-click **Software Inventory Client Agent**.

7. On the **General** tab, select the **Enable software inventory on clients** check box.

8. Click **Full schedule**.

9. Click **Schedule**.

10. On the **Schedule** dialog box, verify that the **Start** date is the same as, or prior to, today's date.

11. Verify that **Recurrence pattern** is set to **Interval**.

12. Set **Recur every** to **1 days**, and then click **OK**.

13. On the **Inventory Collection** tab, delete the .exe file type by selecting the **.exe** file type and clicking the **delete** (the X) icon.

14. To inventory all the files in the root of the system drive, perform the following steps:

    a. Click the **New** ✳ icon. The **Inventoried File Properties** dialog box appears.

    b. Type ***.exe** in the **Name** box, and then click **Set**.

    c. On the **Path Properties** dialog box, click **Variable or path name**, and then in the **Location** box, type **%SystemDrive%**

    d. Verify the **Search subdirectories** check box is selected.

    e. Click **OK** twice.

15. In the **Software Inventory Client Agent Properties** dialog box, click **Apply**.

16. On the **File Collection** tab, click the **New** ✳ icon.

17. In the **Name** box, type ***.ini**

Note If the aggregate of the collected files exceeds the default setting of 128 kilobytes (KB), the Software Inventory Agent will not collect *any* files. The maximum setting is 20,480 KB. The maximum number of rules is 64.

---

18. In the **Maximum size [KB]** box, type or select **10000**.

Note By increasing the maximum size for the collected files, you can ensure the Software Inventory Agent will be able to collect files.

---

19. Click **OK** twice.

20. Close the SMS Administrator console.

▶ **To force a policy update on the Advanced Client**

1. On the Bonn virtual machine, click **Start**, and then click **Control Panel**.

2. Click **Performance and Maintenance**, and then click **Systems Management**.

3. On the **Actions** tab, click **Machine Policy Retrieval & Evaluation Cycle**, and then click **Initiate Action**.

4. In the **Machine Policy Retrieval & Evaluation Cycle** message box, click **OK**.

Note   Be sure to wait about two minutes for the policy update to complete before moving on to the next step.

---

5. On the **Components** tab, verify that the **SMS Inventory Agent** has a status of **Enabled**.

6. Click **OK**.

7. Close the Control Panel.

▶ **To view Software Inventory policy on the client**

Note   The SMS 2003 Toolkit 1 is not included as part of the default SMS 2003 installation. However, for the purposes of this course, the SMS 2003 Toolkit 1 has been installed on the appropriate virtual machines.

If you want to install the toolkit, you can download the SMS Toolkit 1 from the Microsoft Download Center.

---

1. On the Bonn virtual machine, click **Start**, point to **All Programs**, point to **SMS 2003 Toolkit 1**, and then click **Policy Spy**.

2. On the **Actual** tab, expand **Machine** and then expand **CollectibleFileItem**.

3. Click **FileItemID="{...}"**.

   The policy appears in the lower pane.

Note   If the policy does *not* appear, you may have to wait for a couple more minutes. Occasionally, SMS takes longer than the typical two to three minutes to update policies.

---

4. Review the policy details and note the following entries:

```
string FileSpec = "*.ini";
string SearchPath = "*";
```

Note You have already updated the policy. However, you can also force the policy to update by using Policy Spy by performing the following steps:

a. On the **Tools** menu, click **Request Machine Assignments**.

b. On the **Tools** menu, click **Evaluate Machine Policy**.

c. Review the updated policy details.

Although these steps will expedite the updating process, it might take several minutes for the policy details to be refreshed.

5. Close Policy Spy.

▶ **To force a software inventory and file collection cycle on the Advanced Client**

Note The file collection cycle occurs automatically on the Advanced Client when the software inventory cycle occurs on a schedule.

1. On the Bonn virtual machine, click **Start**, and then click **Control Panel**.

2. Click **Performance and Maintenance**, and then click **Systems Management**.

3. On the **Actions** tab, click **Software Inventory Cycle**, and then click **Initiate Action**.

4. In the **Software Inventory Cycle** message box, click **OK**.

5. Click **File Collection Cycle**, and then click **Initiate Action**.

6. In the **File Collection Cycle** message box, click **OK**.

7. Click **OK**.

8. Close the Control Panel.

Note Be sure to wait about two minutes for the policy update to complete before moving on to the next step.

▶ **To verify a successful inventory collection**

1. On the Dublin virtual machine, click **Start**, point to **All Programs**, click **Systems Management Server**, and then select the **SMS Administrator Console**.

2. In the console tree, expand **Site Database (001 – NWTraders)**, expand **Collections**, and then click **All Systems**.

3. In the details pane, right-click **Bonn**, point to **All Tasks**, and then click **Start Resource Explorer**.

4. In the Resource Explorer console tree, expand **Software**, and then click **Collected Files**.

5. In the details pane, right-click **SMSCfg.ini**, point to **All Tasks**, and then click **View File** to view the file in Notepad.

6. Review the Smscfg.ini file.

   This file contains a list of installed SMS components and their versions on Bonn.

7. Close the file and then close any open windows.

8. Leave Glasgow and Dublin and Bonn running.

Reflection question

How can you configure hardware and software inventory to minimize the impact on your network?

_____

_____

_____

Lesson: Extending Inventory Collection

- **What Is the SMS_def.mof File?**
- **How to Modify the SMS_def.mof File**
- **How SMS Uses WMI in Hardware Inventory Collection**
- **What Are MIF Files?**
- **How to Enable or Disable MIF File Collection**
- **How to Create MIF Files**
- **How to Submit a NOIDMIF File to the Client**

Introduction

In your role as SMS administrator you may want to extend inventory collection beyond the default inventory collection attributes. You might be responsible for configuring current software inventory rules and file collection to collect additional file types or files that your organization needs. You might also be responsible for extending the hardware inventory collection to collect additional hardware inventory data.

This lesson describes how you can modify the inventory collection attributes to collect the specific data that your organization needs.

Lesson objectives

After completing this lesson, you will be able to:

- Describe the purpose of the SMS_def.mof file.
- Modify the SMS_def.mof file.
- Describe how SMS uses Microsoft Windows Management Instrumentation (WMI) in hardware inventory collection.
- Describe the purpose of Management Information Format (MIF) files.
- Enable or disable a MIF file collection.
- Create a MIF file.
- Submit a MIF file to the client.

What Is the SMS_def.mof File?

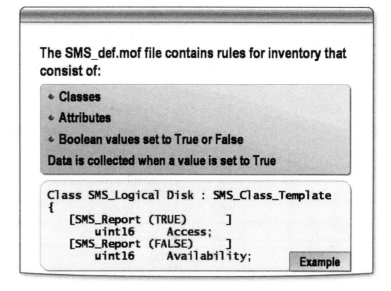

The SMS_def.mof file contains rules for inventory that consist of:

* Classes
* Attributes
* Boolean values set to True or False

Data is collected when a value is set to True

```
Class SMS_Logical Disk : SMS_Class_Template
{
    [SMS_Report (TRUE)        ]
        uint16       Access;
    [SMS_Report (FALSE)       ]
        uint16       Availability;
```

Example

SMS_def.mof is a file that lists the hardware attributes that are collected by SMS. You can customize the SMS_def.mof file so that SMS collects the hardware attributes that are needed by your organization.

For example, you want to determine which computers in your network have printers attached to them, and the properties of those printers. By default, hardware inventory does not report that information. By modifying the SMS_def.mof file, you can extend hardware inventory to report information about those printers.

SMS_def.mof consists of a list of attributes and classes or groups of related attributes. Each class and attribute is assigned a Boolean value of True or False. The attributes and classes that are set to True are collected, and those set to False are not.

If additional hardware inventory is required, or if there is data being collected that is not required, hardware inventory can be configured to accommodate these desired changes.

An example from the SMS_def.mof default attributes file

SMS_def.mof lists classes and attributes in the following format:

```
[SMS_Report(TRUE),
SMS_Group_Name("Boot Configuration"),
ResID(400),ResDLL("SMS_RXPL.dll"),
SMS_Class_ID("MICROSOFT|BOOT_CONFIGURATION|1.0")]
class Win32_BootConfiguration : SMS_Class_Template
{
    [SMS_Report(TRUE)]
string  BootDirectory;
    [SMS_Report(FALSE)]
string  ConfigurationPath;
    [SMS_Report(TRUE)]
string  LastDrive;
    [SMS_Report(TRUE),key]
string  Name;
```

In the preceding example, the class is set to True. When a class is set to True, any attributes with the key property are collected, even if the individual attributes are set to False.

How SMS uses the SMS_def.mof file to configure inventory

SMS uses the SMS_def.mof file that is stored in the SMS site server to create the appropriate Advanced Client policy for Advanced Clients. When the Inventory Client Agent runs on Advanced Clients, it uses the Advanced Client policy to collect only the attributes that are enabled in the SMS_def.mof file.

When the Hardware Inventory Client Agent runs on the Legacy Client to collect inventory, it reads the SMS_def.mof file and collects only the attributes that are enabled in the SMS_def.mof file.

Where SMS_def.mof is stored

The SMS_def.mof file is stored in the \SMS\Inboxes\clifiles.src\Hinv directory on the site server and in a copy of the file that is stored on the site's Legacy Clients.

How to Modify the SMS_def.mof File

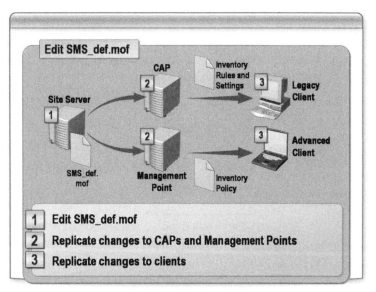

You can adjust the hardware inventory configuration by modifying the SMS_def.mof file on the site server. Editing SMS_def.mof is the means for configuring any changes to hardware inventory for all clients in SMS. Although you do not find SMS_def.mof on Advanced Clients, changes made to the original master SMS_def.mof are immediately applied to the site database and then propagated to Advanced Clients as new policies by means of Management Points. Legacy Clients all receive their own local copies of the modified master SMS_def.mof from their CAP.

The process of editing the SMS_def.mof file and distributing these changes to SMS clients consists of the following stages:

1. *Edit the SMS_def.mof file.* You use a text file editor to change the class and property reporting settings in the SMS_def.mof file. Each property and class has an SMS_Report flag. To include a property or class in inventory, set the SMS_Report flag to True. To remove a property or class from inventory, set the SMS_Report flag to False.

2. *Replicate the changes to the CAP.* The CAP receives a copy of the file from the site server. The file is accessible by the legacy clients and is stored in \CAP_Site\Clifiles.box\Hinv\sms_def.mof.

   For the management point, the file is translated into advanced client policies and stored in the site database. The SMS_def.mof file itself is not stored in the database—just the data that is generated by this file. The Management Point will receive the policies when an advanced client makes a request.

3. *Replicate the changes to the clients.* During the policy refresh cycle, the advanced client will apply the policies that reflect the changes to the SMS_def.mof from the management point. The legacy client will obtain a copy of the SMS_def.mof from the CAP during its next scheduled configuration refresh cycle. Both legacy and advanced clients will then apply this "template" during the next hardware inventory cycle.

Considerations for modifying SMS_def.mof

Considerations for modifying SMS_def.mof are as follows:

- Changes to the SMS_def.mof file should be documented.

- Making back-up copies of the SMS_def.mof file is strongly recommended especially when applying SMS Service Packs since the Service Pack may change the default SMS_def.mof file and override the current settings.

- A test environment would verify that your changes achieve the desired database results before rolling the file out in a production environment.

- Other sites on which you plan to include these changes will need the file manually copied to their respective site servers.

- Before making any changes, verify that the component you may want to add is not already in the file in a disabled state.

Note For a detailed explanation of using and editing the SMS_def.mof file, see Chapter 2 of the *Microsoft Systems Management Server 2003 Operations Guide*.

Considerations for distributing SMS_def.mof

Considerations for distributing SMS_def.mof are as follows:

- *Realize that changes to SMS_def.mof do not automatically propagate throughout the SMS hierarchy*. Although changes to SMS_def.mof are automatically propagated to all clients at the SMS site, they are not propagated to any other sites. You must make the same changes to the SMS_def.mof at other sites, or copy the SMS_def.mof to those sites.

- *Be careful when copying SMS_def.mof from other sites*. Different sites might be running a different version or service pack of SMS. The version of the SMS_def.mof that you copy might not include changes you or Microsoft has made in the SMS_def.mof at the destination site.

- *Make changes to the copy of the SMS_def.mof file on the site server*. Do not place custom SMS_def.mof files on Legacy Clients or CAPs. If you do, those files are used temporarily and then overwritten. At each daily client refresh cycle, the SMS_def.mof on the CAP is compared with the copy on the client, and if these copies are different, the copy on the CAP is copied to the client, overwriting any custom SMS_def.mof file that exists on the client. Copies of the SMS_def.mof file also exist on Legacy Clients, but you should not modify them. The SMS client automatically updates these copies when necessary.

How SMS Uses WMI in Hardware Inventory Collection

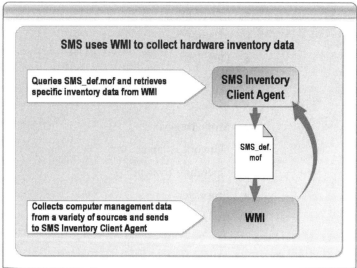

Windows Management Instrumentation (WMI) is a management infrastructure in Microsoft Windows® that collects computer management data from a wide variety of sources and makes it accessible by means of standard interfaces.

SMS uses WMI extensively to collect hardware inventory. The SMS client inventory agent retrieves data from WMI. The agent does not retrieve all the data from the WMI. Instead, it retrieves specific data based on hardware inventory rules stored on the clients. These hardware inventory rules are defined by SMS_def.mof, as described in the previous topic.

WMI provides approximately 1,500 hardware properties for client computers, such as:

- Device ID of a tape drive.

- Manufacturer of a CD-ROM drive.

- Current size of the registry.

- Primary partition of a disk.

The SMS client inventory agents query these classes for hardware inventory data.

Additional information that WMI can provide

WMI provides data in a large number of classes that might not be currently defined in SMS_def.mof. For example, WMI includes software classes, including operating system configuration and entities, installed software, software configuration, and other objects, such as objects for the logged-on user.

As an SMS administrator, you can modify the SMS_def.mof file to collect additional information from WMI. For example, to gather information about computers with uninterruptible power supplies, enable the section of the file with the heading, "Uninterruptible Power Supply."

What is collected by default?

By default, the SMS_def.mof is configured to use WMI to collect hardware inventory information for common hardware devices and properties such as:

- CD-ROM
- Monitor
- Disk Drive
- PC BIOS
- Memory
- Motherboard
- Network Adapter
- Operating System
- Processor
- Video Controller

What Are MIF Files?

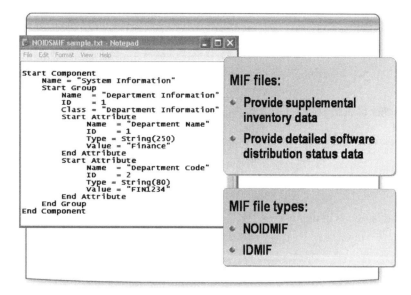

Management Information Format (MIF) files are files that are based on the Desktop Management industry standard. The MIF standard defines how text files can be used to represent computer management information.

You can use MIF files to provide supplemental information about SMS client computers or other resources during hardware inventory. MIFs can also provide detailed software distribution status information. SMS collects the MIFs and stores their contents in the SMS site database, where you can use their data in the same way that you use default SMS inventory data.

Types of MIF files

SMS supports two types of MIF files:

- *NOIDMIF*. Custom NOIDMIF files extend the current inventory set by adding new inventory properties to each client. You can collect additional information about each computer, such as asset or office numbers.

- *IDMIF*. Custom IDMIF files extend the current inventory set by adding new architectures to the database. IDMIFs, allow you to collect information about entities such as shared network printer or non-system items. IDMIF files can also be used to add stand-alone computers to the SMS site database.

Differences between IDMIF files and NOIDMIF files

IDMIF files are identical to NOIDMIF files, with these exceptions:

- IDMIF files must have a header that provides architecture, and a unique ID. NOIDMIF files are automatically given a similar header by the system during processing on the client.

- IDMIF files must include a top-level group with the same class as the architecture being added or changed, and that group must include at least one property.

- Like NOIDMIF files, IDMIF files have key properties that must be unique. Any class that has more than one instance must have at least one key property defined; otherwise subsequent instances will overwrite previous instances.

Note For more information about extending hardware inventory and MIF files in particular, see Chapter 3, "Advanced Inventory Collection," in the *Microsoft Systems Management Server 2003 Operations Guide*. You can find this guide in the Additional Reading section of the Student Materials compact disc. You can also refer to the SMS Administrator's Companion, pages 352-353, for examples of when and why you would use NOIDMIF and IDMIF files.

Benefits of using MIF files

If you use custom MIF files, hardware inventory can help in tracking asset depreciation by collecting purchase dates of the computers in the organization. By using this data, the administrator can determine the total depreciation of assets in the organization. This can prevent paying unnecessary taxes on assets that have depreciated and can help in the planning of future hardware purchases.

Disadvantages of using MIF files

- *Security*. Collecting IDMIFs or NOIDMIFs can be a security risk, so you can disable their collection if that risk is significant to you. For more information about IDMIF and NOIDMIF security issues, see the "Inventory Collection" section in Chapter 5, "Understanding SMS Security," in the *Microsoft Systems Management Server 2003 Concepts, Planning, and Deployment Guide*.

- *Network performance*. If you modify the SMS_def.mof file or create custom MIF files to add information to inventory, consider the performance effects. Adding information, such as the Microsoft Win32® classes, Win32_LogEvent, Win32_Account, or Win32_Directory, can slow network and system performance, as they may generate network calls to collect data from network services.

How to Enable or Disable MIF File Collection

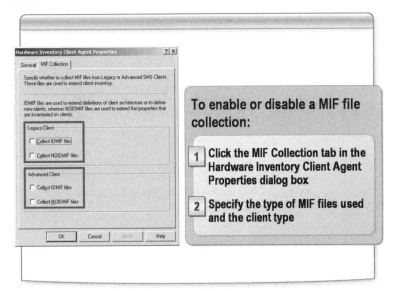

You must enable MIF collection before you can collect and store data from MIF files. Newly installed SMS 2003 sites have MIF collection disabled by default. SMS 2003 sites that have been upgraded from SMS 2.0 have MIF collection enabled by default.

Procedure

To enable or disable MIF file collection:

1. In the **Hardware Inventory Client Agent Properties** dialog box. click the **MIF Collection** tab.

2. Select or clear the options to collect IDMIF or NOIDMIF files for the Legacy Client and Advanced Client.

How to Create MIF Files

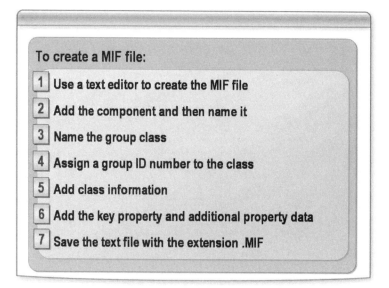

To create a MIF file:

1 Use a text editor to create the MIF file

2 Add the component and then name it

3 Name the group class

4 Assign a group ID number to the class

5 Add class information

6 Add the key property and additional property data

7 Save the text file with the extension .MIF

The most common way to use a NOIDMIF file is to create a new class that cannot be collected through the SMS_def.mof file and then store the collected data in the SMS site database. IDMIF files are identical to NOIDMIF files, with a few exceptions detailed below.

To create an IDMIF you must:

- Add the architecture

- Add the unique ID

Procedure to create MIF files

You can create NOIDMIF files by using the text editor. If you are using a text editor to create a NOIDMIF file, you will type a series of commands to create a new class. The high-level steps are as follows:

1. Use a text editor to create the MIF file.

2. Add a component and then name it.

3. Name the group class.

4. Assign a group ID number to the class.

5. Add class information.

6. Add the key property and additional property data.

7. Save the text file with the extension .mif.

An example from an IDMIF file

An IDMIF file lists classes and attributes in the following format:

```
//Architecture<Media Equip>
//UniqueID<awesome101>
Start Component
     Name = "Video Equipment"
     Start Group
          Name = "MediaEquip"
          ID = 1
          Class =  "MediaEquip"
          Key = 1
               Start Attribute
                    Name = "corp"
                    ID = 1
                    Access = Name = READ-ONLY
                    Storage = Specific
                    Type = String(20)
                    Value ="Great"
               End Attribute
          End Group
```

How to Submit a NOIDMIF File to the Client

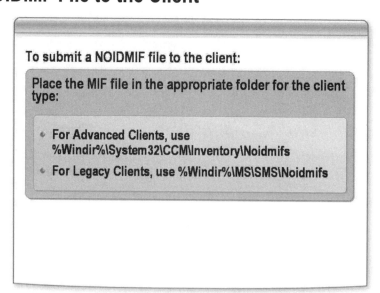

To submit a NOIDMIF file to the client:

Place the MIF file in the appropriate folder for the client type:

- For Advanced Clients, use %Windir%\System32\CCM\Inventory\Noidmifs
- For Legacy Clients, use %Windir%\MS\SMS\Noidmifs

When you customize hardware inventory by using NOIDMIF files, you must leave the NOIDMIF in the NOIDMIFS folder on the client. The custom MIF file is used at each hardware inventory cycle when the extended classes and properties are collected. If the NOIDMIF file is not found on the client during hardware inventory, the extended classes and properties are deleted and you must submit the NOIDMIF file again by replacing it in the NOIDMIFS folder on the client.

To submit the NOIDMIF file to the client, place it in the appropriate folder on the client computer. The folder you choose depends on the client type:

- For Advanced Clients, store NOIDMIF files in the following folder:

  %Windir%\System32\CCM\Inventory\Noidmifs

- For Legacy Clients, store NOIDMIF files in the following folder:

  %Windir%\MS\SMS\Noidmifs

Tip   The safest method on both clients is to use the folder that the following registry subkey points to:

HKLM\Software\Microsoft\SMS\Client\Configuration\Client Properties\ NOIDMIF Directory.

The next time hardware inventory runs, the NOIDMIF file is included in the process, and the new properties and classes are added to the SMS site database.

Practice: Extending an Inventory Collection

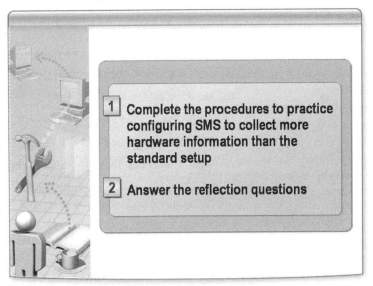

Instructions

Complete the procedures to practice configuring SMS to collect more hardware information than the standard setup. Answer the reflection questions that follow.

In this practice, use the following values:

Variable	Value
Virtual machine—SMS Site 1	Dublin
Dublin Administrator	JaePa (Jae Pak)
Virtual machine—Domain controller	Glasgow
Domain Administrator	Administrator

Procedure

▶ **Modify the sms_def.mof on the site server**

1. Verify that Glasgow and Dublin virtual machines are running.

2. In the space provided below, write the *current date and time* on the Dublin virtual machine. You will need this information to verify that the SMS configuration was successfully updated.

_____

3. On Dublin virtual machine, click **Start**, click **Run**, type **C:\SMS\Inboxes\Clifiles.src\Hinv** and then click **OK**.

   Windows Explorer opens and displays the folder and its files.

4. Open the **Sms_def.mof** file using Notepad:

   a. Double-click **sms_def.mof**.

   b. In the **Windows** message box, click **Select the program from a list**, and then click **OK**.

   c. Click **Notepad** in the **Programs** list, clear the check box for **Always use the selected program to open this kind of file**, and then click **OK**.

Caution The site server creates a copy of this file called Sms_def.mof.bak on C:\SMS\data\hinvarchive\. If you have any problems modifying the file in this practice, you can replace your file with a copy of the correct file from this location.

5. Search for the first occurrence of the **CD-ROM** attribute:

    a. On the **Edit** menu, click **Find**.

    b. In the **Find what** box, type **CD-ROM**, and then click **Find Next**.

        The first occurrence is highlighted.

    c. Click **Cancel** to dismiss the **Find** dialog box.

6. In the **SMS_Group_Names** attribute for **CD-ROM**, replace the word **TRUE** with **FALSE** (on the line above CD-ROM).

    Verify that your changes appear like the sample below:

```
[ SMS_Report      (FALSE),
  SMS_Group_Name ("CD-ROM"),
  SMS_Class_ID   ("MICROSOFT|CDROM|1.0") ]
```

7. Repeat steps 5 and 6 for the **Desktop Monitor** and **IDE Controller** attributes. Verify your changes appear like the samples below:

    *   **Desktop Monitor**

```
[ SMS_Report      (FALSE),
  SMS_Group_Name ("Desktop Monitor"),
  SMS_Class_ID   ("MICROSOFT|DESKTOP_MONITOR|1.0") ]
```

    *   **IDE Controller**

```
[ SMS_Report      (FALSE),
  SMS_Group_Name ("IDE Controller"),
  SMS_Class_ID   ("MICROSOFT|IDE_CONTROLLER|1.0") ]
```

8. On the **File** menu, click **Save**.

9. Close any open windows.

▶ **To verify the SMS configuration for hardware inventory has been successfully modified**

1. Click **Start**, and then click **Run**.

2. In the **Open** dialog box, type **C:\SMS\Logs\dataldr.log**, and then click **OK**.

    The Dataldr.log opens in SMS Trace.

3. On the **Tools** menu, click **Filter**.

4. In the **Filter Settings** dialog box, select the **Filter when the Time** check box.

5. Under **Filter when the Time** section, select **is after** from the drop-down list.

6. Leave the date as the default, and then type in the time that you wrote at the beginning previous task.

7. Click **OK**.

8. Verify that the following entries appear in the log file:

```
SMS_DEF.Mof change detected
Removing DataItem id(......) from DataItem table (no longer set
for hinv reporting)
Removing DataItem id(......) from DataItem table (no longer set
for hinv reporting)
Removing DataItem id(......) from DataItem table (no longer set
for hinv reporting)
End of cimv2\sms-to-policy conversion; returning 0x0
```

If your file contains theses entries (there may be additional lines of text interspersed), the database has been successfully updated.

Important Be sure to go back into the **Filter** dialog box and remove the previously applied filter settings (that is, clear the **Filter when the Time** check box).

---

9. Close SMS Trace.

10. Leave the Glasgow and Dublin and Bonn virtual machines running.

Note For a detailed explanation of the use and editing of the Sms_def.mof file, refer to Chapter 2 of the *Microsoft Systems Management Server 2003 Operations Guide*.

You can find this guide in the Additional Reading section of the Student Materials compact disc.

Lesson: Configuring Software Metering

- What Is Software Metering?
- The Components of Software Metering
- How Software Metering Works
- How to Create a Software Metering Rule
- How to Configure the Software Metering Client Agent
- How to Verify the Installation and Operation of Software Metering
- How to Isolate Problems with Software Metering

Introduction

In this lesson, you will learn about software metering and how the Software Metering Client Agent is configured and enabled. By using this feature, you can monitor program usage on SMS client computers, track license compliance.

Lesson objectives

After completing this lesson, you will be able to:

- Describe what software metering is.
- Identify the components of software metering.
- Describe how software metering works.
- Create a software metering rule.
- Configure the Software Metering Client Agent.
- Verify the installation and operation of software metering.
- Isolate problems with software metering.

What Is Software Metering?

Software Metering is the process of gathering detailed data on program usage from client computers in an SMS site

Types of data collected:

- Program usage information
- File information
- Program information

Software metering allows you to monitor program usage on Systems Management Server client computers. Using software metering, you can collect detailed program and usage information, including user name, file description, start time, and end time. Software metering data can be conveniently summarized to produce useful reports that can help you plan software purchases in your organization.

Software metering is supported on Legacy Clients and Advanced Clients. Software metering also monitors program usage on SMS clients that are running Microsoft Terminal Server Services. Software metering rules are enforced on all remote desktops with an open session to the Terminal Server computer that is an SMS client, and software metering data is collected from these desktops. However, all the remote desktop computers will share a single computer name, which is the Terminal Server computer name.

The Components of Software Metering

Component	Description
Software Metering Rules	Configuration rules provide data to monitor program usage
Software Metering Client Agent	Uses software metering rule to collect and report metered data
Client Access Points (CAPs)	• Receive legacy client metering reports • Provide software metering rules to Legacy clients
Management Points	• Receive Advanced client metering reports • Provide software metering rules to Advanced Clients
Software Metering Processes on the Site Server	• Processes client reports and passes data to the site database • Creates/prepares software metering rules
Queries and Reports	Displays summarized data

Software metering is supported on Legacy Clients, Advanced Clients, and SMS clients running Terminal Services. The software metering components are:

- *Software metering rules.* These rules represent the programs you want to monitor on each client. The rules are enforced on all remote desktops with an open session to the terminal server that is an SMS client. Programs monitored typically have .exe or .com file name extensions.

- *Software Metering Client Agent.* This agent runs the software metering rules on the client and collects and reports metered data back to the site.

- *The CAP and Management Point site systems.* The CAP receives the Legacy Client metering reports while the Management Point receives the Advanced Client reports. The reports are then passed to the site server and eventually to the site database.

- *Software Metering server component.* The site server runs the Software Metering Processor which is one of many processes managed by the SMS Executive. This component is responsible for creating rules, processing incoming client reports, and passing the data to the site database.

- *Queries and reports.* The data that is collected from the clients is summarized in the site database by scheduled SQL tasks. The summarized data is then available to reports and queries.

How Software Metering Works

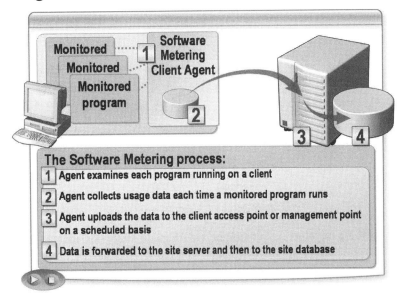

The Software Metering Client Agent must be enabled before the process of collecting program usage data can begin.

The software metering process occurs as follows:

1. The Software Metering Client Agent examines each program running on the client and determines if the program file's header information matches a specified rule for the SMS site to which the client is assigned.

2. The agent collects usage data each time a monitored program runs on the client, regardless of whether the client is connected to the network.

3. The agent uploads the data to the client access point or management point on its next Software Metering Usage Report cycle. If the client is not connected to the network, the data remains on the client and is uploaded to the SMS site the next time the client connects to the network.

4. The data is forwarded from the CAP or management point to the site server.

5. The data is added to the site database, and, if a rule was created as a higher-level parent site, the data is propagated to the higher-level SMS sites.

How rules and metered data are stored

SMS uses WMI to store software metering rules and collected data. The metering rules that you configure are stored in the SMS site database and passed to the Management Point when an Advanced Client makes a request. The rules for Legacy Clients are copied to Client Access Points. The rules are then propagated to SMS Legacy Clients during the Software Metering Client Agent's next update cycle, which is set to every seven days for Legacy Clients and retrieved during the next policy retrieval cycle for Advanced Clients by default.

Metered data collected by the agent

During the software metering process, the Software Metering Client Agent collects the following detailed program information.

Usage information	File information	Program information
• Start time	• File ID	• Company name
• End time	• File name	• Product name
• Meter data ID	• File version	• Product version
• Resource ID (computer name)	• File description	• Product language
• User name	• File size	
• Users in Terminal Services sessions		
• Whether it is still running		

How to view the metered data

To facilitate viewing and analyzing metered data, SMS provides sample software metering reports that can be used with the SMS Reporting feature. You can access the reports from the SMS Administrator console.

The data that is collected from the clients is summarized in the site database by scheduled SQL tasks. The summarized data is then available to reports and queries. Although these can be customized, there are several predefined reports and queries available from the SMS Administrator console.

Queries use Windows Management Instrumentation Query Language (WQL) to gather metering data from WMI without directly accessing the database. Reports query the database directly using SQL statements.

How to Create a Software Metering Rule

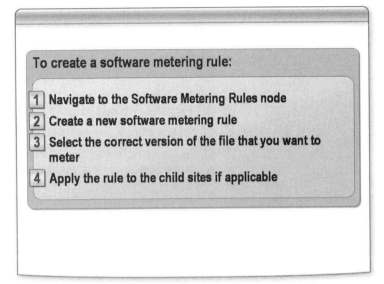

To create a software metering rule:

1 Navigate to the Software Metering Rules node

2 Create a new software metering rule

3 Select the correct version of the file that you want to meter

4 Apply the rule to the child sites if applicable

You must create and configure software metering rules to specify the applications to be monitored by the clients. These steps are performed from the SMS Administrator console and apply to the entire site.

Any process you see running on a client's task manager can be monitored. The filename can be a .com or .exe file. Although you can meter versions of the same file, wildcard characters are also admissible.

Procedure

To create and configure a software metering rule:

1. In the SMS Administrator console, expand Site Database (*site code – site name*) and then click **Software Metering Rules**.

2. Right-click **Software Metering Rules**, point to **New**, and then click **Software Metering Rule**.

   The **Software Metering Rule Properties** dialog box opens.

3. On the **General** tab, browse for the executable file that is associated with the application you wish to meter, and then select it.

   The remaining fields will be populated with information obtained from the file's header.

   If you cannot browse for the file, enter the file name and the remaining fields manually.

4. Verify **This rule applies to the specified site and all its child sites** is selected to apply this rule to child sites where the client agent is enabled.

   Note   The clients will refresh their local rules once every seven days for the Legacy Client and once every hour for Advanced Clients.

How to Configure the Software Metering Client Agent

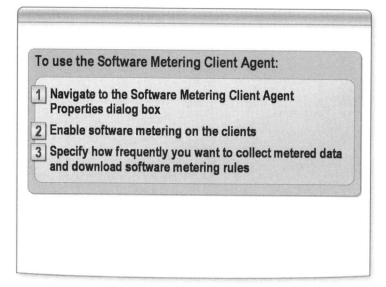

To use the Software Metering Client Agent:

1. Navigate to the Software Metering Client Agent Properties dialog box
2. Enable software metering on the clients
3. Specify how frequently you want to collect metered data and download software metering rules

The client must have the Software Metering Client Agent enabled to monitor applications that are launched into memory. The agent will apply the rules you created from the SMS Administrator console to compile the data into a report. This report is eventually sent to the site and accessible to queries and reports from WMI.

Procedure

When you configure the Software Metering Client Agent, the changes that you make in the **Software Metering Client Agent Properties** dialog box are valid for the entire SMS site.

To enable the Software Metering Client Agent:

1. In the SMS Administrator console, navigate to the **Client Agents** node under **Site Settings**.

2. In the details pane, right-click **Software Metering Client Agent**, and then click **Properties**.

   The **Software Metering Client Agent Properties** dialog box opens.

3. On the **General** tab, select **Enable Software metering on clients**.

4. On the **Schedule** tab, specify how frequently you want to collect program usage data and how often software metering rules are downloaded.

   You can view the metered data after the collection cycle is complete.

Note To avoid network performance problems, do not schedule downloads too frequently. The default download schedule is weekly for Legacy Clients and the polling for Advance Clients is hourly.

How to Verify the Installation and Operation of Software Metering

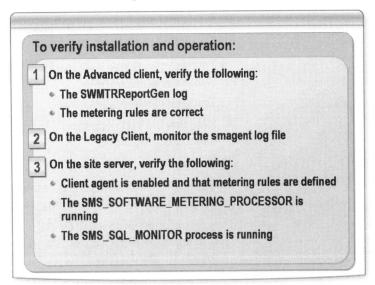

To verify installation and operation:

1 On the Advanced client, verify the following:
  * The SWMTRReportGen log
  * The metering rules are correct

2 On the Legacy Client, monitor the smagent log file

3 On the site server, verify the following:
  * Client agent is enabled and that metering rules are defined
  * The SMS_SOFTWARE_METERING_PROCESSOR is running
  * The SMS_SQL_MONITOR process is running

You can verify that software metering is installed and operational by checking the status of the SMS Software Metering Client Agent or querying the WMI Instrumentation Test tool.

Procedures

To verify that the agent is installed and running successfully on the clients:

1. On the Advanced Client, use SMS Trace to monitor the \%windir%\system32\ccm\logs\SWMTRReportGen.log log file.

   a. While the log is open, in Control Panel, open **Systems Management**.

   b. On the **Actions** tab, force a Software Metering Usage Report Cycle.

   c. Verify that an entry indicating that a report was successfully generated appears.

   d. Verify that Mtrmgr.log contains the appropriate strings.

   For example, if you launched Calc.exe, you would verify that the following string appears:

   Tracking creation Id=… PID=…\calc.exe appears.

   Note that the PID corresponds to the decimal value that this application has in Task Manager.

2. On the Advanced Client, use PolicySpy to verify that the software metering rules are correct.

   a. Click the **Actual** tab, and then expand **CCM_SoftwareMeteringRule**.

   b. Verify the details of each rule.

3. On the Legacy Client, use SMS Trace to monitor the \%windir%\ms\sms\logs\smagent.log log file.

   a. While this log is open, launch some of the metered applications.

   b. Verify that the appropriate strings appear in the log.

      For example, if you launched Calc.exe, you would verify that the following string appears:

      Tracking creation Id=… PID=…\calc.exe appears.

      Note that the PID corresponds to the decimal value that this application has in Task Manager.

4. On the site server, verify the following:

   a. Verify that the client agent is enabled, and that metering rules have been defined using the SMS Administrator console.

   b. Verify that the SMS_SOFTWARE_METERING_PROCESSOR is running using SMS Service Manager. This processor prepares the client reports for the database.

   c. Verify that the SMS_SQL_MONITOR process is running using SMS Service Manager. This process summarizes the raw data.

Note   Since the default for collecting data from the client is seven days and summarization takes place once a day, you might wait for up to eight days for the first data to be viewable. Therefore, summarized data will not be immediately forthcoming.

How to Isolate Problems with Software Metering

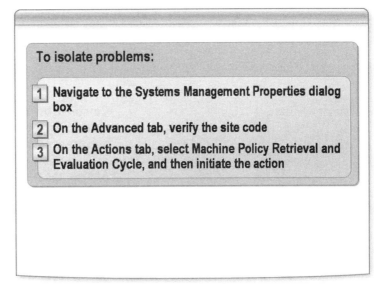

To isolate problems:

1. Navigate to the Systems Management Properties dialog box
2. On the Advanced tab, verify the site code
3. On the Actions tab, select Machine Policy Retrieval and Evaluation Cycle, and then initiate the action

If you encounter problems with software metering, some factors you can check include the SMS site number and the policies.

Procedure to view the SMS site number

Verify the SMS site code. Check the site number to make sure that you are monitoring the right site.

To view the SMS site code:

1. In Control Panel, double-click the **Systems Management** icon.

   The **Systems Management Properties** dialog box appears.

2. Click the **Advanced** tab and verify that the correct site code is displayed.

Procedure to refresh policies on the Advanced Client

Refresh the policies. Ensure that the policies are up to date.

To refresh policies on the Advanced Client:

1. In Control Panel, open **Systems Management**.

2. On the **Actions** tab, select **Machine Policy Retrieval & Evaluation Cycle**.

3. Click **Initiate Action**.

Procedure to refresh policies on the Legacy Client

To refresh policies on the Legacy Client:

1. In Control Panel, open **Systems Management**.

2. On the **Sites** tab, select a site.

3. Click **Update Configuration**.

Practice: Using Software Metering

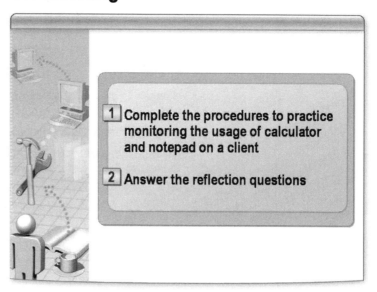

Instructions

Complete the procedures to practice monitoring the usage of calculator and notepad on a client. Answer the reflection questions that follow.

In this practice, use the following values:

Variable	Value
Virtual machine—SMS Site 1	Dublin
Dublin administrator	JaePa (Jae Pak)
Virtual machine—domain controller	Glasgow
Domain administrator	Administrator
Virtual machine—SMS Advanced Client	Bonn
Bonn administrator	SMartinez (Sandra Martinez)

Procedures

▶ **To create a rule to meter the Windows calculator**

1. Verify that Glasgow and Dublin virtual machines are running.

2. On the Dublin virtual machine, click **Start**, point to **All Programs**, point to **Systems Management Server**, and then click **SMS Administrator Console**.

3. On the console tree of the SMS Administrator console, expand **Site Database (001 – NWTraders)**, and then click **Software Metering Rules**.

4. Right-click **Software Meeting Rules**, point to **New**, and then click **Software Metering Rule**.

5. In the **Software Metering Rule Properties** dialog box, on the **General** tab, in the **Name** box, type **CalcRule**, and then click **Browse**.

6. In the **Open** dialog box, browse to C:\WINDOWS\system32\.

7. Click **calc.exe**, and then click **Open**.

8. In the **Version** box, type * (asterisk).

9. Click **OK**.

▶ **To create a rule to meter Notepad**

1. On the console tree of the SMS Administrator console, right-click **Software Metering Rules**, point to **New**, and then click **Software Metering Rule**.

2. Right-click **Software Meeting Rules**, point to **New**, and then click **Software Metering Rule**.

3. In the **Software Metering Rule Properties** dialog box, on the **General** tab, in the **Name** box, type **NoteRule** and then click **Browse**.

4. In the **Open** dialog box, browse to C:\WINDOWS\system32\.

5. Click **notepad.exe**, and then click **Open**.

6. In the **Version** box, type * (asterisk).

7. Click **OK**.

▶ **To enable the Software Metering Client Agent**

1. On the console tree of the SMS Administrator console, under **Site Database (001 – NWTraders)**, expand **Site Hierarchy**, expand **001 NWTraders**, expand **Site Settings**, and then click **Client Agents**.

2. In the details pane, right-click **Software Metering Client Agent**, and then click **Properties**.

3. In the **Software Metering Client Agent Properties** dialog box, on the **General** tab, select the **Enable software metering on clients** check box.

4. On the **Schedule** tab, under the **Data collection schedule** area, click **Schedule**.

5. In the **Schedule** dialog box, in the **Recur every** box, type or select **1**, and then click **OK**.

6. On the **Schedule** tab, under the **Metering rules download schedule** area, click **Schedule**.

7. In the **Schedule** dialog box, in the **Recur every** boxes, type or select **3**, select **hours**, and then click **OK**.

8. On the **Software Metering Client Agent Properties** dialog box, click **OK**.

9. Close the SMS Administrator console.

► **To force a refresh of the client's configuration**

1. On the Bonn virtual machine, click **Start**, and then click **Control Panel**.

2. Click **Performance and Maintenance**, and then click **Systems Management**.

3. On the **Actions** tab, click **Machine Policy Retrieval & Evaluation Cycle**, and then click **Initiate Action**.

4. Click **OK** twice.

> **Note** Be sure to wait about two minutes for the policy update to complete before moving on to the next step. (The Component status will not automatically refresh while the Systems Management Properties box is open.)

5. Click **Systems Management**, then click the **Components** tab, and verify that the status of the **SMS Software Metering Agent** appears as **Enabled**.

6. Click **OK**.

7. Close any open windows.

► **To create test data on the client**

1. On the Bonn virtual machine, click **Start**, point to **All Programs**, point to **Accessories**, and then click **Notepad**.

2. Click **Start**, point to **All Programs**, point to **Accessories**, and then click **Calculator**.

3. Close and open the Windows Calculator and Notepad several times.

   This will generate test metering data in the log files.

► **To force a usage report on the client**

1. On the Bonn virtual machine, click **Start**, and then click **Control Panel**.

2. Click **Performance and Maintenance**, and then click **Systems Management**.

3. On the **Actions** tab, click **Software Metering Usage Report Cycle**, and then click **Initiate Action**.

4. In the **Software Metering Usage Report Cycle** message box, click **OK**.

> **Note** You will need to wait about one minute before proceeding to the next step.

5. Click **Machine Policy Retrieval & Evaluation Cycle**, and then click **Initiate Action**.

6. In the **Machine Policy Retrieval & Evaluation Cycle** message box, click **OK**.

7. Click **OK**, and then close any open windows.

▶ **To examine the MeterRules.MRX rule file created on the CAP**

1. On the Dublin virtual machine, click **Start**, and then click **Windows Explorer**.

2. In Windows Explorer, browse to C:\CAP_001\swmproc.box\data\..

3. Right-click **MeterRules.MRX**, and then click **Open With**.

4. In the **Caution** message box, click **Open With**.

5. In the **Windows** message box, click **Select the program from a list**, and then click **OK**.

6. Click **Internet Explorer**, and then click **OK**.

7. Verify that **CalcRule** and **NoteRule** are enabled by finding the following lines in the file (type the **RuleID** in each space provided):

   • **CalcRule**

   ```
   <MeterRule Enabled="TRUE" ExplFileName="calc.exe"
   ...
   RuleID="_____"
   ```

   • **NoteRule**

   ```
   <MeterRule Enabled="TRUE" ExplFileName="notepad.exe"
   ...
   RuleID="_____"
   ```

8. Close any open windows.

▶ **To verify the metering on the client**

1. On the Bonn virtual machine, click **Start**, point to **All Programs**, point to **SMS 2003 Toolkit 1**, and then click **SMS Trace**.

2. In the **SMS Trace** message box, click **Yes**.

3. Maximize the SMS Trace window, and then, on the **File** menu, click **Open**.

4. In the **File name** box, type **C:\Windows\system32\CCM\logs\mtrmgr.log** and then click **Open**.

5. Scroll to the bottom of the log file and look for one of the following entries:

   • Calculator

   ```
   Creation event received for process xxx
   Process ID xxx is for process C:\WINDOWS\system32\calc.exe
   Found match against RuleID 00100yyy
   Tracked usage for process xxx
   ```

   • Notepad

   ```
   Creation event received for process xxx
   Process ID xxx is for process C:\WINDOWS\system32
   \notepad.exe
   Found match against RuleID 00100yyy
   Tracked usage for process xxx
   ```

   One of these set of lines is generated each time you open the Windows Calculator or Notepad.

The **Process ID** *xxx* corresponds to the decimal value that this application has in task manager.

The **RuleID 00100***yyy* is the rule number automatically assigned when you created each software metering rule; the number displayed will match the number you recorded for each rule in the previous task.

The **Found match** and **Tracked usage** lines both indicate that the client is metering.

6. Verify that the client is metering by performing the following steps:

   a. With SMS Trace still open and maximized, click **Start**, point to **All Programs**, point to **Accessories**, and then click **Calculator**.

   b. Minimize the **Calculator** window after it opens.

   c. Notice that a new log entry has been generated in the **mtrmgr.log** file for **calc.exe** that is identical to that shown in step 4; the only detail that changes is the **Product ID**.

   d. Open several more instances of the Calculator, and you will see the SMS Trace log register each process, verifying that the client is metering.

7. Close all open windows.

Note In the next module, you will use SMS reports to view software metering data on the site server.

Reflection questions

1. Can Software Metering account for the same application running locally, as well as from a Terminal Services or Remote Desktop session?

   _____

   _____

   _____

2. Can applications be monitored if the client is either disconnected, or logged off from the network?

   _____

   _____

   _____

3. If the name of the executable file has been altered, can software metering still track usage?

   _____

   _____

   _____

Discussion: Collecting Inventory and Software Metering

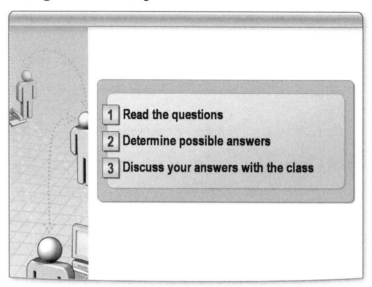

Review questions

1. A department in your organization has deployed a user application with expensive per-user licenses. How can you use software inventory and software metering to help ensure that your organization is getting the most value from this application?

   _____

   _____

   _____

2. Your organization wants to use software inventory and file collection but needs to avoid unnecessary client processes. How can you configure software inventory and file collection to accomplish this goal?

   _____

   _____

   _____

3. The data collected through inventory collection and software metering is historical. If that usage activity changes rapidly in your organization, what can you do to ensure that you are collecting the most accurate information?

_____

_____

_____

4. In what situations would you use or modify each of the following inventory files?

    -   IDMIF

    -   NOIDMIF

    -   SMS_def.mof

_____

_____

_____

Microsoft®

Module 6: Querying and Reporting Data

Contents

Overview

- Introduction to the Architecture of Data and Status Queries
- Creating and Running Queries
- Configuring and Deploying a Reporting Point
- Configuring and Running Reports
- Creating and Running Dashboards

Introduction

You can create and run queries to locate objects in a Microsoft® Systems Management Server (SMS) site database that match your query criteria. Queries are most useful for extracting information related to resource discovery, inventory data, and status messages. Reports allow system administrators to easily organize and display information about the computers managed by SMS. Reports are managed in the SMS Administrator console, but they are viewed in either the SMS Administrator console or Microsoft Internet Explorer. In this module, you will create, run, and view queries and reports. You will also learn how to deploy the reporting point site system.

Objectives

After completing this module, you will be able to:

- Describe the architecture of data and status queries.

- Create and run queries.

- Configure and deploy a reporting point.

- Configure and run reports.

- Create and run dashboards.

Lesson: Introduction to the Architecture of Data and Status Queries

---

- What Is a Query?
- What Is an SMS Object Type?
- SMS Object Types Available for Building Queries
- Required and Optional Elements of an SMS Query
- The Role of the System Class in Identifying Inventory Data

Introduction

The purpose of a database query is to return information based on a set of criteria. The process begins when you create a query statement that defines the information you need. The query engine then searches the database for entries that match your criteria. The query result then displays the data that matched your criteria.

The process is the same for SMS queries. This lesson discusses the architecture that supports data queries and status message queries, in addition to various elements that comprise a query.

Lesson objectives

After completing this lesson, you will be able to:

- Describe a query.
- Describe an SMS object type.
- Describe the SMS object types that are available for building queries.
- Describe the required and optional elements of an SMS query.
- Describe the role of the system class in identifying inventory data.

What Is a Query?

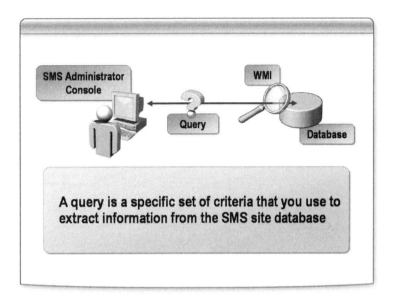

A query is a specific set of criteria that you use to extract information from the SMS site database. SMS queries store the criteria for sets of database objects that you want to find. A query searches the SMS site database for objects that match the query's criteria. Other SMS features, including reporting, collections, and status message queries, can query against objects within the SMS site database. You can also create stand-alone named queries, which are stored in the SMS site database and can be run from within the SMS Administrator console. The results that are returned by a named query appear in the details pane of the SMS Administrator console.

Queries can return information about most types of SMS objects, including sites, advertisements, packages, and named queries themselves. Queries are most commonly used to extract information related to users, user groups, discovered resources, and inventory data.

Queries are never run directly against the SQL database. SMS relies on the Windows Management Instrumentation (WMI) layer to expose its database information to the SMS Administrator console and other tools.

What Is an SMS Object Type?

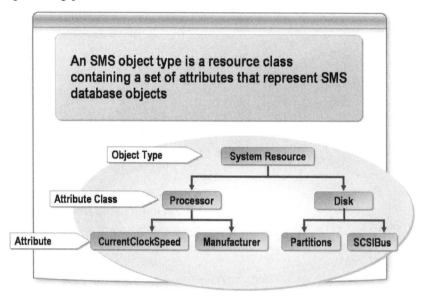

An SMS object type is a resource class containing a set of attributes that represent SMS database objects such as clients, users, user groups, packages, or advertisements. Each object type has specific attributes that describe those objects.

An attribute is the specific property for which the query searches. The attributes are organized into one or more attribute classes. Attribute classes group related attributes within an object type and contain the set of attributes that define the class. For example, the **System Resource** object type contains an attribute class called **Processor** with attributes such as **CurrentClockSpeed** and **Manufacturer**, and another attribute class called **Disk Driver** with attributes such as **Partitions** and **SCSIBus**. You use the attributes within an attribute class to construct a query.

When you create a query by using the SMS Query Builder, you can use the attributes of only one SMS object type at a time. By default, the System Resource object type is selected. You can use the <unspecified> object type to query against more than one SMS object type at a time.

SMS object types are WMI classes, and SMS attributes are WMI properties. Attribute classes are directly analogous to SQL table columns and Web-Based Enterprise Management (WBEM) properties.

SMS Object Types Available for Building Queries

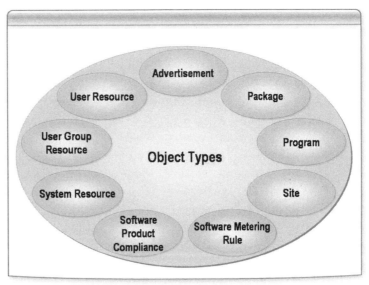

Following are brief descriptions of SMS object types that are available for building queries.

Object type	Description
Advertisement	A single attribute class with attributes representing the data in an SMS advertisement. SMS advertisements are used to alert users that software distributions are available.
Package	A single attribute class with attributes representing the data in an SMS package. Packages are basic units of software distribution, including programs and the source files required to run them.
Program	A single attribute class with attributes representing the data in an SMS program. Programs are software distribution command lines that run the program or command.
Site	A single attribute class with attributes representing an SMS site object.
Software Metering Rule	A single attribute class with attributes representing the data in an SMS software metering rule. A software metering rule represents a program that you want to monitor. In each rule, you specify an executable's file name, a version, and a language.
Software Product Compliance	A single attribute class with attributes related to product compliance. This object can help you to enforce product compliance by identifying clients that are not in compliance.

(continued)

Object type	Description
System Resource	Many attribute classes that together characterize the discovery data and inventory data of a system resource. Discovery data is characterized by a single attribute class called System Resource, and the inventory data is characterized by the other classes of the System Resource object type, for example, Logical Disk.
User Group Resource	A single attribute class representing the discovery data for User Group objects.
User Resource	A single attribute class representing the discovery data for User objects. This object type represents SMS users in an SMS site hierarchy.
Unspecified	When you do not specify an object type, you can only create a query by using WQL in the Query Language view. This can be useful for creating free-form WQL queries to run against classes other than those listed above, or to run against more than one SMS class.

Required and Optional Elements of an SMS Query

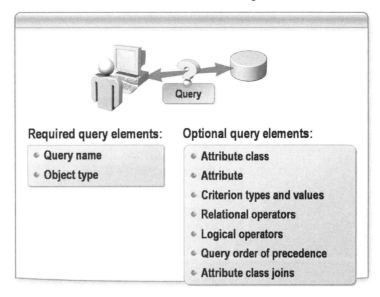

In case you need to create a query to suit a specific information need, there are certain elements that you must provide, and there are other elements that you might or might not need to provide, depending on your particular circumstance.

Required SMS query elements

You must specify the following elements in each query. They are found in the SMS Query Builder on the **General** tab of the **Query Properties** dialog box or on dialog boxes that open from that tab.

- *Query name*. This element is a unique name that identifies the query. The query name appears in Queries in the SMS Administrator console.

- *Object type*. This element is an SMS database object that defines the scope of the query. You must designate only one object type for each query. By default, SMS selects the System Resource object type.

Optional SMS query elements

Attribute class and attribute are not required elements. If you do not define a class or an attribute, SMS defaults to all classes or attributes. These elements are found in the SMS Query Builder on the **General** tab of the **Query Properties** dialog box.

- *Attribute class*. This element is a container object that groups related attributes. The attributes of an object type are organized into one or more attribute classes. The attribute classes that you can select include all attribute classes belonging to the object type for the current query. In the **Select Attribute** dialog box, you can select from a list of attribute classes for the object type you selected for this query, and then select an attribute of that class.

- *Attribute*. This element is the specific property for which the query searches. In the **Select Attribute** dialog box, you can select from the list of attributes for the attribute class you have chosen.

If you choose to refine your query, you will need to specify additional query elements. You can use the **Criteria** and **Joins** tabs of the **Query Statement Properties** dialog box to refine the query further.

The optional SMS query elements on these tabs include:

- *Criterion types and values.* You can use a criterion type to create an expression that compares a query attribute to a specified value or to another attribute. The criterion type that you select determines what is compared to the query attribute.

- *Relational operators.* Relational operators define how an expression's value is compared to the specified attribute. The relational operators that are available depend on the data type of the attribute.

- *Logical operators.* In SMS, you can use logical operators to join two expressions within a query. The logical operators permitted in SMS are AND, OR, and NOT.

- *Query order of precedence.* Before you can obtain the results you want, you must understand the order in which WMI Query Language (WQL) evaluates the logical operators. On the **Criteria** tab of the **Query Statement Properties** dialog box, the expressions are evaluated from top to bottom, except for expressions in parentheses, which always come first. In WQL, expressions are evaluated in the following order:

  1. Expressions within parentheses

  2. Expressions preceded by NOT

  3. Expressions joined by AND

  4. Expressions joined by OR

- *Attribute class joins.* You use attribute class join operations to specify how to combine data from two different attribute classes. When you use an attribute from an attribute class that is not yet in the query, the SMS Query Builder automatically creates a new join for this attribute class. Suitable joins are automatically created when the query is built. Users typically do not need to use the **Joins** tab of the **Query Statement Properties** dialog box. However, there are certain kinds of queries that can only be expressed by manually entering new joins or by modifying the ones that are automatically created.

The Role of the System Class in Identifying Inventory Data

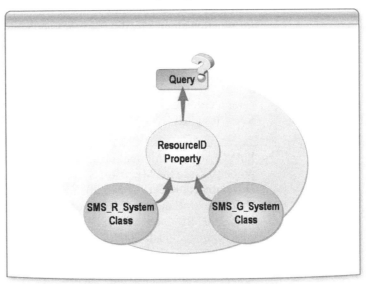

How queries use system classes

When you build an SMS query, you specify the attribute or attributes within an object type that the query uses to search the SMS site database. Any database objects that match one or more specified attributes are returned by the query.

An object type is a class containing a set of attributes that represent an SMS database object, such as a client, a user, a user group, a package, or an advertisement. The set of attributes for an object type describes the object. Related attributes are grouped together into attribute classes.

Note SMS object types are WMI classes, and SMS attributes are WMI properties.

Primary system classes

Most of the queries that you create are based on the following classes:

- *The SMS_R_System class*. SMS_Resource is the parent class of all discovery classes: SMS_R_System, SMS_R_User, and SMS_R_UserGroup. The SMS_R_System class contains discovery data for all discovered computers. This class includes properties (attributes) such as IPAddress, OperatingSystemNameandVersion, and Name (system name).

- *The SMS_G_System classes*. SMS_G_System is the parent class for all inventory classes. For example, the SMS_G_System_LOGICAL_DISK attribute class contains information about a client's logical disk drive, such as Availability, Name, FileSystem, and FreeSpace.

The ResourceID property links the SMS_R_System class and the SMS_G_System classes.

How SMS collects inventory data

If you configure hardware inventory on your SMS site, the Hardware Inventory Client Agent gathers information about the hardware on each client. If you configure software inventory, the Software Inventory Client Agent collects information about specific file types and collects the files you specify. SMS passes this information through the client access point (CAP) or management point (MP) to the site server and incorporates hardware and software information into the SMS site database. When the data is available, you can use a query to obtain data from the SMS site database about clients that meet certain criteria, such as all clients that have less than 256 megabytes (MB) of RAM installed.

Note For more information about SMS object classes, attributes, and properties, see the Microsoft Systems Management Server 2003 Software Development Kit. The SMS 2003 SDK is an excellent source for information about the SMS database and its object classes and attributes. To download the SMS 2003 SDK, see the MSDN® Web site at http://www.microsoft.com/smserver/downloads/2003.

Practice: Describing the Architecture of Data and Status Queries

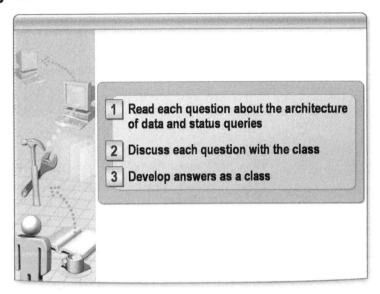

Instructions

Read the following questions about the architecture of data and status queries, discuss possible answers with other students, and then develop answers as a class.

Discussion questions

1. What are the SMS object types that you can query on?

   _____

   _____

   _____

2. What is the difference between a data query and status query?

   _____

   _____

   _____

Lesson: Creating and Running Queries

- How to Create and Run a Data Query
- Demonstration: How to Use a Data Query
- How to Create and Run a Status Message Query
- Demonstration: How to View a Status Message Query
- How to Export and Import Queries
- What Are Security Rights?
- How to Configure Class and Instance Security on Queries
- Demonstration: How to Configure Class and Instance Security on Queries
- How to View WQL Query Statements
- Analogous Concepts in SQL Server and WMI
- Demonstration: How to View WQL Query Statements

Introduction

SMS 2003 provides many predefined queries that you can either use as delivered or modify. For example, by running queries, you can retrieve the list of all clients running a specific operating system or all clients with an almost full hard disk drive. This information helps you to anticipate software and hardware upgrades and can help you to make other administrative decisions.

Lesson objectives

After completing this lesson, you will be able to:

- Create and run a data query.
- Create and run a status message query.
- Export and import queries.
- Describe security rights.
- Configure class and instance security on queries.
- View WQL query statements.
- Describe analogous concepts in Microsoft SQL Server™ and WMI.

How to Create and Run a Data Query

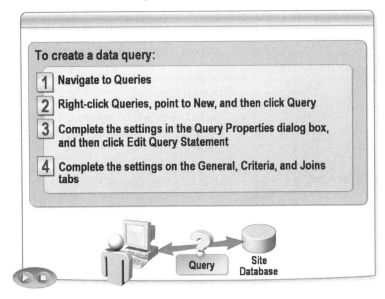

To create a data query:

1 Navigate to Queries

2 Right-click Queries, point to New, and then click Query

3 Complete the settings in the Query Properties dialog box, and then click Edit Query Statement

4 Complete the settings on the General, Criteria, and Joins tabs

Query Site Database

You can create and run queries to locate objects in an SMS site that match your query criteria. These objects include items such as specific types of computers or user groups. Queries can return most types of SMS objects, including sites, collections, packages, and saved queries themselves. However, queries are most useful for extracting information related to resource discovery, inventory data, and status messages.

Guidelines for creating a data query

To create a query, you must have Create permission for the Query security object class.

When you create a query, you will need to specify a minimum of two parameters: where to search and what to search for. For example, to find out the amount of hard disk space that is available on all personal computers in an SMS site, you can create a query to search the System Resource object type and search for available hard disk space.

After you create an initial query, you can specify additional query criteria. For example, you can specify that the query results include only personal computers with more than 100 MB of available hard disk space. You can also modify how results are displayed so that you can view the results in an order that is meaningful to you. For example, you can specify that the results be ordered by the amount of available hard disk space in either ascending or descending order.

Procedure to create a data query

To create a data query:

1. In the SMS Administrator console, navigate to Queries by expanding **Systems Management Server** and then **Site Database**.

2. Right-click **Queries**, point to **New**, and then click **Query**.

3. Complete the settings in the **Query Properties** dialog box, and then click **Edit Query Statement**.

4. In the **Query Statement Properties** dialog box, complete the settings on the following tabs:

    *   Use the **General** tab to specify the attributes to be returned in the results of the query, the order in which the attribute results are presented within columns, and how they are sorted.

    *   Use the **Criteria** tab to refine query criteria and limit the results that are returned.

    *   Use the **Joins** tab to combine data from two different attribute classes or to modify an existing join operation. Joins refine your query and help ensure that useful data returns.

Guidelines for running a data query

You need Read permission to run a query; if you do not have Read permission for a query, that query will not display in the list of queries available to you in the SMS Administrator console. Query results are limited to the security objects for which you have Read permission.

When a query is run, SMS searches the SMS site database for objects that match the query criteria. The results of the query appear in the details pane of the SMS Administrator console.

You can modify how these results are displayed by using the **General** tab in the **Query Statement Properties** dialog box.

You can modify the order in which the query results are displayed by moving the query attributes up or down in the table. The order of the attributes in this table, from top to bottom, is the order in which they are displayed within the query results columns, from left to right. In other words, the first attribute listed in this table is displayed in the first column on the left and the last attribute listed in this table is displayed in the last column on the right.

You can also modify how query results are sorted. The sort order determines the order in which the results are displayed within the columns. Choose from ascending, descending, or unsorted. To modify the sort order, select a query attribute, and then click **Properties**.

Finally, after a query is run, you can rearrange the result columns in the details pane. The rearranged order will be saved as a user preference across sessions.

Procedure to run a data query

To run a data query:

1. In the SMS Administrator console, navigate to Queries by expanding **Systems Management Server** and **Site Database**, and then click **Queries**.

2. Right-click the query that you want to run, and then click **Run Query**.

    The results of the query appear in the details pane of the SMS Administrator console. However, if you run the query from the details pane (rather than from the console tree), you must right-click the query, click **Run Query**, right-click the query again, and then click **Open** to view the results.

    Note Some invalid queries do not generate errors. Therefore, if a query does not return data, it might be invalid. Review the query to ensure that, for example, it is not querying a resource for a value that the resource does not possess.

Demonstration: How to Use a Data Query

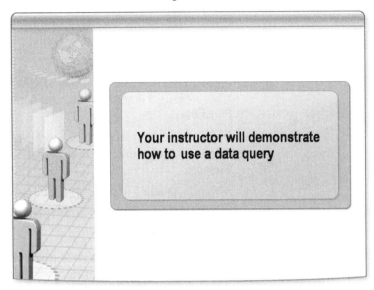

In this demonstration, you will see how to use a data query.

Your instructor will use the following values in this demonstration.

Variable	Value
Virtual Computer—SMS Site 1	Dublin
Dublin Administrator	JaePa (Jae Pak)
Virtual machine—domain controller	Glasgow
Domain administrator	Administrator

Important   These steps are included for your information and you should not attempt to perform them in the classroom.

Demonstration steps performed by instructor only

▶ **To use a data query**

1. If you have not already done so, log the Glasgow virtual machine on to the NWTRADERS domain with a user name of **Administrator** and a password of **P@ssw0rd**.

   After the Glasgow virtual machine opens, you can minimize it.

2. If you have not already done so, log the Dublin virtual machine on to the NWTRADERS domain with a user name of **JaePa** and a password of **P@ssw0rd**.

3. On the Dublin virtual machine, click **Start**, point to **All Programs**, point to **Systems Management Server**, and then click **SMS Administrator Console**.

4. In the console tree of the SMS Administrator console, expand **Site Database (001 – NWTraders)**, expand **Queries**, and then click **All Non-Client Systems**.

   Note The details pane displays **There are no items to show in this view**.

5. Right-click **All Non-Client Systems**, and then click **Run Query**.

   Note The details pane now displays **Glasgow** and **Paris**.

6. Close the SMS Administrator console.

7. Leave the Glasgow and Dublin virtual machines running.

How to Create and Run a Status Message Query

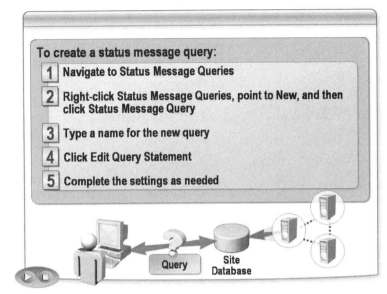

To create a status message query:

1. Navigate to Status Message Queries

2. Right-click Status Message Queries, point to New, and then click Status Message Query

3. Type a name for the new query

4. Click Edit Query Statement

5. Complete the settings as needed

Query   Site Database

SMS status messages report information about SMS component behavior and data flow. SMS status messages are categorized by severity and type.

A status message query is a query that is specific to status messages. In the SMS Administrator console, Status Message Queries contains all status message queries that are currently defined in the SMS site database.

Important Because an SMS site database can store tens of thousands of status messages, it is recommended that you restrict the number of messages that you view at one time.

Guidelines for creating a status message query

You must have Create permission for the Query security object class to perform this procedure.

To create a status message query, use the **Status Message Query Properties** dialog box to enter a name for the query, to specify the attributes that are returned in the query results, and to determine how the results are displayed in the details pane of the SMS Administrator console.

Procedure to create a status message query

To create a status message query:

1. In the SMS Administrator console, navigate to Status Message Queries by expanding **Systems Management Server**, expanding **Site Database**, and then expanding **System Status**.

2. Right-click **Status Message Queries**, point to **New**, and then click **Status Message Query**. This opens the **Status Message Query Properties** dialog box.

3. In the **Name** box, type a name for the new query (up to 50 printable characters).

4. Click **Edit Query Statement**. This opens the **Query Statement Properties** dialog box.

Note Site database queries are different from status message queries. Do not paste text from a standard SMS query into a status message query.

---

5. Complete the settings as needed on the **Criteria** tab, and then click **OK**.

Guidelines for running a status message query

You need Read permission to run a query; if you do not have Read permission for a query, that query will not display in the list of queries available to you in the SMS Administrator console. You also need Read permission to the Status Messages class to read the individual messages.

After you run the status message query, all messages that match the query criteria you specified will appear in the Status Message Viewer main window. Status Message Viewer is the primary tool for viewing status messages that are stored in an SMS site database. Status Message Viewer is similar to Event Viewer, but it has additional capabilities that allow you to:

- Export and print status messages.

- Start multiple viewers to compare messages for troubleshooting.

- Select multiple rows of messages to create your own grouping.

- Copy messages to the Clipboard (with tab-delimited columns) to support pasting to applications such as Microsoft Office Excel and Microsoft Office Word.

- Delete status messages (if you have permission to do so).

- Find, filter, or sort on each column.

- Specify which columns are displayed and specify their order and width.

- Select the font used in the Status Message Viewer.

- Select additional startup and refresh options. (Options are automatically saved when you exit Status Message Viewer.)

Procedure to run a status message query

To run a status message query:

1. In the SMS Administrator console, navigate to Status Message Queries by expanding **Systems Management Server** and **Site Database**, and then click **Status Message Queries**.

2. In the details pane, right-click the status message query you want to run, and then click **Show Messages**.

After Status Message Viewer runs, all messages that match the query criteria that you specified will appear in the Status Message Viewer main window.

Tip SMS2003StatusMessages.xls is a downloadable troubleshooting tool that lists all status messages generated by SMS 2003. You can filter messages by message ID, by message type (such as error messages, warning messages), or by the component that generates the message. The link to this spreadsheet is included on the Internet links pages of the Student Materials compact disc.

Demonstration: How to View a Status Message Query

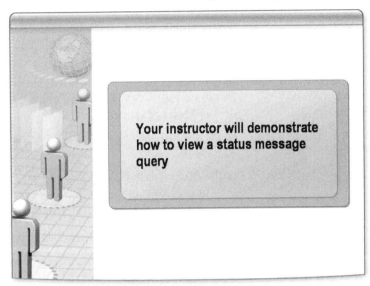

In this demonstration, you will see how to use a status message query.

Your instructor will use the following values in this demonstration.

Variable	Value
Virtual machine—SMS Site 1	Dublin
Dublin Administrator	JaePa (Jae Pak)
Virtual machine—domain controller	Glasgow
Domain administrator	Administrator

Important   These steps are included for your information and you should not attempt to perform them in the classroom.

Demonstration steps performed by instructor only

▶ **To view a status message query**

1. Verify that the Glasgow and Dublin virtual machines are running.

2. On the Dublin virtual machine, click **Start**, point to **All Programs**, point to **Systems Management Server**, and then click **SMS Administrator Console**.

3. In the console tree of the SMS Administrator console, expand **Site Database (001 – NWTraders)**, expand **System Status**, and then click **Status Message Queries**.

4. In the details pane, right-click **All Status Messages**, and then click **Show Messages**.

5. In the **All Status Messages** dialog box, click **Select data and time**, and then select **1 day ago**.

6. Click **OK**.

7. Review the results of the query.

8. Close the SMS Status Message Viewer window and the SMS Administrator console.

9. Leave the Glasgow and Dublin virtual machines running.

How to Export and Import Queries

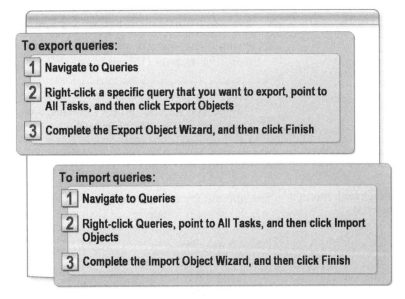

You can use the export and import object wizards to export and import individual or multiple collections, queries, or reports. Both the export and the import processes work with Managed Object Format (MOF) files. MOF is a standard text file that contains computer management information in a standard format that can be loaded into the SMS site database.

Occasionally, you might want to share a query with administrators of other SMS sites. To accomplish this, you can use the Export Object Wizard to export query object definitions from your SMS site database to a MOF file.

You can use the Import Object Wizard to import these MOF files back into the site's database or into another site's database. However, when running a query that was imported from another site, the wizard runs against the current site's database.

Guidelines for exporting a query

You can use the Export Object Wizard to export individual collections, queries, or reports or multiples of one type of object, such as several reports. When you export a query, the query's definitions are written to a MOF file that then can be imported. However, the query's Object ID is not written to that MOF file. This prevents an existing query from being accidentally replaced if the MOF file is imported and the Object ID of the imported query matches the Object ID of an existing query.

To use the Export Object Wizard, you must have Read permission for any object that you want to export.

You can use the Export Object Wizard to export objects from only one object class at a time. MOF files that are created by using the Export Object Wizard contain only one object class.

Procedure to export a query

To export a query:

1. In the SMS Administrator console, navigate to Queries by expanding **Systems Management Server** and **Site Database**, and then click **Queries**.

2. Right-click a specific query that you want to export, point to **All Tasks**, and then click **Export Objects** to open the Export Object Wizard.

Note If you want to export more than one query at a time, navigate to Queries and then right-click **Queries** to open the Export Object Wizard. Select the queries you want to export, and then complete the wizard.

---

3. Complete the Export Object Wizard, and then click **Finish**.

Guidelines for importing a query

The Import Object Wizard guides you through the steps that are necessary to import collections, queries, or reports into the SMS site database from a MOF file. To use the Import Object Wizard, you must have class Create permission for each object type that you want to import.

When you import queries, ensure that none of the imported queries has the same name as an existing query. If you do import a query with the same name, the data for the existing query is replaced without warning. To change the name of a query in a MOF file, you can open and edit the MOF file with any text editor.

You can use the Import Object Wizard to import user-created MOF files that contain objects from multiple object classes. However, if you do not have Create permission for all object classes in an MOF file, some objects might not be imported. For example, if an MOF file contains both reports and collections and you have Create permission only for the Reports object class, the collections are not imported.

Procedure to import a query

To import a query:

1. In the SMS Administrator console, navigate to Queries by expanding **Systems Management Server** and **Site Database**, and then click **Queries**.

2. Right-click **Queries**, point to **All Tasks**, and then click **Import Objects** to open the Import Object Wizard.

3. Complete the Import Object Wizard, and then click **Finish**.

What Are Security Rights?

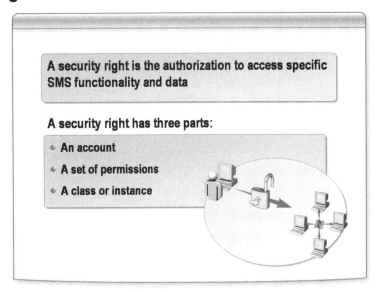

SMS 2003 grants access to its functionality based on security rights. Configuring SMS security means creating various security rights so that SMS administrators have access to certain functionality and data. A security right has three parts:

- *An account*. The Windows User account or group name to which the security right applies, such as Ben Smith, administrator, or power users.

- *A set of permissions*. The type of action that is permitted, such as read, create, or delete.

- *A class or instance*. The entity on which the permission acts. Security objects can be either a class (such as all queries) or an instance (such as a particular query).

SMS administrators who do not have permissions for all entities in the SMS Administrator console will only see those entities for which they have permissions.

Security Rights lists all the currently defined security rights in the SMS system. By default, SMS creates every possible security right for these two users:

- The user who installed SMS

- NT AUTHORITY\SYSTEM (the local system account)

When Security Rights is selected, the details pane contains the following columns:

- *Name*. A Windows user or user group to whom the security right applies.

- *Class*. The class of security objects to which the security right applies.

- *Instance*. The instance of a security object to which the security right applies. If the right applies to a class, this column contains (All Instances).

- *Permissions*. The permissions enabled for a security right.

How to Configure Class and Instance Security on Queries

To create a security right:

1 Navigate to Security Rights

2 Right-click Security Rights, click New, and then click either
   Class Security Right or Instance Security Right

3 Select the user to which you want to grant permissions

4 Select the permissions you want the security right to have

To modify a security right:

1 Navigate to Security Rights

2 Right-click a security right, and then click Properties

3 Modify the permissions

Guidelines for creating a security right

You must have Modify permission for the Site security object class or instance to perform this procedure.

When you create a security right for a collection, SMS enables Read permission by default.

Procedure to create a security right

To create a security right:

1. In the SMS Administrator console, navigate to Security Rights by expanding **Systems Management Server** and then **Site Database**.

2. Right-click **Security Rights**, point to **New**, and then click either **Class Security Right** or **Instance Security Right**.

3. In the **Security Right Properties** dialog box, select the **User Name** to whom you want to give the security right.

Note The list of users from which you can make your selection only includes users who have existing rights to other objects in SMS.

4. Select the **Class** or **Instance** (for example, All Systems, Advertisement, Collection, Package, Query, and so forth).

5. Select the permissions you want the security right to have (for example, Administer, Delegate, Modify, Read, and so forth).

Note The list of permissions that appears depends on the class or instance you select.

Guidelines for modifying a security right

To modify a security right, you must have Modify permission for the Site security object class or instance.

You should not modify (or remove) the SMS rights for the local system account (NT Authority\SYSTEM). This version of SMS does not use those rights, but future versions or tools might require those rights.

Procedure to modify a security right

To modify a security right:

1. In the SMS Administrator console, navigate to Security Rights by expanding **Systems Management Server** and **Site Database**, and then click **Security Rights**.

2. In the details pane, right-click a security right, and then click **Properties**.

3. In the **Security Right Properties** dialog box, modify the permissions. Click the various permissions to toggle between selected and unselected.

Demonstration: How to Configure Class and Instance Security on Queries

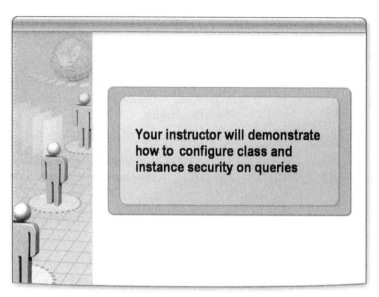

In this demonstration, you will see how to configure class and instance security on queries. Your instructor will use the following values in this demonstration.

Variable	Value
Virtual machine—SMS Site 1	Dublin
Dublin Administrator	JaePa (Jae Pak)
Virtual machine—domain controller	Glasgow
Domain administrator	Administrator

Important These steps are included for your information. Do not attempt to perform them in the classroom. If you perform these steps in the classroom environment, you might leave your computer in an incorrect state for upcoming practices.

▶ **To configure class and instance security on queries**

1. Verify that the Glasgow and Dublin virtual machines are running.

2. On the Dublin virtual machine, click **Start**, point to **All Programs**, point to **Systems Management Server**, and then click **SMS Administrator Console**.

3. In the console tree of the SMS Administrator console, expand **Site Database (001 – NWTraders)**, and then click **Queries**.

4. In the details pane, right-click **All Client Systems**, and then click **Properties**.

5. To give the Administrator all rights to *all* queries:

   a. On the **Security** tab, in the **Class security rights** section, click the **New** icon.

   b. In the **User name** box, type **NWTRADERS\Administrator**

   c. In the **Permissions** box, select all items.

   d. Click **OK**.

6. To give Judy Lew all security rights to this query instance:

   a. In the **Instance security rights** section, click the **New** icon.

   b. In the **User name** box, type **NWTRADERS\JudyLe**

   c. In the **Permissions** field, select all items.

   d. Click **OK**.

7. Click **OK**.

8. Close the SMS Administrator console.

9. Leave the Glasgow and Dublin virtual machines running.

How to View WQL Query Statements

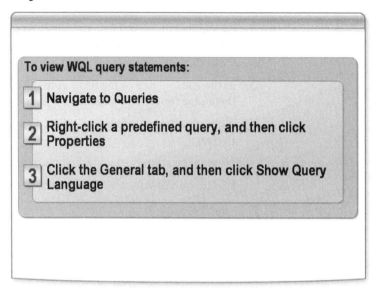

To view WQL query statements:

1 Navigate to Queries

2 Right-click a predefined query, and then click Properties

3 Click the General tab, and then click Show Query Language

You can create and edit query statements by:

- Using the **Query Statements Properties** dialog box in Query Design view and using the command buttons and properties on the **General**, **Criteria**, and **Joins** tabs.

- Using the **Query Statements Properties** dialog box in Query Language view and typing a WQL query statement into the **Query Statement** box.

SMS queries are similar to queries you might use with SQL Server, but SMS queries are defined in WQL (WMI Query Language), which is part of the WMI standard. You do not need to know WQL to build queries, but it is helpful to know WQL if you are building more complex queries.

Important   Use the Query Language view only if you have a good working knowledge of WQL. If you enter a query that is not valid (for example, one that is not syntactically correct), you will get an error message. If the query statement that you edit uses features of WQL that are not supported in the Query Design view, you cannot return to the Query Design view. However, you can still save and attempt to run the query.

Procedure

To view the WQL query statement associated with a predefined query:

1. In the SMS Administrator console, navigate to Queries by expanding **Systems Management Server** and **Site Database**, and then click **Queries**.

2. Right-click a predefined query and then click **Properties**.

3. Click **Edit Query Statement**.

4. In the **Query Statement Properties** dialog box, click the **General** tab, and then click **Show Query Language**.

   The WQL query statement appears in the Query statement text box.

Tip   To learn more about WQL, you can review WQL statements associated with the predefined queries provided in the SMS Administrator console.

Analogous Concepts in SQL Server and WMI

Conceptual Element	SQL Server	WMI
Individual items	Rows	Instances
The characteristics of items	Columns	Properties
Containers of columns and rows	Tables	Classes
Container of tables	Databases	Namespaces
Program code that functions on data	Stored procedures	Methods
Table characteristics	Table characteristics	Class qualifiers

SQL Server and WMI are radically different systems serving completely different purposes. WMI can store some data, but it is not built for the efficient large-scale storage and retrieval of data for which SQL Server is built. The programming interfaces are also completely different. However, relating some SQL Server concepts to roughly equivalent WMI concepts can help you to better understand WMI. The following table lists some analogous concepts in SQL Server and WMI.

Conceptual element	SQL Server	WMI
Individual items	Rows	Instances
The characteristics of items	Columns	Properties
Containers of columns and rows	Tables	Classes
Container of tables	Databases	Namespaces
Program code that functions on data	Stored procedures	Methods
Table characteristics	Table characteristics	Class qualifiers

Note A knowledge of WMI is a key requirement for scripting administrative tasks in SMS. Complete information about WMI and WQL can be found in the Microsoft Windows® Management Instrumentation Software Development Kit, which is available for download from the MSDN® Web site at http://msdn.microsoft.com.

Demonstration: How to View WQL Query Statements

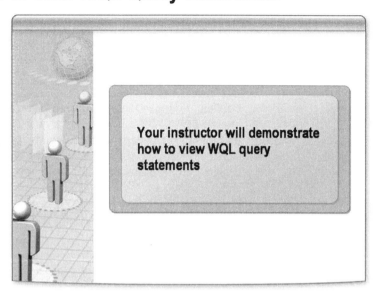

In this demonstration, you will see how to view WQL query statements.

Your instructor will use the following values in this demonstration.

Variable	Value
Virtual machine—SMS Site 1	Dublin
Dublin Administrator	JaePa (Jae Pak)
Virtual machine—domain controller	Glasgow
Domain administrator	Administrator

Important These steps are included for your information and you should not attempt to perform them in the classroom.

Demonstration steps performed by instructor only

▶ **To view WQL query statements**

1. Verify that the Glasgow and Dublin virtual machines are running.

2. On the Dublin virtual machine, click **Start**, point to **All Programs**, point to **Systems Management Server**, and then click the **SMS Administrator Console**.

3. In the console tree of the SMS Administrator console, expand **Site Database (001 – NWTraders)**, expand **System Status**, and then click **Status Message Queries**.

4. In the details pane, right-click **SQL Tasks Created, Modified, or Deleted**, and then click **Properties**.

   The **SQL Tasks Created, Modified, or Deleted Status Message Query Properties** dialog box appears.

5. In the **SQL Tasks Created, Modified, or Deleted Status Message Query Properties** dialog box, click **Edit Query Statement**.

6. In the **SQL Tasks Created, Modified, or Deleted Query Statement Properties** dialog box, click **Show Query Language**.

    Use this tab to work in the Query Language view. The query statement text area displays the query syntax. You can compose or edit a query manually by using WMI Query Language (WQL) commands. Statements can contain up to 4,096 characters.

    Caution   Use the Query Language view only if you have a good working knowledge of WQL. If you enter a query that is not valid (for example, one that is not syntactically correct), you will get an error message. If the query statement that you edit uses features of WQL that are not supported in design view, you cannot return to design view. However, you can still save and run the query.

7. Click **Show Query Design** to return to design view.

8. Click **Cancel** twice.

9. Close the SMS Administrator console.

10. Leave the Glasgow and Dublin virtual machines running.

Practice: Creating and Running Queries

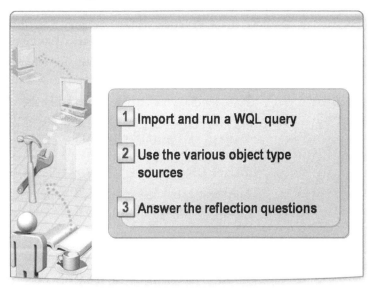

Instructions

Complete the procedures to practice creating your own custom query by importing, then modifying, an existing query. Then you will restrict access to this custom report. After you complete the procedures, answer the reflection questions.

In this practice, use the following values.

Variable	Value
Virtual machine—SMS Site 1	Dublin
Dublin Administrator	JaePa (Jae Pak)
Virtual machine–domain controller	Glasgow
Domain administrator	Administrator

Procedures

▶ **To import and run a WQL query**

1. If you have not already done so, log the Glasgow virtual machine on to the NWTRADERS domain with a user name of **Administrator** and a password of **P@ssw0rd**.

   After the Glasgow virtual machine opens, you can minimize it.

2. If you have not already done so, log the Dublin virtual machine on to the NWTRADERS domain with a user name of **JaePa** and a password of **P@ssw0rd**.

3. On the Dublin virtual machine, click **Start**, point to **All Programs**, point to **Systems Management Server**, and then click the **SMS Administrator Console**.

4. In the console tree of the SMS Administrator console, expand **Site Database (001 – NWTraders)**, right-click **Queries**, point to **New**, and then click **Query**.

5. In the **Query Properties** dialog box, in the **Name** box, type **Practice 'J' Users Query**, and then click **Import Query Statement**.

6. In the **Browse Query** dialog box, click **All Users**, and then click **OK**.

7. In the **Query Properties** dialog box, click **Edit Query Statement**.

8. In the **Practice 'J' Users Query Statement Properties** dialog box, on the **General** tab, click **Show Query Language**.

9. On the **Query Language** tab, type **where UniqueUserName like '%j%'** at the end of the Query statement.

   Verify that your change appears like the sample below:

   ```
   ...ResourceId, ResourceType, UniqueUserName from sms_r_user
   where UniqueUserName like '%j%'
   ```

10. Click **OK** twice.

11. In the console tree of the SMS Administrator console, expand **Queries** (if it isn't already expanded), and then click **Practice 'J' Users Query**.

   Note   The details panel shows **There are no items to show in this view**.

12. In the console tree, right-click **Practice 'J' Users Query**, and then click **Run Query**.

   Caution   Be sure to run queries from the console tree of the SMS Administrator console—*not* from the details panel! If you try to run a query in the details pane, no results will appear.

13. In the details pane, verify that the query returns **JaePa** and **JudyLe** in the **User Name** column.

14. Leave the SMS Administrator console open.

▶ **To set access restrictions to the query**

1. If you haven't already done so, in the console tree of the SMS Administrator console, expand **Site Database (001 – NWTraders)**, expand **System Status**, and then expand **Queries**.

2. Right-click **Practice 'J' Users Query** and then click **Properties**.

3. In the **Practice 'J' Users Query Statement Properties** dialog box, click the **Security** tab.

4. To give Sandra Martinez the permission to Read for this query instance.

   a. In the **Instance security rights** section, click the **New** icon.

   b. In the **User name** box, type **NWTRADERS\SMartinez**

   c. In the **Permissions** box, select **Read**.

   d. Click **OK**.

   e. Verify that **SMartinez** is displayed under the **Instance security rights** section with **Read** permissions.

5. In the **Practice 'J' Users Query Properties** dialog box, click **OK**.

6. Close the SMS Administrator console.

7. Leave the Glasgow and Dublin virtual machines running.

Reflection questions   Take a moment to think about your organization and its potential business needs.

1. What are the differences between queries and reports?

   _____

   _____

   _____

   _____

   _____

   _____

2. Why are attribute classes important when creating and using queries?

   _____

   _____

   _____

   _____

   _____

   _____

Lesson: Configuring and Deploying a Reporting Point

- **What Is a Reporting Point?**
- **The SMS Reporting Architecture**
- **What Is Report Viewer?**
- **How to Enable a Reporting Point**
- **Demonstration: How to Enable a Reporting Point**
- **Methods for Verifying the Installation of the Reporting Point**
- **Demonstration: How to Verify the Installation of the Reporting Point**
- **Reporting Point Security**
- **Demonstration: How to View Reporting Security**

Introduction

The SMS Reporting feature is implemented through the reporting point site system, which is installed on an IIS Server. In this lesson, you will learn how to configure and deploy the reporting point and verify its installation. You will also implement reporting security.

Lesson objectives

After completing this lesson, you will be able to:

- Describe the purpose and function of a reporting point.
- Describe the reporting architecture.
- Describe the purpose and function of the Report Viewer.
- Enable a reporting point.
- Describe the methods for verifying the reporting point installation.
- Identify methods to enhance reporting point security.

What Is a Reporting Point?

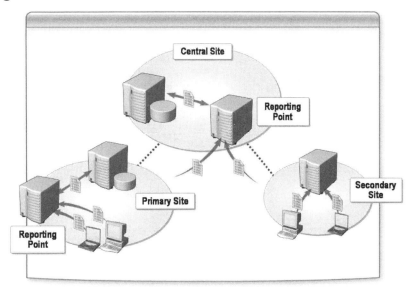

Before you can begin using SMS reporting, you must enable one or more of your site systems as a reporting point. A reporting point is a site system role that stores files that are used by Report Viewer and stores reports and dashboards.

Since reporting points communicate only with the local site database, you implement reporting points only on your primary sites, not on your secondary sites. When you set up a reporting point, SMS creates a designated Uniform Resource Locator (URL) that users can use to access that reporting point. If you anticipate heavy demand for reports in your site, you can create more than one reporting point and then point different groups of users to the different reporting point URLs.

The SMS Reporting Architecture

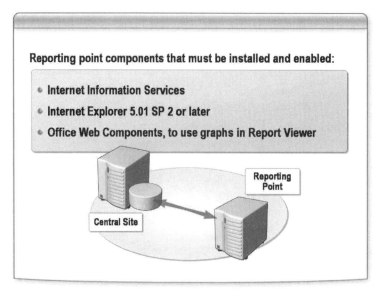

Reporting point components that must be installed and enabled:

- Internet Information Services
- Internet Explorer 5.01 SP 2 or later
- Office Web Components, to use graphs in Report Viewer

Central Site

Reporting Point

For a site system to function as a reporting point, the following requirements must be met:

- The site system server must have Microsoft Internet Information Services (IIS) installed and enabled.

- Microsoft Internet Explorer 5.01 Service Pack 2 or later must be installed on any server or client that uses Report Viewer.

- To use graphs in the reports, Microsoft Office Web Components must be installed.

Important   Upgrading a computer that is running IIS to Microsoft Windows Server™ 2003 requires that IIS be locked down by the IIS Lockdown tool. If you have an SMS reporting point on a computer running a Windows 2000 Server family operating system and you do not run the IIS Lockdown tool before you upgrade that server to Windows Server 2003, your reporting point will not be operable after the operating system upgrade. To reinstate reporting functionality, you must enable IIS after the upgrade by invoking IIS Manager in Administrative Tools.

Microsoft Office Web components

To display report data as a chart by using Report Viewer, you must have a licensed copy of Microsoft Office Web Components installed on the reporting point site system. Microsoft Office Web Components is a collection of Component Object Model (COM) controls that allow you to publish interactive data as part of a Web page. Used with Internet Explorer version 5.01 or later, Office Web Components allow you to view a published control (spreadsheet, chart, or database) on a Web page and to view data access pages.

Because organizations use various versions of Microsoft Office, the Office Web Components are not included on the SMS 2003 compact disc. However, the Office Web Components are installed with all Office 2003 editions, all Office XP editions, and all Office 2000 editions except Office 2000 Small Business.

What Is Report Viewer?

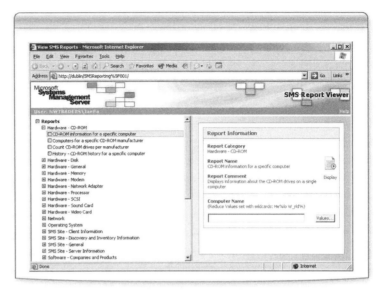

SMS 2003 uses files that are hosted on a reporting point to display database information in Report Viewer. *Report Viewer* is a browser-based application that you can start either from within the SMS Administrator console or by using a URL in Internet Explorer. When a user runs a report, the results are based on the data that is retrieved by the report's SQL statement. The SQL statement accesses read-only SQL Server views instead of SMS site database tables. The report retrieves the specified data and displays it in an Internet Explorer window.

When you set up a reporting point, SMS creates a designated URL that users can use to access that reporting point. To balance a heavy demand for reports in a larger site, you can enable more than one reporting point and then point different groups of users to different URLs for each reporting point. When you start Report Viewer from the SMS Administrator console, you select the specific reporting point that you want to use.

Interoperability issues with Report Viewer in a mixed-version hierarchy

Because client data from SMS 2.0 sites propagates to SMS 2003 sites, reports that you run in SMS 2003 sites include data from SMS 2.0 sites that was propagated to the SMS 2003 site database. However, the following interoperability issues exist with Report Viewer in a mixed-version hierarchy:

- You cannot use SMS 2003 Report Viewer to view reports that are created by Crystal Reports in SMS 2.0 sites.

- You cannot use the SMS 2003 Report Viewer to access an SMS 2.0 site database.

In both these circumstances, you can continue to use a stand-alone version of SMS 2.0 Crystal Reports to view SMS 2.0 reports, or the Web Reporting tool that is included with either of the SMS 2.0 feature packs.

How to Enable a Reporting Point

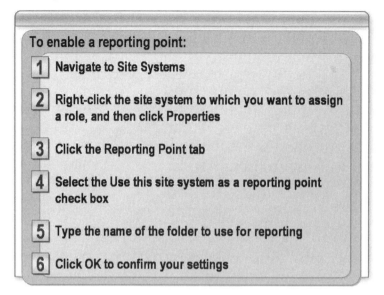

To enable a reporting point:

1 Navigate to Site Systems

2 Right-click the site system to which you want to assign a role, and then click Properties

3 Click the Reporting Point tab

4 Select the Use this site system as a reporting point check box

5 Type the name of the folder to use for reporting

6 Click OK to confirm your settings

To create and enable a reporting point, you must have Modify permissions for the SMS site.

Procedure

To enable a reporting point:

1. In the SMS Administrator console, navigate to Site Systems by expanding **Systems Management Server**, **Site Database**, **Site Hierarchy**, the appropriate site name, and **Site Settings**, and then click **Site Systems**.

2. Right-click the site system to which you want to assign a role, and then click **Properties**.

3. In the **Site System Properties** dialog box, click the **Reporting Point** tab.

4. Select the **Use this site system as a reporting point** check box.

5. In the **Report folder** box, type the name of the folder under the root folder for SMS 2003 to use for reporting. The default folder name is http://servername/SMSReporting_site code.

    In the **URL** box, the URL that users can use to access reports appears as a read-only field. The URL is determined based on the site server name and the report folder name.

6. Click **OK** to confirm your settings.

Tip The SMS 2003 Troubleshooting Flowchart bundle consists of flowcharts to help you troubleshoot SMS 2003 during the course of your day-to-day tasks. The Reporting Point Setup flowchart guides you through the tasks and decision points involved in this process. This bundle is available as an executable file at the Microsoft Download Center. The link to this bundle is included on the Internet links pages of the Student Materials compact disc.

Demonstration: How to Enable a Reporting Point

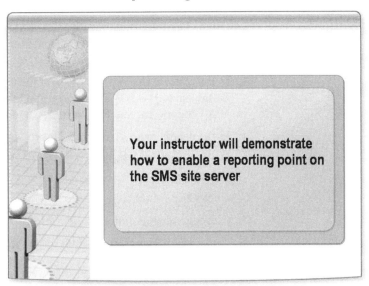

In this demonstration, you will see how to enable a reporting point. Your instructor will use the following values in this demonstration.

Variable	Value
Virtual machine—SMS Site 1	Dublin
Dublin Administrator	JaePa (Jae Pak)
Virtual machine—domain controller	Glasgow
Domain administrator	Administrator

Important These steps are included for your information. Do not attempt to perform them in the classroom. If you perform these steps in the classroom environment, you might leave your computer in an incorrect state for upcoming practices.

Demonstration steps performed by instructor only

▶ **To enable a reporting point on the SMS site server**

1. Verify that the Glasgow and Dublin virtual machines are running.

2. On the Dublin virtual machine, click **Start**, point to **All Programs**, point to **Systems Management Server**, and then click **SMS Administrator Console**.

3. In the console tree of the SMS Administrator console, expand **Site Database (001 – NWTraders)**, expand **Site Hierarchy**, expand **001-NWTraders**, expand **Site Settings**, and then click **Site Systems**.

4. In the details pane, right-click **Dublin**, and then click **Properties**.

5. On the **Reporting Point** tab, select the **Use this site system as a reporting point** check box.

6. Click **OK**.

7. Close the SMS Administrator console.

8. Leave the Glasgow and Dublin virtual machines running.

Methods for Verifying the Installation of the Reporting Point

Method	Action
Computer Management	View the default Web site
Windows Explorer	View C:\Inetpub\wwwroot\SMSReporting_*sitecode*
Trace32 or Notepad	View the reporting point deployment log files
SMS Site Component Manager in SMS Administrator console	View the status messages for the reporting point
IIS Manager	Browse the reporting folder

You can use the following methods to verify the reporting point installation:

Method	Action
Computer Management	View the default Web site to verify that the SMS_REPORTING_POINT service (in the Services node) and the reporting point Web site in IIS (in the IIS node) appear.
Windows Explorer	View C:\Inetpub\wwwroot\SMSReporting_*sitecode* to verify the installed files and folders.
Trace32 or Notepad	View the reporting point deployment log files Rsetup.log and SMSReportingInstall.log.
SMS Site Component Manager in SMS Administrator console	View the status messages for the reporting point.
IIS Manager	Browse the reporting folder to verify that IIS is working and that you have permissions to run reporting.

Demonstration: How to Verify the Installation of the Reporting Point

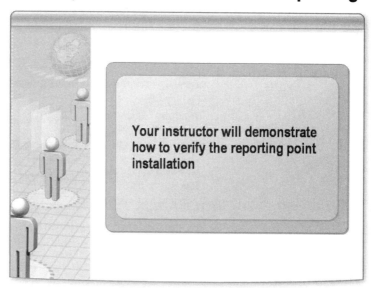

Your instructor will demonstrate how to verify the reporting point installation

In this demonstration, you will see how to verify the installation of a reporting point. First you will see how to add a user to the SMS Reporting Users group. You will also see the basic Web application on Internet Explorer and how to configure its security settings.

Your instructor will use the following values in this demonstration.

Variable	Value
Virtual machine—SMS Site 1	Dublin
Dublin Administrator	JaePa (Jae Pak)
Virtual machine—domain controller	Glasgow
Domain administrator	Administrator

Important These steps are included for your information and you should not attempt to perform them in the classroom.

Demonstration steps performed by instructor only

▶ **To add user to SMS Reporting Users group**

1. Verify that the Glasgow and Dublin virtual machines are running.

2. On the Dublin virtual machine, click **Start**, point to **All Programs**, point to **Administrative Tools**, and then click **Computer Management**.

3. Expand **Local Users and Groups**, and then click **Groups**.

4. In the details pane, right-click **SMS Reporting Users**, and then click **Properties**.

5. In the **SMS Reporting Users Properties** dialog box, click **Add**.

6. In the **Select Users, Computers, or Groups** dialog box, click **Advanced**, and then click **Find Now**.

7. In the **Search Results** list, click **Jae Pak**, and then click **OK**.

8. Click **OK** twice, and then close the Computer Management window.

▶ **To set Internet Explorer security settings for http://dublin**

1. On the Dublin virtual machine, click **Start**, point to **All Programs**, and then click **Internet Explorer**.

2. Select the **In the future, do not show this message** check box if the following error dialog displays: "Microsoft Internet Explorer's Enhanced Security Configuration is currently enabled on your server," and then click **OK**.

3. In Internet Explorer, on the **Tools** menu, click **Internet Options**.

4. In the **Internet Options** dialog box, on the **Security** tab, click **Local intranet**, and then click **Sites**.

5. In the **Add this Web site to the zone** box, type **http://dublin** and then click **Add**.

6. Verify that the **Require server verification** check box is cleared, then click **Close**, and then click **OK**.

7. Close Internet Explorer.

▶ **To verify the reporting point installation**

1. On the Dublin virtual machine, click **Start**, point to **All Programs**, point to **Systems Management Server**, and then click **SMS Administrator Console**.

2. In the console tree of the SMS Administrator console, expand **Site Database (001 – NWTraders)**.

3. Right-click **Reporting**, point to **All Tasks**, point to **Run**, and then click **Dublin**.

   This brings up the SMS Report Viewer.

Note It may take a minute or two to load the list of reports.

---

4. Expand **Reports** (if not already expanded).

   All configured and processed reports will be available from this screen.

5. Close the SMS Report Viewer and then close the SMS Administrator console.

6. Leave the Glasgow and Dublin virtual machines running.

Reporting Point Security

To improve reporting point security:

Reporting Point

- Apply service packs and security-related hotfixes

- Do not put your reporting point servers on the Internet

- Carefully manage membership in the SMS Reporting Users group

- Use the latest version of IIS

- Disable IIS functions that you do not require

- Put IIS on servers that are separate from other applications, or on servers with few other functions

- Use IIS security lockdown and other IIS security tools

- Configure SMS object security for each report

Why IIS security is so important

SMS 2003 relies on IIS to support the reporting point, server locator point, BITS-enabled distribution point, and management point site systems. Well-maintained IIS security helps to ensure the integrity of these SMS site systems and Recovery Expert installations.

If IIS is installed on SMS site servers when the site is running in SMS advanced security, IIS security is especially important because:

- The site server's computer account has administrative privileges on other computers that are site systems on the site. IIS runs by using the local system account, which is the only account with the right to use the computer account. This typically is the case only on site servers.

- When using advanced security, the SMS site server manages its local files and registry entries by using the local system account. Software running in the local system account context of IIS has equal access to those files and registry entries.

Security recommendations

To enhance the security of your reporting points, we recommend the following practices:

- Apply service packs and security-related hotfixes as they become available.

- Do not put your reporting point servers on the Internet.

- Carefully manage membership in the SMS Reporting Users group. The users of SMS Reports must have access to the SMS reporting point. By default, all members of the Administrators and SMS Reporting Users groups have access to the reporting point. However, the SMS Reporting Users group does not have any members by default; this allows administrators to assign the appropriate security rights to specific users or groups of users.

- Use the most recent version of IIS. Usually this means using the most recent available operating system.

- Disable IIS functions that you do not require.

- Put IIS on servers that are separate from other applications, or on servers with few other functions.

- Use IIS security lockdown and other IIS security tools, which are explained below.

- Configure SMS object security for each report. For example, you can specify which users have Read, Modify, or Administer permissions on the report.

IIS security tools

IIS provides three sets of security tools.

- *Lockdown tools*. There are two lockdown tools for IIS servers that support SMS site systems. Both tools are included in SMS 2003 Toolkit 1.

  - *IIS Lockdown 2.1 Template*. This tool secures IIS 5.0 on computers running Windows 2000 Server that host SMS site systems (including BITS-enabled distribution points, management points, reporting points, and server locator points) and Recovery Expert installations.

  - *URLScan 2.5 Template*. This tool secures IIS 6.0 on computers running Windows Server 2003 that host SMS site systems (including BITS-enabled distribution points, management points, reporting points, and server locator points) and Recovery Expert installations.

- *Application protection modes*. You can implement three IIS application protection modes: low, medium, and high. High application protection mode is the most secure and isolates the application files from the IIS files at the process level. SMS 2003 uses IIS 5.0 high application protection mode.

- *Application pools*. In IIS 6.0, you can implement application pools, which are similar to high application protection mode. Application pools are more efficient and enable the use of new IIS 6.0 features, such as automatic application restarts, called the worker process Isolation Mode. To determine which mode IIS 6.0 is in, right-click the **Web Sites** node in the IIS administrative tool and then click **Properties**. The Isolation Mode is indicated on the **Service** tab.

Demonstration: How to View Reporting Security

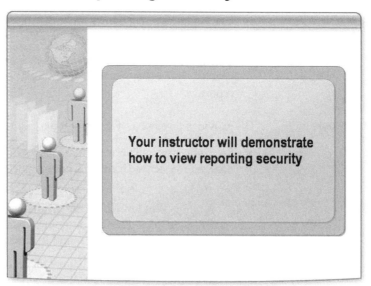

In this demonstration, you will see how to view reporting security. Your instructor will use the following values in this demonstration.

Variable	Value
Virtual machine—SMS Site 1	Dublin
Dublin Administrator	JaePa (Jae Pak)
Virtual machine—domain controller	Glasgow
Domain administrator	Administrator

Important These steps are included for your information. Do not attempt to perform them in the classroom. If you perform these steps in the classroom environment, you might leave your computer in an incorrect state for upcoming practices.

▶ **To view SMS reporting security**

1. Verify that the Glasgow and Dublin virtual machines are running.

2. On the Dublin virtual machine, click **Start**, point to **All Programs**, point to **Systems Management Server**, and then click **SMS Administrator Console**.

3. In the console tree of the SMS Administrator console, expand **Site Database (001 – NWTraders)**, expand **Reporting**, and then click **Reports**.

4. In the details pane, right-click **All inventoried files on a specific computer** and then click **Properties**.

5. Click the **Security** tab.

   Use this tab to set the default security rights on security objects. To see this tab, you must have Administrator permission on at least one security object. There are two types of security rights you can modify: Class and Instance.

   • Class security rights are the user accounts and security permissions set for *the current* security object class.

   • Instance security rights are the same as Class security rights, except that they contain the security rights on the current *instance* of the security object, that is, the current report.

   You can create, modify, and delete security rights from this tab.

   Note   These security settings apply only to SMS security, not IIS security.
   ---

6. Click **Cancel**.

7. Close the SMS Administrator console.

8. Leave the Glasgow and Dublin virtual machines running.

Practice: Configuring and Deploying a Reporting Point

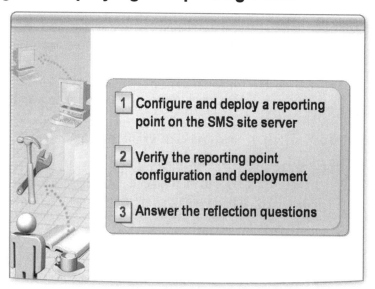

Instructions

Complete the procedures to practice configuring and deploying a reporting point, including how to add a user to the SMS Reporting Users group and configuring the basic Web Application on Internet Explorer and its security settings. Then answer the reflection questions.

In this practice, use the following values.

Variable	Value
Virtual machine—SMS Site 1	Dublin
Dublin Administrator	JaePa (Jae Pak)
Virtual machine—domain controller	Glasgow
Domain administrator	Administrator

Procedures

▶ **To configure and deploy a reporting point on the SMS site server**

1. On the Dublin virtual machine, click **Start**, point to **All Programs**, point to **Systems Management Server**, and then click **SMS Administrator Console**.

2. In the console tree of the SMS Administrator console, expand **Site Database (001 – NWTraders)**, expand **Site Hierarchy**, expand **001-NWTraders**, expand **Site Settings**, and then click **Site Systems**.

3. Right-click **Dublin**, and then click **Properties**.

4. On the **Reporting Point** tab, select the **Use this site system as a reporting point** check box, and then click **OK**.

Note This installation will take about two minutes.

▶ **To add user to SMS Reporting Users group**

1. Verify that the Glasgow and Dublin virtual machines are running.

2. On the Dublin virtual machine, click **Start**, point to **All Programs**, point to **Administrative Tools**, and then click **Computer Management**.

3. Expand **Local Users and Groups**, and then click **Groups**.

4. In the details pane, right-click on **SMS Reporting Users**, and then click **Properties**.

5. In the **SMS Reporting Users Properties** dialog box, click **Add**.

6. In the **Select Users, Computers, or Groups** dialog box, click **Advanced**, and then click **Find Now**.

7. In the **Search Results** list, click **Jae Pak**, and then click **OK**.

8. Click **OK** twice, and then close the **Computer Management** window.

▶ **To set Internet Explorer security settings for http://dublin**

1. On the Dublin virtual machine, click **Start**, point to **All Programs**, and then click **Internet Explorer**.

2. Select the **In the future, do not show this message** check box if the following error dialog displays: "Microsoft Internet Explorer's Enhanced Security Configuration is currently enabled on your server," and then click **OK**.

3. In Internet Explorer, on the **Tools** menu, click **Internet Options**.

4. In the **Internet Options** dialog box, on the **Security** tab, click **Local Intranet**, and then click **Sites**.

5. In the **Add this Web site to the zone** box, type **http://dublin** and then click **Add**.

6. Verify that the **Require server verification** check box is cleared, click **Close**, and then click **OK**.

7. Close Internet Explorer.

Reflection question   What are the prerequisites for installing a reporting point?

_____

_____

_____

Procedures

▶ **To verify the reporting point configuration and deployment**

1. On the Dublin virtual machine, in the SMS Administrator console, expand **Site Database (001 – NWTraders)** if needed, and then click **Reporting**.

2. Right-click **Reporting**, point to **All Tasks**, point to **Run**, and then click **Dublin**.

   This brings up the SMS Report Viewer.

   Note It may take a minute or two to load the list of reports.

   ---

3. Expand **Reports** (if not already expanded).

   All configured and processed reports will be available from this screen.

4. Close the SMS Report Viewer when done viewing reports.

5. Close the SMS Administrator console.

6. Leave the Glasgow and Dublin virtual machines running.

Reflection questions

1. What must be installed if you want to see graphs in reports?

   _____

   _____

   _____

2. What can you do to further secure your IIS server?

   _____

   _____

   _____

   _____

Lesson: Configuring and Running Reports

- **What Is an SMS Report?**
- **Report Categories for Predefined Reports**
- **How to Filter the List of Reports**
- **How to Use the Report Viewer to Run a Predefined Report**
- **Demonstration: How to View and Filter Predefined Reports**
- **How to Create a Link to another Report**
- **How to Export and Import Reports**

Introduction

SMS 2003 provides a comprehensive set of predefined secure reports with information about the client computers across the SMS hierarchy and the current state of managed systems across an organization. You can provide management and other SMS users with reports that can be viewed in Internet Explorer. Reports include a wide range of information, including:

- Hardware and software inventory.
- Computer configuration details and status.
- Software deployment, deployment errors, and usage status.

Lesson objectives

After completing this lesson, you will be able to:

- Describe an SMS report.
- Identify report categories for predefined reports.
- Filter the view of the list of reports.
- Use the Report Viewer to run a predefined report.
- Create a link to another report.
- Export and import reports.

What Is an SMS Report?

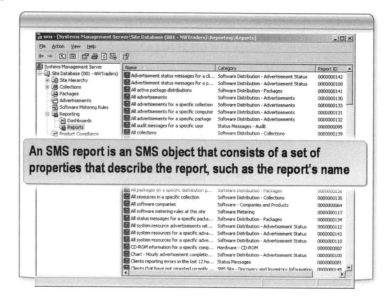

An SMS report is an SMS object that consists of a set of properties that describe the report, such as the report's name

Definition

A report is an SMS object that consists of a set of properties that describe the report, such as the report's name. The primary property in a report's definition is its SQL statement, which specifies the data that needs to be retrieved from the SMS site database and be displayed. The report's SQL statement definition queries read-only views in the SMS site database. These views emulate the WQL information accessed through the SMS query designer.

An SMS report displays information from the SMS site database in an organized format.

Types of reports

SMS 2003 provides many predefined reports. These reports can display a variety of information, such as hardware inventory data, software inventory data, software distribution information, software update status, software metering information, and status messages data. You can use predefined reports to retrieve and display data about your site, such as clients that are low on disk space, or clients that have a specific network card.

For many administrators, these reports provide sufficient information to administer their computer infrastructures and SMS systems. However, you might find that your information needs extend beyond the predefined reports. In this case, you can create your own reports or copy and modify predefined reports to better meet your needs.

Important   To create a custom report, you must have a working knowledge of SQL and of the tables and views of the site database. For more information about creating reports, see Chapter 11, "Creating Reports," in the *Microsoft Systems Management Server 2003 Operations Guide* on the Additional Reading page of your Student Materials compact disc.

Uses of reports

Reporting is useful for site maintenance. You can run reports as you need them, or you can schedule reports to run on a regular basis to help detect and diagnose problems early. For example, if there is a problem with a specific client, you can run a report that displays that client's recent errors. To ensure continued site health, you can regularly run a report that displays site status. Other reports, such as reports that display software distribution status and software usage, can also help with site maintenance.

A report can link to other related information, such as another report, or a URL. Links provide quick access to additional relevant information. For example, you can link a report that lists discovered computers to a report that provides recent error messages. Every discovered computer that is displayed has a link to error messages associated with that computer.

A report can also have prompts. You can use prompts to limit the report's scope based on information that the user enters when the report runs. For example, you can specify a report that retrieves all the clients running a certain product and you can include a prompt for the user to provide a product name. Every time that the report runs, the user enters a product name and the report displays the clients that are running the specified product.

Report Categories for Predefined Reports

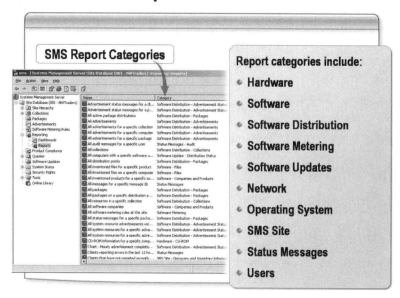

SMS 2003 provides more than 150 predefined reports that you can use to gather important information from your site database. These reports are grouped in several categories in order to provide a quick method for seeing the relationships and differences between reports.

The report categories for predefined reports include the following higher-level categories. Many of these categories contain sub-categories.

- Hardware
- Software
- Software Distribution
- Software Metering
- Software Update
- Network
- Operating System
- SMS Site
- Status Messages
- Users

How to Filter the List of Reports

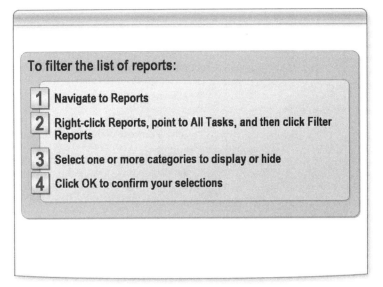

To filter the list of reports:

1 Navigate to Reports

2 Right-click Reports, point to All Tasks, and then click Filter Reports

3 Select one or more categories to display or hide

4 Click OK to confirm your selections

In the SMS Administrator console, you can filter the list of reports by categories. You can then sort the list to quickly locate a specific report.

Procedure

To filter the list of reports:

1. In the SMS Administrator console, navigate to Reports by expanding **Systems Management Server**, **Site Database**, and **Reporting**.

2. Right-click **Reports**, point to **All Tasks**, and then click **Filter Reports**.

3. In the **Filter Reports** dialog box, select one or more categories, and then click the **Display/Hide** button above the **Categories** list.

   In the **Categories** box, the **Display** column value for the selected category or categories switches between **Yes (Display)** and **No (Hide)**.

4. Click **OK** to confirm your selections.

How to Use the Report Viewer to Run a Predefined Report

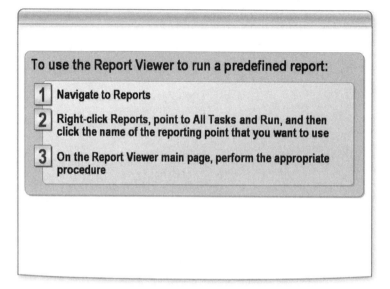

To use the Report Viewer to run a predefined report:

1 Navigate to Reports

2 Right-click Reports, point to All Tasks and Run, and then click the name of the reporting point that you want to use

3 On the Report Viewer main page, perform the appropriate procedure

You use Report Viewer to display the list of available reports and to run reports. When Report Viewer runs, it displays only the reports that the user has permission to view. The reports are categorized to help you locate a specific report that you need to run. When a user runs a report, the results are based on the data that is retrieved by the report's SQL statement. The SQL statement accesses read-only SQL Server views, instead of SMS site database tables. The report retrieves the specified data and displays it in Internet Explorer.

You can start Report Viewer either from the SMS Administrator console or by typing the designated URL for a reporting point in the **Address** box of Internet Explorer.

Important   Reports cannot be run until at least one reporting point is created for the site.

Procedure

To use the Report Viewer to run a predefined report:

1. In the SMS Administrator console, navigate to Reports by expanding **Systems Management Server**, **Site Database**, and **Reporting**.

2. Right-click **Reports**, point to **All Tasks**, point to **Run**, and then click the name of the reporting point that you want to use to start Report Viewer.

3. On the Report Viewer main page, perform one of the following procedures:

   - In the reports tree, expand a category to view a list of reports in that category for which you have Read permission. To run a report, click the report, enter values for any required parameters, and then click **Display**.

   - To view the list of dashboards, click **Dashboards**.

   - To view the list of reports that are designated to appear on the Computer Details page, click **Computer Details**. Report Viewer will only display those reports for which you have Read permission.

   - To view the list of supplemental reports, expand **Supplemental Reports**. Supplemental reports are reports that you or others create outside of SMS and that you place in the Supplemental Reports folder on a reporting point. If you have multiple reporting points, you must place a supplemental report on each of the reporting points from which you want users to access the report. Supplemental reports do not appear in the SMS Administrator console; they only appear in Report Viewer. However, the Supplemental Reports item does not appear in the Report Viewer tree until you install at least one supplemental report file on the reporting point.

Demonstration: How to View and Filter Predefined Reports

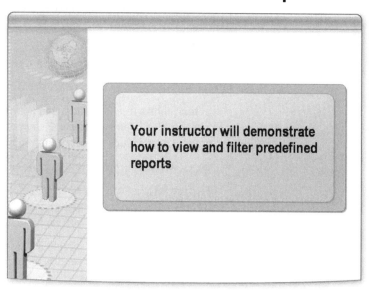

In this demonstration, you will see the list of predefined reports in SMS Administrator console and identify reports that map to common SMS system administrator functions. Then you will see how to filter the list of reports. Finally, you will see how to view predefined reports by using the Report Viewer. Your instructor will use the following values in this demonstration.

Variable	Value
Virtual machine—SMS Site 1	Dublin
Dublin Administrator	JaePa (Jae Pak)
Virtual machine—domain controller	Glasgow
Domain administrator	Administrator

Important   These steps are included for your information and you should not attempt to perform them in the classroom.

Demonstration steps performed by instructor only

▶ **To view the predefined reports in SMS Administrator console**

1. Verify that the Glasgow and Dublin virtual machines are running.

2. On the Dublin virtual machine, click **Start**, point to **All Programs**, point to **Systems Management Server**, and then click **SMS Administrator Console**.

3. In the console tree of the SMS Administrator console, expand **Site Database (001 – NWTraders)**, expand **Reporting**, and then click **Reports**.

4. Click the **Category** column heading to sort the reports by category.

▶ **To filter the list of reports**

1. In the console tree, right-click **Reports**, click **All Tasks**, and then click **Filter Reports**.

2. In the **Categories** list, use the following steps to select particular categories of reports to display in the details pane of the SMS Administrator console:

   a. Verify that **Hardware – CD-ROM** is selected.

   b. Scroll to the bottom of the list, hold down SHIFT, and then click **Users** to select all categories.

   c. Click the **Hide/Display** button so that **Display** column is set to **No** for all categories.

   d. Click **Users** so that is the only category selected.

   e. Hold down CTRL, and then click **Software Metering** (so that you have two categories selected).

   f. Scroll up, then use CTRL to select three additional categories:

      • Hardware – Processor

      • Operating System

      • SMS Site – Discovery and Inventory Information

   g. Click the **Hide/Display** button.

      You should have five categories with **Yes** in the **Display** column.

   h. Click **OK**.

      The categories of reports you selected appear in the details pane.

   i. Click the **Category** column heading to sort the list by category.

      Notice that only reports from the five selected categories are displayed.

▶ **To view predefined reports by using the Report Viewer**

1. In the console tree, right-click **Reports**, point to **All Tasks**, point to **Run**, and then click **Dublin**.

Note After the SMS Report Viewer opens, it may take a minute or two to load the list of reports.

---

2. In the View SMS Reports window, review the predefined SMS reports.

3. Close the View SMS Reports window and the SMS Administrator console.

4. Leave the Glasgow and Dublin virtual machines running.

How to Create a Link to Another Report

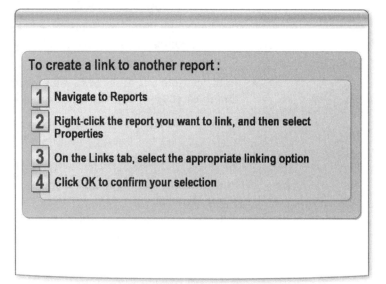

To create a link to another report:

1 Navigate to Reports

2 Right-click the report you want to link, and then select Properties

3 On the Links tab, select the appropriate linking option

4 Click OK to confirm your selection

You can use a link in a source report to provide users with ready access to additional data, such as more detailed information about each of the items in the source report. For example, you might link a report that lists all site codes to another report that lists all recent error messages for a given site code. The source report passes a specific site code to the target report, based on the line item in the source report about which the user chooses to obtain more information. A report can only be configured with one link, and that link can only connect to a single target.

Procedure

To create a link to another report:

1. In the SMS Administrator console, navigate to Reports by expanding **Systems Management Server**, **Site Database**, and **Reporting**, and then click **Reports**.

2. Right-click the name of the report that you want to link, and then click **Properties**.

3. On the **Links** tab, select one of the following options in the **Link type** box:

   - **No Link**. Click this option if you do not want to link to another report or target.

   - **Link to another report**. Click this option to link to another report. Click **Select**, and then select a target report from the Report list. If the target report requires prompts, you must designate the column in the source report that is used to provide data for each prompt. To designate a column, double-click a prompt to open its properties. In the **Column** box, type the report column number, and then click **OK**.

   - **Link to Computer Details**. Click this option to link to the **Computer Details** page. The source report must contain a column that contains computer name data. In the **Computer name column** box, specify which column contains computer names.

- **Link to Status Message Details**. Click this option to link to the **Status Message Details** page. The source report must contain a column that specifies status message record ID data. In the Record ID column box, specify which column contains record IDs.

- **Link to URL**. Click this option to link the report to the resource specified in the **URL** box.

4. Click **OK** to confirm your selection.

Note To take advantage of report links, a user must have the appropriate security rights to a report's link target. For example, if a report links to the Status Message Details page to view status message details, a user must have Read permission for the Status Message object. Or, if a report links to another report to view the link target report, the user must have Read permission for the Report object instance or for the Report class.

How to Export and Import Reports

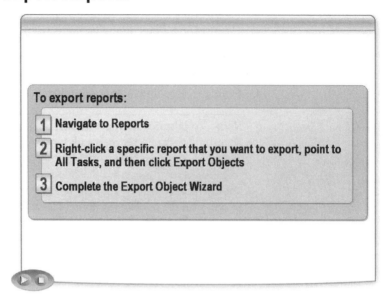

To export reports:

1. Navigate to Reports

2. Right-click a specific report that you want to export, point to All Tasks, and then click Export Objects

3. Complete the Export Object Wizard

You can export and import reports by using the Export Object Wizard and the Import Object Wizard. SMS 2003 exports reports by writing report object definitions, which are the properties that define a report, to a file. Only the report object definitions are exported or imported, not report data. You can use exported report files to share reports with other SMS administrators, or to import reports that you obtained from other SMS administrators or other sources.

The report ID is unique for each report. When you export a report, the report ID is not written to the MOF file. This prevents you from accidentally replacing an existing report by importing an MOF file in which a report ID for an imported report matches that of an existing report. When you import reports, SMS assigns each imported report a new report ID.

Guidelines for exporting a report

You can use the Export Object Wizard to export objects from only one object class (reports, collections, or queries) at a time. MOF files that are created by using the Export Object Wizard contain only one object class.

To export a report, you must have Read permission for the Reports security object class or instance.

Caution   When exporting reports, do not use an MOF file name that is the same as an existing MOF file name in the same folder. If you do, the data for the existing file will be overwritten without warning.

Procedure to export a report

To export a report:

1. In the SMS Administrator console, navigate to Reports by expanding **Systems Management Server**, **Site Database**, and **Reporting**, and then click **Reports**.

   Note If you want to export more than one report at a time, navigate to Reports, and then right-click **Reports** to open the Export Object Wizard. Select the reports you want to export, and then complete the wizard.

2. Right-click a specific report that you want to export, point to **All Tasks**, and then click **Export Objects** to open the Export Object Wizard.

3. Complete the Export Object Wizard.

Guidelines for importing a report

To import a report, you must have Create permission for the Reports security object class or instance.

You can use the Import Object Wizard to import user-created MOF files that contain objects from multiple object classes. However, you must have Create permission for all object classes in an MOF file. Any objects for which you do not have permission are not imported. For example, if you import an MOF file that contains report and collection objects but you have Create permission only for the Reports object class, the collection objects are not imported.

   Caution When importing reports, the properties of the existing report are overwritten without warning if you import a report with the same name and category as a report already in the database. To avoid this, open the MOF file by using Notepad or another text file application and review the object names against the names of existing objects in the SMS site database before importing the file.

Procedure to import a report

To import a report:

1. In the SMS Administrator console, navigate to Reports by expanding **Systems Management Server**, **Site Database**, and **Reporting**, and then click **Reports**.

2. Right-click **Reports**, point to **All Tasks**, and then click **Import Objects** to open the Import Object Wizard.

3. Complete the Import Object Wizard.

Practice: Configuring and Running Reports

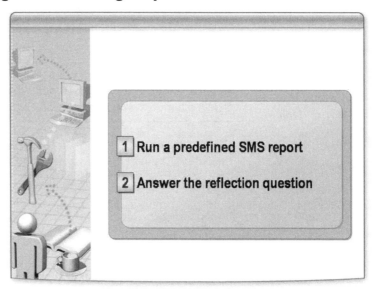

Instructions

Complete the procedures to practice running a predefined SMS report to view data about the clients that were deployed in previous modules. Then answer the reflection question.

In this practice, use the following values.

Variable	Value
Virtual machine—SMS Site 1	Dublin
Dublin Administrator	JaePa (Jae Pak)
Virtual machine—domain controller	Glasgow
Domain Administrator	Administrator

Procedure

▶ **To run a predefined report by using the Report Viewer**

1. Verify that the Glasgow and Dublin virtual machines are running.

2. On the Dublin virtual machine, click **Start**, point to **All Programs**, point to **Accessories**, and then click **Command Prompt**.

3. In the **Command Prompt** window, type **C:\SMS\Bin\i386\RunMeterSumm.exe SMS_001**, and then press ENTER.

4. In the **Command Prompt** window, review the results, and then close the **Command Prompt** window.

Important   Due to the limitations of the virtual machine classroom environment, you must run RunMeterSumm.exe to display reports containing software metering data. This is because these reports display *summarized* data, and the SQL summarization task only summarizes data that is older than seven days. Running RunMeterSumm.exe causes SMS to summarize software metering data regardless of when the data was collected. RunMeterSumm.exe is a tool provided on your course compact disc.

---

5. On the Dublin virtual machine, click **Start**, point to **All Programs**, point to **Systems Management Server**, and then click **SMS Administrator Console**.

6. In the console tree of the SMS Administrator console, expand **Site Database (001 – NWTraders)**, and then expand **Reporting**.

7. Right-click **Reports**, point to **All Tasks**, point to **Run**, and then click **Dublin**.

Note   It may take a minute or two to load the list of reports.

---

8. In the console tree of the **View SMS Reports** window, expand **Software Metering**, and then click **Users that have run a specific metered software program**.

9. In the details pane, under the **Rule Name** area, click **Values**.

10. In the **Select Value – Web Page Dialog** dialog box, click **CalcRule**.

11. In the details pane, under the **Month (1 – 12)** area, click **Values**.

12. In the **Select Value – Web Page Dialog** dialog box, click *the appropriate value*.

13. In the details pane, under the **Year** area, click **Values**.

14. In the **Select Value – Web Page Dialog** dialog box, click *the appropriate value*.

15. In the details pane, in the upper-right corner, click the **Display** icon.

16. The SMS Report page displays the report. This report displays that the total usage for Calc.exe for the month and year you specified.

17. Close any SMS Reports windows and the SMS Administrator console.

18. Leave the Glasgow and Dublin virtual machines running.

Reflection question

Your instructor performed a demonstration using a particular report. Why is the "Computers assigned but not installed for a particular site" report useful?

_____

_____

_____

Lesson: Creating and Running Dashboards

- What Is a Dashboard?
- Guidelines for Using Dashboards
- How to Create and Use Dashboards
- Demonstration: How to Create and Use a Dashboard

Introduction

Reporting also supports dashboards, which display sets of reports in Report Viewer. Using a single dashboard, you can monitor information about a variety of SMS objects or systems.

Lesson objectives

After completing this lesson, you will be able to:

- Describe a dashboard.
- Identify guidelines for using dashboards.
- Create and use dashboards.

What Is a Dashboard?

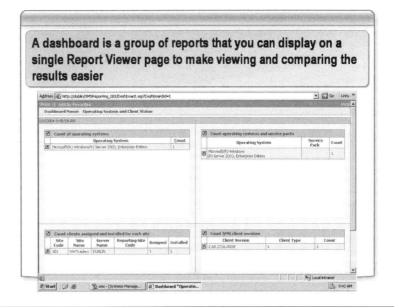

A dashboard is a group of related reports that you can display on a single Report Viewer page to make viewing and comparing the results easier. You can use dashboards with the reports included with SMS (and any custom reports you have created), provided that these reports do not use prompts. There are approximately 40 predefined reports of the approximately 160 reports that can be included in a dashboard.

Like reports, you manage dashboards in the SMS Administrator console, but you view them using Report Viewer.

Some suggested uses for dashboards include:

- Grouping your most commonly used reports on a single page.

- Grouping reports that show related types of information about the hardware or software of managed computers. For instance, you can build a dashboard that provides a complete view of software updates compliance throughout your organization

SMS dashboards can be viewed from any computer with access to a reporting point.

Important   Dashboards are not subject to SMS security. However, users are able to view reports in a dashboard based on their security rights.

Guidelines for Using Dashboards

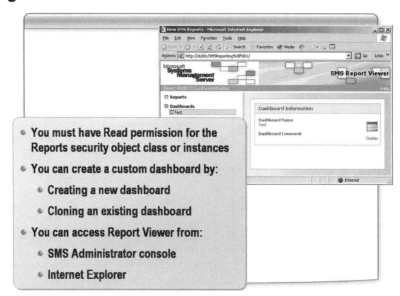

Follow these guidelines for using dashboards:

- To include a report in a dashboard, you must have Read permission for the Reports security object class or the report instance. Dashboard users must also have Read permission for the Reports security object class or instances to view the results of reports included in a dashboard.

- You can create your own custom dashboard or copy an existing dashboard and modify it to meet your needs. You cannot export or import a dashboard.

  - When you create a new dashboard, you determine the number of reports that it can contain by specifying the number of rows and columns. You can limit the height of the cells in which the reports display to minimize the size of the dashboard window. The default height for each report cell is 250 pixels. When you define the number of cells in a dashboard, you can select the reports that you want to display in the cells.

  - Cloning a dashboard is the easiest way to create a new dashboard based on an existing dashboard. After cloning, you can modify the properties and reports of the new copy to suit your needs.

- You run dashboards by using Report Viewer. You can start Report Viewer either from the SMS Administrator console or by entering the dashboard's unique URL in the **Address** box in Internet Explorer.

How to Create and Use Dashboards

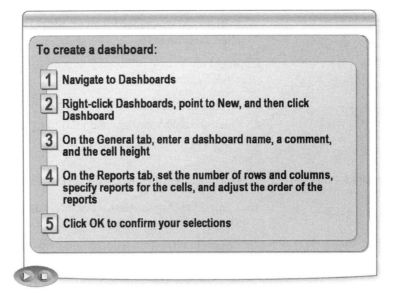

To create a dashboard:

1 Navigate to Dashboards

2 Right-click Dashboards, point to New, and then click Dashboard

3 On the General tab, enter a dashboard name, a comment, and the cell height

4 On the Reports tab, set the number of rows and columns, specify reports for the cells, and adjust the order of the reports

5 Click OK to confirm your selections

Procedure to create a dashboard

To create a dashboard:

1. In the SMS Administrator console, navigate to Dashboards by expanding **Systems Management Server**, **Site Database**, and then **Reporting**.

2. Right-click **Dashboards**, point to **New**, and then click **Dashboard**.

3. On the **General** tab, enter a dashboard name, a comment, and the cell height.

4. On the **Reports** tab, set the number of rows and columns, specify reports for the cells, and adjust the order of the reports.

5. Click **OK** to confirm your selections.

Procedure to modify a dashboard

To modify a dashboard:

1. In the SMS Administrator console, navigate to Dashboards by expanding **Systems Management Server**, **Site Database**, and **Reporting**, and then click **Dashboards**.

2. Right-click the dashboard that you want to modify, and then click **Properties**.

3. On the **General** tab, modify the settings as needed.

4. On the **Reports** tab, modify the settings as needed.

5. Click **OK** to confirm your selections.

Procedure to clone a dashboard

To clone a dashboard:

1. In the SMS Administrator console, navigate to Dashboards by expanding **Systems Management Server**, **Site Database**, and **Reporting**, and then click **Dashboards**.

2. Right-click the dashboard you want to clone, point to **All Tasks**, and then click **Clone**.

3. In the **New Dashboard Name** box, type a name, and then click **OK**.

4. Open the dashboard and then modify the properties as needed.

5. Click **OK** to confirm your selections.

Procedure to run dashboard

To run a dashboard by using the SMS Administrator console:

1. In the SMS Administrator console, navigate to Dashboards by expanding **Systems Management Server**, **Site Database**, and then **Reporting**.

2. Right-click **Dashboards**, point to **All Tasks**, point to **Run**, and then click the name of the reporting point that you want to use to start Report Viewer.

    The list of dashboards appears under **Dashboards** on the Report Viewer main page.

3. Select a dashboard, and then click **Display**.

Demonstration: How to Create and Use a Dashboard

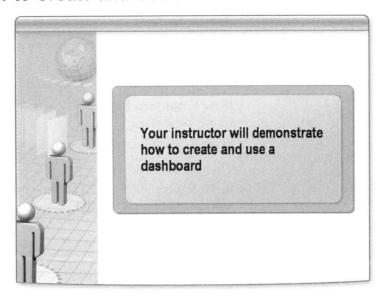

Your instructor will demonstrate how to create and use a dashboard

In this demonstration, you will see how to create and use a dashboard. Dashboards are created in SMS and published to IIS. During a pause in the demonstration, you will be given a reflection question to discuss with class.

Your instructor will use the following values in this demonstration.

Variable	Value
Virtual machine—SMS Site 1	Dublin
Dublin Administrator	JaePa (Jae Pak)
Virtual machine—domain controller	Glasgow
Domain administrator	Administrator

Important These steps are included for your information. Do not attempt to perform them in the classroom. If you perform these steps in the classroom environment, you might leave your computer in an incorrect state for upcoming practices.

Demonstration steps performed by instructor only

▶ **To create and use a dashboard**

1. Verify that the Glasgow and Dublin virtual machines are running.

2. On the Dublin virtual machine, click **Start**, point to **All Programs**, point to **Systems Management Server**, and then click **SMS Administrator Console**.

3. In the console tree of the SMS Administrator console, expand **Site Database (001 – NWTraders)**, and then expand **Reporting**.

4. Right-click **Dashboards**, point to **New**, and then click **Dashboard**.

5. On the **General** tab, in the **Name** box, type **Demo Dashboard**

6. On the **Reports** tab, in the **Dashboard dimensions** area, enter **1** for the number of rows and then verify that the number of columns is **2**.

7. Click **Set**.

8. In the **Dashboard Reports** box, double-click the first dashboard position (row 1, column 1).

9. In the **Reports** list, select **Sites by hierarchy with time of last site status update**.

10. Click **OK**.

11. In the **Dashboard Reports** box, double-click the second dashboard position (row 1, column 2).

12. In the **Reports** list, select **Count clients for each site**.

13. Click **OK**, and then click **OK**.

14. In the details pane, right-click **Demo Dashboard**, point to **All Tasks**, point to **Run**, and then click **Dublin**.

15. Review the dashboard.

16. Close the SMS Administrator console and any open windows.

17. Leave the Glasgow and Dublin virtual machines running.

Practice: Creating and Running Dashboards

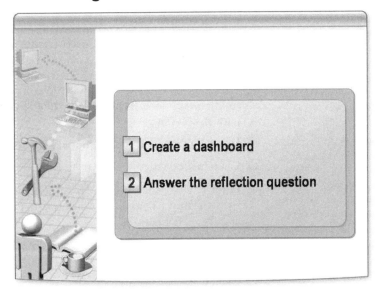

1. Create a dashboard
2. Answer the reflection question

Instructions

Complete the procedures to practice creating a dashboard. Then answer the reflection question.

In this practice, use the following values.

Variable	Value
Virtual machine—SMS Site 1	Dublin
Dublin Administrator	JaePa (Jae Pak)
Virtual machine—domain controller	Glasgow
Domain administrator	Administrator

Procedure

▶ **To create a dashboard**

1. Verify that the Glasgow and Dublin virtual machines are running.

2. On the Dublin virtual machine, click **Start**, point to **All Programs**, point to **Systems Management Server**, and then click **SMS Administrator Console**.

3. In the console tree of the SMS Administrator console, expand **Site Database (001 – NWTraders)**, and then expand **Reporting**.

4. Right-click **Dashboards**, point to **New**, and then click **Dashboard**.

5. In the **Dashboard Properties** dialog box, on the **General** tab, in the **Name** box, type **Operating Systems and Client Status**

6. On the **Reports** tab, in the **Dashboard Reports** box, double-click the first dashboard position (row 1, column 1).

7. In the **Reports** list, select **Count of operating systems**.

8. Click **OK**.

9. In the **Dashboard Reports** box, double-click the second dashboard position (row 1, column 2).

10. In the **Reports** list, select **Count operating systems and service packs**.

11. Click **OK**.

12. In the **Dashboard Reports** box, double-click the third dashboard position (row 2, column 1).

13. In the **Reports** list, select **Count clients assigned and installed for each site**.

14. Click **OK**.

15. In the **Dashboard Reports** box, double-click the fourth dashboard position (row 2, column 2).

16. In the **Reports** list, select **Count SMS client versions**.

17. Click **OK** twice.

18. In the details pane of the SMS Administrator console, right-click **Operating Systems and Client Status** dashboard, point to **All Tasks**, point to **Run**, and then click **Dublin**.

    The **Operating Systems and Client Status** dashboard opens and runs the reports.

19. Review the dashboard.

20. On the **File** menu, click **Close**.

21. Close the SMS Administrator console and any open windows.

22. Leave the Glasgow and Dublin virtual machines running.

Reflection questions

1. Why are reports more efficient than queries?

   _____

   _____

   _____

2. You would like to create a dashboard with your favorite reports but the list of available reports does not include all your favorite reports. What is the most likely cause of the shorter list?

   _____

   _____

   _____

Discussion: Querying and Reporting Data

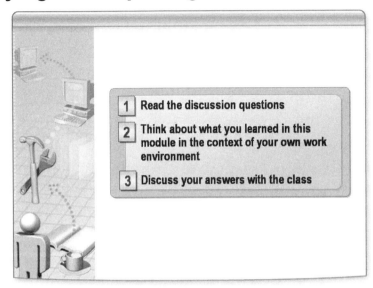

1. What is the main issue that you and your users will encounter when running a query or a report? Why?

   _____

   _____

   _____

   _____

2. You have enabled hardware and software inventory. You can browse inventory using Resource Explorer, but you cannot run any report in the Reports node. What is mostly likely the cause for the problem?

   _____

   _____

   _____

   _____

3. When you are designing your dashboard, why is the list of selectable reports considerably less than the total of 159 reports?

_____

_____

_____

Module 7: Preparing an SMS Site for Software Distribution

Contents

Overview

- Explaining How SMS Distributes Software
- Managing Distribution Points
- Configuring Software Distribution and the Advertised Programs Client Agent

---

Introduction

In this module, you will learn about the Microsoft® Systems Management Server (SMS) software distribution process. You will learn about the flow of software distribution and the roles played by the site, the SMS objects used to distribute software, and the SMS client. Finally, you will learn how to prepare the site for software distribution by allocating distribution points and configuring the SMS client.

Objectives

After completing this module, you will be able to:

- Explain how SMS distributes software.

- Manage distribution points.

- Configure software distribution and the Advertised Programs Client Agent.

Lesson: Explaining How SMS Distributes Software

* The Benefits of SMS Software Distribution
* How the Client Handles Software Distribution
* Administrative Tasks Involved in the Software Distribution Process
* The Process of Configuring Site Settings in Software Distribution
* The SMS Objects Used to Distribute Software
* The Monitoring Phase of Software Distribution

Introduction

In this lesson, you will learn about the key elements and events in the SMS software distribution process. This lesson will give you a broad overview of the software distribution process that you will learn about in this module and in Module 8, "Managing Software Distribution."

Lesson objectives

After completing this lesson, you will be able to:

- Describe the benefits of the SMS software distribution process.
- Explain how the client handles the software distribution process.
- Identify the administrative tasks involved in the software distribution process.
- Define the site settings in the software distribution process.
- Identify the SMS objects used to distribute software.
- Explain the monitoring phase of software distribution.

The Benefits of SMS Software Distribution

SMS software distribution:

- Eliminates the process of providing thousands of software compact discs to users, along with programs and instructions
- Reduces user errors
- Allows users to successfully run programs and install software without needing to know how to run these programs or which setup options are best for them
- Allows you to centrally define and control how and when programs run on client computers

Using SMS software distribution eliminates the inefficient process of providing thousands of software compact discs to users, along with programs and instructions. The automated process of program distribution eliminates user errors such as entering incorrect values in prompts, running incorrect programs, or entering incorrect arguments. By using software distribution, users can successfully run programs and install software without needing to know how to run these programs or which setup options are best for them. Users do not need to manage their own software installations. Instead, you centrally define and control how and when programs run on client computers.

How the Client Handles Software Distribution

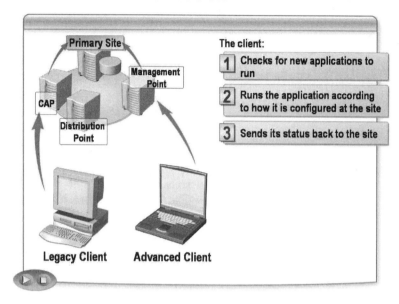

The process

During software distribution, the client computer:

1. Checks for new applications to run.

   • Legacy Clients communicate with a client access point (CAP).

   • Advanced Clients communicate with the management point (MP).

2. Runs the application according to how it was configured at the site. For example, the client might automatically download the installation files before running installation.

   • Client receives application files from the distribution point.

3. Sends its status back to the site. For example, if the program runs successfully, the client sends a status message that indicates the installation was successful.

Actions the administrator can perform during the software distribution process

You can:

- Make queries on the status and use the Report Viewer to view reports.

- Perform software metering to monitor the usage of the applications that you have distributed.

- Check the status of the client. You can check the state of clients in the hierarchy. You can run queries on status messages to detect any problems that clients might be having, such as:

  - The client is failing to download a program.

  - The client is unnecessarily running a program again.

  - The client successfully started the program, and the program ended successfully or failed.

Tip You can monitor a client's status only if it creates status messages and these status messages reach the site server. However, if the client, the CAP, or the management point is experiencing problems that prevent status messages from reaching the site server, you will not be aware of any problems. To detect clients from which you are missing status messages, you need to run a query that returns all clients that have not reported a status message within the expected time interval.

Administrative Tasks Involved in the Software Distribution Process

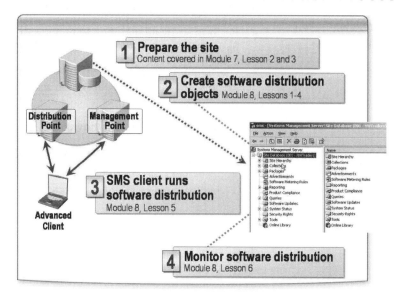

Tip This slide is broken down in the next three topics, explaining the four administrative tasks involved in the software distribution process in more detail.

There are several administrative tasks you must do for the software distribution process to succeed. These tasks are outlined in this module and also in Module 8, "Managing Software Distribution."

The SMS software distribution feature automates the distribution of programs to SMS clients. These programs run on the client computers to perform tasks such as installing software or scanning the clients' hard drives for viruses.

The overall software distribution process is explained by the following four phases:

1. **Preparing the site for software distribution**.

   The tasks in this phase are covered in Lesson 2 and Lesson 3 of this module.

2. **Creating the SMS software distribution objects**:

   - Determine who receives the software (create collection).

   - Determine what software to distribute (create package).

   - Determine how the package is run (create program).

   - Tie the first three software distribution objects in an instruction (create advertisement).

   The tasks in this phase are covered in Lessons 1, 2, 3, and 4 of Module 8, "Managing Software Distribution."

3. **SMS client runs software distribution**.

   When the client receives the advertisement, the client agent follows the instructions to deploy the software.

   The tasks in this phase are covered in Lesson 5 of Module 8, "Managing Software Distribution."

4. **Monitoring software distribution**.

   SMS allows you to gather data and produce reports on software distribution. Using these methods, you can check the status of the SMS client and/or servers.

   The tasks in this phase are covered in Lesson 6 of Module 8, "Managing Software Distribution."

The Process of Configuring Site Settings in Software Distribution

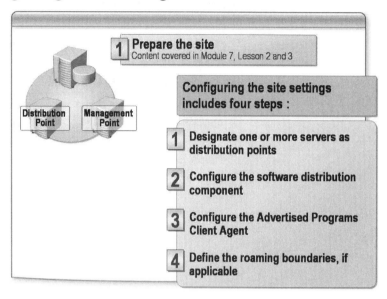

Tip   This slide illustrates the first administrative task involved in the software distribution process, as outlined in the previous topic, "Administrative Tasks Involved in the Software Distribution Process."

The first step in preparing SMS to distribute software is configuring the site settings. This configuration process includes four steps:

1. Designate one or more servers as distribution points.
2. Configure the software distribution component.
3. Configure the Advertised Programs Client Agent.
4. Define the roaming boundaries, if applicable.

The order in which you configure these site components does not affect the software distribution process.

The SMS Objects Used to Distribute Software

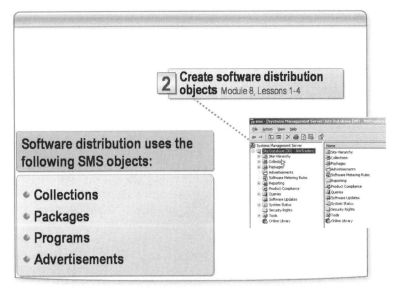

Tip This slide illustrates the second administrative task involved in the software distribution process, as outlined in the topic before last, "Administrative Tasks Involved in the Software Distribution Process."

To properly distribute software to your clients, you must create the four distribution objects: collections, packages, programs, and advertisements.

Note If you use a pre-defined collection, you do not have to create your own collection.

You create a software distribution package and program and then advertise the program that you want the clients to run. Advertising the program makes a program available to a specified target collection. You must create the collection, package, and program before you create the advertisement. The advertisement contains the name of the program, the name of the target collection, and the scheduling information. However, the site's clients will not be able to receive advertised programs until you enable the Advertised Programs Client Agent on the site's clients. Once the software distribution objects are created, you can reuse one or more of them for future software distribution.

Note Software distribution objects will be discussed in Module 8, "Managing Software Distribution."

The Monitoring Phase of Software Distribution

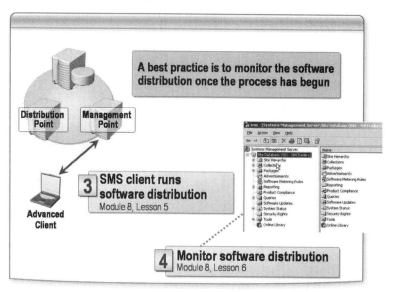

Tip This slide illustrates the third and fourth administrative tasks involved in the software distribution process, as outlined in the third topic of this lesson, "Administrative Tasks Involved in the Software Distribution Process."

Once the SMS client runs software distribution, the final phase of the software distribution process is to monitor the software distribution. SMS allows you to gather data and produce reports on software distribution. Using these methods, you can check the status of the SMS client and/or servers.

The tasks in this phase are covered in Lesson 6 of Module 8, "Managing Software Distribution."

Practice: Explaining How SMS Distributes Software

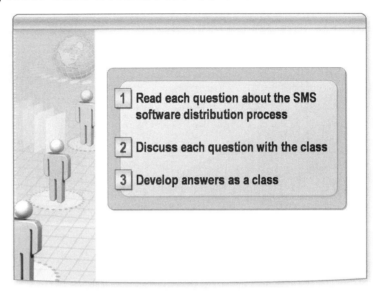

Instructions   Discuss the following questions on the SMS software distribution process with the class.

Discussion questions   1. Does the order in which you configure the site components make a difference?

_____

_____

_____

2. Does the order in which you configure the SMS software distribution objects make a difference?

_____

_____

_____

3. What is the correct sequence of steps for distributing software?

_____

_____

_____

Lesson: Managing Distribution Points

- The Benefits of BITS, Delta Replication, and Compression In Managing Network Performance
- Guidelines for Configuring a Site System to Be a Distribution Point
- What is a Distribution Point Group?
- Demonstration: How to Configure a Distribution Point and a Distribution Point Group

Introduction

In this lesson, you will learn how to manage a distribution point as part of site configuration. You will learn the strategic importance of distribution point functionality in managing peak use of network bandwidth.

Lesson objectives

After completing this lesson, you will be able to:

- Describe the benefits of BITS, delta replication, and compression in managing network performance.
- Describe the guidelines for configuring a site system to be a distribution point.
- Explain a distribution point group.
- Configure a distribution point and a distribution point group.

The Benefits of BITS, Delta Replication, and Compression in Managing Network Performance

SMS manages network performance by:

- Using BITS to provide checkpoint restart download of packages from distribution points to Advanced Clients

- Using delta replication to only send the updated package files that have changed since the last time the package was distributed

- Using compression to automatically compress package source files when it sends the package to other SMS sites

When you use SMS to distribute an application, SMS sends the package source files to distribution points. SMS provides software distribution capabilities that help you manage network bandwidth between an SMS site and distribution points. These capabilities also help to reduce the load on the network link between the site where distribution is configured and the child sites. Network bandwidth is often a significant issue, especially when distributing large software applications such as Microsoft Windows® XP. BITS, delta replication, and compression all help in reducing the load on the network.

SMS also provides software distribution settings that allow Advanced Clients to better handle situations such as non-continuous connectivity to the network and slow link connections.

The benefits of BITS technology and the BITS-enabled distribution point

Software distribution can use Background Intelligent Transfer Service (BITS) technology, which can transfer files from distribution points that are BITS-enabled. BITS is supported only on Advanced Clients. Legacy Clients use Server Message Block (SMB).

To protect your Advanced Clients from excessive bandwidth consumption, enable BITS on your distribution points that serve Advanced Clients. If an interruption of your network connection occurs, BITS provides checkpoint restart download of packages by resuming within the file after the network connection is restored and if the client connects to the same distribution point. If you connect to a new distribution point, it restarts at the beginning of the file. The standard Server Message Block also provides checkpoint restart, but not at the same level within a file as BITS does.

Plan to have both your CAPs and distribution points on the same reliable high-speed connection as the site server. Although these site systems can function over a wide area network (WAN), the consequences can be detrimental and potentially cause significant network activity on your WAN.

If multiple SMS clients exist at a remote location, you might want to consider having a local distribution point to serve these SMS clients.

Important BITS requires Microsoft Internet Information Services (IIS) on the distribution point and that you enable BITS on the distribution point through SMS.

The benefits of delta replication

When SMS 2003 updates the source files for a package, and the source files have already been distributed to child SMS 2003 sites as local distribution points, it only sends the updated files in the package that have changed since the last time the package was distributed. Delta replication minimizes the network traffic between sites and to local distribution points, especially when the package being sent is large and the changes to that package are relatively small. Therefore, in most cases, delta replication greatly reduces network traffic.

Note A file is considered to be changed if it has been renamed or moved, or if its contents have changed.

Delta replication also occurs within each site to its distribution points. The files that have changed are transferred to the distribution points.

By default, the originating site keeps the differences between the current version of a package and the previous five versions. If a child site has one of the previous five versions of the package, the originating site will send the appropriate changes to the child site. If the child site has an older version of the package, the originating site will send the entire package.

If the originating site sends the changed files for a package but the child site no longer has the package or the package has been altered at the child site, the child site will send a status message to the originating site reporting the problem.

The benefits of compression

File compression helps streamline software distribution by reducing the load on the network. SMS automatically compresses package source files when it sends the package source files to other SMS sites. By default, files distributed within the originating site are not compressed. When compressed packages are sent to other sites, the other sites decompress the package and then distribute it to the distribution points.

If the source files are on removable media such as compact discs, you can have SMS create a compressed version of the source files in the event you assign a new distribution point to the package. SMS stores the compressed file and uses it instead of the original source files as a source for distribution.

Guidelines for Configuring a Site System to Be a Distribution Point

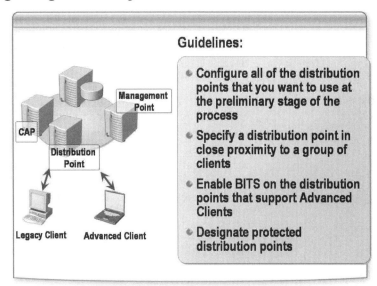

At installation, SMS assigns the distribution point role to the site server.

Follow these guidelines when configuring a site system to be a distribution point:

- *Configure all of the distribution points that you want to use at the preliminary stage of the process.* In this manner, you can select from existing distribution points when you distribute packages. You can create additional distribution points to reduce the load on the site server and provide access to all client computers in your site. When software distribution in your SMS system includes multiple sites, a distribution point is specified by default in each site to ensure access by client computers assigned to different sites.

- *Specify a distribution point in close proximity to a group of clients.* It is recommended that you locate distribution points as close to the clients as possible to minimize network travel connections over WAN links.

- *Enable BITS on the distribution points that support Advanced Clients.* To protect your Advanced Clients from excessive bandwidth consumption, enable BITS on your distribution points that serve Advanced Clients. If an interruption of your network connection occurs, BITS provides checkpoint restart download of packages by resuming within the file after the network connection is restored and if the client connects to the same distribution point.

- *Designate protected distribution points.* The protected distribution point is designed to protect distribution points from unwanted client access. The SMS administrator specifies which boundaries Advanced Clients must be in to use the protected distribution point. Any clients outside those boundaries are unable to access packages from that distribution point. For example, when an SMS client uses a slow or unreliable network link, you might want to ensure that the SMS client only accesses a protected distribution point that supports the boundary that the client is in.

  If there is a WAN connection between SMS site servers, you must be aware of and carefully consider bandwidth usage. Advanced Clients choose a distribution point by sending a Content Location Request to the local management point. The Advanced Client then receives a list of distribution points it can use. The Advanced Client lists the distribution points in order by IP subnet, Active Directory site, and SMS site when making package source file requests. The Advanced Client chooses the first distribution point it finds. Advanced Clients in a remote roaming configuration, and Legacy Clients, choose a distribution point randomly.

  For example, an organization implements SMS in its corporate campus with distribution points spread across several subnets. You might want to restrict access to a distribution point to clients in one building on the corporate campus. Therefore, you would enable a particular distribution point as a protected distribution point, limiting access to clients in the subnets of that building.

Note   For more information about distribution points, see Chapter 15, "Deploying and Configuring SMS Sites," in the *Microsoft Systems Management Server 2003 Concepts, Planning, and Deployment Guide* on the Additional Reading page of your Student Materials compact disc.

What Is a Distribution Point Group?

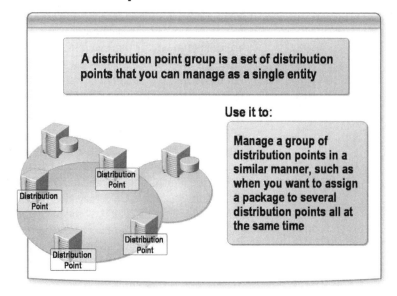

A *distribution point group* is a set of distribution points that you can manage as a single entity. A distribution point group simplifies management tasks when a site includes more distribution points than you can manage individually. You can use distribution point groups to quickly create a diverse collection of distribution points, such as those in multiple sites.

Note   Distribution point groups are useful at the site to which the SMS Administrator console is connected.

If you want to use a regular set of distribution points, you can create a group of all the distribution points and then assign packages to the distribution point group, instead of to the individual distribution points. You can create as many distribution point groups as you need.

Note   For more information about distribution point groups, see Chapter 15, "Deploying and Configuring SMS Sites," in the *Microsoft Systems Management Server 2003 Concepts, Planning, and Deployment Guide* on the Additional Reading page of your Student Materials compact disc.

Demonstration: How to Configure a Distribution Point and a Distribution Point Group

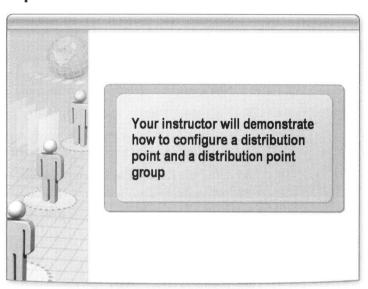

Your instructor will demonstrate how to configure a distribution point and a distribution point group

In this demonstration, you will see how to configure a distribution point and a distribution point group.

Your instructor will use the following values in this demonstration.

Variable	Value
Virtual machine—SMS Site 1	Dublin
Dublin administrator	JaePa (Jae Pak)
Virtual machine—domain controller	Glasgow
Domain administrator	Administrator

Important   These steps are included for your information. Do not attempt to perform them in the classroom. If you perform these steps in the classroom environment, you might leave your computer in an incorrect state for upcoming practices.

Demonstration steps performed by instructor only

▶ **To configure a distribution point and distribution point group**

1. Verify that the Glasgow and Dublin virtual machines are running.

2. On the Dublin virtual machine, click **Start**, point to **All Programs**, point to **Systems Management Server**, and then click the **SMS Administrator Console**.

3. In the console tree of the SMS Administrator console, expand **Site Database (001 – NWTraders)**, expand **Site Hierarchy**, expand **001 – NWTraders**, expand **Site Settings**, and then click **Site Systems**.

4. Right-click **Dublin**, and then click **Properties**.

5. On the **Distribution Point** tab, verify that the **Use this site system as a distribution point** check box is selected.

6. Select the **Enable Background Intelligent Transfer Service (BITS)** check box.

7. Click the **New** icon.

8. In the **Distribution Point Group Properties** dialog box, in the **Name** box, type **DPGroup1**

9. Verify that the **Include this site system in this distribution point group** check box is selected.

10. Click **OK** twice.

11. Close the SMS Administrator console.

12. Leave the Glasgow and Dublin virtual machines running.

Note Although the Distribution Point site role has been enabled, the actual share will not exist on the site system until at least one package is configured to use this Distribution Point. Steps to verify the creation of the share can then be performed.

Practice: Managing Distribution Points

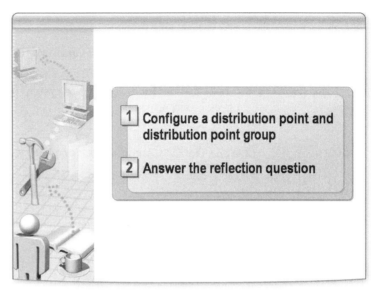

Instructions

Complete the procedures to practice configuring a distribution point and verifying the configuration. Then answer the reflection question.

Use the following values.

Variable	Value
Virtual machine—SMS Site 1	Dublin
Dublin administrator	JaePa (Jae Pak)
Virtual machine—domain controller	Glasgow
Domain administrator	Administrator

Procedure

▶ **To configure a distribution point and distribution point group**

1. If you have not already done so, log the Glasgow virtual machine on to the NWTRADERS domain with a user name of **Administrator** and a password of **P@ssw0rd**.

    After the Glasgow virtual machine opens, you can minimize it.

2. If you have not already done so, log the Dublin virtual machine on to the NWTRADERS domain with a user name of **JaePa** and a password of **P@ssw0rd**.

3. On the Dublin virtual machine, click **Start**, point to **All Programs**, point to **Systems Management Server**, and then click the **SMS Administrator Console**.

4. In the console tree of the SMS Administrator console, expand **Site Database (001 – NWTraders)**, expand **Site Hierarchy**, expand **001 – NWTraders**, expand **Site Settings**, and then click **Site Systems**.

5. Right-click **Dublin**, and then click **Properties**.

6. On the **Distribution Point** tab, verify that the **Use this site system as a distribution point** check box is selected.

7. Select the **Enable Background Intelligent Transfer Service (BITS)** check box.

8. Click the **New** ⚹ icon.

9. In the **Distribution Point Group Properties** dialog box, in the **Name** box, type **DPGroup1**

10. Verify that the **Include this site system in this distribution point group** check box is selected.

11. Click **OK** twice.

12. Close the SMS Administrator console.

13. Leave the Glasgow and Dublin virtual machines running.

Note   Although the Distribution Point site role has been enabled, the actual share will not exist on the site system until at least one package is configured to use this Distribution Point. Steps to verify the creation of the share can then be performed.

Reflection question

Clair Hector is the director of IT and Jae Pak is the systems administrator for Northwind Traders. Clair and Jae are considering adding distribution points to sites in the Northwind Traders hierarchy. Clair has asked Jae to identify issues with adding distribution point servers.

What are the network management issues concerning distribution points, and why are they important?

_____

_____

_____

_____

_____

Lesson: Configuring Software Distribution and the Advertised Programs Client Agent

- **What Is the Advanced Client Network Access Account?**
- **Software Distribution Component Settings that Administrators Typically Specify**
- **Guidelines for Configuring the Software Distribution Component**
- **Demonstration: How to Configure the Software Distribution Component**
- **Advertised Programs Client Agent Settings that Administrators Typically Specify**
- **Demonstration: How to Configure the Advertised Programs Client**
- **Demonstration: How to Verify the Download of Agent Policy on the Advanced Client**

Introduction

In this lesson, you will learn how to make the necessary configuration changes to enable software distribution for SMS clients using the Advertised Programs Client Agent.

Lesson objectives

After completing this lesson, you will be able to:

- Describe the Advanced Client Network Access Account.

- Identify the software distribution component settings that administrators typically specify.

- Describe the guidelines for configuring the software distribution component.

- Configure the Software Distribution component.

- Identify the Advertised Programs Client Agent settings that administrators typically specify.

- Configure the Advertised Programs Client Agent.

- Verify the download of Agent Policy on the Advanced Client.

What Is the Advanced Client Network Access Account?

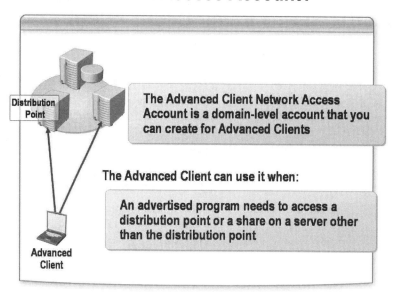

Software distribution accounts are used to access content on SMS clients. The accounts are used in both standard security and advanced security sites. The Legacy Client uses the Legacy Client Software Installation Account, and the Advanced Client uses the Advanced Client Network Access Account.

The *Advanced Client Network Access Account* is a domain-level account that you can create for Advanced Clients. The Advanced Client can use this account when an advertised program needs to access a distribution point or a share on a server other than the distribution point. Consequently, this account must have the appropriate permissions on the share that the advertised program accesses. After the SMS client has tried using its computer account and the logged on user account to connect to the distribution point, the client attempts to connect by using the Advanced Client Network Access Account.

Software Distribution Component Settings that Administrators Typically Specify

Software Distribution component settings that administrators typically specify on the General tab:

- The drive on the site server on which compressed package files are stored
- The number of threads to allocate to package processing
- The user name and password for the Legacy Client Software Installation Account
- The user name and password for the Advanced Client Network Access Account

The Software Distribution component is configured with defaults that are appropriate for most SMS installations. However, you can use the SMS Administrator console to specify these settings as needed. You configure the SMS Software Distribution component by using either the **General** tab or the **Retry Settings** tab in the **Software Distribution Properties** dialog box. The following table introduces the software distribution settings that you typically specify.

The Setting to Specify	The Tab to Use	Information About the Setting
The drive on the site server on which compressed package (.pkg) files created by SMS are stored	**General** tab	SMS creates a compressed version of a package source folder when the package is sent to a different site, or when the package properties are set to create and reference a compressed copy of the package source folder.
The number of threads to allocate to package processing	**General** tab	By default, the processing thread limit is three, but valid entries range from one to seven threads. As you allow more threads, SMS can process more packages concurrently.
The user name and password for the Legacy Client Software Installation Account	**General** tab	You use this option by specifying an account that can run advertised programs on Legacy Clients. By default, programs can run in the logged-on user's context or in a local administrator account. If you choose the local administrator account, then you use the SMSCliToknLocalAcct.

(continued)

The Setting to Specify	The Tab to Use	Information About the Setting
The user name and password for the Advanced Client Network Access Account	**General** tab	By default, the Advanced Client accesses distribution points by using the logged-on user's account or by using the computer account if no user is logged on. If these accounts do not have the appropriate access permissions, the client uses the Advanced Client Network Access Account.
The retry settings for updating distribution points	**Retry Settings** tab	You can set the number of retries for the Distribution Manager to distribute package source files to distribution points. You set the number of retries and the delay intervals between them.
The retry settings for updating CAPs	**Retry Settings** tab	You can set the number of retries for the Advertisement Manager to distribute advertisements and package information to CAPs.

Guidelines for Configuring the Software Distribution Component

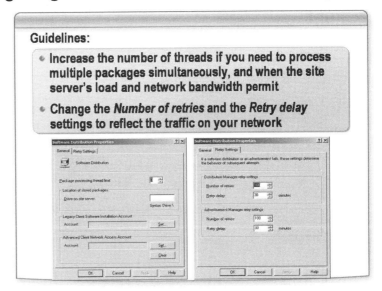

Guidelines:

* Increase the number of threads if you need to process multiple packages simultaneously, and when the site server's load and network bandwidth permit
* Change the *Number of retries* and the *Retry delay* settings to reflect the traffic on your network

There are certain guidelines you should follow when configuring the software distribution component. These guidelines are listed in the following table.

The Setting to Specify	Guidelines
The number of threads to allocate to package processing	For most installations, the default value is best. However, in cases in which the site server's load and network bandwidth permit, you might want to increase the number of threads if you need to process multiple packages simultaneously.
	Be aware that only one package will be compressed at a time, and only one package will be decompressed at a time.
The user name and password for the Advanced Client Network Access Account	You must create this account manually as a domain user account with the rights needed to access the required network resources. If the account must be used in multiple domains because users might use resources from multiple domains, the domains should be set to trust each other so that the account can be used on the resources on all the domains.
The retry settings for updating distribution points and CAPs	By default, retries are set to 100, but valid entries range from 1 to 1,000 retries. The default retry delay value is 30 minutes, but valid entries range from 1 through 1,440 minutes. Change these settings to reflect the traffic on your network.
	Be aware that retries can generate significant network traffic. Generally, the lighter the network traffic, the more often you can set the number of retries.

Demonstration: How to Configure the Software Distribution Component

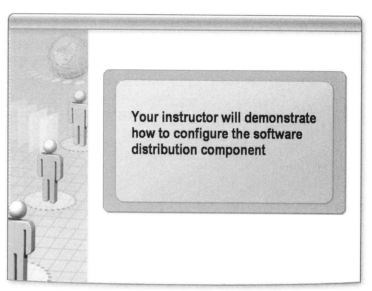

In this demonstration, you will see how to configure the software distribution component.

Your instructor will use the following values in this demonstration.

Variable	Value
Virtual machine—SMS Site 1	Dublin
Dublin administrator	JaePa (Jae Pak)
Virtual machine—domain controller	Glasgow
Domain administrator	Administrator

Important These steps are included for your information. Do not attempt to perform them in the classroom. If you perform these steps in the classroom environment, you might leave your computer in an incorrect state for upcoming practices.

Demonstration steps performed by instructor only

▶ **To configure the software distribution component**

1. Verify that the Glasgow and Dublin virtual machines are running.

2. On the Dublin virtual machine, click **Start**, point to **All Programs**, point to **Systems Management Server**, and then click **SMS Administrator Console**.

3. Expand **Site Database (001 – NWTraders)**, expand **Site Hierarchy**, expand **001 – NWTraders**, expand **Site Settings**, and then click **Component Configuration**.

4. Right-click **Software Distribution**, and then click **Properties**.

5. In **Software Distribution Properties** dialog box, under the **Advanced Client Network Access Account** area, click **Set**.

6. In the **Windows User Account** dialog box, in the **User name** box, type **NWTRADERS\SMS_Net_Access**

7. In the **Password** and **Confirm Password** boxes, type **P@ssw0rd**

8. Click **OK** twice.

9. Close the SMS Administrator console.

10. Leave the Glasgow and Dublin virtual machines running.

Advertised Programs Client Agent Settings that Administrators Typically Specify

Advertised Programs Client Agent settings that administrators typically specify on the General tab:

* Enable or disable the agent
* Whether you want Legacy Clients to be able to change agent settings
* Program or policy polling intervals
* For Advanced Clients, whether you want a new program notification icon to open Add or Remove Programs

The role of the Advertised Programs Client Agent is to facilitate software distribution at the client. The client agent runs on the client's computer and primarily allows clients to receive and run programs that you advertise.

Configuring the Advertised Programs Client Agent should be one of the first steps you take in preparing the site for software distribution. After enabling software distribution, SMS installs the Advertised Programs Client Agent on all Legacy Client computers within the site and enables the SMS Software Distribution Agent on all Advanced Client computers within the site. Before using SMS software distribution, examine the configuration of the Advertised Programs Client Agent and adjust the configuration as necessary. You adjust the configuration by using either the **General** tab or the **Notification** tab in the **Advertised Programs Client Agent Properties** dialog box. Each setting is introduced in the following table.

The Setting to Specify	The Tab to Use
Enable or disable the Advertised Programs Client Agent	**General** tab
Whether you want Legacy Clients to be able to change Agent settings	**General** tab
Program or Policy polling intervals	**General** tab
For Advanced Clients, whether you want a new program notification icon to open Add or Remove Programs	**General** tab
Display a visual indicator when new advertisements are received	**Notification** tab
Play a sound when new advertisements are received	**Notification** tab
Provide a countdown and countdown length when scheduled programs are set to run	**Notification** tab
Play countdown sounds when a scheduled program is about to run	**Notification** tab
Show a status icon in the notification area for advertised programs	**Notification** tab

Options that you select apply to all client computers in the site. Clients requiring different settings must be assigned to a separate SMS site. In some situations, you will want to give the Legacy Client the ability to change Agent settings. Some of these settings include the ability to turn off notifications, to specify how frequently to check for new programs, to be notified when new advertised programs are available, or when a scheduled program is about to run.

Note For more information on the role of the Advertised Programs Client Agent, refer to Managing Software Installation at the Client in Module 8, "Managing Software Distribution."

Demonstration: How to Configure the Advertised Programs Client Agent

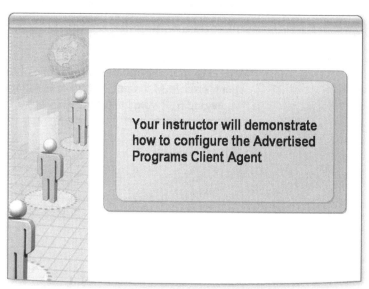

In this demonstration, you will see how to configure the Advertised Programs Client Agent.

Your instructor will use the following values in this demonstration.

Variable	Value
Virtual machine—SMS Site 1	Dublin
Dublin administrator	JaePa (Jae Pak)
Virtual machine—domain controller	Glasgow
Domain administrator	Administrator

Important   These steps are included for your information. Do not attempt to perform them in the classroom. If you perform these steps in the classroom environment, you might leave your computer in an incorrect state for upcoming practices.

Demonstration steps performed by instructor only

▶ **To configure the Advertised Programs Client Agent**

1. Verify that the Glasgow and Dublin virtual machines are running.

2. On the **Dublin** virtual machine, click **Start**, point to **All Programs**, point to **Systems Management Server**, and then click **SMS Administrator Console**.

3. Expand **Site Database (001 – NWTraders)**, expand **Site Hierarchy**, expand **001 – NWTraders**, expand **Site Settings**, and then click **Client Agents**.

4. Right-click **Advertised Programs Client Agent**, and then click **Properties**.

5. On the **General** tab, select the **Enable software distribution to clients** check box.

6. In the **Legacy Client settings** area, select the **Clients cannot change agent settings** check box, and then verify that the **Program polling interval (minutes)** is set to **60**.

7. In the **Advanced Client settings** area, verify that the **Policy polling interval (minutes)** is set to **60**, and then select the **New program notification icon opens Add or Remove Programs** check box.

Important   It is not recommended that you decrease the program polling interval default setting of 60 minutes for either the Legacy Client or the Advanced Client. A lower setting can cause unnecessary network traffic.

---

8. On the **Notification** tab, select the **Display a notification message** check box, and then click **OK**.

9. Close the SMS Administrator console.

10. Leave the Glasgow and Dublin virtual machines running.

Demonstration: How to Verify the Download of Agent Policy on the Advanced Client

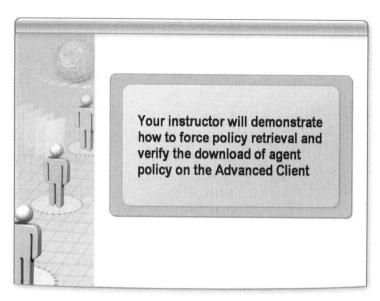

In this demonstration, you will see how to verify the download of agent policy on the Advanced Client by using Policy Spy.

Your instructor will use the following values in this demonstration.

Variable	Value
Virtual machine—SMS Site 1	Dublin
Dublin administrator	JaePa (Jae Pak)
Virtual machine—domain controller	Glasgow
Domain administrator	Administrator
Virtual machine—SMS Advanced Client	Bonn
Bonn administrator	SMartinez (Sandra Martinez)

Important   These steps are included for your information. Do not attempt to perform them in the classroom. If you perform these steps in the classroom environment, you might leave your computer in an incorrect state for upcoming practices.

Demonstration steps performed by instructor only

▶ **To force policy retrieval on the client**

1. Log the Bonn virtual machine on to the NWTRADERS domain with a user name of **SMartinez** and a password of **P@ssw0rd**.

2. On the Bonn virtual machine, click **Start**, and then click **Control Panel**.

3. Click **Performance and Maintenance**, and then click **Systems Management**.

4. In the **Systems Management Properties** dialog box, on the **Actions** tab, click **Machine Policy Retrieval & Evaluation Cycle**, and then click **Initiate Action**.

5. On the **Machine Policy Retrieval & Evaluation Cycle** message box, click **OK**.

Note   Be sure to wait about two minutes for the policy update to complete before moving to the next step.

---

6. On the **Components** tab, verify that the **SMS Software Distribution Agent** component appears and that its status is **Enabled**.

7. Click **OK**.

8. Close the Control Panel.

▶ **To verify the download of agent policy on the Advanced Client**

1. On the Bonn virtual machine, click **Start**, point to **All Programs**, point to **SMS 2003 Toolkit 1**, and then click **Policy Spy**.

2. Click the **Actual** tab, expand the **Machine** folder, and then expand **CMM_SoftwareDistributionClientConfig**.

3. Click **SiteSettingsKey=[1]**.

   The policy appears in the lower pane.

4. Verify there is a line that states **Enabled=True**.

5. Close Policy Spy.

6. Leave the Glasgow, Dublin, and Bonn virtual machines running.

Practice: Configuring Software Distribution and the Advertised Programs Client Agent

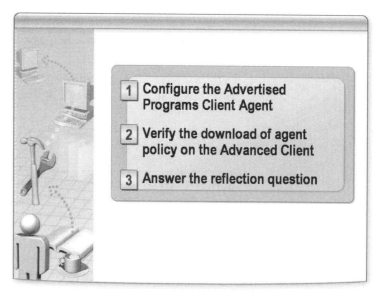

1 Configure the Advertised Programs Client Agent

2 Verify the download of agent policy on the Advanced Client

3 Answer the reflection question

Instructions

Complete the procedures to practice configuring the Advertised Programs Client Agent and verifying the download of agent policy on the Advanced Client. Then answer the reflection question.

Use the following values.

Variable	Value
Virtual machine—SMS Site 1	Dublin
Dublin administrator	JaePa (Jae Pak)
Virtual machine—domain controller	Glasgow
Domain administrator	Administrator
Virtual machine—SMS Advanced Client	Bonn
Bonn administrator	SMartinez (Sandra Martinez)

Procedures

▶ **To configure the Advertised Programs Client Agent**

1. Verify that the Glasgow and Dublin virtual machines are running.

2. On the Dublin virtual machine, click **Start**, point to **All Programs**, point to **Systems Management Server**, and then click **SMS Administrator Console**.

3. Expand **Site Database (001 – NWTraders)**, expand **Site Hierarchy**, expand **001 – NWTraders**, expand **Site Settings**, and then click **Client Agents**.

4. Right-click **Advertised Programs Client Agent**, and then click **Properties**.

5. On the **General** tab, select the **Enable software distribution to clients** check box.

6. In the **Legacy Client settings** area, select the **Clients cannot change agent settings** check box, and then verify that the **Program polling interval (minutes)** is set to **60**.

7. In the **Advanced Client settings** area, verify that the **Policy polling interval (minutes)** is set to **60**, and then select the **New program notification icon opens Add or Remove Programs** check box.

> **Important** It is not recommended that you decrease the program polling interval default setting of 60 minutes for either the Legacy Client or the Advanced Client. A lower setting can cause unnecessary network traffic.

8. On the **Notification** tab, select the **Display a notification message** check box, and then click **OK**.

9. Close the SMS Administrator console.

▶ **To force policy retrieval on the client**

1. Log the Bonn virtual machine on to the NWTRADERS domain with a user name of **SMartinez** and a password of **P@ssw0rd**.

2. On the Bonn virtual machine, click **Start**, and then click **Control Panel**.

3. Click **Performance and Maintenance**, and then click **Systems Management**.

4. In the **Systems Management Properties** dialog box, on the **Actions** tab, click **Machine Policy Retrieval & Evaluation Cycle**, and then click **Initiate Action**.

5. On the **Machine Policy Retrieval & Evaluation Cycle** message box, click **OK**

> **Note** Be sure to wait about two minutes for the policy update to complete before moving to the next step.

6. On the **Components** tab, verify that the **SMS Software Distribution Agent** component appears and that its status is **Enabled**.

7. Click **OK**.

8. Close the Control Panel.

▶ **To verify the download of agent policy on the Advanced Client**

1. On the Bonn virtual machine, click **Start**, point to **All Programs**, point to **SMS 2003 Toolkit 1**, and then click **Policy Spy**.

2. Click the **Actual** tab, expand the **Machine** folder, and then expand **CMM_SoftwareDistributionClientConfig**.

3. Click **SiteSettingsKey=[1]**.

   The policy appears in the lower pane.

4. Verify that there is a line that states **Enabled=True**.

5. Close Policy Spy.

6. On the Bonn virtual machine, on the **Action** menu, click **Close**.

7. Verify that **Save state and save changes** is selected in the drop-down list, and then click **OK**.

   The Bonn virtual machine begins to shut down.

8. Leave the Glasgow and Dublin virtual machines running.

Reflection question

If you allowed Legacy Clients the ability to change agent settings, what settings could they change?

_____

_____

_____

_____

Discussion: Preparing an SMS Site for Software Distribution

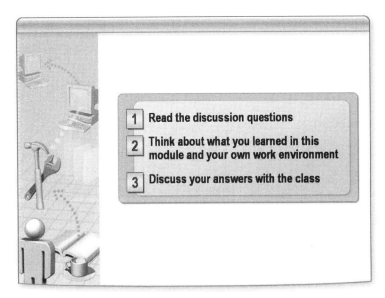

1. Broadly speaking, what types of collections could you use in your organization? How might the use of these collections streamline software distribution?

   _____

   _____

   _____

   _____

   _____

2. How does SMS software distribution give you flexibility in deploying applications to users in your organization?

   _____

   _____

   _____

3. You are responsible for configuring the Advertised Programs Client Agent within your organization. What must you consider? Why might you need to assign some clients to different SMS sites?

    _____

    _____

    _____

    _____

Module 8: Managing Software Distribution

Contents

Overview

- Configuring Software Distribution Objects Using a Software Distribution Methodology
- Creating and Configuring Collections
- Creating and Configuring Packages
- Creating and Configuring Advertisements and Managing Software Installation at the Client
- Monitoring Software Distribution

Introduction

The Microsoft® Systems Management Server (SMS) software distribution feature automates the distribution of programs to SMS clients. These programs run on the client computers to perform tasks such as installing software or scanning the client's hard drives for viruses.

In this module, you will learn to distribute software to SMS clients by creating a package and then advertising a program from the package to a collection of clients. In Module 7, the first stage of the software distribution sequence was discussed. This module will build upon the previous module and discuss the three remaining stages of the distribution sequence.

Objectives

After completing this module, you will be able to:

- Explain the sequence of the software distribution methodology.
- Create and configure collections.
- Create and configure packages.
- Create and configure advertisements.
- Monitor software distribution.

Lesson: Configuring Software Distribution Objects Using a Software Distribution Methodology

- How Software Distribution Objects Are Created
- What Is a Collection?
- What Do Packages and Programs Do?
- What Are Advertisements?
- How the Configuration of Software Distribution Objects Is Verified
- How the Distribution of Files on the Distribution Point Is Verified

Introduction

In this lesson, you will learn how to use a methodology to reliably distribute software in an enterprise. The principles of the software distribution methodology will help enforce a pattern of behavior which will minimize the possibility of errors.

Lesson objectives

After completing this lesson, you will be able to:

- Describe how software distribution objects are created.
- Describe what collections are.
- Describe what packages and programs do.
- Describe what advertisements are.
- Verify the configuration of software distribution objects.
- Verify the distribution of files on the distribution point.

How Software Distribution Objects Are Created

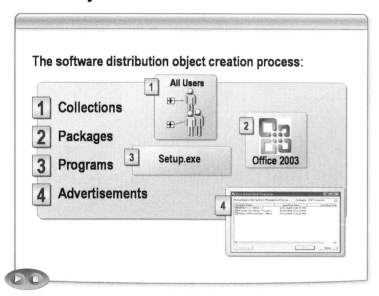

The distribution of software has a specific sequence that needs to be followed to ensure proper distribution. In Module 7, the first stage of the distribution sequence was discussed: that of configuring site settings. The next stage of the sequence is to create software distribution objects. This second stage has four parts:

1. Creating and Configuring Collections
2. Creating and Configuring Packages
3. Creating Programs
4. Creating and Configuring Advertisements

When you use software distribution, the inefficiency of sending out thousands of CDs containing programs and instructions is eliminated. Each of the four software distribution objects must be configured to define and control how and when programs will run on client computers and to determine how much user management will be involved.

The configuring of each object will be discussed in more detail in this module.

What Is a Collection?

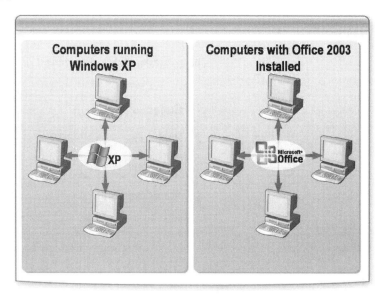

A collection is a set of resources in a site. The set is defined by membership rules. Collections are used to distribute software, view the inventories of clients, and access clients for remote control sessions. Examples of collections are all Microsoft Windows® XP Systems or all computers with Microsoft Office 2003 installed.

SMS includes many predefined collections that are useful in most SMS sites. You can also create your own collections based on discovery or inventory data such as all computers with a specific amount of disk space.

How collections are created

An administrator creates a collection by defining rules that add individual resources to the collection. Rules used to define the collection's member list are referred to as the collection's *membership rules*. SMS evaluates the membership rules to determine which resources should become members of that collection.

When you create a collection, SMS adds all resources that fit the membership rules you have specified for the collection. When SMS adds a new resource to the SMS site database, it also adds the resource to any collections that are appropriate the next time those collections are updated. You can configure a collection to be automatically updated according to a specified schedule. You can also update a collection's membership list on demand.

If you distribute software to a collection and then subsequently modify the membership rules for that collection, the modification affects the software distribution to the resources in that collection. Clients that are removed from the collection do not receive the advertisement, but any program that was installed while the client was a member of the collection remains. New members of the collection will receive the advertisement.

Purpose of collections

In the context of software distribution, collections are designed to gather resources into manageable groups and are designed to answer the question "Who will this be distributed to?" You will learn more about collections in Lesson 2, "Creating and Configuring Collections."

What Do Packages and Programs Do?

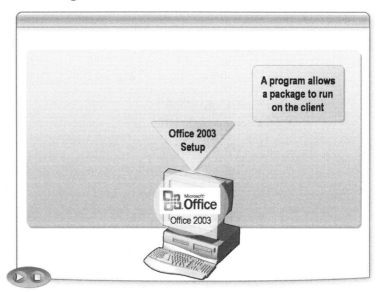

The next two software distribution objects that are found in the software distribution sequence are packages and programs.

Packages

Packages consist of three components that you will create and manage:

- The package definition, which sometimes includes the package source files
- The program that carries out the package task
- The process of distributing the packages to distribution points so that clients can access source files for the program that has been targeted to them

Creating packages can be as simple as manually naming the package itself. However, packages are not useful until they have SMS programs that specify which command line should be run in the packages to accomplish certain functions (such as setup or uninstallation). Because packages that contain files also need to be distributed to distribution points, defining which distribution points should be used for a package can also be important.

Creating a package object is the same as creating other SMS objects. The only required property is a name.

Packages answer the question "What will be distributed?"

Programs

After you create a package, you must create one or more programs. A program is actually a component of a package. Programs are commands that run on targeted client computers, for example, a program could be an executable file (.exe), a script, a batch file, or an operating system command. Programs answer the question "How will software be distributed?"

Programs have a wide range of configurable options, such as:

- Security context
- Supported platforms
- Environment requirements
- Run once for each user or once per computer
- Dependent programs
- The distribution point to access for package source files.

You will learn more about packages and programs in Lesson 3, "Creating and Configuring Packages."

What Are Advertisements?

An advertisement is an object configured by the site administrator on an SMS site, which in turn becomes a notification or a policy for the client

Advertised programs are found in Control Panel:

 Add or Remove Programs

 Run Advertised Programs

When you are ready to make a program in a package available to clients, you advertise the program to a target collection. Advertisements answer the question "Distribute when, to whom, and how often?" On Advanced Clients, newly advertised programs will be listed both in **Add or Remove Programs** in Control Panel or **Run Advertised Programs**. On Legacy Clients, advertised programs will be listed in **Advertised Programs** in Control Panel.

What is an advertisement?

An advertisement is an object configured by the site administrator on an SMS site, which in turn becomes a notification or a policy for the client.

On Legacy Clients, an advertisement is a notification that the site server sends to the client access points (CAPs) specifying that a software distribution program is available for clients.

On Advanced Clients, an advertisement is a policy that the management point will retrieve when a client requests policy.

How advertisements work

SMS uses collections to determine which clients receive an advertisement for a program. You will learn more about advertisements in Lesson 4, "Creating and Configuring Advertisements."

How the Configuration of Software Distribution Objects Is Verified

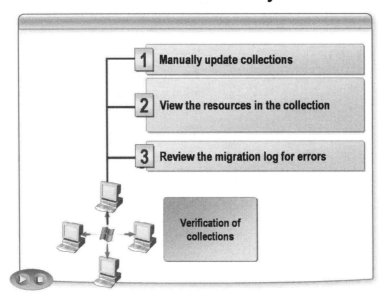

After software distribution objects have been configured, it is not difficult to verify that they have been created and configured.

Verifying collections

To verify collections you should:

1. Manually update collections.

2. View the resources in the collection.

3. View the Colleval.log file. This will let you know if troubleshooting is necessary.

Verifying packages

When one or more distribution points have been specified, a package folder will be created and can be viewed in two different locations. First, you can look in *x*:\SMSPKG*x*$ (where *x* is the drive that contains the package folder). This will list the individual folders containing the package files. The names of these will be the package IDs. Second, you can use the Report Viewer to view the **All packages** report. This can show you all packages for a distribution point. Finally, you can check Package Status from the SMS Administrator console to determine if the package was successfully sent to the distribution point.

Note SMSPKG*x*$ does not have to be saved on the C: drive. You can create an administrator share wherever it is most appropriate for your environment.

Verifying programs and advertisements

The easiest way to verify both programs and advertisements is to look for them in the SMS Administrator console. This is enough to know that they were configured and created. Programs are found by expanding the specific package node on the SMS Administrator console. Advertisements has its own node located on the SMS Administrator console.

Always verify files on CAPs to see if advertisements are available to Legacy Clients. If for some reason you cannot verify the advertisement on the CAP you have to look at Offermgr.log on the site server to see if the advertisement was successfully created and sent to the CAP. To verify that advertisement policy was successfully created for Advanced Clients, see Policypv.log,

How the Distribution of Files on the Distribution Point Is Verified

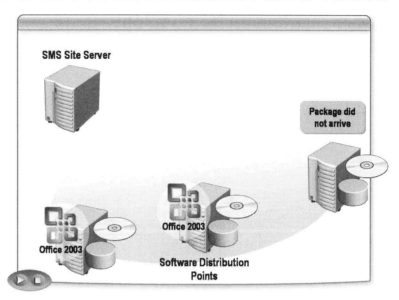

The Package Status Summarizer, which is available in the SMS Administrator console, provides a quick view of how many distribution points have successfully made the package available, how many are still retrying, and how many have failed. If the numbers do not look right, you can double-click any package to see more information, or you can right-click and then click **Show Messages** to see the informational, warning, and error messages that have been generated.

This topic will be covered in more detail in Lesson 6, "Monitoring Software Distribution."

Practice: Configuring Software Distribution Objects Using a Software Distribution Methodology

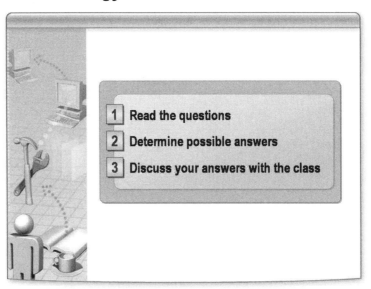

Instructions

Read the following reflection questions, determine possible answers, and then discuss your answers with the class.

Reflection questions

1. What is the difference between a package and a program?

_____

_____

_____

2. Why is it important to update a collection if you create or modify it?

_____

_____

_____

3. In your work environment, what types of programs do you think you will advertise?

    _____

    _____

    _____

Lesson: Creating and Configuring Collections

- How Collections Are Used in the Software Distribution Process
- How to Create and Configure Collections
- How to Verify the Updating of Collections with the SMS Administrator Console and Server Log Files
- Demonstration: How to Create a Collection with a Direct Membership Rule
- Demonstration: How to Verify the Created Collection
- Demonstration: How to Create a Collection with a Rule Based on a Query
- How to Create a Subcollection
- Demonstration: How to Create a Subcollection
- How Collections Are Propagated Down an SMS Hierarchy

Introduction

In this lesson you will learn how collections are used in the software distribution process. You also learn how to create and manage collections.

Lesson objectives

After completing this lesson, you will be able to:

- Describe how collections are used in the software distribution process.
- How to create collections.
- Verify the updating of collections with the SMS Administrator console and server log file.
- Create a subcollection.
- Describe how collections are propagated down an SMS hierarchy.

How Collections Are Used in the Software Distribution Process

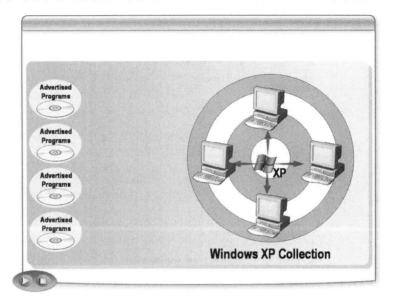

Collections serve as targets for SMS operations, primarily software distribution. By using collections, you can perform an SMS operation on every member of the collection at the same time. For example, when you want to distribute software to clients with certain minimum hardware requirements, you can use a collection of clients that meet those hardware requirements. A client must be in a collection before you can perform any SMS operation on that client.

You can use collections to group resources in a logical order instead of the physical order of groups such as sites. Collections also provide a manageable view into the SMS site database by partitioning the data into useful categories. Collections gather resources according to user-defined criteria.

How to Create and Configure Collections

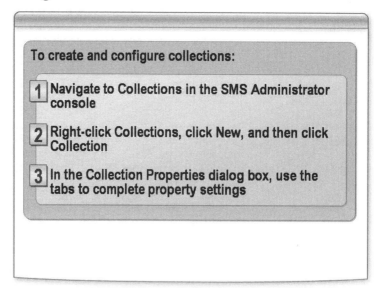

To create and configure collections:

1. Navigate to Collections in the SMS Administrator console

2. Right-click Collections, click New, and then click Collection

3. In the Collection Properties dialog box, use the tabs to complete property settings

During the stage of the software distribution sequence in which you create software distribution objects, you first have to create and configure collections.

To create a collection, you first create it, and then you specify its properties. You set the properties according to how your organization organizes users, user groups, and computers for software distribution and other tasks. You must have the appropriate permissions to create or modify collections.

Procedure to a create a collection

To create a new collection:

1. Navigate to Collections in the SMS Administrator console.

2. Right-click **Collections**, point to **New**, and then click **Collection**.

3. In the **Collection Properties** dialog box, use the tabs to complete property settings.

When creating collections, you will be specifying certain properties. There are four tabs in the **Collection Properties** dialog box.

The purpose of the collection properties tabs

Tab Name	Purpose
General	The General tab is where you will name your collection.
Membership rules	Specifying Membership Rules is also known as defining resource groups. Membership rules are based on one of the following:

- SMS query

  - SMS will search for all resources that match the defined query. All the resources returned by the query will become members of the collection. For example, your query may be designed to find all resources with 256 megabytes (MB) of RAM. Query-based rules can also specify collection limiting, which means it will be limited to resources found in other collections.

- Specific resource or group (direct membership rule)

  - Membership rules can be targeted toward individual resources, such as a list of users, user groups, or SMS clients. The targeted resources become permanent members of the collection. For example, you could create a small collection for a test deployment of an application you want to distribute.

* You can use the Create Direct Membership Rules Wizard to assist you in creating the membership rules you would like to specify for a collection.

Another property located on the Membership Rules tab is the schedule. You can specify a schedule for when you would like the collection to be updated. You can also manually update collection membership when desired outside the scheduled updates. Because new resources will be added to your company, they will need to be part of a collection to be able to receive any new software that becomes available through advertised programs.

Tab Name	Purpose
Advertisements	The Advertisements tab allows you to specify which programs you would like to make available for the new collection. This tab is used to view advertisements targeted to the collection. It is not used for configuring the advertisement.
Security	The Security tab allows you to specify what rights users will have on either all collections (object class) or the specific collection (instance).

When collections are updated

SMS periodically evaluates resources against the membership rules. When hardware and software configurations on individual computers change, SMS removes those computers from collections or adds new computers to collections according to the membership rules of the collections at the next collection update cycle. By keeping collections current, SMS ensures that your software distributions always go to all the computers that meet your collection criteria, including those computers that were added to the network after you created the collection.

When to modify a collection

After a collection has been created, it can be modified at any time. You may need to change the update schedule for a collection or make a new advertised program available to a collection.

Procedure to modify a collection

To modify a collection:

1. In the SMS Administrator console, navigate to Collections.

2. Right-click the collection you want to modify and then click **Properties**.

3. In the **Collection Properties** dialog box, change the appropriate properties.

How to Verify the Updating of Collections with the SMS Administrator Console and Server Log Files

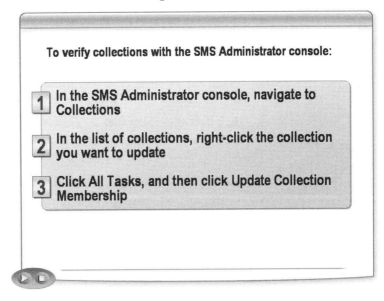

When dealing with collections, it is important to make sure that they are updated on a regular basis. When you create a collection, you can set it to update automatically on a schedule. You can also manually update collections if the need arises.

Procedure to update a collection

In the SMS Administrator console, you can manually update a collection.

To update a collection in the SMS Administrator console:

1. In the SMS Administrator console, navigate to Collections.

2. In the list of collections, right-click the collection you want to update.

3. Point to **All Tasks**, and then click **Update Collection Membership**.

Verifying collections with server log files

Server log files are mainly used to troubleshoot problems. You can also verify the update of a collection in the server log files if something unexpected happens with the update of your collection. This can be used if your collection is updating on a schedule.

Procedures to verify collections were updated

You can view the server log files in two ways: by using the SMS Trace tool or by navigating to the Logs folder.

To use the SMS Trace Tool to view server log files:

1. Click **Start**, point to **All Programs**, and then point to **SMS 2003 Tool Kit 1**.

2. Click **SMS Trace**. The SMS Trace window will appear.

3. On the **File** menu, click **Open**. All the log files will appear in the details pane of the SMS Trace window.

4. Click the **colleval.log** file, and then click **Open**.

To use Log folder to view server log files:

1. Click **Start** and then click **My Computer**.

2. Double-click **Local Disk**.

3. Double-click the **SMS** folder.

4. Double-click the **Logs** folder. All the logs will appear in the details pane.

Demonstration: How to Create a Collection with a Direct Membership Rule

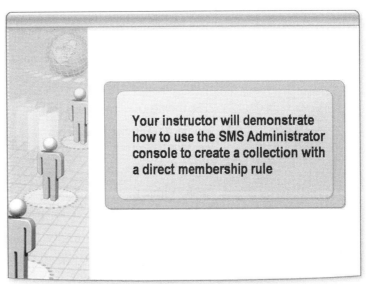

In this demonstration, you will see how to create a collection with a direct membership rule.

Your instructor will use the following values in this demonstration.

Variable	Value
Virtual machine—SMS Site 1	Dublin
Dublin Administrator	JaePa (Jae Pak)
Virtual machine—domain controller	Glasgow
Domain administrator	Administrator

Important These steps are included for your information. Do not attempt to perform them in the classroom. If you perform these steps in the classroom environment, you might leave your computer in an incorrect state for upcoming practices.

Demonstration steps performed by instructor only

▶ **To create a collection with a direct membership rule**

1. If you have not already done so, log the Glasgow virtual machine on to the NWTRADERS domain with a user name of **Administrator** and a password of **P@ssw0rd**.

    After the Glasgow virtual machine opens, you can minimize it.

2. If you have not already done so, log the Dublin virtual machine on to the NWTRADERS domain with a user name of **JaePa** and a password of **P@ssw0rd**.

3. On the Dublin virtual machine, click **Start**, point to **Programs**, point to **Systems Management Server**, and then click **SMS Administrator Console**.

4. In the SMS Administrator console, expand **Site Database (001 – NWTraders)**, and then click **Collections**.

5. Right-click **Collections**, point to **New**, and then click **Collection**.

   The **Collection Properties** dialog box will open.

6. On the **General** tab, type **Demo 1 Collection** in the **Name** box.

7. On the **Membership Rules** tab, create a membership rule by clicking the

   New membership rule [icon] icon.

   a. The Create Direct Membership Rule Wizard will open. Click **Next**.

   b. On the **Search for Resources** page, in the **Resources class** list, select **System Resource**.

   c. In the **Attribute name** list, select **Name**.

   d. In the **Value** field, type **Bonn**

   e. Click **Next**.

   f. On the **Collection Limiting** page, click **Browse**.

   g. Click **All Systems**, and then click **OK**.

   h. Click **Next**.

   i. Under **System Resources**, select the **Bonn** check box, and then click **Next**.

   j. Click **Finish**.

8. Set the schedule to update the collection.

   a. On the **Membership Rules** tab, verify that the **Update this collection on a schedule** check box is selected.

   b. Click **Schedule**.

      The **Schedule** dialog box will open.

   c. Verify that the **Start** date is the same as, or prior to, today's date.

   d. Verify that **Recurrence pattern** is set to **Interval**.

   e. Set **Recur every** to **3 days**, and then click **OK**.

9. Click **OK** to close the **Collection Properties** dialog box.

10. Close the SMS Administrator console.

11. Leave the Glasgow and Dublin virtual machines running.

Demonstration: How to Verify the Created Collection

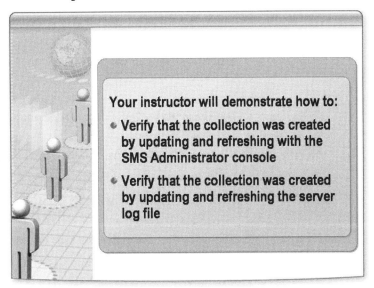

In this demonstration, you will see how to verify the created collection by refreshing the SMS Administrator console and viewing the server log file (Colleval.log).

Your instructor will use the following values in this demonstration.

Variable	Value
Virtual machine—SMS Site 1	Dublin
Dublin Administrator	JaePa (Jae Pak)
Virtual machine—domain controller	Glasgow
Domain administrator	Administrator

Important These steps are included for your information. Do not attempt to perform them in the classroom. If you perform these steps in the classroom environment, you might leave your computer in an incorrect state for upcoming practices.

Demonstration steps performed by instructor only

▶ **To verify that the collection was created by refreshing the SMS Administrator console**

1. Verify that Glasgow and Dublin virtual machines are running.

2. On the Dublin virtual machine, click **Start**, point to **All Programs**, point to **Systems Management Server**, and then click **SMS Administrator Console**.

3. In the console tree of the SMS Administrator console, expand **Site Database (001 – NWTraders)**, expand **Collections**, and then click **Collections**.

4. Right-click **Collections**, and then click **Refresh**.

5. In the details pane, verify that **Demo 1 Collection** is displayed.

6. Write the Collection ID for the **Demo 1 Collection** here: _____ .

▶ **To verify that the collection was created by viewing the server log file**

1. On the Dublin virtual machine, click **Start**, and then click **Windows Explorer**.

2. In the **Folders** list, browse to **C:\SMS\Logs**.

3. In the details list, double-click the file **colleval.log**.

4. Review the log to verify that **Demo 1 Collection** was created:

   a. In the **SMS Trace** window, on the **Tools** menu, click **Find**.

   b. In the **Find what** box, type the *Collection ID* previously recorded, and then click **Find**.

   c. Verify that **Demo 1 Collection** was created.

5. Close any open windows.

6. Leave the Glasgow and Dublin virtual machines running.

Demonstration: How to Create a Collection with a Rule Based on a Query

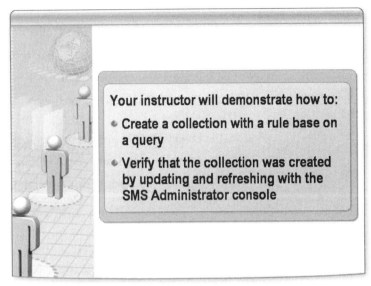

In this demonstration, you will see how to create a collection with a rule based on a query. You will also see how to verify the collection by refreshing the SMS Administrator console.

Your instructor will use the following values in this demonstration.

Variable	Value
Virtual machine—SMS Site 1	Dublin
Dublin Administrator	JaePa (Jae Pak)
Virtual machine—domain controller	Glasgow
Domain administrator	Administrator

Important   These steps are included for your information. Do not attempt to perform them in the classroom. If you perform these steps in the classroom environment, you might leave your computer in an incorrect state for upcoming practices.

Demonstration steps performed by instructor only

▶ **To create a collection with a rule based on a query**

1. Verify that Glasgow and Dublin virtual machines are running.

2. On the Dublin virtual machine, click **Start**, point to **All Programs**, point to **Systems Management Server**, and then click **SMS Administrator Console**.

3. In the SMS Administrator console, expand **Site Database (001 - NWTraders)**, and then click **Collections**.

4. Right-click **Collections**, point to **New**, and then click **Collection**.

   The **Collection Properties** dialog box will open.

5. In the **Name** box, type **Demo 3 Collection**

6. On the **Membership Rules** tab, click the **New query** icon.

   The **Query Rule Properties** dialog box will open.

7. In the **Name** box, type **Demo 3 Collection**

8. In the **Resource class** list, verify that **System Resource** is selected.

9. Click **Import Query Statement**.

10. In the **Browse Query** dialog box, click **All Client Systems**, and then click **OK**.

11. In the **Query Rule Properties** dialog box, click **OK**.

12. Set the schedule to update the collection.

    a. Verify that the **Update this collection on a schedule** check box is selected.

    b. Click **Schedule**.

       The **Schedule** dialog box will open.

    c. Verify that the **Start** date is the same as, or prior to, today's date.

    d. Verify that **Recurrence pattern** is set to **Interval**.

    e. Set **Recur every** to **3 days**, and then click **OK**.

13. Click **OK** to close the **Collection Properties** dialog box.

▶ **To verify that the collection was created by refreshing the SMS Administrator console**

1. In the console tree of the SMS Administrator console, right-click **Collections**, and then click **Refresh**.

2. Verify that **Demo 3 Collection** exists.

3. In the console tree of the SMS Administrator console, click once on **Demo 3 Collection**. In the details pane, verify that Dublin, Bonn, and Perth are members of the collection. (Perth may not appear yet due to timings.)

4. Leave the Glasgow and Dublin virtual machines running.

How to Create a Subcollection

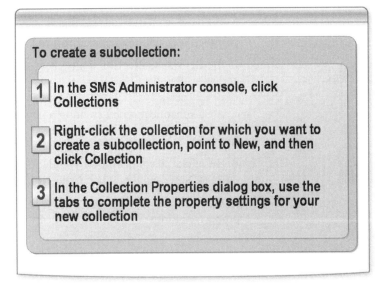

To create a subcollection:

1. In the SMS Administrator console, click Collections

2. Right-click the collection for which you want to create a subcollection, point to New, and then click Collection

3. In the Collection Properties dialog box, use the tabs to complete the property settings for your new collection

In addition to resources, collections can contain other collections, which are called subcollections. Subcollections are not members of the parent collection. A collection can be a subcollection of multiple collections. This is important because it means that multiple instances of a collection can appear throughout the hierarchy. This also means that you can delete one instance of a collection and still have other instances of that same collection appear elsewhere as subcollections.

Subcollections function in the same way as nested distribution lists within an e-mail system. The nested distribution list has its own identity and is simply a convenient way of gathering the diverse set of groups that form the distribution list. In the same way, subcollections are a convenient way to gather several diverse groups of resources into a single group to be acted on in some way.

You can create subcollections in two ways:

- By linking the collection to another existing collection
- By creating a new collection under an existing collection

Procedures

To create a subcollection by linking to another collection:

1. In the SMS Administrator console, click **Collections**.
2. Right-click the collection for which you want to create a subcollection, point to **New**, and then click **Link to Collection**.
3. In the **Browse Collection** dialog box, select the collection that you want to add as a subcollection.

To create a subcollection by creating a new collection:

1. In the SMS Administrator console, click **Collections**.
2. Right-click the collection for which you want to create a subcollection, point to **New**, and then click **Collection**.
3. In the **Collection Properties** dialog box, use the tabs to complete the property settings for your new collection.

Demonstration: How to Create a Subcollection

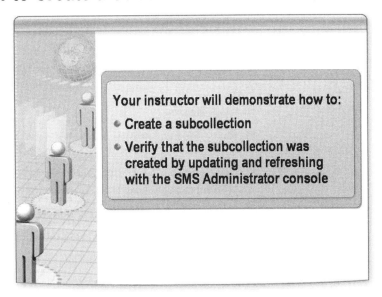

In this demonstration you will see how to create a subcollection.

Your instructor will use the following values in this demonstration.

Variable	Value
Virtual machine—SMS Site 1	Dublin
Dublin Administrator	JaePa (Jae Pak)
Virtual machine—domain controller	Glasgow
Domain administrator	Administrator

Important   These steps are included for your information. Do not attempt to perform them in the classroom. If you perform these steps in the classroom environment, you might leave your computer in an incorrect state for upcoming practices.

Demonstration steps performed by instructor only

▶ **To create a subcollection**

1. Verify that Glasgow and Dublin virtual machines are running.

2. On the Dublin virtual machine, click **Start**, point to **All Programs**, point to **Systems Management Server**, and then click **SMS Administrator Console**.

3. In the SMS Administrator console, expand **Site Database (001 – NWTraders)**, and then expand **Collections**.

4. Right-click **Demo 1 Collection**, point to **New**, and then click **Collection**.

   The **Collection Properties** dialog box will open.

5. In the **Name** box, type **Demo 4 Collection**

6. On the **Membership Rules** tab, click the New query ⬚ icon.

   The **Query Rule Properties** dialog box will open.

7. In the **Name** box, type **XP Systems**

8. In the **Resource class** list, verify **System Resource** is selected.

9. Click **Limit to collection**.

10. Click **Browse**.

11. In the **Browse Collection** list, click **All Windows XP Systems**, and then click **OK** twice.

12. Repeat steps 6-11, typing **2003 Systems** in the **Name** box and selecting **All Windows Server 2003 Systems** from the **Browse Collection** list.

13. Set the schedule to update the collection.

    a. Verify that the **Update this collection on a schedule** check box is selected.

    b. Click **Schedule**.

       The **Schedule** dialog box will open.

    c. Verify that the **Start** date is the same as, or prior to, today's date.

    d. Verify that **Recurrence pattern** is set to **Interval**.

    e. Set **Recur every** to **3 days**, and then click **OK**.

14. Click **OK** to close the **Collection Properties** dialog box.

▶ **To verify that the subcollection was created by refreshing the SMS Administrator console**

1. In the SMS Administrator console, expand **Site Database (001 - NWTraders)**.

2. Right-click **Collections**, and then click **Refresh**.

3. Expand Demo 1 Collection, and then verify that **Demo 4 Collection** exists.

4. Leave the Glasgow and Dublin virtual machines running.

How Collections Are Propagated Down an SMS Hierarchy

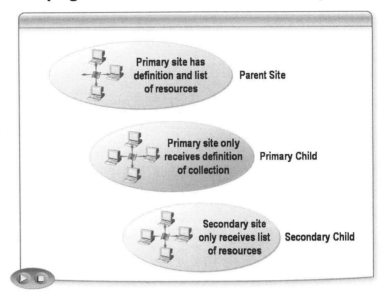

When you create collections at a parent site, SMS propagates them to lower-level primary and secondary sites. You can modify or delete collections only at the site that they were created in. At child sites, you cannot modify collections that were propagated from an upper-level site. Unlike collections, queries are not propagated down a hierarchy to lower-level sites.

Primary child sites

When SMS propagates a collection, primary child sites receive only the definition of the collection. This includes the collection's general data and its membership rules, but it does not include the actual list of clients that are members of that collection. Each primary child site evaluates the propagated collection's membership rules. If the collection is based on a query, the query runs against the current SMS site database.

Secondary child sites

When SMS propagates a collection, secondary child sites receive only the list of resources that are members of the collection. They do not receive the collection definition. Because secondary sites do not maintain their own database, the secondary site's parent site evaluates the collection's membership rules for the secondary site and generates the membership list. The membership list includes resources from only the secondary site. When a collection is re-evaluated at the parent site, the parent site sends updated membership lists to its secondary sites. The members are stored in a file cache on the secondary site server.

Practice: Creating a Collection with a Direct Membership Rule

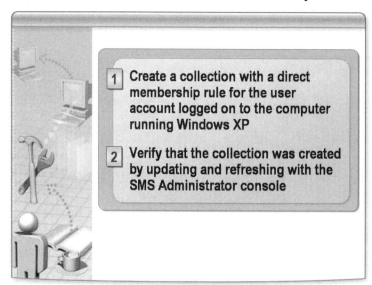

Instructions

Complete the procedures to practice creating a collection with a direct membership rule for the user logged on to the computer running Windows XP. Then answer the reflection question that follows

Use the following values.

Variable	Value
Virtual machine—SMS Site 1	Dublin
Dublin Administrator	JaePa (Jae Pak)
Virtual machine—domain controller	Glasgow
Domain administrator	Administrator

Procedure

▶ **To create a collection with a direct membership rule for the user account logged on to a computer running Windows XP**

1. If you have not already done so, log the Glasgow virtual machine on to the NWTRADERS domain with a user name of **Administrator** and a password of **P@ssw0rd**.

   After the Glasgow virtual machine opens, you can minimize it.

2. Log the Dublin virtual machine on to the NWTRADERS domain with a user name of **JaePa** and a password of **P@ssw0rd**.

3. On the Dublin virtual machine, click **Start**, point to **All Programs**, point to **Systems Management Server**, and then click **SMS Administrator Console**.

4. In the SMS Administrator console, expand **Site Database (001 - NWTraders)**, and then click **Collections**.

5. Right-click **Collections**, point to **New**, and then click **Collection**.
   The **Collection Properties** dialog box will open.

6. In the **Name** box, type **Practice 2 Collection**

7. On the **Membership Rules** tab, click the **New Membership rule** icon.
   The Create Direct Membership Rule Wizard will open.

8. Click **Next**.

9. On the **Search for Resources** page, in the **Resource class** list, select **User Resource**.

10. In the **Attribute name** list, select **User Name**.

11. In the **Value** box, type **%SMartinez%**

12. Click **Next**.

13. On the **Collection Limiting** page, click **Browse**.

14. In the **Browse Collection** list, click **All Users**, and then click **OK**.

15. On the **Collection Limiting** page, click **Next**.

16. On the **Select Resources** page, select the **NWTRADERS\SMartinez (Sandra Martinez)** check box, and then click **Next**.

17. On the **Completing the Create Direct Membership Rule Wizard** page, click **Finish**.

18. Click **OK** to close the **Collection Properties** dialog box.

▶ **To verify that the collection was created**

1. In the console tree of the SMS Administrator console, expand **Site Database (001 - NWTraders)** if needed.

2. Right-click **Collections**, and then click **Refresh**.

3. Verify that **Practice 2 Collection** is displayed in the details pane.

4. Leave the Glasgow and Dublin virtual machines running.

Practice: Creating a Collection with a Rule Based on a Query

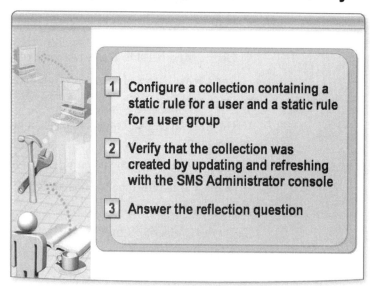

Instructions

Complete the procedures to practice configuring a collection containing a static rule for a user and a static rule for a user group. Then answer the reflection question that follows.

Use the following values.

Variable	Value
Virtual machine—SMS Site 1	Dublin
Dublin Administrator	JaePa (Jae Pak)
Virtual machine—domain controller	Glasgow
Domain administrator	Administrator

Procedure

▶ **To use the SMS Administrator console to create a collection by using a query-based membership rule**

1. Verify that Glasgow and Dublin virtual machines are running.

2. On the Dublin virtual machine, click **Start**, point to **All Programs**, point to **Systems Management Server**, and then click **SMS Administrator Console**.

3. In the console tree of the SMS Administrator console, expand **Site Database (001 – NWTraders)**, and then click **Collections**.

4. Right-click **Collections**, point to **New**, and then click **Collection**.

   The **Collection Properties** dialog box will open.

5. In the **Name** box, type **Practice 3 Collection**

6. Create a query for users in the domain group.

   a. On the **Membership Rules** tab, click the **New query** icon.

   b. The **Query Rule Properties** dialog box will open.

   c. In the **Name** box, type **Practice 3 Rule 1**

   d. In the **Resource class** list, select **User Resource**.

   e. Click **Edit query statement**.

      The **Practice 3 Rule 1 Query Statement Properties** dialog box will open.

   f. On the **Criteria** tab, click the **New** icon.

      The **Criterion Properties** dialog box will open.

   g. In the **Criterion type** list, verify **Simple value** is selected, and then click **Select**.

   h. The **Select Attribute** dialog box will open.

   i. In the **Attribute class** list, select **User Resource**.

   j. In the **Attribute** list, select **User Group Name**.

   k. Click **OK**.

   l. On the **General** tab of the **Criterion Properties** dialog box, click **Values**.

   m. In the **Values** list, select **NWTRADERS\Domain Users**.

   n. Click **OK** four times.

7. In the **Collection Properties** dialog box, verify that the **Membership rules** box contains **Practice 3 Rule 1**.

8. Set the schedule to update the collection.

   a. Verify that the **Update this collection on a schedule** check box is selected.

   b. Click **Schedule**.

      The **Schedule** dialog box will open.

   c. Verify that the **Start** date is the same as, or prior to, today's date.

   d. Verify that **Recurrence pattern** is set to **Interval**.

   e. Set **Recur every** to **3 days**, and then click **OK**.

9. Click **OK** to close the **Collection Properties** dialog box.

▶ **To verify that the collection was created**

1. In the console tree of the SMS Administrator console, expand **Site Database (001 - NWTraders)** if needed.

2. Right-click **Collections**, and then click **Refresh**.

3. Verify that **Practice 3 Collection** is displayed beneath Collections.

4. In the console tree of the SMS Administrator console, expand **Collections**, and then click once on **Practice 3 Collection**. In the details pane, verify that each domain user appears as a collection member.

5. Close the SMS Administrator console.

6. Leave the Glasgow and Dublin virtual machines running.

Reflection Question

What are some direct membership rules or rules based on queries that would apply to your work environment?

_____

_____

_____

Practice: Creating and Configuring Collections

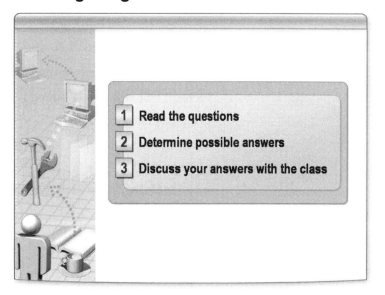

Instructions

Read the following reflection questions, determine possible answers, and then discuss your answers with the class.

Discussion questions

1. Why would you create a collection by using a rule based on a query?

   _____

   _____

   _____

2. Why would you create a collection by using a direct membership rule?

   _____

   _____

   _____

Lesson: Creating and Configuring Packages

* The Relationship Between Packages and Programs
* How to Create a Package and Configure Its Properties
* Package Configuration Options
* How to Create a Program
* How to Distribute Packages to Distribution Points
* Demonstration: How to Create Packages and Programs
* How to Verify That a Package Has Reached the Distribution Point

Introduction

In this lesson, you will learn how SMS packages are used to encapsulate the instructions used to install software. You will learn various methods of creating packages and take advantage of the various SMS features for managing packages.

Lesson objectives

After completing this lesson, you will be able to:

■ Describe the relationship between packages and programs.

■ Create a package and configure its properties.

■ Describe package configuration options.

■ Create a program.

■ Distribute packages to distribution points.

■ Verify that a package has reached the distribution point.

The Relationship Between Packages and Programs

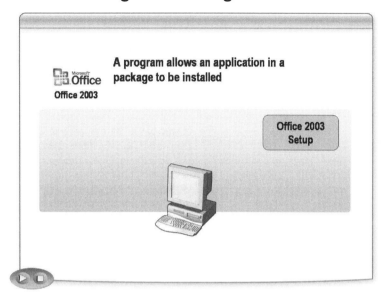

In SMS software distribution, the methods for configuring packages and programs are closely related. The files that a program requires when it runs are called package source files. Most packages contain package source files, though a program can also run programs that are already present on the target computer. A package must be created first, so that the necessary program can run.

A package is the basic unit of software distribution and contains the files that a program needs to run.

Programs are a subset of packages

When you create a new package, you will see that, underneath the newly created package in the SMS Administrator console hierarchy, there are three objects: Access Accounts, Distribution Points, and Programs. You cannot distribute software to clients without having created a program. After a package has been created, you need to configure program properties so clients can run the application in the package.

How to Create a Package and Configure Its Properties

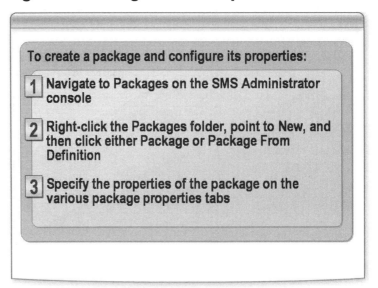

After you decide what you want to distribute, you must create a package for the software to be distributed, using the SMS Administrator console to create the package.

For more information about package development (package definition files) for software distribution, go to http://www.microsoft.com/smserver/downloads/ 2003/default.asp.

Procedure

To create a package:

1. In the SMS Administrator console, navigate to **Packages**.

2. Right-click the **Packages** folder, point to **New**, and then click either **Package** or **Package From Definition**.

3. Specify the properties of the package on the various package properties tabs.

Tab Name	Purpose of Tab
General	The only required field on the General tab is the name of the new package.
Data Source	This tab is used to specify if the package has source files and, if so, where they are located. It is also important to make sure that the source files are specified to be on a shared directory. You will browse for the appropriate source files on the Data Source tab.
Data Access	On the Data Access tab, you can specify the package to be accessed through a common SMS share. You can use a non-SMS shared folder for your data access, but in doing that, you run a higher risk of errors in distribution because the correct permissions are not configured for non-SMS shares.

(continued)

Tab Name	Purpose of Tab
Distribution Settings	The Distribution Settings tab is where you specify the sending priority. A best practice is to use medium priority. High priority can be used, but should be saved for emergencies, antivirus software, and security updates. Packages are sent to child sites according to the priority schedule specified here.
Reporting	The Reporting tab is used to specify how SMS identifies whether installation status MIF files generated by a client apply to a package.
Security	The Security tab allows you to specify users' rights to this specific package or to the Packages class.

Package Configuration Options

> Other package configuration options to consider are:
>
> * Sub-objects
> * Source directories
> * Package compression
> * Package definition file

When creating a package, there are other configuration options to be considered.

Sub-objects

When a new package has been created, three sub-objects are created beneath the package in the site hierarchy. These sub-objects are:

- Access Account. Specifies what type of accounts will have access to the package source files.

- Distribution Points. Specifies where the packages will be located for user access.

- Programs. Specify what command line program is to be run on the target computers.

Package source directories

If a package contains source files and the site is running in standard security mode, be sure that the package source files are accessible by the SMS Service account. Create this folder the same way you create any other folder on your computer. The package source folder can be a folder on a drive, or it can be the drive itself, including a CD drive. The package source folder can be on a remote computer if the remote computer is accessible by the SMS Service account for standard security or accessible to the site server computer account for advanced security. For remote drives, always specify the package source folder by using the Universal Naming Convention (UNC).

Note If the package does not specify any source files, the client will try to run the program from its local files or drives.

When you have created a package source folder, you must designate it as such so that SMS will use it for package source files.

Important It is a best practice to use source files for software distribution.

Package compression

SMS automatically compresses package source files before sending them out to other sites. The receiving site will decompress the package and then distribute to the distribution points. Compressing the package source files saves your network bandwidth space when sending the package source files to child sites. If the source files are on removable media such as CDs, you can have SMS create a compressed version of the source files. SMS stores the compressed file and uses it instead of the original source files for distribution within the local site.

To create a compressed version of the source files for your package, navigate to the package you want to compress in the SMS Administrator console. Next, right-click the package and then click **Properties**. Click the **Data Source** tab and enter the source folder, if one has not already been specified. Then select **Use a compressed copy of the source directory**.

What is a package definition file?

A package definition file is a specially formatted file describing a package and one or more programs. A package definition file is created outside the SMS Administrator console. Use a package definition file as an alternative to manually creating a package definition in the SMS Administrator console. If you already have a package definition file, import the file into a wizard. SMS immediately creates the package definition and programs. Many Microsoft products and third-party applications ship with their own package definition files, and SMS Installer can create a package definition file for any packages it creates.

Package definition files have an extension of .sms. You can also import Windows Installer files as package definition files in SMS 2003.

How to Create a Program

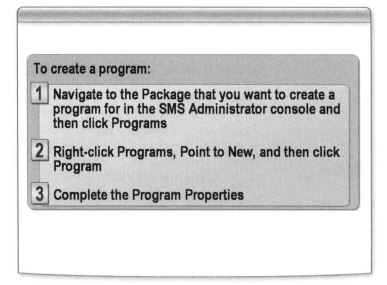

To create a program:

1 Navigate to the Package that you want to create a program for in the SMS Administrator console and then click Programs

2 Right-click Programs, Point to New, and then click Program

3 Complete the Program Properties

Once you have created and configured a package, you must create a program. A program is a command that runs on clients. Most often programs will be in the form of an executable (.exe, .vbs, .bat) file or a Windows Installer command (.msi) file.

Procedure

To create a program:

1. Navigate to the package that you want to create a program for in the SMS Administrator console. The folders Access Accounts, Distribution Points, and Programs will appear.

2. Right-click **Programs**, point to **New**, and then click **Program**.

3. Complete the program properties.

The purpose of the program properties tabs?

Tab Name	Purpose of tab
General	On the General tab you will need to identify the program name and the command line. These properties are required when you create a program. By default, the package source folder appears, if it exists and is accessible. If not, the root folder of the current computer appears.
Requirements	The options on the Requirements tab are all optional. Here you can set properties such as: • Estimated disk space • Maximum allowed run time • Specify client platforms where program can run • Additional requirements to appear in Advertised Programs in Control Panel

(continued)

Tab Name	Purpose of tab
Environment	On the Environments tab you can specify: • Whether the program should run only when a user is logged on, only when a user is not logged on, or regardless of whether a user is logged on • Whether the program should run with users' rights or administrative credentials • Allow the user to interact with the desktop • The drive mode or the type of connection that will be used for accessing the distribution points • The computer to reconnect the drive to the distribution point each time the user logs on
Advanced	On the Advanced tab you can specify: • To run another program first—Allows you to force a dependent program to run before the existing one • Additional run-time options, such as that the program should run once for every user that logs on • Suppress program notifications—Allows for hidden applications without user notification • Disable program—This is so new instances of the advertised program can run
Windows Installer	This tab is used to specify the Windows Installer product information to enable installation source management. Refer to Module 2, "Exploring SMS Site Architecture," for information on Windows Installer.

How to Distribute Packages to Distribution Points

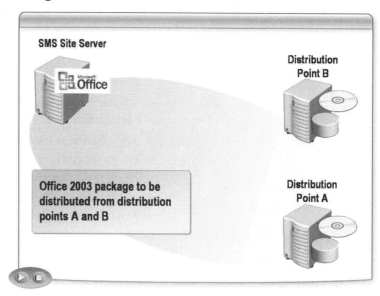

You must specify at least one distribution point for each package you create containing source files. Packages that do not use source files do not need distribution points assigned.

When you specify distribution points for a package, SMS places a copy of the package source files on each distribution point specified. SMS can also update package source files on distribution points according to your schedule, or you can update them manually.

Manage Distribution Points Wizard

For assistance with distribution point management tasks, you can use the Manage Distribution Points Wizard. By using the Manage Distribution Points Wizard, you can:

- Copy the package to new distribution points.
- Refresh the package on selected distribution points.

  This is used to recover distribution points. The wizard assumes that all the information required to restore a distribution point and its packages was previously configured.

- Update all distribution points with a new package source version.

  This is used when the package content has changed. The package will be assigned a new version to reflect the change in the packages content.

- Remove the package from selected distribution points.

You need to specify which distribution points you want to use to distribute your package. To do this you will need to use the Manage Distribution Points Wizard.

Procedure

To assign a new distribution point to distribute a package:

1. In the SMS Administrator console, expand **Packages**.

2. Click the package for which you want to set a distribution point.

3. Right-click **Distribution Points**, point to **All Tasks**, and then click **Manage Distribution Points**. The Manage Distribution Points Wizard will appear.

4. Click **Next**.

5. On the **Manage Distribution Points** page, click **Copy the package to new distribution points**.

6. Click **Next**. The copy package page will appear, showing all distribution points that are not currently storing the package.

7. Click the desired distribution point.

8. Click **Finish**. The package will be copied to the selected distribution point.

Note If your site has a large amount of distribution points, you can group some of the distribution points to make them more manageable. You can then distribute packages to a specified group rather than having to distribute to individual distribution points.

SMS distributes to distribution points serially (one after another). It may take a significant period before the package source files have been distributed to all distribution points for the package.

You should wait until all distribution points are updated with the package source files before creating advertisements for the package source files to reduce the chance of a client accessing the files from a remote distribution point.

Demonstration: How to Create Packages and Programs

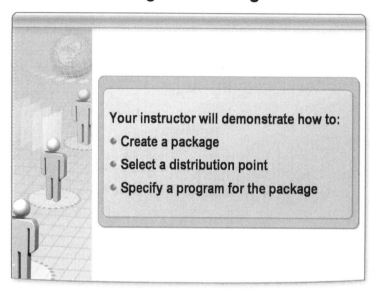

In this demonstration, you will see how to create packages and programs.

Your instructor will use the following values in this demonstration.

Variable	Value
Virtual machine—SMS Site 1	Dublin
Dublin Administrator	JaePa (Jae Pak)
Virtual machine—domain controller	Glasgow
Domain administrator	Administrator

Important These steps are included for your information. Do not attempt to perform them in the classroom. If you perform these steps in the classroom environment, you might leave your computer in an incorrect state for upcoming practices.

Demonstration steps performed by instructor only

▶ **To create a package**

1. Verify that Glasgow and Dublin virtual machines are running.

2. On the Dublin virtual machine, click **Start**, point to **All Programs**, point to **Systems Management Server**, and then click **SMS Administrator Console**.

3. In the SMS Administrator console, expand **Site Database (001 – NWTraders)**, and then click **Packages**.

4. Right-click **Packages**, point to **New**, and then click **Package**.

   The **Package Properties** dialog box will open.

5. On the **General** tab, in the **Name** box, type **Demo 5 Package**

6. On the **Data Source** tab, select the **This package contains source files** check box.

7. Click **Set**.

   The **Set Source Directory** dialog box will open.

8. Click **Local drive on the site server**.

9. Click **Browse**.

   The **Browse for Folder** dialog box will open.

10. Expand **Local Disk (C:)**, click **C:\2596**, and then click **OK** twice.

11. Verify that **Always obtain files from source directory** is selected.

12. Select the **Update distribution points on a schedule** check box.

13. Set the schedule to every 3 days.

    a. Click **Schedule**.

       The **Schedule** dialog box will open.

    b. Verify that the **Start** date is the same as, or prior to, today's date.

    c. Verify that **Recurrence pattern** is set to **Interval**.

    d. Set **Recur every** to **3 days**, and then click **OK**.

14. Click **OK** to close the **Package Properties** dialog box.

▶ **To select a distribution point**

1. In the console tree of the SMS Administrator console, under **Site Database (001 – NWTraders)**, expand **Packages** (if needed), and then expand the **Demo 5 Package**.

2. Click **Access Accounts** and verify that Administrators and Users exist.

3. Right-click **Distribution Points**, point to **New**, and then click **Distribution Points**.

   The New Distribution Points Wizard will open.

4. If the **Welcome to the New Distribution Points Wizard** page appears, click **Next**.

5. Select the **Dublin** check box.

6. Click **Finish**.

▶ **To specify a program for the package**

1. In the console tree of the SMS Administrator console, under **Demo 5 Package**, right-click **Programs**, point to **New**, and then click **Program**.

   The **Program Properties** dialog box will open.

2. In the **Name** box, type **Demo 5 Program**

3. Click **Browse**.

   The **Open** dialog box will open.

4. Browse to **C:\2596\VisioViewer**.

5. Select the Microsoft Visio® Viewer installer (**vviewer.exe**), and then click **Open**.

6. Click the **Requirements** tab.

   Note that you can enter package-size and time-required-to-run values that users can use to decide whether to run the package immediately or at a later time.

7. Click **This program can run only on the specified client platforms**.

8. Select the **All x86 Windows XP** check box from the platform list, and then click **OK**.

9. Leave the Glasgow and Dublin virtual machines running.

How to Verify That a Package Has Reached the Distribution Point

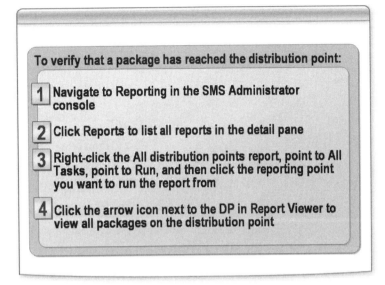

To verify that a package has reached the distribution point:

1. Navigate to Reporting in the SMS Administrator console

2. Click Reports to list all reports in the detail pane

3. Right-click the All distribution points report, point to All Tasks, point to Run, and then click the reporting point you want to run the report from

4. Click the arrow icon next to the DP in Report Viewer to view all packages on the distribution point

After you have distributed packages to distribution points, you need to verify that the packages have reached their destinations.

SMS has a predefined report that is called All distribution points. You can navigate to **Reports** in the SMS Administrator console to see a list of all available reports. This report allows you to view all packages on a specific distribution point. If a package has not reached the distribution point, check the package status summary. The steps for viewing the package status summary will be covered in Lesson 6, "Monitoring Software Distribution."

Procedure

To view the All distribution points report:

1. Navigate to **Reporting** in the SMS Administrator console.

2. Click **Reports**. All reports will be listed in the detail pane.

3. Right-click the **All distribution points** report, point to **All Tasks**, point to **Run**, and then click on the reporting point you want to run the report from.

4. The Report Viewer will display with the distribution point listed. Click the **arrow** icon next to the distribution point. All packages on the distribution point will appear.

Note   You can also use the System Status or Package Status to view the distribution of packages to distribution points. Additionally, you can verify the files in the package folder on the distribution point.

Practice: Creating a Package

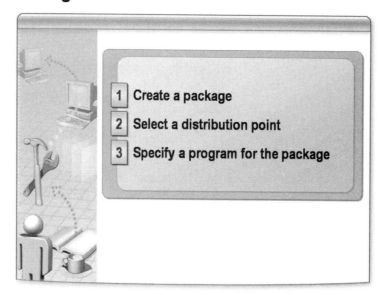

1. Create a package
2. Select a distribution point
3. Specify a program for the package

Instructions

Complete the procedures to practice creating a package for the Visio Viewer 2002. Then answer the reflection question that follows.

Be sure the package and program files:

■ Are installed with administrator rights.

■ Run silently (in a hidden desktop).

■ Run unattended (automatically, from the command line).

■ Require no logged-on user.

■ Are uncompressed.

Use the following values:

Variable	Value
Virtual machine—SMS Site 1	Dublin
Dublin Administrator	JaePa (Jae Pak)
Virtual machine—domain controller	Glasgow
Domain administrator	Administrator

Procedure

▶ **To create a package**

1. Verify that Glasgow and Dublin virtual machines are running.

2. On the Dublin virtual machine, click **Start**, point to **All Programs**, point to **Systems Management Server**, and then click **SMS Administrator Console**.

3. In the console tree of the SMS Administrator console, expand **Site Database (001 – NWTraders)**, and then click **Packages**.

4. Right-click **Packages**, point to **New**, and then click **Package**.

   The **Package Properties** dialog box will open.

5. On the **General** tab, in the **Name** box, type **Practice 5 Package**

6. On the **Data Source** tab, select the **This package contains source files** check box.

7. Click **Set**.

   The **Set Source Directory** dialog box will open.

8. Click **Local drive on the site server**.

9. Click **Browse**.

   The **Browse for Folder** dialog box will open.

10. Expand **Local Disk (C:)**, click **C:\2596**, and then click **OK**.

11. In the **Set Source Directory** dialog box, click **OK**.

12. Verify that **Always obtain files from source directory** is selected.

13. Select the **Update distribution points on a schedule** check box.

14. Set the schedule to every 3 days.

    a. Click **Schedule**.

       The **Schedule** dialog box will open.

    b. Verify that the **Start** date is the same as, or prior to, today's date.

    c. Verify that **Recurrence pattern** is set to **Interval**.

    d. Set **Recur every** to **3 days**, and then click **OK**.

15. Click **OK** to close the **Package Properties** dialog box.

▶ **To specify a program for the package**

1. On the Dublin virtual machine, in the SMS Administrator console, expand **Packages** (if needed), expand **Practice 5 Package**, right-click **Programs**, point to **New**, and then click **Program**.

   The **Program Properties** dialog box will open.

2. In the **Name** box, type **Practice 5 Program**

3. Click **Browse**.

   The **Open** dialog box will open.

4. Browse to **C:\2596\VisioViewer**.

5. Click **Visio Viewer** installer (**vviewer.exe**), and then click **Open**.

6. In the **After running** list, verify that **No action required** is selected.

7. Click the **Requirements** tab.

   Note that you can enter package-size and time-required-to-run values that users can use to decide whether to run the package immediately or at a later time.

8. Click **This program can run only on the specified client platforms**.

9. Select the **All x86 Windows XP** check box from the platform list.

10. On the **Environment** tab, in the **Program can run** list, select **Whether or not a user is logged on**.

11. Verify **Run with administrative rights** is selected, and then click **OK**.

▶ **To select a distribution point**

1. On the Dublin virtual machine, in the SMS Administrator console, expand **Site Database (001 – NWTraders)**, expand **Packages**, and then expand **Practice 5 Package**.

2. Click **Access accounts** and verify that Administrators and Users exist.

3. Right-click **Distribution Points**, point to **New**, and then click **Distribution Points**.

   The New Distribution Points Wizard will open.

4. If the **Welcome to the New Distribution Points Wizard** page appears, click **Next**.

5. Select the **Dublin** check box, and then click **Finish**.

6. Close the SMS Administrator console.

7. Leave the Glasgow and Dublin virtual machines running.

Practice: Configuring Packages

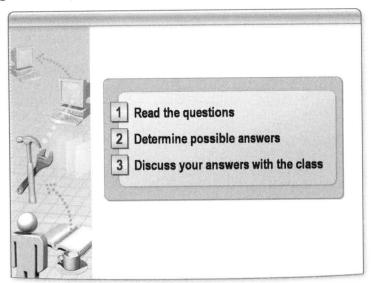

Instructions

Discuss the following questions about configuring packages, determine possible answers, and then discuss them with your classmates.

Discussion questions

1. After configuring the properties on a package, you notice there is no distribution server configured. What action should you take?

_____

_____

_____

2. What types of packages would you distribute with a high priority?

_____

_____

_____

3. Does setting a high sending priority on a package mean that the package will use the sender exclusive of any other SMS process contending for the sender?

_____

_____

_____

Lesson: Creating and Configuring Advertisements and Managing Software Installation at the Client

- How to Create an Advertisement
- What Are the Advertisement Configuration Options?
- Options for Managing Remote Downloads for a Package
- How to Retrieve User and Machine Policy
- How the Client Runs Advertised Programs
- The Role of the Agent in Software Distribution
- Demonstration: How to Create and Configure an Advertisement

Introduction

In this lesson, you will learn how installation instructions are delivered to clients by means of advertisements. You will learn how advertisements are targeted using collections and how they can be scheduled for voluntary and assigned installations. You will learn to configure how Advanced Clients download and run programs from distribution points, although this will not be tested until Module 11, "SMS Hierarchies."

Lesson objectives

After completing this lesson, you will be able to:

- Create an advertisement.
- Describe the advertisement configuration options.
- Describe the options for managing remote downloads for a package.
- Retrieve a user or machine policy.
- Describe how the client runs advertised programs.
- Describe the role of the agent in software distribution.

How to Create an Advertisement

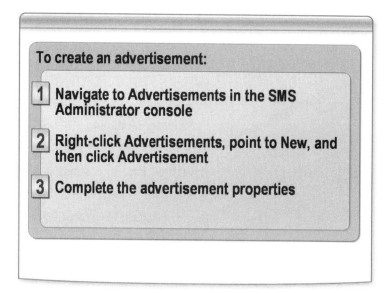

To create an advertisement:

1 Navigate to Advertisements in the SMS Administrator console

2 Right-click Advertisements, point to New, and then click Advertisement

3 Complete the advertisement properties

The final software distribution object that needs to be created and configured is the advertisement. Advertisements are created to specify when and how often a program will run.

Procedure

To create an advertised program:

1. In the SMS Administrator console, navigate to **Advertisements**.

2. Right-click **Advertisements**, point to **New**, and then click **Advertisement**.

3. Complete the advertisement properties. To do this:

    a. On the **General** tab, name the advertisement.

    b. In the **Package** list, select the appropriate package.

    c. In the **Program** list, select the appropriate program.

    d. In the **Collection** box, type the name of the collection this advertisement is to go to. If you do not know the exact name of the collection, click the **Browse** button to search for the collection you need.

    e. On the **Schedule** tab, specify the date and time the advertisement will be made available.

    f. Specify the advertisement expiration. This is optional.

    g. Set the priority of the advertisement. This is optional.

    h. On the **Schedule** tab, you schedule when the advertised program is mandatory to run on clients.

    i. On the **Advanced Client** tab, you specify whether to run the advertised program from a distribution point, or to download the package and then run it locally. This includes configuring package source access for both local and remote clients.

What Are the Advertisement Configuration Options?

Advertisement Scheduling Options

> Mandatory: Program is run after an event (for example, on logon or logoff or at a specific date and time)

> Optional: Allows users to run the advertised program when they want to

Additional Advertisement Properties

> Run the advertised program from a DP or download the package and run it locally

> Using remote DPs when the client is considered to be remotely roaming

---

For software distribution, there are two scheduling options for configuring the advertisements properties as well as additional properties to configure downloading and running programs from a distribution point.

Mandatory assignment

When you assign a program, you are making that program mandatory; the advertised program will run automatically on the client. When assigning programs, you can also make scheduled assignments and event assignments. Scheduled assignments allow you to specify the start date and time for the program to run. Event-driven assignments are run when the specified event occurs.

You might want to schedule advertisements to run outside of your organization's normal business hours to avoid the busiest times on the network. For example, you might schedule one advertisement to run at midnight, and another to run at 2:00 A.M.

Voluntary advertisement

When assigning programs, you can choose to allow users to run the program independently of assignments. This option is found on the **Schedule** tab of the **Advertised Programs Properties** dialog box. When you enable this option, the advertisement is still mandatory and will run according to the schedule for each assignment, but users are also allowed to run the program when they want.

Note If no mandatory assignment is specified, the advertisement becomes voluntary by default. Users can run the advertised program when they want.

Advertisements to Advanced Clients

Advertisements to Advanced Clients include some additional options. These are found on the **Advanced Client** tab in the **Advertisements Properties** dialog box. These additional options are:

- Whether to run the advertised program from a distribution point or download the package and then run it locally.

- Whether to use remote distribution points when local distribution points are not available.

Options for Managing Remote Downloads for a Package

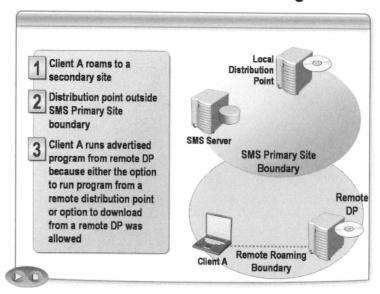

By default, advanced clients do not run advertised programs unless a local distribution point is available. The client must be within the boundaries of an SMS site, and that site must have at least one distribution point with the package for the advertised program. The remote distribution points are either within the roaming boundaries of the client's assigned site or the roaming boundaries of the site that the client has roamed to.

You can allow the advertised program to run by setting the **Download program from a remote distribution point** option. This is most appropriate when the package is large, or when the clients have slow network links to the remote distribution points.

You can also allow the advertised program to run from a remote distribution point by setting the **Run program from a remote distribution point** option. This is most appropriate when the package is small, or when the programs needed to run the advertised program are a small fraction of the package.

Configuring the advertisement to support access to remote distribution points is done on the **Advanced Client** tab in the **Advertisement Properties** dialog box.

How to Retrieve a User or Machine Policy

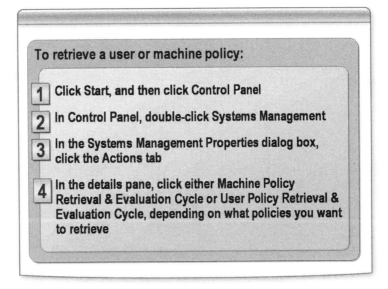

To retrieve a user or machine policy:

1. Click Start, and then click Control Panel

2. In Control Panel, double-click Systems Management

3. In the Systems Management Properties dialog box, click the Actions tab

4. In the details pane, click either Machine Policy Retrieval & Evaluation Cycle or User Policy Retrieval & Evaluation Cycle, depending on what policies you want to retrieve

The Advanced Client retrieves user and machine policy on a cycle. Administrators can change the cycle of the Advanced Client if they do not want to use the default cycle of once every hour. Policies are sometimes created for software distribution objects; therefore the retrieval of these policies is actually the application of these policies to users and machines.

You can also retrieve policies manually if you want them to be retrieved before the automatic cycle runs.

Procedure

To manually retrieve a user or machine policy:

1. Click **Start**, and then click **Control Panel**.

2. In Control Panel, double-click **Systems Management**.

3. In the **Systems Management Properties** dialog box, click the **Actions** tab.

4. In the details pane, click either **Machine Policy Retrieval & Evaluation Cycle** or **User Policy Retrieval & Evaluation Cycle**, depending on what policies you want to retrieve.

5. Click **Initiate Action**.

Note For Legacy Clients, you will need to start the **Advertised Programs Monitor** in **Control Panel**, and then click **Refresh** on the view menu (F5).

How the Client Runs Advertised Programs

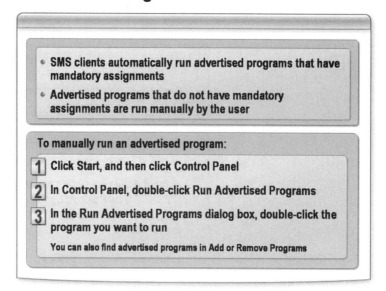

- SMS clients automatically run advertised programs that have mandatory assignments
- Advertised programs that do not have mandatory assignments are run manually by the user

To manually run an advertised program:

1. Click Start, and then click Control Panel
2. In Control Panel, double-click Run Advertised Programs
3. In the Run Advertised Programs dialog box, double-click the program you want to run

You can also find advertised programs in Add or Remove Programs

---

When the SMS client detects new advertised programs, the program will either be made available to the user in the Control Panel or will be run automatically. When configuring advertised programs, you set properties to either make the advertised programs mandatory or voluntary. Mandatory means that the program is required. Mandatory advertised programs can either be set to run without user intervention or they can be configured to require user input. Voluntary advertised programs are not required and the user initiates the program running.

You will configure mandatory assignments for most software that does not require end user intervention. There might be times, however, when you do not want to create a mandatory assignment.

For example, you might want to run a pilot test for new software. Not everyone will have the time to perform the pilot test. Therefore the advertisement should have no assignments, so that only those who have time to run the installation can manually run it.

Procedure

To manually run an advertised program on an Advanced Client:

1. Click **Start**, and then click **Control Panel**.

2. In Control Panel, double-click either **Run Advertised Programs** or **Add Remove Programs**.

3. In the **Run Advertised Programs** dialog box, double-click the program you want to run.

   If you click on **Add or Remove Programs** from Control panel, you then click **Add New Programs**. All programs available on your network will appear.

Note   On Legacy Clients, advertised programs are run by double-clicking **Advertised Programs** in Control Panel.

The Role of the Advertised Program Agent in Software Distribution

> **For the Advanced Client, the Advertised Program agent:**
>
> - Runs programs that the user initiates
> - Runs assigned programs
> - Manages package downloads and the local cache of downloaded packages

> **For the Legacy Client, the Advertised Program agent:**
>
> - Runs programs that the user initiates from the Advertised Programs Wizard
> - Runs assigned programs

The Advertised Programs Client Agent that you configure in the SMS Administrator console determines how the software distribution agent on SMS clients installs and runs applications. The client agent monitors the distribution to determine whether it completes successfully and it reports the distribution status back to the client's assigned site.

The software distribution agent on both the Advanced Client and the Legacy Client assesses advertisements to determine whether they are enabled, active, and not expired. It also determines if the program is appropriate for the client operating system and service pack, based on the program's properties as configured by the SMS administrator. The agent runs programs that users select from Add or Remove Programs or Run Advertised Programs in the Control Panel. Legacy Clients use the Advertised Programs Wizard. It also initiates assigned programs without user intervention. The agent displays an icon in the notification area of the taskbar if the program was configured to display it.

The role of the agent for Advanced Clients

Advanced Clients periodically check the management point to determine if any advertisements (as policies) are applicable to the client. The SMS Software Distribution Agent maintains a list of the advertisements that are not assignments (that is, advertisements that are not automatically run), allowing the users to run them when it is convenient. The Agent also launches assigned programs at the configure time. Users at Advanced Clients can view and run programs by using either Add or Remove Programs or Run Advertised Programs in Control Panel.

On Advanced Clients, the agent also manages package downloads and the local cache of downloaded packages. If the client downloads a package and the network connection is interrupted, the client resumes the download when the network connection is restored.

The role of the agent for Legacy Clients

On Legacy Clients, the agent manages programs that the user initiates from the Advertised Programs Wizard, and it also runs assigned programs. The SMS administrator can configure the Advertised Programs Client Agent to allow Legacy Clients to override administrator settings on the client through Advertised Programs Monitor in Control Panel.

Demonstration: How to Create and Configure an Advertisement

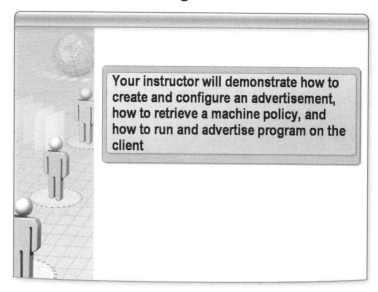

In this demonstration, you will see how to create and configure an advertisement, how to retrieve a machine policy, and how to run an advertised program on the client.

Your instructor will use the following values in this demonstration.

Variable	Value
Virtual machine—SMS Site 1	Dublin
Dublin Administrator	JaePa (Jae Pak)
Virtual machine—domain controller	Glasgow
Domain administrator	Administrator
Virtual machine—SMS Advanced Client	Bonn
Bonn Administrator	SMartinez (Sandra Martinez)

Important These steps are included for your information. Do not attempt to perform them in the classroom. If you perform these steps in the classroom environment, you might leave your computer in an incorrect state for upcoming practices.

▶ **To create an advertisement**

1. Verify that the Glasgow and Dublin and Bonn virtual machines are running.

2. On the Dublin virtual machine, click **Start**, point to **All Programs**, point to **Systems Management Server**, and then click **SMS Administrator Console**.

3. In the console tree of the SMS Administrator console, expand **Site Database (001 – NWTraders)**, and then click **Advertisements**.

4. Right-click **Advertisements**, point to **New**, and then click **Advertisement**.

5. In the **Advertisement Properties** dialog box, in the **Name** box, type **Demo 6 Advertisement**

6. In the **Package** list, select **Demo 5 Package**.

7. In the **Program** list, select **Demo 5 Program**.

8. Click **Browse**.

   The **Browse Collection** dialog box will open.

9. In the **Browse Collection** list, click **Demo 3 Collection**.

10. Click **OK**.

11. Clear the **Include members of subcollections** check box.

12. On the **Schedule** tab, click the **New** ⚡ icon.

13. In the **Assignment Schedule** dialog box, click **Assign immediately after this event**.

14. Verify **As soon as possible** is selected from the list.

15. Click **OK**.

16. On the **Advanced Client** tab, click **Download program from distribution point**.

17. Click **Download program from a remote distribution point**.

   The client is not roaming; this option is being selected just for demonstration purposes.

18. Click **OK**.

19. Close the SMS Administrator console.

▶ **To retrieve machine policy**

1. Log the Bonn virtual machine on to the NWTRADERS domain with a user name of **SMartinez** and a password of **P@ssw0rd**.

2. On the **Bonn** virtual machine, click **Start**, and then click **Control Panel**.

3. Click **Performance and Maintenance**, and then click **Systems Management**.

4. On the **Actions** tab, click **Machine Policy Retrieval & Evaluation Cycle**, and then click **Initiate Action**.

5. On the **Machine Policy Retrieval & Evaluation Cycle** dialog box, click **OK**.

6. On the **Systems Management Properties** message box, click **OK**.

7. Close the Control Panel.

8. Leave the Glasgow, Dublin, and Bonn virtual machines running.

▶ **To run an advertised program on the client**

1. Verify that the Glasgow, Dublin, and Bonn virtual machines are running.

2. On the Bonn virtual machine, wait for the **Assigned Program About to Run** update balloon to appear.

3. Click the balloon to display the **Program Countdown Status** dialog box.

Note   If the balloon disappears, you can double-click the icon that appears in the right corner of the task bar. (Hovering the cursor over the icon displays the text "An assigned program is about to run.")

---

4. The **Program Countdown Status** dialog box displays the time remaining until the advertised program automatically runs; you can let the timer go to 0, or you can click **Run** at any time to manually run the advertised program.

5. After the **Welcome to Microsoft Visio Viewer 2002 Setup Wizard** page is displayed, click **Next** if needed.

6. In the **User name** box, type **Student** and then click **Next**.

7. Select the **I accept the terms in the License Agreement** check box, and then click **Next**.

8. Verify the **Open all Visio drawings...** check box is selected, and then click **Install**.

9. Click **OK**.

10. On the Bonn virtual machine, on the **Action** menu, click **Close**.

11. Verify that **Save state and save changes** is selected in the list, and then click **OK**.

   The Bonn virtual machine begins to shut down.

12. Leave the Glasgow and Dublin virtual machines running.

Practice: Creating an Advertisement to Install the Visio Viewer

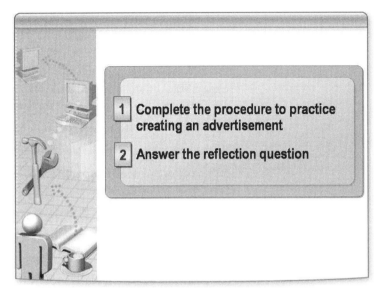

Instructions

Complete the procedures to practice creating an advertisement for the Visio Viewer 2002, retrieving a user policy, and running an advertised program on the client. Then answer the reflection question that follows

The advertisement should:

- Be mandatory.

- Download as soon as possible.

- Download before running.

- Be able to use a remote distribution point.

- Give users two to five minutes to click the boxes.

Use the following values.

Variable	Value
Virtual machine—SMS Site 1	Dublin
Dublin Administrator	JaePa (Jae Pak)
Virtual machine—domain controller	Glasgow
Domain administrator	Administrator
Virtual machine—SMS Advanced Client	Bonn
Bonn Administrator	SMartinez (Sandra Martinez)

Procedure

▶ **To create an advertisement**

1. Verify that the Glasgow and Dublin virtual machines are running.

2. On the Dublin virtual machine, click **Start**, point to **All Programs**, point to **Systems Management Server**, and then click the **SMS Administrator Console**.

3. In the SMS Administrator console, expand **Site Database (001 – NWTraders)**, and then click **Advertisements**.

4. Right-click **Advertisements**, point to **New**, and then click **Advertisement**.

   The **Advertisement Properties** dialog box will open.

5. In the **Advertisement Properties** dialog box, in the **Name** box, type **Practice 7 Advertisement**

6. In the **Package** list, select **Practice 5 Package**.

7. In the **Program** list, select **Practice 5 Program**.

8. Click **Browse**.

   The **Browse Collection** dialog box will open.

9. In the **Browse Collection** list, click **Practice 2 Collection**, and then click **OK**.

10. Clear the **Include members of subcollections** check box.

11. On the **Schedule** tab, click the **New** ⋇ icon.

12. In the **Assignment Schedule** dialog box, click **Assign immediately after this event**, select **As soon as possible**, and then click **OK**.

13. On the **Advanced Client** tab, click **Download program from distribution point**.

14. Click **Download program from a remote distribution point**.

   The client will not be roaming. This is for demonstration purposes only.

15. Click **OK**.

16. Close the SMS Administrator console.

17. Leave the Glasgow and Dublin virtual machines running.

▶ **To retrieve a user policy**

1. Log the Bonn virtual machine on to the NWTRADERS domain with a user name of **SMartinez** and a password of **P@ssw0rd**.

2. On the **Bonn** virtual machine, click **Start**, and then click **Control Panel**.

3. Click **Performance and Maintenance**, and then click **Systems Management**.

4. On the **Actions** tab, click **User Policy Retrieval & Evaluation Cycle**, and then click **Initiate Action**.

5. On the **User Policy Retrieval & Evaluation Cycle** dialog box, click **OK**.

6. On the **Systems Management Properties** message box, click **OK**.

7. Close the Control Panel.

8. Leave the Glasgow, Dublin, and Bonn virtual machines running.

▶ **To run an advertised program on the client**

1. Verify that the Glasgow, Dublin, and Bonn virtual machines are running.

2. On the Bonn virtual machine, wait for the **Assigned Program About to Run** update balloon to appear.

3. Click the balloon to display the **Program Countdown Status** dialog box.

Note   If the balloon disappears, you can double-click the icon that appears in the right corner of the task bar. (Hovering the cursor over the icon displays the text "An assigned program is about to run.")

---

4. The **Program Countdown Status** dialog box displays the time remaining until the advertised program automatically runs; you can let the timer go to 0, or you can click **Run** at any time to manually run the advertised program.

   The advertised program does not appear to run. Use C:\Windows\System32\CCM\Logs\Execmgr.log to see if the program started. You might want to start Task Manager to view or stop running processes.

   According to Execmgr.log and Task Manager, did the advertised program start successfully? Is the Visio Viewer setup (vviewer.exe) process running? If the process is running, why might you not see the Visio Viewer setup on the Desktop? What configuration option in **Practice 5 Program** might cause the Visio Viewer setup not to appear?

   To run the Visio Viewer setup, use the SMS Administrator console on Dublin to reconfigure the advertised program such that you can run the program correctly. Because the advertisement you created has already run once, you may need to create a new advertisement.

Note   For a comprehensive set of steps to complete this procedure, please refer to Appendix B: "Course 2596B, *Managing Microsoft Systems Management Server 2003* – Troubleshooting Practices Answer Key" on your Student Materials compact disc. Also, you must fix this problem before proceeding.

---

5. After the **Welcome to Microsoft Visio Viewer 2002 Setup Wizard** page is displayed, click **Next** if needed.

6. In the **User name** box, leave the default, and then click **Next**.

7. Select the **I accept the terms in the License Agreement** page, and then click **Next**.

8. Verify the **Open all Visio drawings...** check box is selected, and then click **Install**.

9. Click **OK**.

10. On the Bonn virtual machine, on the **Action** menu, click **Pause**.

    The Bonn virtual machine dims indicating it is paused.

11. Leave the Glasgow, Dublin, and Bonn virtual machines running.

Reflection questions

1. In what situations might an advertisement be configured as mandatory?

    _____

    _____

    _____

2. When might an SMS administrator request that a user force policy retrieval using the control panel?

    _____

    _____

    _____

Lesson: Monitoring Software Distribution

- Standard Reports for Software Distribution
- How to Use the Standard Reports for Software Distribution
- Methods to Monitor the Software Distribution Process
- How to Check Status Information for Advertisements and Packages
- Locations of Software Distribution Log Files
- Demonstration: How to Use Reports and Status Information

Introduction

In this lesson, you will learn how to use reporting and status information to monitor a software distribution process. You will learn how to isolate problems related to software distribution.

Lesson objectives

After completing this lesson, you will be able to:

- Describe standard reports for software distribution.
- Use standard reports for software distribution.
- Monitor the software distribution process.
- View status information for advertisements and packages.
- Locate files for software distribution objects.

Standard Reports for Software Distribution

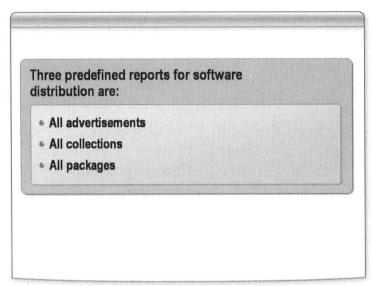

SMS 2003 provides a number of predefined reports that you can use to quickly gather a wide variety of information about your SMS operations. Three of the predefined reports are All advertisements, All collections, and All packages.

To read a report, you must be a member of the SMS Reporting Users user group on the reporting point.

How to Use the Standard Reports for Software Distribution

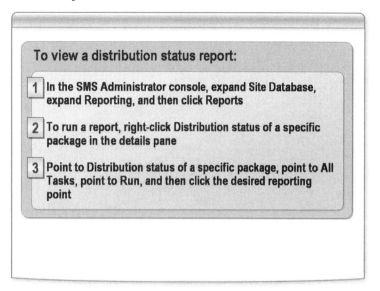

There are several reports that can be viewed in the SMS Administrator console and the Report Viewer, not all of which pertain to software distribution. You will want to view the report for the distribution status of a specific package.

Procedures

To view reports with SMS Administrator console:

1. In the SMS Administrator console, expand **Site Database**, expand **Reporting**, and then click **Reports**. The list of reports for which you have Read permissions will appear in the details pane.

2. To see reports for a specific package, right-click **Distribution status of a specific package** in the details pane, point to **All Tasks**, point to **Run**, and then click the desired reporting point to run the report.

To filter the list of reports:

1. After you have navigated to Reports in the SMS Administrator console, right-click **Reports**, point to **All Tasks**, and then click **Filter Reports**.

2. In the **Filter Reports** dialog box, select one or more categories in the **Categories** list, and then click **Display/Hide**.

To view reports with Report Viewer:

1. In the SMS Administrator console, expand **Site Database**, and then expand **Reporting**.

2. Right-click **Reports**, point to **All Tasks**, and then point to **Run**.

3. On the **Run** menu, click the name of the reporting point that you want to use to start Report Viewer. Report Viewer will start on the main page.

4. On the Report Viewer main page, perform one of the following procedures:

    *   In the reports tree, expand a category to view a list of reports in the category for which you have Read permission. To run a report, click the report, enter values for any required parameters, and then click **Display**.

    *   To view the list of dashboards, click **Dashboards**.

    *   To view the list of reports that are designated to appear on the Computer Details page, click **Computer Details**. Only reports for which you have Read permission appear on this page.

    *   To view the list of supplemental reports, expand **Supplemental Reports**.

Methods to Monitor the Software Distribution Process

Monitoring software distribution can be done using:

- Software Distribution Reports
- Advertisements Summary Status
- Package Status Summary

You might want to consider using SMS reports to monitor the status of packages and advertisements. SMS reports return a significant amount of useful status information. You can also use status message queries to directly obtain the status of advertisements or package distributions. You can use such queries in reports to display status information in a more effective manner.

After you distribute software, you can monitor the distribution by viewing SMS status messages. For example, if you advertise a program to run a virus scan each night at midnight, you might want to check every morning to see if all the clients have run the program. You can see this information at a glance in the main Advertisement Status console item. This console item displays every advertisement and includes status information.

The package status summary provides information about each package. You can select a package to see the information on a site-by-site basis. You can also select any site to see information for that package on a distribution point-by-distribution point basis. At any level (package, site, or distribution point), you can view the status messages that were used to create the statistics.

Procedure to view the package status summary

To view the package status summary:

1. In the SMS Administrator console, click **System Status**.

2. Expand the node for **Package Status**. All packages will appear.

3. Click the package for which you want to view the status. Information will appear in the details pane.

The Advertisement Status summary provides information about each advertisement, and then you can select an advertisement to see the information about a site-by-site basis. At either level (package or site), you can view the status messages that were used to create the statistics displayed in the status summary.

Procedure to view the advertisement summary status

To view the advertisement summary status:

1. In the SMS Administrator console, click **System Status**.

2. Expand the **Advertisement Status** node. All advertisements will appear.

3. Click the advertisement for which you want to view the status. Information will appear in the details pane.

You can also use software distribution reports to monitor status. Software distribution reports were discussed in an earlier in this lesson.

How to Check Status Information for Advertisements and Packages

To check an advertisement status:

1. In the SMS Administrator console, expand Site Database, expand System Status, expand Advertisement Status, and then click the desired advertisement

2. Right-click the desired site

3. Select Show Messages

4. To view all status messages, click All

5. To view selected messages, click Received, Failures, Program Started, Program Errors, or Program Success

The SMS status system gives you a good view of how the distribution of your packages to distribution points is progressing and provides meaningful information about each advertised program.

SMS updates package status each time there is a change in the condition of a package.

You can simultaneously advertise multiple programs in multiple sites. All the status messages generated by any component within your organization are collected by the status system, filtered, and processed to display meaningful information about each advertisement. You can either view the advertisement summary information, or you can view the status messages that produced the summary information.

Procedure to check advertisement status

▶ **To check the advertisement status**

1. In the SMS Administrator console, expand **Site Database**, expand **System Status**, expand **Advertisement Status**, and then click the desired advertisement.

2. Right-click the desired site code and then point to **Show Messages**.

   • To view all status messages, click **All**.

   • To view selected messages, click **Received**, **Failures**, **Programs Started**, **Program Errors**, or **Program Success**.

You can use status summaries for quick information and use console items for more detailed information regarding package distribution. Under each summary, you can get the information you need at the most appropriate level. SMS updates package status each time there is a change in the condition of a package.

**Procedure to check
package status**

▶ **To check the package status**

1. In the SMS Administrator console, expand **Site Database**, expand **System Status**, and then expand **Package Status**.

2. Right-click the desired package, and then point to **Show Messages**.

3. To view all status messages, click **All**.

4. To view selected messages, click **Errors**, **Warnings**, or **Info**.

5. To view status information for a specific site, select the desired package from the console tree. The package status information for each site appears in the details pane.

6. To view status messages associated with a particular site for the package you selected, select the site you want in the details pane, right-click it, and then click **Show Messages**. To view all status messages, click **All**. For selected messages, click **Errors**, **Warnings**, or **Info**.

7. To view package status information for a specific distribution point, select the package you want, and then select the site you want in the console tree. The package status information for each distribution point for the selected package and site appears in the details pane.

8. To view the status messages associated with a particular distribution point for the selected package, select the distribution point you want in the details pane, right-click the distribution point, and then click **Show Messages**. To view all the status messages associated with the distribution point for the package, click **All**. To view selected messages, click **Errors**, **Warnings**, or **Info**.

Locations of Software Distribution Log Files

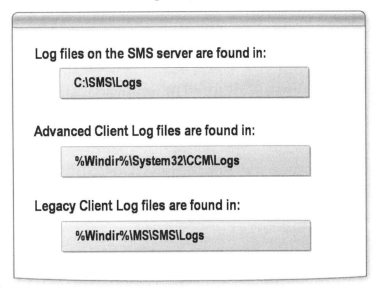

To track software distribution processes, you might need to check the log files on the SMS server or on the client. The SMS server keeps logs for collection, packages, and advertisements. The client keeps log files about execution.

The log files on the SMS server are found in C:\SMS\Logs, assuming that SMS was installed on drive C. The Advanced Client log files can be found in %Windir%\System32\CCM\Logs. Legacy Client log files are stored in %Windir%\MS\SMS\Logs.

The following table shows the software distribution object, where its log file is located, and its corresponding log file.

Distribution object	Log files	Where located
Collection	Colleval.log	C:\SMS\Logs
Package	Distmgr.log	C:\SMS\Logs
Program	Execmgr.log	%Windir%\System32\CCM\Logs
Advertisement for Advanced Clients	Policypv.log	C:\SMS\Logs
Advertisement for Legacy Clients	Offermgr.log	C:\SMS\Logs

Note The above table assumes that SMS was installed on the C: drive. It is possible that SMS will be installed on a different drive in your work environment.

Demonstration: How to Use Reports and Status Information

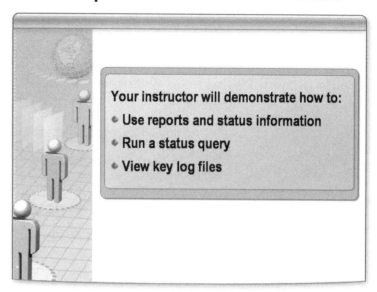

In this demonstration you will run reports, review status messages, and review log files that will help verify software distribution.

Your instructor will use the following values in this demonstration.

Variable	Value
Virtual machine—SMS Site 1	Dublin
Dublin Administrator	JaePa (Jae Pak)
Virtual machine—domain controller	Glasgow
Domain administrator	Administrator

Important   These steps are included for your information. Do not attempt to perform them in the classroom. If you perform these steps in the classroom environment, you might leave your computer in an incorrect state for upcoming practices.

Demonstration steps performed by instructor only

▶ **To use reports and status information**

1. Verify that Glasgow and Dublin virtual machines are running.

2. On the Dublin virtual machine, click **Start**, point to **All Programs**, point to **Systems Management Server**, and then click **SMS Administrator Console**.

3. In the SMS Administrator console, expand **Site Database (001 – NWTraders)**, and then click **Advertisements**.

4. In the details pane, find the **Advertisement ID** column, and then write the ID number in the space below:

   Demo 6 Advertisement ID: _____

5. In the console tree pane, expand **Reporting**, right-click **Reports**, point to **All Tasks**, point to **Run**, and then click **Dublin**.

   The SMS Report Viewer will open.

6. Expand **Software Distribution – Advertisement Status**, and then click **Status of a specific advertisement**.

7. In the **Report Information** pane, type the Advertisement ID you wrote down in step 4 into the **Advertisement ID** box, and then click the **Display** icon to launch the **Status of a specific advertisement** report.

   This report reveals the percentage of total adverts that clients have successfully received.

8. Close all SMS Report Viewer windows, but leave open the SMS Administrator console.

▶ **To run a status query**

1. On the Dublin virtual machine, in the console tree of the SMS Administrator console, expand **System Status**, and then click **Status Message Queries**.

2. Right-click **All Status Messages for a Specific Advertisement at a Specific Site**, and then click **Show Messages**.

   The **All Status Messages for a Specific Advertisement at a Specific Site** dialog box will open.

3. In the **Prompted value:** section, verify that **Property Value** is selected, then click **Load existing**, and then click the down arrow.

4. Click **OK** on the **All existing values for this prompt will be loaded into the list at this time** message box.

5. Select the first advertisement value in the list, and verify the same value is displayed for **Property Value**.

6. In the **Prompted value:** section, click **Site Code**, click **Load existing**, and then click the **down arrow**.

7. Click **OK** on the **All existing values for this prompt will be loaded into the list at this time** message box.

8. Select **001** in the list, and verify the same value is displayed for **Site Code**.

9. In the **Prompted value:** section, click **Time**, click **Select date and time**, and then select **1 day ago** in the list.

10. Click **OK**.

    The **SMS Status Message viewer** window will open.

11. Double-click any message to review status, and then close any open windows.

► **To view key log files**

1. On the Dublin virtual machine, click **Start**, and then click **Windows Explorer**.

2. In Windows Explorer, browse to **C:\SMS\Logs**.

3. Double-click **Distmgr.log**.

4. In **SMS Trace**, on the **Tools** menu, click **Filter**.

5. In the **Filter Settings** dialog box, select the **Filter when the Entry Text** check box, select **contains**, type **successfully created/updated**, and then click **OK**.

   The results will reveal the last time that packages were updated on the distribution point.

6. Verify that the scheduled update is occurring at the specified time as configured in the package's properties.

7. Close SMS Trace and Windows Explorer.

8. Leave the Glasgow and Dublin virtual machines running.

Practice: Running Standard Reports on Software Distribution

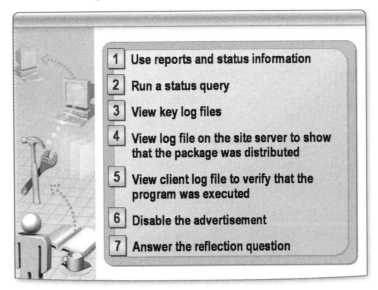

Instructions

In this practice, complete the procedures to run standard reports, run a status query, view key log files, verify client log file, and then disable any advertisements you have created. After completing all procedures, answer the reflection that follows.

Use the following values.

Variable	Value
Virtual machine—SMS Site 1	Dublin
Dublin Administrator	JaePa (Jae Pak)
Virtual machine—domain controller	Glasgow
Domain administrator	Administrator
Virtual machine—SMS Advanced Client	Bonn
Bonn Administrator	SMartinez (Sandra Martinez)

Procedure

▶ **To use reports and status information**

1. Verify that Glasgow and Dublin virtual machines are running.

2. On the Dublin virtual machine, click **Start**, point to **All Programs**, point to **Systems Management Server**, and then click **SMS Administrator Console**.

3. In the SMS Administrator console, expand **Site Database (001 – NWTraders)**, expand **Reporting**, and then click **Reports**.

4. In the details pane, right-click **All advertisements**, point to **All Tasks**, point to **Run**, and then click **Dublin**.

   The SMS Report Viewer will open.

5. Click the arrow next to the advertisement name to launch the **Status of a specific advertisement** report.

   This report reveals the percentage of total advertisements that clients have successfully received.

6. Close SMS Report Viewer.

▶ **To run a status query**

1. On the Dublin virtual machine, in the console tree of the SMS Administrator console, under **Site Database (001 – NWTraders)**, expand **System Status**, and then select **Status Message Queries**.

2. Right-click **All Status Messages for a Specific Advertisement at a Specific Site**, and then click **Show Messages**.

   The **All Status Messages for a Specific Advertisement at a Specific Site** dialog box will open.

3. In the **Prompted value:** section, verify **Property Value** is selected, then click **Load existing**, and then click the down arrow.

4. Click **OK** on the **All existing values for this prompt will be loaded into the list at this time** message box.

5. Select the first advertisement value in the list, and verify the same value is displayed for **Property Value**.

6. In the **Prompted value:** section, click **Site Code**, click **Load existing**, and then click the down arrow.

7. Click **OK** on the **All existing values for this prompt will be loaded into the list at this time** message box.

8. Select **001** in the list, and verify the same value is displayed for **Site Code**.

9. In the **Prompted value:** section, click **Time**, click **Select date and time**, and then select **2 days ago** in the list.

10. Click **OK**.

    The **SMS Status Message viewer** window will open.

11. Double-click any message to review status, and then close any open windows when done.

▶ **To view key log files**

1. On the Dublin virtual machine, click **Start**, and then click **Windows Explorer**.

2. In Windows Explorer, browse to **C:\SMS\Logs**.

3. Double-click **Distmgr.log**.

4. In **SMS Trace**, on the **Tools** menu, click **Filter...**

5. In the **Filter Settings** dialog box, select the **Filter when the Entry Text** check box, select **contains**, type **successfully created/updated** and then click **OK**.

   The results will reveal the last time that packages were updated on the distribution point.

6. Close SMS Trace.

▶ **To view client log file to verify that the program was executed**

1. On the Bonn virtual machine, on the **Action** menu, click **Resume**.

2. Click **Start**, point to **All Programs**, point to **Accessories**, and then click **Windows Explorer**.

3. Navigate to **C:\Windows\System32\CCM\Logs**.

4. Open and review the **Execmgr.log** file.

   This log will show that the program was executed. Do a search for "**Program exit code**". If the code number is **0**, the program above the line was successful.

5. Close any open windows.

▶ **To disable advertisements**

Note   To enable a subsequent practice to function properly, at this point you will have to disable all advertisements that you have created.

---

1. On the Dublin virtual machine, click **Start**, point to **All Programs**, point to **Systems Management Server**, and then click **SMS Administrator Console**.

2. In the SMS Administrator console, expand **Site Database (001 – NWTraders)**, and then click **Advertisements**.

3. In the details pane, right-click **Practice 7 Advertisement**, point to **All Tasks**, and then click **Disable Program**.

4. Click **Yes** in the **Are you sure you want to disable this program?** message box.

Note   Repeat steps 3 and 4 for each new advertisement you created.

---

5. Close any open windows.

6. Leave the Glasgow, Dublin, and Bonn virtual machines running.

Reflection Question   What report data is useful in your organization, and who would need the data?

_____

_____

_____

Lab A: Using SMS Software Distribution to Deploy an Office Application

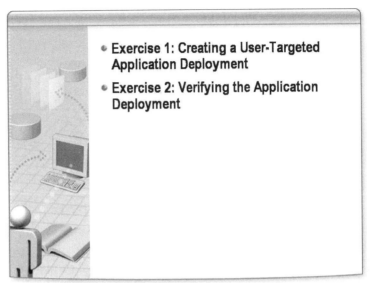

- Exercise 1: Creating a User-Targeted Application Deployment
- Exercise 2: Verifying the Application Deployment

In this lab, you will install Microsoft Office PowerPoint® Viewer 2003. Read the scenario and then complete the exercises that follow.

Tip If you need to, you can refer to the steps you performed in the previous practices in this module for guidance and support.

Objectives

After completing this lab, you will be able to:

- Deploy an application by using SMS.

- Verify the status of an SMS application deployment.

Note This lab focuses on the concepts in this module and as a result might not comply with Microsoft security recommendations.

Scenario

You are the SMS administrator for a medium-sized company. You receive an e-mail message from your boss that reads as follows:

"We have purchased PowerPoint Viewer 2003 and want to deploy this as a pilot to all the sales staff's computers. Because this is a pilot, we want our sales staff to be able to decide whether they want to install the product. However, I want to be able to get information on how many sales staff members install the product so that we can determine whether we will go forward and implement this more widely. Some of the sales staff take their laptops home to work, so they might choose to download the viewer from home, so make sure to configure this so that they can see the estimated download time and resource usage. Thanks."

Estimated time to complete this lab: 30 minutes

Exercise 1
Creating a User-Targeted Application Deployment

In this exercise, you will deploy an application with SMS by creating a collection, a package, and an advertisement. You will also verify the creation of each of these items.

In this lab, use the following values.

Variable	Value
Virtual machine—SMS Site 1	Dublin
Dublin Administrator	JaePa (Jae Pak)
Virtual machine—domain controller	Glasgow
Domain administrator	Administrator
Virtual machine—SMS Advanced Client	Bonn
Bonn Administrator	SMartinez (Sandra Martinez)

▶ **To update all Windows XP computers**

1. Verify that the Glasgow and Dublin virtual machines are running.

2. On the Dublin virtual machine, click **Start**, point to **All Programs**, point to **Systems Management Server**, and then click **SMS Administrator Console**.

3. In the console tree of the SMS Administrator console, expand **Site Database (001 NWTraders)**, expand **Collections**, and then click **All Windows XP Systems**.

4. In the results pane, verify that Bonn is a member of the collection. If Bonn does *not* appear, perform the following steps:

    a. Right-click **All Windows XP Systems**, point to **All Tasks**, and then click **Update Collection Membership**.

    b. In the **All Windows XP Systems** dialog box, click **OK**.

    c. Right-click **All Windows XP Systems**, and then click **Refresh**.

▶ **To create a collection of sales staff with Windows 2000 or later systems**

1. On the Dublin virtual machine, in the SMS Administrator console, expand **Site Database (001 NWTraders)**, and then click **Collections**.

2. Right-click **Collections**, point to **New**, and then click **Collection**.

3. In the **Collection Properties** dialog box, in the **Name** box, type **Sales Computers**

4. On the **Membership Rules** tab, click the **New query** icon.

    The **Query Rule Properties** dialog box will open.

5. In the **Name** box, type **Sales Computers**

6. In the **Resource class** list, select **System Resource**.

7. Click **Limit to Collection**.

8. Click **Browse**.

9. In the **Collections** list, select **All Windows XP Systems**, and then click **OK**.

10. Click **OK**.

11. Repeat steps 4 through 9 to create another rule and use the following values:

    a. Name: **Sales Computers 2**

    b. Collection: **All Windows 2000 Professional Systems**

12. Repeat steps 4 through 9 to create another rule and use the following values:

    a. Name: **Sales Computers 3**

    b. Collection: **All Windows Server 2003 Systems**

13. Set the schedule to every 3 days.

    a. Click Schedule.

        The **Schedule** dialog box will open.

    b. Set **Recur every** to **3 days**.

    c. Click **OK**.

14. In the **Sales Computers Collection Properties** dialog box, click **OK**.

► **To verify that the collection was created by refreshing the SMS Administrator console**

1. On the Dublin virtual machine, in the SMS Administrator console, expand **Site Database (001 NWTraders)**.

2. Right-click **Collections**, and then click **Refresh**.

3. Verify that Sales Computers exists.

4. In the console tree, click **Sales Computers**.

5. Verify that Bonn, Glasgow, Dublin, and Paris appear in the collection.

► **To create a package for PowerPoint Viewer 2003**

1. On the Dublin virtual machine, in the SMS Administrator console, expand **Site Database (001 NWTraders)**, and then click **Packages**.

2. Right-click **Packages**, point to **New**, and then click **Package**.

    The **Package Properties** dialog box will open.

3. On the **General** tab, in the **Name** box, type **Sales Computers PowerPoint Viewer 2003**.

4. On the **Data Source** tab, select the **This package contains source files** check box.

5. Click **Set**.

    The **Set Source Directory** dialog box will open.

6. Click **Local drive on the site server**.

7. Click **Browse**.

    The **Browse for Folder** dialog box will open.

8. Click **C:\2596\ppviewer**, and then click **OK**.

9. In the **Set Source Directory** dialog box, click **OK**.

10. Verify that **Always obtain files from source directory** is selected.

11. Select the **Update distribution points on a schedule** check box.

12. Set the schedule to monthly.

    a. Click **Schedule**.

       The **Schedule** dialog box will open.

    b. Set the **Recurrence pattern** to **Monthly**.

    c. Click **OK**.

13. In the **Package Properties** dialog box, click **OK**.

▶ **To specify a program for the package**

1. On the Dublin virtual machine, in the SMS Administrator console, expand **Site Database (001 NWTraders)**, expand **Packages**, and then expand the **Sales Computers PowerPoint Viewer 2003**.

2. Right-click **Programs**, point to **New**, and then click **Program**.

The **Program Properties** dialog box will open.

3. In the **Name** box, type **Sales Computers PowerPoint Viewer 2003**.

4. Click **Browse**.

The **Open** dialog box will open.

5. Select **ppviewer.exe**.

6. Click **Open**.

7. On the **Requirements** tab, in the **Estimated disk space** box, type **2** and then select **MB**.

8. In the **Maximum allowed run time** box, type **10**

9. Click **This program can only run on specified client programs**, and then select the **All Windows Server 2003**, **All x86 Windows 2000**, and **All x86 Windows XP** check boxes.

10. Click the **Environment** tab.

11. In the **Program can run** list, ensure that **Only when a user is logged on** is selected.

12. Click **Run with Administrative rights**.

13. Select the **Allow users to interact with this program** check box.

14. Click **OK**.

▶ **To select a distribution point after the program has been created**

1. On the Dublin virtual machine, in the SMS Administrator console, expand **Site Database (001 NWTraders)**, expand **Packages**, and then expand **Sales Computers PowerPoint Viewer 2003**.

2. Click **Access Accounts** and verify that Administrators and Users exist.

3. Right-click **Distribution Points**, point to **New**, and then click **Distribution Points**.

   The New Distribution Points Wizard will open.

4. On the **Welcome to the New Distribution Points Wizard** page, click **Next**.

5. Select the **Dublin** check box.

6. Click **Finish**.

▶ **To create an advertisement for the package**

1. On the Dublin virtual machine, in the SMS Administrator console, expand **Site Database (001 NWTraders)**, and then select **Advertisements**.

2. Right-click **Advertisements**, point to **New**, and then click **Advertisement**.

   The **Advertisement Properties** dialog box will open.

3. In the **Name** box, type **Sales Computers PowerPoint Viewer 2003**.

4. In the **Package** list, select **Sales Computers PowerPoint Viewer 2003**.

5. In the **Program** list, select **Sales Computers PowerPoint Viewer 2003**.

6. Click **Browse**.

   The **Browse Collection** dialog box will open.

7. In the **Collection** list, select **Sales Computers**.

8. Click **OK**.

9. Click the **Advanced Client** tab.

10. Click **Download program from distribution point**.

11. Click **Download program from a remote distribution point**.

    This is selected for demonstration purposes only. The client will not actually be roaming.

12. Click **OK**.

13. Close any open windows.

14. Leave the Glasgow, Dublin, and Bonn virtual machines running.

Exercise 2
Verifying the Application Deployment

In this exercise, you will:

1. Force policy retrieval from the client.

2. Find the Sales Computers PowerPoint Viewer 2003 advertisement on the client.

3. Install the PowerPoint Viewer 2003.

4. Use reports and status information on the site server to track advertisements.

5. View key log files on the site server to show that the package was distributed.

▶ **To force policy retrieval from the client**

1. If you haven't already, log the Bonn virtual machine on to the NWTRADERS domain with a user name of **SMartinez** and a password of **P@ssw0rd**.

2. On the Bonn virtual machine, click **Start**, and then click **Control Panel**.

3. Click **Performance and Maintenance**, and then click **Systems Management**.

4. On the **Actions** tab, click **Machine Policy Retrieval & Evaluation Cycle**.

5. Click **Initiate Action**.

   The **Machine Policy Retrieval & Evaluation Cycle** message box will open.

6. Click **OK** twice.

7. Close the Control Panel

Note You might need to wait a few minutes before proceeding to the next procedure.

▶ **To find the Sales Computers PPViewer advertisement on the client**

1. On the Bonn virtual machine, look in the System Tray for the **New Program Available** icon and then click on it.

2. The **Run Advertised Programs** dialog box will open.

3. Select the advertised program, and then click **Run**.

4. The **Program Download Required** dialog box appears. Select the **Run program automatically when download completes** check box, and then click **Download**.

5. Follow the normal software installation procedures.

Note If the **New Program Available** icon does not appear in the System Tray, click **Start**, and then click **Control Panel**. Next, click **Add or Remove Programs** and then click **Run Advertised Programs**. Then follow steps 2 through 5 above.

---

6. In the **Run Advertised Programs** dialog box, click **Close**.

7. Close any open windows.

▶ **To view client log file to verify that the program was executed**

1. On the Bonn virtual machine, click **Start**, point to **All Programs**, point to **Accessories**, and then click **Windows Explorer**.

2. In Windows Explorer, browse to **C:\Windows\System32\CCM\Logs**.

3. Open and review the Execmgr.log.

   This log will show that the program was executed. Scroll to the bottom of the log and look for a Program exit code of 0.

4. Close Notepad and Windows Explorer.

5. Close any open windows.

6. On the Bonn virtual machine, on the **Action** menu, click **Close**.

7. Verify that **Save state and save changes** is selected in the list, and then click **OK**.

   The Bonn virtual machine begins to shut down.

8. Leave the Glasgow and Dublin virtual machines running.

▶ **To use reports and status information to track advertisements on the site server**

1. On the Dublin virtual machine, in the SMS Administrator console, expand **Site Database (001 NWTraders)**, expand **Reporting**, and then click **Reports**.

2. Right-click **All advertisements**, point to **All Tasks**, point to **Run**, and then click **Dublin**.

   The **SMS Report** window will open.

3. Open the **Sales Computers PowerPoint Viewer 2003** advertisement by clicking the arrow to the left of the advertisement name.

4. Review the status of the advertisement.

5. On the **File** menu, click **Close**.

▶ **To run a status message query for the advertisement**

1. On the Dublin virtual machine, in the SMS Administrator console, expand **Site Database (001 NWTraders)**, and then click **Advertisements**.

2. In the details pane, find the **Advertisement ID** for the **Sales Computers PPViewer** advertisement.

   Write down the advertisement ID to use in step 5.

3. In the SMS Administrator console, expand **Site Database (001 NWTraders)**, expand **System Status**, and then click **Status Message Queries**.

4. Right-click **All Status Messages for a Specific Advertisement at a Specific Site**, and then click **Show Messages**.

   The **All Status Messages for a Specific Advertisement at a Specific Site** dialog box will open.

5. Click **Load existing**, click the **down arrow**, in the **SMS Status Message Viewer** dialog box click **OK**, and then select the advertisement that matches the advertisement ID in step 2.

6. Click **Site Code**, and in the **Value** area, click **Specify** and type **001**

7. Click **Time**.

8. Click **date and time**, and then select **1 hour ago**.

9. Click **OK**.

   The **SMS Status Message viewer** window will open.

10. Double-click any message to review status.

11. Close the SMS Status Message Viewer window

▶ **To view a log file on the site server to show that the package was distributed**

1. On the Dublin virtual machine, minimize the SMS Administrator console.

2. Click **Start**, and then click **Windows Explorer**.

3. In Windows Explorer, browse to **C:\SMS\Logs**.

4. Open and review the Distmgr.log.

5. This log will show how the package was distributed.

   Do a search for the word "copying" to find the line that shows how the package was distributed.

6. Close SMS Trace and Windows Explorer.

Discussion: Managing Software Distribution

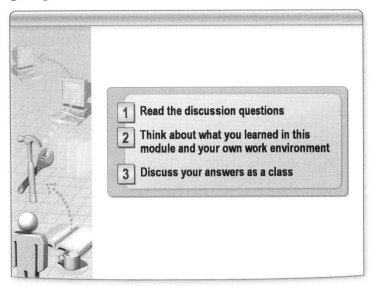

1. How can you configure software distribution of an application to minimize end-user disruption?

   _____

   _____

   _____

   _____

2. You want to distribute Microsoft Office, and you want users to have a choice to install either without the need to configure any options, or install and choose the options they want. What is the most efficient way to configure this distribution?

   _____

   _____

   _____

3. You suspect that clients might not be installing an application that you configured as a mandatory assignment. What would you check on the SMS site to verify and locate the problem?

    _____

    _____

    _____

    _____

Module 9: Implementing SMS Software Update Tools and Managing Update Deployment

Contents

Overview

- Explaining How the SMS Software Updates Process Works
- Installing the Software Update Scanning Tools
- Performing Software Update Inventory
- Deploying and Verifying Software Updates

Introduction

In this module, you will learn to implement Microsoft® Systems Management Server (SMS) software update scanning tools and manage the deployment of security and Microsoft Office updates.

Objectives

After completing this module, you will be able to:

- Describe the SMS software update process
- Install the software update scanning tools
- Perform a software update inventory
- Deploy and verify software updates

Lesson: Explaining How the Software Update Process Works

- **How SMS Is Used to Manage Software Updates**
- **Differences in Software Update Management for Windows Update Services and SMS 2003**
- **How SMS Determines Which Software Updates Are Needed**
- **How SMS Distributes Software Updates**

Introduction

In this lesson, you will learn about the major components and processes of SMS software update inventory and update distribution.

Lesson objectives

After completing this lesson, you will be able to:

- Describe how SMS is used to manage software updates.
- Describe differences in software update management for Microsoft Windows® update services and SMS 2003 software update management.
- Describe how SMS determines which software updates are needed.
- Describe how SMS distributes software updates.

How SMS Is Used to Manage Software Updates

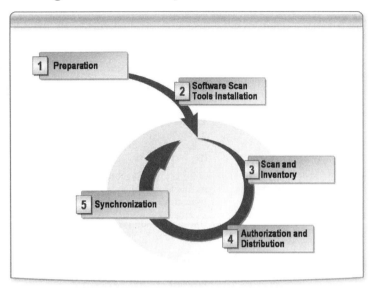

The SMS software update process

The process of managing software updates with SMS consists of multiple phases. The first two phases occur one time only. The subsequent phases are ongoing and occur on a regular cycle as determined by the configuration of the software update management tools and the needs of the enterprise. The five phases are described as follows.

1. Preparation phase

   Collect information about the computers and software in the enterprise, and become informed about the latest security developments and technology.

2. Scan tools installation phase

   Download, install, and deploy the software updates scan tools in the enterprise.

3. Software updates scan and inventory phase

   Program and advertisement settings for the software updates scan tool package control the scan component, which analyzes the current state of installed and applicable software updates on SMS client computers. The more often you run the software update scanning tools, the more current will be the information that is collected and propagated through the site.

4. Software updates authorization and distribution phase

   Use the Distribute Software Updates Wizard to authorize updates for distribution.

5. Software updates catalog synchronization phase

   In this automated process, the software inventory scan components on SMS client computers are updated with the latest software updates catalog data from Microsoft.

Differences in Software Update Management for Windows Update Services and SMS 2003

Feature	Windows Update Services	SMS 2003 with Software Update Management
Platforms supported	Windows 2000 and later	Windows NT 4.0 SP6a and later
Updates for Microsoft products	Windows OS + components	Windows OS + components Microsoft Exchange Server Microsoft SQL Server Microsoft Office
Updates for non-Microsoft products	None	Basic software distribution feature can be used
Installation control	End user	Administrator
Enterprise features	None	Software/hardware inventory Software distribution Scheduling and targeting
Reporting	Reporting from each computer	Rich reporting feature
Deployment	None	Ongoing process

SMS 2003 Software Update Management tools

SMS 2003 Software Update Management feature provides several tools, including the following:

- Security Update Inventory Tool

- Microsoft Office Inventory Tool for Updates

- Distribute Software Updates Wizard

- SMS Reporting

These tools are described in the following lesson, "Installing the Software Update Scanning Tools."

Key differences between Microsoft Windows update services and SMS 2003 with Software Update Management

There are some key differences between Microsoft Windows update services and SMS 2003 with Software Update Management. The differences are outlined in the following table.

Feature	Windows Update Services	SMS 2003 with Software Update Management
Platform support	Windows 2000 and later	Microsoft Windows NT® 4.0 SP 6a and later.
Updates for Microsoft products	Updates only to the Windows operating system and its components	Updates to Windows operating system, its components, Microsoft Exchange Server, Microsoft SQL Server™, and Microsoft Office.
Updates for non-Microsoft products	Not supported	Basic software distribution feature of SMS can be used to deploy updates for non-Microsoft products.
Control	User decides which updates to install and when	Corporate administrator controls all aspects of update installation. The user experience can be fully configured.
Enterprise features	None	Rich set of enterprise features for software and hardware inventory, bandwidth-aware software distribution, sophisticated scheduling, and targeting.
Reporting	Local computer reporting from each computer only	Rich reporting driven by rich data in the SQL Server database.
Deployment	No deployment required	Requires detailed planning for new customers (simple for existing SMS customers). Ongoing administration process depends on richness and complexity of enterprise.

How SMS Determines Which Software Updates Are Needed

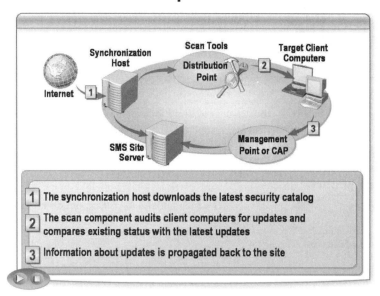

The SMS software update inventory function identifies which software applications and software updates have been installed and which need to be installed.

The process

The process of determining the needed updates is performed on a regular schedule. This process is controlled by the advertisement settings for the software update scan and inventory tool package. The process occurs as follows:

1. The SMS site synchronization host periodically downloads the latest version of the security catalog (Mssecure.cab) from Microsoft.

2. An advertisement instructs the client to run the scan component of the software update scanning tool for the Security Update Inventory Tool or for the Microsoft Office Inventory Tool for Updates (Scanwrapper.exe for both tools). The following actions take place:

    a. The scan component of the Security Update Inventory Tool uses the technology of the Microsoft Baseline Security Analyzer (which is built into the tools) and the security updates database to audit SMS client computers for installed and applicable updates. It compares this information to the latest security catalog (Mssecure.cab) to determine which updates are missing.

    b. Information about the missing updates is converted to hardware inventory data and stored in Windows Management Instrumentation (WMI).

3. The hardware inventory process takes the information from WMI on the client and sends it to the site with the rest of the hardware inventory data.

The software update scanning tools are described in more detail later in this module. These tools are described in the following lesson, "Installing the Software Update Scanning Tools."

How SMS Distributes Software Updates

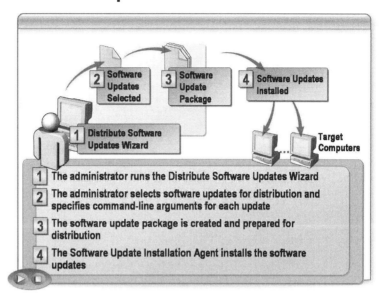

The process	SMS 2003 distributes software updates through the Distribute Software Updates Wizard. This wizard allows you to authorize updates and then distribute them through the following process:

1. The administrator runs the Distribute Software Updates Wizard.

    Running the wizard allows you to create or update software update packages. The information the wizard displays is based on the software update data that was collected during the scanning phase on the targeted clients.

2. The administrator selects the software updates for distribution and specifies the correct command-line arguments for each update.

3. The Distribute Software Updates Wizard does the following:

    a. Downloads the source files for the specified software updates from the Microsoft downloads site (provided the update supports automated downloads).

    b. Stores the source file on the specified package source shared folder.

    c. Creates or updates the necessary packages, programs, and advertisements for distributing the software updates to SMS clients.

    d. Creates an SMS program containing commands to run the Software Updates Installation Agent for every software update package. The software update packages replicate to distribution points in the site, and the programs are advertised to the clients.

4. The Software Updates Installation Agent runs on the clients and installs the appropriate software updates that have been authorized. The agent runs the scan component before installation of the updates to ensure that it installs only the needed software updates.

Practice: Explaining How the Software Update Process Works

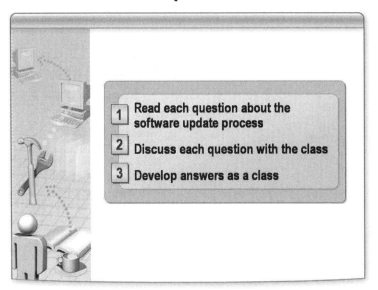

Instructions

Read the following questions about the software update process, discuss possible answers with other students, and then develop answers as a class. Do not move on to the next lesson until you can explain how the software update process works.

Scenario

Clair Hector is the director of the Information Technology (IT) department for Northwind Traders. Jae Pak is the system administrator in charge of managing the day-to-day operations of the network and server environment. To better understand what is needed to implement software update management, Clair has asked Jae to gather information about how SMS manages software updates.

Discussion questions

1. What software update tools are used in the software update management process? What functionality do they provide?

_____

_____

_____

_____

_____

2. What additional features does SMS Software Update Management provide over Windows Update?

_____

_____

_____

_____

_____

3. How can you obtain the latest security catalog?

_____

_____

_____

_____

_____

Lesson: Installing the Software Update Scanning Tools

- What Are the Software Update Scanning Tools?
- How to Install the Software Update Scanning Tools
- Demonstration: How to Install the Software Update Scanning Tools
- SMS Objects Created by the Software Update Scanning Tools
- Demonstration: How to View SMS Objects Created by the Software Update Scanning Tools

Introduction

In this lesson, you will learn about the software update scanning tools for Microsoft Office and security updates. You will also learn how to install these tools.

Lesson objectives

After completing this lesson, you will be able to:

- Describe the software update scanning tools.
- Install the software update scanning tools.
- Describe the SMS objects that are created by the software update scanning tools.
- View SMS objects created by the software update scanning tools

What Are the Software Update Scanning Tools?

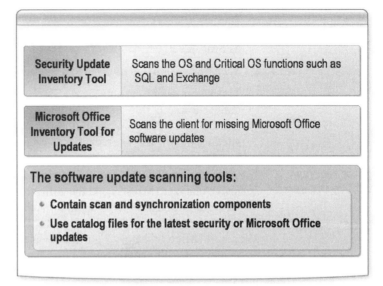

What are software update scanning tools?

The *software update scanning tools* are tools that administrators can use to help find updates, determine which updates their client computers already have, and determine which updates are needed. These tools include the following:

- *The Security Update Inventory Tool*

    This tool scans an SMS client computer's operating system and operating system functions and provides a detailed status of the presence or absence of known security updates from Microsoft.

- *Microsoft Office Inventory Tool for Updates*

    This tool scans an SMS client computer and provides a detailed inventory of the presence or absence of known updates to Microsoft Office.

The tools are periodically updated and are not included or installed automatically with SMS but must be downloaded and installed from the Microsoft SMS Web site.

The Security Update Inventory Tool and the Microsoft Office Inventory Tool for Updates are not dependent on each other. You can use either tool without using the other, or you can use both. The software update scanning tools are not installed on SMS sites by default.

The tools are packaged in their respective installation programs: SecurityPatch_*xxx*.exe or OfficePatch_*xxx*.exe, where *xxx* is the locale version code for the package. Each installer package contains two main components:

The scan and synchronization components

- *Scan component (Scanwrapper.exe)*

  This component runs on the SMS client computers in your enterprise and, when configured as an advertised program, scans for installed or applicable (not yet installed) updates. It stores the data gathered in WMI for collection as SMS inventory data.

- *Synchronization component (Syncxml.exe for both tools)*

  This component runs on a single SMS client computer that has an Internet connection. It periodically downloads the latest Security Updates Catalog and Office Updates Database. It then uses SMS distribution points in your site to send the latest version of the catalog to SMS client computers.

Catalogs for security and MS Office Updates

The Security Updates Catalog (Mssecure.cab) is used by the Microsoft Baseline Security Analyzer (MBSA) and the software update scanning tools to determine which security updates are installed on your computers and which are applicable. The Microsoft Office Updates Database (Invcif.exe) is used by the Microsoft Office Inventory Tool for Updates to determine which Office updates are installed on your computer and which are applicable. The synchronization component automatically downloads the latest version of this database on a regular basis and distributes it to the computers in your enterprise by using SMS distribution points.

You can obtain the Security Updates Catalog and Microsoft Office Updates Database files from the Microsoft Web site. The installer for each of the software update scanning tools installs the catalog the first time it runs. After that, the synchronization host periodically downloads the updated security catalog.

How to Install the Software Update Scanning Tools

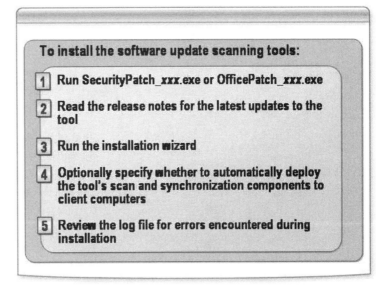

To install the software update scanning tools:

1. Run SecurityPatch_xxx.exe or OfficePatch_xxx.exe

2. Read the release notes for the latest updates to the tool

3. Run the installation wizard

4. Optionally specify whether to automatically deploy the tool's scan and synchronization components to client computers

5. Review the log file for errors encountered during installation

The procedures for installing the Security Update Inventory Tool and the Microsoft Office Inventory Tool for Updates are identical.

Procedure

To install either of the tools:

1. Run SecurityPatch_xxx.exe or OfficePatch_xxx.exe (where xxx is the three-digit language code) from the folder of your choice on the SMS site server.

2. Click **Release Notes** and read the release notes for the latest update on the tool.

3. The installation wizard will lead you through the process of installing and configuring the Installer Tool and will download these files:

   - The Scan Tool (Scanwrapper.exe) and the Security Update Bulletin Catalog (Mssecure.cab) are downloaded for SecurityPatch_xxx.exe.

   - The Microsoft Office Inventory Tool for Updates (Invcm.exe) and the Microsoft Office Updates Database (Invcif.exe) are downloaded for OfficePatch_xxx.exe.

4. During setup, you can choose whether to deploy the scan and the synchronization components automatically to client computers by using SMS distribution points. The wizard will also allow you to download a tool for enhanced Web-based reporting for the inventory results.

5. Review the %temp%\advertisement.log log file to view any errors encountered during installation. The log file is automatically displayed by the Installation Wizard.

Demonstration: How to Install the Software Update Scanning Tools

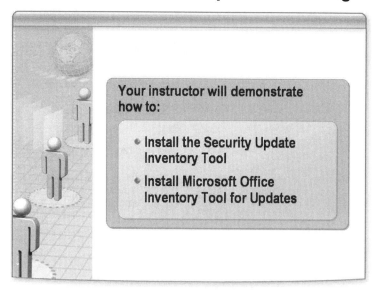

Introduction

In this demonstration, your instructor will show you how to install the Security Update Inventory Tool. The tool will create collections, advertisements, and a package as part of the installation. Your instructor will also run a similar installation of the Microsoft Office Inventory Tool for Updates.

Note Successful installation typically requires access to the Internet, but the virtual machine classroom environment does not have Internet access. Therefore, the installations in these procedures have been preconfigured to work in the classroom. To configure a computer to install these tools without access to the Internet, see the Help files included with the tools.

Your instructor will use the following values in this demonstration.

Variable	Value
Virtual machine—SMS Site 1	Dublin
Dublin Administrator	JaePa (Jae Pak)
Virtual machine—domain controller	Glasgow
Domain administrator	Administrator
Virtual machine—SMS Advanced Client	Bonn
Bonn Administrator	SMartinez (Sandra Martinez)

Important These steps are included for your information. Do not attempt to perform them in the classroom. If you perform these steps in the classroom environment, you might leave your computer in an incorrect state for upcoming practices.

Demonstration steps performed by instructor only

▶ **To install the Security Update Inventory Tool**

1. Verify that the Glasgow virtual machine is running. If Glasgow is not running, log it on to the NWTRADERS domain with a user name of **Administrator** and a password of **P@ssw0rd**.

   After the Glasgow virtual machine opens, you can minimize it.

2. Verify that the Dublin virtual machine is running. If Dublin is not running, log it on to the NWTRADERS domain with a user name of **JaePa** and a password of **P@ssw0rd**.

3. Log the Bonn virtual machine on to the NWTRADERS domain with a user name of **SMartinez** and a password of **P@ssw0rd**.

   After the Bonn virtual machine opens, you can minimize it.

4. On the Dublin virtual machine, click **Start**, and then click **Windows Explorer**.

5. In **Windows Explorer**, browse to **C:\2596\InvTools**, and then double-click **SecurityPatch_ENU.exe**.

6. In the Security Update Inventory Tool Installation Wizard, on the **Welcome** page, click **Next**.

7. On the **License Agreement** page, click **Accept**, and then click **Next**.

8. On the **Select Destination Directory** page, verify that the default destination path is **C:\Program Files\SecurityPatch**, and then click **Next**.

9. In the **Security Update Inventory Tool Installation** message box, click **Yes**.

10. On the **Scan Tool Download** page, click **Next**.

11. On the **Ready to Install** page, click **Next**.

12. On the **Distribution Settings** page, in the **Package name** box, type **Security Scan** and then click **Next**.

13. On the **Database Updates** page, leave the default of Dublin in the **Obtain updates using** box, and then click **Next**.

14. On the **Test Computer** page, type **Bonn** in the **Test computer** box, and then click **Next**.

15. On the **Ready to Install** page, click **Next**.

    The installation might take one to two minutes.

16. On the **Installation Completed** page, click **Finish**.

Note You will verify that the Security Update Inventory Tool was successfully installed in the demonstration "How to View SMS Objects Created by the Software Update Scanning Tools" later in this lesson.

► **To install Microsoft Office Inventory Tool for Updates**

1. On the Dublin virtual machine, with the **InvTools** folder still open in **Windows Explorer**, in the details pane, double-click **OfficePatch_ENU.exe**.

2. In the Microsoft Office Inventory Tool for Updates Installation Wizard, on the **Welcome** page, click **Next**.

3. On the **License Agreement** page, click **Accept**, and then click **Next**.

4. On the **Select Destination Directory** page, leave the default destination path of **C:\Program Files\OfficePatch**, and then click **Next**.

5. In the **Microsoft Office Inventory Tool for Updates Installation** message box, click **Yes**.

6. On the **Office Update Inventory Tool** page, click **Next**.

7. On the **Ready to Install** page, click **Next**.

8. On the **Distribution Settings** page, clear the **Assign Package to all Distribution Points** check box, and then in the **Package name** box, type **Office Scan** and then click **Next**.

9. On the **Database Updates** page, leave the default of Dublin in the **Obtain updates using** box, and then click **Next**.

10. On the **Test Computer** page, type **Bonn** in the **Test computer** box, and then click **Next**.

11. On the **Ready to Install** page, click **Next**.

    The installation might take one to two minutes.

12. On the **Installation Completed** page, click **Finish**.

13. Close any open windows.

14. Leave the Glasgow, Dublin, and Bonn virtual machines running.

Note   You will verify that the Microsoft Office Inventory Tool for Updates was successfully installed in the demonstration "How to View SMS Objects Created by the Software Update Scanning Tools" later in this lesson.

Practice: Installing the Software Update Scanning Tools

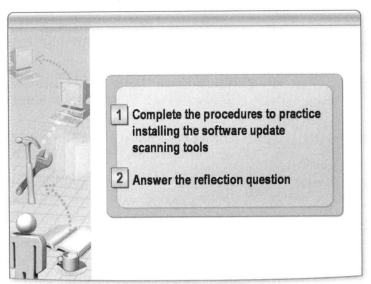

Instructions

Complete the procedures to practice installing the Security Update Inventory Tool (which creates a collection, an advertisement, and a package as part of the installation) and the Microsoft Office Inventory Tool for Updates, and then answer the reflection question that follows.

Note A complete installation should include access to the Internet, but the virtual machine classroom environment does not have Internet access. Therefore, some synchronization functionality will not be available during the following procedures.

In this practice, use the following values.

Variable	Value
Virtual machine—SMS Site 1	Dublin
Dublin Administrator	JaePa (Jae Pak)
Virtual machine—domain controller	Glasgow
Domain administrator	Administrator
Virtual machine—SMS Advanced Client	Bonn
Bonn Administrator	SMartinez (Sandra Martinez)

Procedures

▶ **To install the Security Update Inventory Tool**

1. Verify that the Glasgow virtual machine is running. If Glasgow is not running, log it on to the NWTRADERS domain with a user name of **Administrator** and a password of **P@ssw0rd**.

   After the Glasgow virtual machine opens, you can minimize it.

2. Verify that the Dublin virtual machine is running. If Dublin is not running, log it on to the NWTRADERS domain with a user name of **JaePa** and a password of **P@ssw0rd**.

3. Log the Bonn virtual machine on to the NWTRADERS domain with a user name of **SMartinez** and a password of **P@ssw0rd**.

   After the Bonn virtual machine opens, you can minimize it.

4. On the Dublin virtual machine, click **Start**, and then click **Windows Explorer**.

5. In **Windows Explorer**, browse to **C:\2596\InvTools**, and then double-click **SecurityPatch_ENU.exe**.

6. In the Security Update Inventory Tool Installation Wizard, on the **Welcome** page, click **Next**.

7. On the **License Agreement** page, click **Accept**, and then click **Next**.

8. On the **Select Destination Directory** page, verify that the default destination path is **C:\Program Files\SecurityPatch**, and then click **Next**.

9. In the **Security Update Inventory Tool Installation** message box, click **Yes**.

10. On the **Scan Tool Download** page, click **Next**.

11. On the **Ready to Install** page, click **Next**.

12. On the **Distribution Settings** page, in the **Package name** box, type **Security Scan**

13. Click **Next**.

14. On the **Database Updates** page, leave the default of Dublin in the **Obtain updates using** box, and then click **Next**.

15. On the **Test Computer** page, type **Bonn** in the **Test computer** box.

16. Click **Next**.

17. On the **Ready to Install** page, click **Next**.

    The installation might take one to two minutes.

18. On the **Installation Completed** page, click **Finish**.

▶ **To install Microsoft Office Inventory Tool for Updates**

1. On the Dublin virtual machine, with the **InvTools** folder still open in **Windows Explorer**, in the details pane, double-click **OfficePatch_ENU.exe**.

2. In the Microsoft Office Inventory Tool for Updates Installation Wizard, on the **Welcome** page, click **Next**.

3. On the **License Agreement** page, click **Accept**, and then click **Next**.

4. On the **Select Destination Directory** page, leave the default destination path of **C:\Program Files\OfficePatch**, and then click **Next**.

5. In the **Microsoft Office Inventory Tool for Updates Installation** message box, click **Yes**.

6. On the **Office Update Inventory Tool** page, click **Next**.

7. On the **Ready to Install** page, click **Next**.

8. On the **Distribution Settings** page, clear the **Assign Package to all Distribution Points** check box, and then, in the **Package name** box, type **Office Scan** and then click **Next**.

9. On the **Database Updates** page, leave the default of Dublin in the **Obtain updates using** box, and then click **Next**.

10. On the **Test Computer** page, type **Bonn** in the **Test Computer** box, and then click **Next**.

11. On the **Ready to Install** page, click **Next**.

    The installation might take one to two minutes.

12. On the **Installation Completed** page, click **Finish**.

13. Close any open windows.

14. Leave the Glasgow, Dublin, and Bonn virtual machines running because they will be used in subsequent practices.

Reflection question

What are the differences among the tools contained within the Security Update Scanning Tools for SMS 2003?

_____

_____

_____

_____

SMS Objects Created by the Software Update Scanning Tools

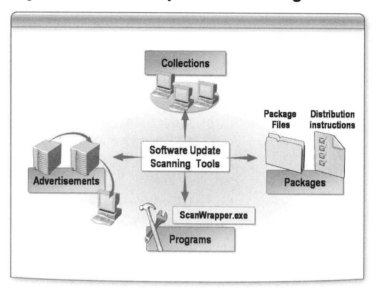

The purpose of default objects

When you initially install software update scanning tools on a site server, the installer program automatically creates the necessary collections, packages, programs, and advertisements needed to deploy the tool components to SMS client computers in your enterprise. These default objects are designed to assist you in deploying the software update scanning tools in your enterprise and to work together with the other software update management components, such as the Distribute Software Updates Wizard.

Guideline for using the default objects

However, in some cases, these default objects are not sufficient to meet the needs of your enterprise. In these cases, it is recommended that you allow the installation program to create the default objects for you automatically, and then create your own collections and create or modify the other objects you need when you finish testing the tools.

The objects created by the software update scanning tools

When you install the software update scanning tools (Security Update Inventory Tool and Microsoft Office Inventory Tool for Updates) on a site server, both tools create three collections, one package, three programs, and two advertisements by default. The default objects that are created are listed in the following table.

Component	Purpose
Collections	
Scan tool collection *Toolname*	The main collection for distributing the scan component to SMS client computers. After installation is completed, the Security Update Inventory Tool program is advertised to this collection. Initially after installation, this collection is restricted by a query limitation to contain the computers that are in the pre-production collection described later.

(*continued*)

Component	Purpose
Collections	
Scan tool (pre-production) collection *toolname* pre-production	Used to test the software update packages that you create with the Distribute Software Updates Wizard. The collection is defined with a direct membership rule that contains the computer you specified as the test computer when you ran the Security Update Inventory Tool installer.
Synchronization component collection *toolname* sync host	If you specified a computer to run the synchronization component when you ran the installer for the Security Update Inventory Tool or the Microsoft Office Inventory Tool for Updates, this collection is created. It is defined by a direct membership rule that contains only the computer you specified, and it receives advertisements from the synchronization program of the scan component package.
Package	
Software update inventory tool package *toolname*	The main package for distributing Security Update Inventory Tool client components to SMS client computers. The package node contains subnodes of Access Accounts, Distribution Points, and Programs. Under the Programs subnode, by default the distribution package contains the three programs described later.
Programs	
Scan component program *toolname*	The generic program for running the scan component on SMS client computers in a production environment.
Scan component expedited program *toolname* expedited	A special program for running the scan component on SMS client computers in an expedited manner in a test environment. The expedited program causes a full hardware inventory cycle. If it is used in your production environment, it can cause serious network and performance issues.
Synchronization component program *toolname*	This program runs the synchronization component on the synchronization host. By default, this program runs the synchronization component (Syncxml.exe) with the following command line for both the Security Update Inventory Tool and the Microsoft Office Inventory Tool for Updates: syncxml.exe /s /site sitename /code sitecode /target packagelocation /package packagename

(*continued*)

Component	Purpose
Advertisements	
Scan component advertisement *toolname*	Advertisement for distributing the scan component to members of the Scan tool collection. Scheduled to run every seven days by default. By default, this advertisement runs the standard (not expedited) scan component program.
Synchronization component advertisement *toolname* sync	Advertisement for the synchronization component to members of the Synchronization component collection. Scheduled to run every seven days by default.

Demonstration: How to View SMS Objects Created by the Software Update Scanning Tools

In this demonstration, your instructor will show you how to review the properties for the components that were created by the Security Update Inventory Tool installation.

Your instructor will use the following values in this demonstration.

Variable	Value
Virtual machine—SMS Site 1	Dublin
Dublin Administrator	JaePa (Jae Pak)
Virtual machine—domain controller	Glasgow
Domain administrator	Administrator
Virtual machine—SMS Advanced Client	Bonn
Bonn Administrator	SMartinez (Sandra Martinez)

Important   These steps are included for your information and you should not attempt to perform them in the classroom.

Demonstration steps performed by instructor only

▶ **To explore the components created by Security Update Inventory Tool**

1. Verify that the Glasgow and Dublin virtual machines are running.

2. On the Dublin virtual machine, open the SMS Administrator console.

3. Expand **Site Database (001 – NWTraders)**, and then expand **Collections**.

4. Right-click the **Security Scan** collection, and then click **Properties**.

   This is the main collection for distributing the scan component to SMS client computers. Upon installation, the Security Update Inventory Tool package is advertised to this collection. Initially after installation, this collection contains only the computers that are contained in the preproduction collection. To change this, remove the collection-limited configuration.

5. Review the properties, and then close the dialog box.

6. Right-click the **Security Scan (pre-production)** collection, and then click **Properties**.

   You can use this collection to test the software update packages that you create with the Distribute Software Updates Wizard. The collection is defined with a direct membership rule that contains the computer you specified as the test computer when you ran the Security Update Inventory Tool Installation Wizard.

7. Review the properties, and then close the dialog box.

8. Right-click the **Security Scan Sync Host** collection, and then click **Properties**.

   If you specified a computer to run the synchronization component when you ran the Security Update Inventory Tool installer, this collection is created. It is defined by a direct membership rule that contains only the computer you specified, and it receives advertisements from the Security Scan Sync program which is part of the Security Scan package.

9. Review the properties, and then close the dialog box.

10. In the console tree of the SMS Administration console, expand **Packages**, and then expand **Security Scan**.

11. Click **Programs**.

12. In the details pane, right-click **Security Scan**, and then click **Properties**.

13. Review the properties, and then close the dialog box.

14. In the details pane, right-click **Security Scan (expedited)**, and then click **Properties**.

   Note Expedited programs are configured to speed the collection of information from the client to the server. This will cause performance issues if used in a production environment. Use this program in a test environment only.

15. Review the properties, and then close the dialog box.

16. In the details pane, right-click **Security Scan Sync**, and then click **Properties**.

    This program runs the Security Update Sync tool on the synchronization host. By default, this program runs the synchronization component (Syncxml.exe) with the following command line:

    syncxml.exe /s /site *siteservername* /code *sitecode* /target *packagelocation* /package *packagename*

17. Review the properties, and then close the dialog box.

18. In the console tree pane, click **Advertisements**.

19. In the details pane, right-click **Security Scan**, and then click **Properties**.

    This advertisement is for distributing the scan component to members of the Security Scan collection. It is scheduled to run every seven days by default. By default, this advertisement runs the standard (not expedited) scan tool program.

20. Review the properties, and then close the dialog box.

21. In the details pane, right-click **Security Scan Sync**, and then click **Properties**.

    This advertisement is for the synchronization component. It is scheduled to run every seven days by default on members of the Security Scan Sync Host collection.

22. Review the properties, and then close the dialog box.

23. Close the SMS Administrator console.

24. Leave the Glasgow, Dublin, and Bonn virtual machines running.

Lesson: Performing Software Update Inventory

- How to Use the Software Update Scanning Tools to Perform Software Update Inventory
- Command-Line Options for the Software Update Scanning Tools
- Demonstration: How to Deploy the Software Update Scanning Tools
- How to Verify the Software Update Inventory Results
- Demonstration: How to Verify Software Update Inventory Results

Introduction

In this lesson, you will learn to deploy the software update scanning tools to perform software update inventory.

Lesson objectives

After completing this lesson, you will be able to:

- Use the scan tools to perform software update inventory.
- Use the command-line options for the software update scanning tools.
- Verify the results of software update inventory.

How to Use the Software Update Scanning Tools to Perform Software Update Inventory

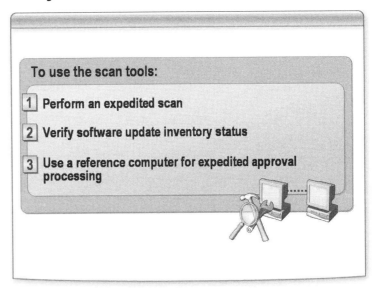

To use the scan tools:

1. Perform an expedited scan

2. Verify software update inventory status

3. Use a reference computer for expedited approval processing

You can use the scan components of the software update scanning tools to conduct an audit of the client computers in your enterprise for installed and applicable software updates. The scan component is Scanwrapper.exe for both security updates and Microsoft Office updates.

The following tasks can help you customize this process to the needs of your enterprise:

1. Perform an expedited scan.

   Expedited scans are performed by forcing the update inventory tool to initiate a hardware inventory cycle immediately after the scan.

2. Verify software update inventory status.

   Verify that the scan has been performed and determine whether the software update inventory data has propagated to the site server.

3. Use a reference computer for expedited approval processing.

   Specify a reference computer to generate baseline software update templates, effectively bypassing the software update inventory process for critical updates you know you need.

Command-Line Options for the Software Update Scanning Tools

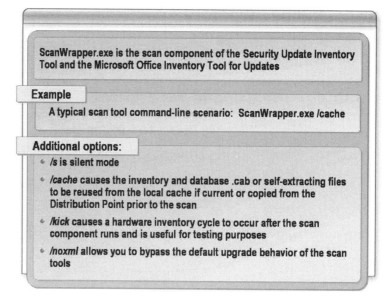

ScanWrapper.exe is the scan component of the Security Update Inventory Tool and the Microsoft Office Inventory Tool for Updates

Example

A typical scan tool command-line scenario: ScanWrapper.exe /cache

Additional options:

- */s* is silent mode
- */cache* causes the inventory and database .cab or self-extracting files to be reused from the local cache if current or copied from the Distribution Point prior to the scan
- */kick* causes a hardware inventory cycle to occur after the scan component runs and is useful for testing purposes
- */noxml* allows you to bypass the default upgrade behavior of the scan tools

---

The scan component for security updates

The security scan component (Scanwrapper.exe) has command-line parameters that you can use to configure how it runs on client computers and how it conducts an audit of the client computers in your enterprise to create an inventory of missing and available security updates.

The Security Update Inventory Tool runs the scan component with the following command line:

Scanwrapper.exe /cache

The scan component for Office updates

The Office scan component (Scanwrapper.exe) has command-line parameters that you can use to configure how it runs on client computers and how it conducts an audit of the client computers in your enterprise to create an inventory of missing and available Microsoft Office updates.

The Microsoft Office Tool for Updates runs the scan component with the following command line:

Scanwrapper.exe /s /cache

Additional options

The following are command-line options for security and Microsoft Office updates.

Parameter	Description
/s	This parameter causes the tool to run in silent mode, which means that no user interface or progress indicators are displayed to the user. You configure this parameter for Microsoft Office updates, not security updates.
/cache	This parameter causes the inventory and database cabinet (.cab) or self-extracting files to be reused from the local cache if they are current. If they are not current, they will be copied from the distribution point prior to the scan.
	Without the /cache parameter, the file copy operation is always performed, regardless of any changes in the .cab file.
	The local cache that is used when running the /cache parameter is secure only for client computers running the NTFS file system. Client computers that are running file allocation table (FAT) file systems can run the scan from a local cache, but the cache is not secure.
/kick	This parameter runs the scan component in an expedited manner. It causes a hardware inventory cycle to occur after the scan tool has run. It also causes the delta inventory resulting from the scan to be forwarded to the SMS site database.
/noxml	SMS 2003 inventory scanning programs upgrade MSXML versions that are earlier than MSXML 3.0 SP 4 and that are not subject to System File Protection (SFP). SMS client computers that are using a version of MSXML in an SFP configuration must be upgraded by using software distribution or other methods.
	You can bypass the default upgrade behavior of the scan tools by editing the appropriate program command line and adding the /noxml switch.

Demonstration: How to Deploy the Software Update Scanning Tools

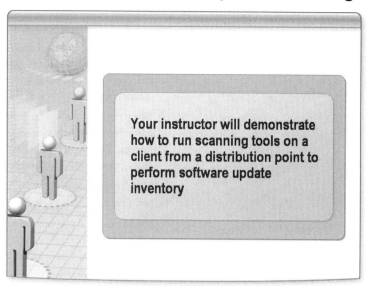

Introduction

In this demonstration, your instructor will show you how to run the scanning tools on your designated test client. The Security Update Inventory Tool installation created a share on the distribution point containing the scanning tools that will be downloaded by the client in accordance with its policies.

Your instructor will use the following values in this demonstration.

Variable	Value
Virtual machine—SMS Site 1	Dublin
Dublin Administrator	JaePa (Jae Pak)
Virtual machine—domain controller	Glasgow
Domain administrator	Administrator
Virtual machine—SMS Advanced Client	Bonn
Bonn Administrator	SMartinez (Sandra Martinez)

Important These steps are included for your information. Do not attempt to perform them in the classroom. If you perform these steps in the classroom environment, you might leave your computer in an incorrect state for upcoming practices.

Because the scan tools depend on hardware inventory, we will enable the Hardware Inventory Client Agent as part of this demonstration.

Demonstration steps performed by instructor only

▶ **To enable hardware inventory**

1. Verify that the Glasgow, Dublin, and Bonn virtual machines are running.

2. On the Dublin virtual machine, click **Start**, point to **All Programs**, point to **Systems Management Server**, and then click **SMS Administrator Console**.

3. In the SMS Administrator console, expand **Site Database (001 – NWTraders)**, expand **Site Hierarchy**, expand **(001 – NWTraders)**, and then expand **Site Settings**.

4. Click **Client Agents**.

5. In the details pane, right-click **Hardware Inventory Client Agent**.

6. Click **Properties**.

7. In the **Hardware Inventory Client Agent Properties** dialog box, verify that the **Enable hardware inventory on clients** check box is selected.

8. Click **OK**.

▶ **To force the policy update on the client**

1. On the Bonn virtual machine, click **Start**, and then click **Control Panel**.

2. Click **Performance and Maintenance**, and then click **Systems Management**.

3. In the **Systems Management Properties** dialog box, click the **Actions** tab.

4. Under **Actions**, click **Machine Policy Retrieval & Evaluation Cycle**, and then click **Initiate Action**.

5. In the **Machine Policy Retrieval & Evaluation Cycle** message box, click **OK**.

    This will force policy update on the client. Although you have forced the policy update, it will still take about two minutes to download and then apply the policies.

    The software update inventory scan will run automatically when the policy is evaluated.

6. Leave the **Systems Management Properties** dialog box open for the next task.

    Note You might need to wait about two minutes before proceeding to the next procedure.

▶ **To initiate the hardware inventory cycle on the client**

1. In the **Systems Management Properties** dialog box, on the **Actions** tab, click **Hardware Inventory Cycle**, and then click **Initiate Action**.

2. In the **Hardware Inventory Cycle** message box, click **OK**.

    Note You might need to wait a few minutes before proceeding to the subsequent demonstration, "How to Verify Software Update Inventory Results."

    ---

3. Close any open windows.

4. Leave the Glasgow, Dublin, and Bonn virtual machines running.

How to Verify the Software Update Inventory Results

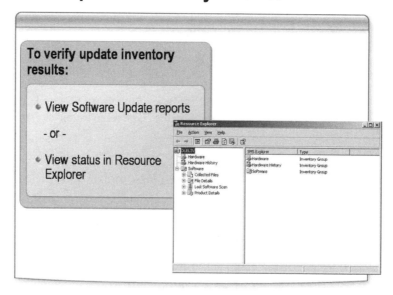

You can verify software update inventory results by using standard reports or Resource Explorer.

Procedures

To view Software Update reports:

1. Navigate to the **Reports** node.

2. Click the category heading to sort the reports by category.

3. Scroll down the list to the **Software Update** category.

4. Select the name of the report you want to run, point to **All Tasks**, point to **Run**, and then click the name of any of the reporting points listed.

   If problems prevent Report Viewer from running from one SMS reporting point, try using another reporting point.

To use Resource Explorer:

1. In the console tree, expand **Systems Management Server**, expand **Site Database**, and then expand **Collections**.

2. Select the collection that contains the SMS client computer for which you want to check the status.

3. In the details pane, right-click the computer, point to **All Tasks**, and then click **Start Resource Explorer**.

4. In the left pane of the **Resource Explorer** window, expand **Hardware**.

   The hardware inventory classes expand in the tree.

5. Click the **Software Updates** node.

   The **Status** column reports the current status of the software update on the SMS client computer. The results appear as instances of a WMI class called Win32_Patchstate. These instances are collected and propagated to the SMS site server using the Hardware Inventory Client Agent.

Demonstration: How to Verify Software Update Inventory Results

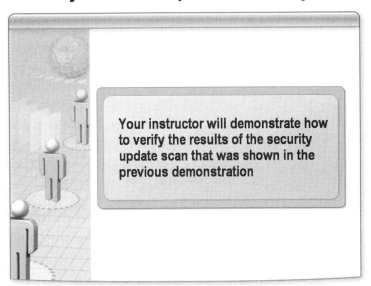

In this demonstration, your instructor will show you how to verify the results of the security update scan that was shown in the previous demonstration.

Your instructor will use the following values in this demonstration.

Variable	Value
Virtual machine—SMS Site 1	Dublin
Dublin Administrator	JaePa (Jae Pak)
Virtual machine—domain controller	Glasgow
Domain administrator	Administrator
Virtual machine—SMS Advanced Client	Bonn
Bonn Administrator	SMartinez (Sandra Martinez)

Important   These steps are included for your information. Do not attempt to perform them in the classroom. If you perform these steps in the classroom environment, you might leave your computer in an incorrect state for upcoming practices.

Demonstration steps performed by instructor only

▶ **To verify the results of the security updates scan**

1. Verify that the Glasgow, Dublin, and Bonn virtual machines are running.

2. On the Dublin virtual machine, click **Start**, point to **All Programs**, point to **Systems Management Server**, and then click **SMS Administrator Console**.

3. In the SMS Administrator console, expand **Site Database (001 – NWTraders)**, expand **Collections**, and then click **All Systems**.

4. In the details pane, right-click **Bonn**, point to **All Tasks**, and then click **Start Resource Explorer**.

5. In the Resource Explorer window, expand **Hardware**, and then click **Software Updates**.

6. Review the list of installed and requested software updates in the details pane.

7. Close the Resource Explorer window.

▶ **To view software updates for the SMS client**

1. On the Dublin virtual machine, in the SMS Administrator console, under **Site Database (001 – NWTraders)**, expand **Reporting**, and then click **Reports**.

2. In the details pane, right-click **Software updates for a specific computer**, point to **All Tasks**, point to **Run**, and then click **Dublin**.

Note   If **Software updates for a specific computer** does not appear, right-click **Reports**, point to **All Tasks**, and then click **Filter Reports**. Verify that all the categories are configured to display.

---

3. In the **Computer Name** box, type **Bonn** and then click the **Display** icon.

4. Review the results of the **Software updates for a specific computer report**.

5. Close any open windows.

6. Leave the Glasgow, Dublin, and Bonn virtual machines running.

Practice: Deploying and Verifying the Software Update Scanning Tools

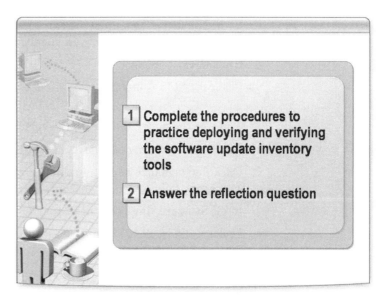

Instructions

Complete the procedures to practice deploying and verifying the software update inventory tools, and then answer the reflection question that follows.

In this practice, use the following values.

Variable	Value
Virtual machine—SMS Site 1	Dublin
Dublin Administrator	JaePa (Jae Pak)
Virtual machine—domain controller	Glasgow
Domain administrator	Administrator
Virtual machine—SMS Advanced Client	Bonn
Bonn Administrator	SMartinez (Sandra Martinez)

Procedures

▶ **To enable hardware inventory**

1. Verify that the Glasgow, Dublin, and Bonn virtual machines are running.

2. On the Dublin virtual machine, click **Start**, point to **All Programs**, point to **Systems Management Server**, and then click **SMS Administrator Console**.

3. In the SMS Administrator console, expand **Site Database (001 – NWTraders)**, expand **Site Hierarchy**, expand **(001 – NWTraders)**, and then expand **Site Settings**.

4. Click **Client Agents**.

5. In the details pane, right-click **Hardware Inventory Client Agent**.

6. Click **Properties**.

7. In the **Hardware Inventory Client Agent Properties** dialog box, select the **Enable hardware inventory on clients** check box.

8. Click **OK**.

9. Leave the SMS Administrator console open.

▶ **To force the policy update on the client**

1. On the Bonn virtual machine, click **Start**, and then click **Control Panel**.

2. Click **Performance and Maintenance**, and then click **Systems Management**.

3. In the **Systems Management Properties** dialog box, click the **Actions** tab.

4. Under **Actions**, click **Machine Policy Retrieval & Evaluation Cycle**, and then click **Initiate Action**.

5. In the **Machine Policy Retrieval & Evaluation Cycle** message box, click **OK**.

    This will force policy to update on the client. Although you have forced the policy to update, it will still take about two minutes to download and apply the policy.

    The software update inventory scan will run automatically when the policy is evaluated.

6. Close the **Systems Management Properties** dialog box.

Note   You might need to wait a few minutes before proceeding to the next procedure.

▶ **To initiate the hardware inventory cycle on the client**

1. Click **Systems Management**.

2. In the **Systems Management Properties** dialog box, in the **Actions** tab, click **Hardware Inventory Cycle**, and then click **Initiate Action**.

3. In the **Hardware Inventory Cycle** dialog box, click **OK**.

Note   You might need to wait a few minutes before proceeding to the next procedure.

---

4. Close the **System Management Properties** dialog box.

5. Close **Control Panel**.

▶ **To verify the results of the security updates scan**

1. On the Dublin virtual machine, in the console tree of the SMS Administrator console, under **Site Database (001 – NWTraders)**, expand **Collections**, and then click **All Systems**.

2. In the details pane, right-click **Bonn**, point to **All Tasks**, and then click **Start Resource Explorer**.

3. In the **Resource Explorer** window, expand **Hardware**, and then click **Software Updates**.

4. Review the list of installed and requested software updates in the details pane.

5. Close the **Resource Explorer** window.

▶ **To view software updates for the SMS client**

1. On the Dublin virtual machine, in the console tree of the SMS Administrator console, under **Site Database (001 – NWTraders)**, expand **Reporting**, and then click **Reports**.

2. In the details pane, right-click **Software updates for a specific computer**, point to **All Tasks**, point to **Run**, and then click **Dublin**.

3. In the **Computer Name** box, type **Bonn** and then click the **Display** icon.

4. Review the results of the software updates for a specific computer report.

5. Close any open windows.

6. Leave the Glasgow, Dublin, and Bonn virtual machines running.

Reflection question

Do the security and office scan tools need to be located and started on the clients? Explain your answer.

_____

_____

_____

Lesson: Deploying and Verifying Software Updates

- Considerations for Planning the Deployment of Software Updates
- How to Distribute Software Updates
- What Is the Distribute Software Updates Wizard?
- Advanced Features of the Distribute Software Updates Wizard
- How to Perform More Complex Software Update Tasks
- Demonstration: How to Distribute Software Updates
- Ways to Verify the Software Update Distribution
- Demonstration: How to Verify the Software Update Distribution

Introduction

In this lesson, you will learn to use the Distribute Software Updates Wizard to distribute software updates that were identified in the software update inventory process.

Lesson objectives

After completing this lesson, you will be able to:

- Describe considerations for planning the deployment of software updates.
- Distribute software updates.
- Describe the purpose of the Distribute Software Updates Wizard.
- Describe the advanced features of the Distribute Software Updates Wizard.
- Perform more complex software update tasks using the Distribute Software Updates Wizard.
- Describe the ways to verify the software update distribution.
- Verify the distribution of software update packages.

Considerations for Planning the Deployment of Software Updates

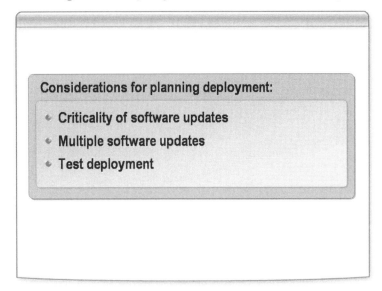

Considerations for planning deployment:

* Criticality of software updates
* Multiple software updates
* Test deployment

Planning considerations for deploying software updates

There are a number of things to consider when planning the deployment of software updates, including the criticality of the updates, the number of updates in a package and how the updates might interact, and test deployment.

■ Criticality of the updates

Every software update released by Microsoft is assigned a security rating, which provides guidance about the urgency with which the update should be handled. You should take the severity rating into account when determining its nature. The following table shows criteria for evaluating criticality.

Rating	Criteria
Critical	A vulnerability whose exploitation could allow the propagation of an Internet worm without user action
Important	A vulnerability whose exploitation could result in compromise of the confidentiality, integrity, or availability of users' data or of the integrity or availability of processing resources
Moderate	A vulnerability whose exploitability is mitigated to a significant degree by factors such as default configuration, auditing, or difficulty of exploitation
Low	A vulnerability whose exploitation is extremely difficult or whose impact is low

■ Multiple software updates

Package source folders contain the files that will be distributed to SMS clients. Although a package can contain more than one update, you might want to limit the size of the package by restricting the number of updates in a package:

* Identify the categories of IT assets to which the package is targeted

* Test the updates

- Test deployment

  Be sure to test an update deployment on one computer and ensure that it works before deploying it to a larger collection of computers. The test should include a preliminary inventory scan. To verify that the tool is working properly, you can review the log file Securitypatch.log in the Temp folder for the account that was used to run the tool.

How to Distribute Software Updates

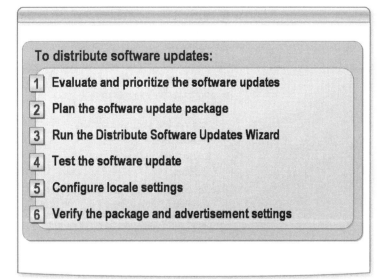

To distribute software updates:

1. Evaluate and prioritize the software updates
2. Plan the software update package
3. Run the Distribute Software Updates Wizard
4. Test the software update
5. Configure locale settings
6. Verify the package and advertisement settings

After you have finished performing software update inventory, you can authorize, download, and distribute software updates by using the Distribute Software Updates Wizard. The Distribute Software Updates Wizard uses the inventory information collected by the software update scanning tools to compile groups of related software updates and to allow you to authorize them for installation.

Procedure

To authorize and distribute software updates:

1. Evaluate and prioritize software updates.
2. Plan the software update packages that will distribute the updates.
3. Run the Distribute Software Updates Wizard.
4. Test the update before authorizing it for distribution.
5. If necessary, configure locale dependencies for each update to accommodate clients in different countries or time zones.
6. Verify the package and advertisement settings you created.

Guidelines for distributing software updates

The following guidelines can help you with the software distribution process:

- Determine which updates are necessary for the SMS client computers in your target collection.

- Group software updates in separate packages according to installation requirements that you determine. This allows you to control deployment more closely.

- Run the wizard from the top-level site in the SMS hierarchy containing the clients to which you want to distribute the updates. If you want to distribute updates to clients throughout the hierarchy, run the wizard from the central site.

What Is the Distribute Software Updates Wizard?

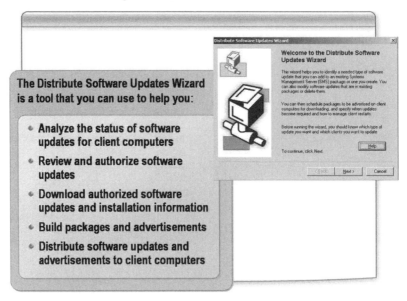

The Distribute Software Updates Wizard is a tool that guides you through several pages that allow you to perform the following actions:

- Use inventory information to analyze the applicable software update status for client computers.

- Review and authorize software updates.

- Download authorized software updates and installation information.

- Build packages and advertisements tailored to specifications for each software update or for a set of updates.

- Distribute software updates and advertisements to client computers by using SMS software distribution.

How to run the wizard

The following procedure describes how to run the Distribute Software Updates Wizard.

To run the Distribute Software Updates Wizard:

1. In the SMS Administrator console, right-click the **Site Database** node, point to **All Tasks**, and then click **Distribute Software Updates**.

2. The **Welcome to the Distribute Software Updates Wizard** page appears.

Considerations for running the Distribute Software Updates Wizard

- Configure the settings of the Distribute Software Updates Wizard according to the needs of your organization and the criticality of the software update.

- If a software update is critical enough to deploy immediately, you can force programs running at the client to close rather than prompt users to save data or postpone the restart of client programs.

- Many updates require command-line options to install successfully. These parameters can be found if you click **Information** in the **Properties** dialog box that is accessed from the **Software Update Status** page.

Advanced Features of the Distribute Software Updates Wizard

Feature	Description
Unattended software update installation	• Control the amount of notification or interaction required by users
Scheduled software update installation	• Schedule software update installations
Dynamic package configuration	• Configure multiple program objects for the same package
Specification of a new software update authorization list	• Use a software update authorization list to determine which software updates **are available** to be installed on SMS client computers

SMS 2003 provides several advanced features that you can use to perform more complex software update tasks, including the following:

- *Configuring unattended software update installation*

  This feature controls the amount of notification or interaction that is required of the user for software update installation.

- *Scheduling software update installation*

  This feature allows you to schedule software update installations to begin at a specific time and end before a specific time.

- *Enabling dynamic package configuration*

  This feature allows you to configure multiple program objects for the same package, and each program object can have its own properties.

- *Specifying a new software update authorization list*

  This feature allows you to select a software update authorization list to determine which software updates are available to be installed on SMS client computers. You might want to do this, for example, if you need to authorize a software update that is newly released and that has not yet been reported as missing on any client computer.

How to Perform More Complex Software Update Tasks

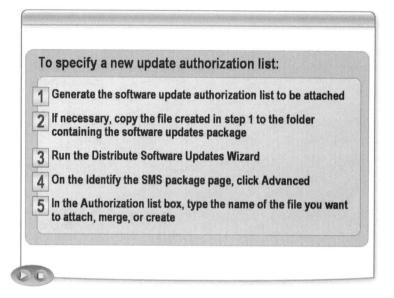

To specify a new update authorization list:

1 Generate the software update authorization list to be attached

2 If necessary, copy the file created in step 1 to the folder containing the software updates package

3 Run the Distribute Software Updates Wizard

4 On the Identify the SMS package page, click Advanced

5 In the Authorization list box, type the name of the file you want to attach, merge, or create

---

Procedure to configure software update packages to install without user notifications

To configure software update packages to install without user notifications:

1. In the SMS Administrator console, navigate to the **Site Database**.

2. Right-click **Site Database**, select **All Tasks**, and then click **Distribute Software Updates**.

3. In the **Distribute Software Updates Wizard**, progress through the wizard and enter the appropriate information. When you complete each page, click **Next** to move on.

4. On the second **Configure Installation Agent Settings** page, ensure that **Perform unattended installation of software updates (recommended)** is selected.

5. On the third **Configure Installation Agent Settings** page, clear the **Use notification balloons or dialogs** check box.

6. If necessary, review the other Software Updates Installation Agent settings that you have configured for this package or program, in particular the settings on the second **Configure Installation Agent Settings** page of the wizard.

7. Under **Specify how long the agent should wait for a user or unresponsive update**, you should set the following:

   a. In the **Wait <N> minutes for user** box, type the number of minutes to wait.

   b. In the **After Countdown** list, select **Install updates**.

   c. Select the **Require updates to be installed as soon as they are advertised** option.

Procedure to configure scheduled software update installations

To configure scheduled software update installations:

1. In the SMS Administrator console, navigate to the **Site Database**.

2. Right-click **Site Database**, select **All Tasks**, and then click **Distribute Software Updates**.

3. In the **Distribute Software Updates Wizard**, progress through the wizard and enter the appropriate information. When you complete each page, click **Next** to move on.

4. On the second **Configure Installation Agent Settings** page, select **Enforce start time and maximum installation time (Advanced Clients and mandatory assignments only)**.

5. In **Maximum installation time (in minutes)**, type the number of minutes you want to allow for the software update installation after the advertisement begins to run.

6. Step through the rest of the wizard.

7. Follow the steps to create an advertisement for the package you just created or modified. On the **Schedule** tab of the **Advertisement Properties** dialog box, under **Advertisement start time**, specify the start time for the scheduled software update installation.

Procedure to enable dynamic configuration by creating a new program object for a package

To enable dynamic configuration by creating a new program object for a package:

1. Run the Distribute Software Updates Wizard to create a software updates package or modify an existing package.

2. On the **Identify the SMS package** page, click **Advanced**.

3. The **Program Item Settings** page opens, displaying the name of the current program. Unless you have previously created a dynamic package, this will be the default program with the name of the package.

4. Click **New** to create a new program object for the package.

   This option is available only if you are modifying an existing software update package.

5. In the **Program name** box, type a name for the new program.

6. Optionally, attach a new software update authorization list to the new program, or merge the contents of an existing authorization list.

Procedure to specify a new update authorization list

To specify a new update authorization list:

1. Generate the new software update authorization list that you want to attach.

2. If necessary, copy the file you created in step 1 to the folder containing the software updates package you want to update.

3. Run the Distribute Software Updates Wizard.

4. On the **Identify the SMS package** page, click **Advanced**.

5. The **Program Item Settings** page appears, displaying the name of the current program and the authorization list attached to that program. Select the program to which you want to attach the new authorization list, or click **New** to create a program.

6. In the **Authorization list** box, type the name of the file you want to attach, merge, or create.

Demonstration: How to Distribute Software Updates

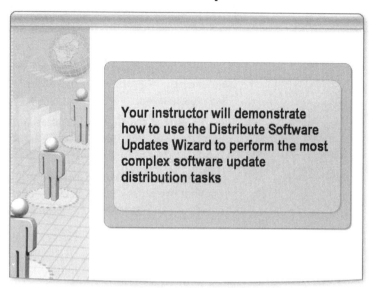

In this demonstration, your instructor will show you how to use the Distribute Software Updates Wizard to perform the most complex software update distribution tasks.

Your instructor will use the following values in this demonstration.

Variable	Value
Virtual machine—SMS Site 1	Dublin
Dublin Administrator	JaePa (Jae Pak)
Virtual machine—domain controller	Glasgow
Domain administrator	Administrator
Virtual machine—SMS Advanced Client	Bonn
Bonn Administrator	SMartinez (Sandra Martinez)

Important These steps are included for your information. Do not attempt to perform them in the classroom. If you perform these steps in the classroom environment, you might leave your computer in an incorrect state for upcoming practices.

Demonstration steps
performed by instructor
only

▶ **To run the Distribute Software Updates Wizard**

1. Verify that the Glasgow, Dublin, and Bonn virtual machines are running.

2. On the Dublin virtual machine, click **Start**, point to **All Programs**, point to **Systems Management Server**, and then click **SMS Administrator Console**.

3. In the SMS Administrator console, expand **Site Database (001 – NWTraders)**, and then click **Software Updates**.

4. In the details pane, in the Name column, right-click **Flaw in NetBIOS Could Lead to Information Disclosure (824105)**, point to **All Tasks**, and then click **Distribute Software Updates**.

5. In the **Distribute Software Updates Wizard**, on the **Welcome** page, click **Next**.

6. On the **Specify a Software Update Type** page, verify that **Select an update type** is selected and that the update type is **MBSA**, and then click **Next**.

7. On the **Create an SMS Package, or modify Packages and Updates** page, click **Next**.

8. On the **Identify the SMS Package** page, in the **Package name** box, type **NetBIOS Update**

9. Click **Advanced**.

   Review the **Program Item Settings** dialog box. These settings are important because they enable you to import a custom authorization list.

10. Click **Cancel** to close the **Program Item Settings** dialog box.

11. Click **Next**.

12. On the **Customize the Organization** page, type **SMS administrator team** in the **Organization** box.

Note   The **Import** button is used to import a file for client users to read when the notification appears to install the update.

---

13. Click **Next**.

14. On the **Select an Inventory Scanning Program** page, leave the default data in the **Inventory Scan Tool package** and **Program name** lists, and then click **Next**.

15. On the **Add and Remove Updates** page, in the **Name** column, select the **Flaw in NetBIOS Could Lead to Information Disclosure (824105)** check box, and then click **Next**.

16. On the **Specify a Source Directory for Files** page, in the **Package source directory** box, delete any existing directory file path, and then type **\\Dublin\C$\2596\Update**

17. Select **I will download the source files myself**, and then click **Next**.

18. In the **Distribute Software Updates Wizard** message box, click **No**.

19. On the **Software Updates Status** page, click **Properties**.

20. In the **Distribute Software Updates Wizard** dialog box, click **Import**.

21. In the **Open** dialog box, in the **Look in** box, browse to **C:\2596\Update** click **WindowsXP-KB824105-x86-ENU.exe**, and then click **Open**.

22. In the **Parameters** box, type **/q /n** to configure the update distribution to run unattended, and then click **OK**.

23. Click **Next**.

24. On the **Update Distribution Points** page, select the **Dublin** check box, and then click **Next**.

25. On the **Configure Installation Agent Settings** page, select the **Collect client inventory immediately (may increase system activity)** check box.

26. In the **Postpone restarts for** list, select **Servers**.

27. Click **Next**.

28. On the next **Configure Installation Agent Settings** page, clear the **Perform unattended installation of software updates (recommended)** check box.

29. In the **After countdown** list, select **Install updates**.

Note If you are performing an unattended assignment you can select the **Enforce start time and maximum installation time (Advanced Client only)** check box. Do not select this option unless you configure a mandatory advertisement.

---

30. Click **Next**.

31. On the next **Configure Installation Agent Settings** page, click **Require updates to be installed as soon as they are advertised**, and then click **Next**.

32. On the **Advertise Updates** page, select the **Advertise** check box, and then click **Browse**.

33. In the **Browse Collection** dialog box, click **All Windows XP Systems**, and then click **OK**.

34. Click **Next**.

35. On the **Completing the Distribute Software Updates Wizard** page, click **Finish**.

36. Close any open windows.

37. Leave the Glasgow, Dublin, and Bonn virtual machines running.

Ways to Verify the Software Update Distribution

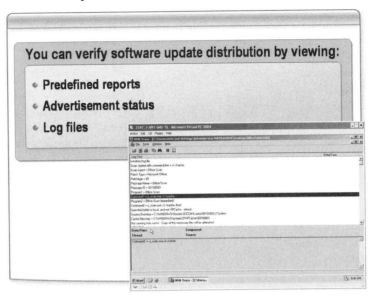

You can verify update distribution by using log files or predefined reports:

- *Predefined reports*

  You can run a predefined report (that is, a default report that is created when you install the SMS site) in the Software Updates category that verifies whether the update was installed. For more information about viewing a report, see *How to Verify the Software Update Inventory Results* in the previous lesson.

- *Advertisement Status*

  You can use the SMS Administrator console to view status messages for software update advertisements.

- *Log files*

  All the software update management client and server components maintain log files that you can use to verify update distribution. The following table lists log files and their locations.

Component	File Name	Location	Description
Security Updates Scan tool (Scanwrapper.exe)	Scanwrapper.log	%Windir%\System32\Ccm\ Logs folder of the SMS client computer.	Log file maintained by scan component on SMS client computer.
Microsoft Office Inventory Tool for Updates (Scanwrapper.exe)	Scanwrapper.log	%Windir%\System32\Ccm\ Logs folder of the SMS client computer.	Log file maintained by scan component on SMS client computer.
Software Updates	Patchinstall.log	%Windir%\System32\Ccm\ Logs folder of the SMS client computer.	Package installation log file maintained by the Software Updates Installation Agent on the SMS client computer.

(*continued*)

Component	File Name	Location	Description
Individual software update files	*qnumber*.log %.	%Windir% folder on SMS client computer.	Installation log maintained by software update installers. Contains information about actual software update installation.
Security Updates Sync Tool (Syncxml.exe)	Securitysyncxml.log	Synchronization host, in the Temp folder of the account running the process (current user if running in attended mode; system temp if running in unattended mode).	Log file for the synchronization component. Used for troubleshooting firewall and authentication issues.
Microsoft Office Inventory Sync Tool for Updates (Syncxml.exe)	Officesyncxml.log	Synchronization host, in the Temp folder of the account running the process (current user if running in attended mode; system temp if running in unattended mode).	Log file for the synchronization component. Used for troubleshooting firewall and authentication issues.

Demonstration: How to Verify the Software Update Distribution

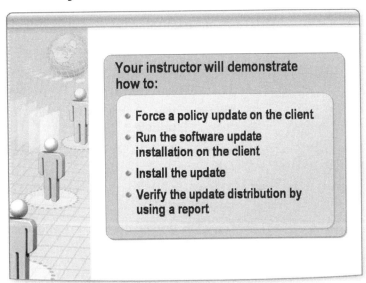

In this demonstration, your instructor will show you how to verify the software update distribution to the client.

Your instructor will use the following values in this demonstration.

Variable	Value
Virtual machine—SMS Site 1	Dublin
Dublin Administrator	JaePa (Jae Pak)
Virtual machine—domain controller	Glasgow
Domain administrator	Administrator
Virtual machine—SMS Advanced Client	Bonn
Bonn Administrator	SMartinez (Sandra Martinez)

Important   These steps are included for your information. Do not attempt to perform them in the classroom. If you perform these steps in the classroom environment, you might leave your computer in an incorrect state for upcoming practices.

Demonstration steps performed by instructor only

▶ **To force a policy update on the client**

1. Verify that the Glasgow, Dublin, and Bonn virtual machines are running.

2. On the Bonn virtual machine, click **Start**, and then click **Control Panel**.

3. Click **Performance and Maintenance**, and then click **Systems Management**.

4. In the **Systems Management Properties** dialog box, click the **Actions** tab.

5. Under **Actions**, click **Machine Policy Retrieval & Evaluation Cycle**, and then click **Initiate Action**.

6. In the **Machine Policy Retrieval & Evaluation Cycle** message box, click **OK**.

   This will force the policy to be updated on the client. It will take about two minutes to update.

7. Click **OK** to close the **Systems Management Properties** dialog box.

8. Close **Control Panel**.

▶ **To run the software update installation on the client**

1. On the Bonn virtual machine, the **Software Updates Installation** icon should appear in the notification area of the taskbar, along with an update balloon. When the icon or the balloon appears, click it.

2. In the **Systems Management Server** dialog box, click **Show Detail**.

3. Click **Install Now**.

4. After the update has finished installing, the Bonn virtual machine will automatically shut down and restart.

▶ **To verify the update**

1. On the Bonn virtual machine, in the **Windows Log On** dialog box, log the Bonn virtual machine on to the NWTRADERS domain with the user name **SMartinez** and the password **P@ssw0rd**.

2. Click **Start**, point to **All Programs**, point to **SMS 2003 Toolkit 1**, and then click **SMS Trace**.

3. On the **File** menu, click **Open**.

4. Verify that the current folder is **C:\Windows\System32\CCM\logs**.

5. Click **PatchInstall.log**.

6. Click **Open**.

7. Search the log for the following entries:

   • Title = Flaw in NetBIOS Could lead to Information Disclosure (824105)

   • Success Code = (0) This entry means that the utility to scan for this update has been applied successfully.

8. Close the **SMS Trace** window.

▶ **To verify the update distribution by using a report**

1. On the Dublin virtual machine, click **Start**, point to **All Programs**, point to **Systems Management Server**, and then click **SMS Administrator Console**.

2. In the SMS Administrator console, expand **Site Database (001 – NWTraders)**, expand **Reporting**, and then click **Reports**.

3. In the details pane, right-click **Software updates for a specific computer**, point to **All Tasks**, point to **Run**, and then click **Dublin**.

4. In the **Computer Name** box, type **Bonn**, and then click the **Display** icon.

5. In the report, view the **Distribution State** column to verify that the **Flaw in NetBIOS Could Lead to Information Disclosure (824105)** update installed.

6. Close any open windows.

7. On the Bonn virtual machine, on the **Action** menu, click **Close**.

8. Verify that **Save state and save changes** is selected, and then click **OK**.

   The Bonn virtual machine begins to shut down.

9. Leave the Glasgow and Dublin virtual machines running.

Practice: Distributing a Software Update

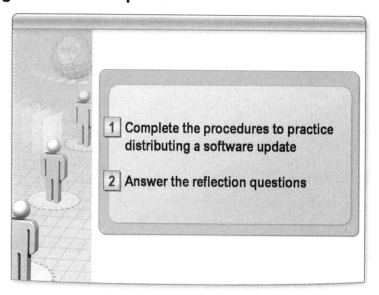

Instructions

Complete the procedure to practice distributing a software update, and then answer the reflection questions that follow.

In this practice, use the following values.

Variable	Value
Virtual machine—SMS Site 1	Dublin
Dublin Administrator	JaePa (Jae Pak)
Virtual machine—domain controller	Glasgow
Domain administrator	Administrator
Virtual machine—SMS Advanced Client	Bonn
Bonn Administrator	SMartinez (Sandra Martinez)

Procedures

▶ **To run the Distribute Software Updates Wizard**

1. Verify that the Glasgow, Dublin, and Bonn virtual machines are running.

2. On the Dublin virtual machine, click **Start**, point to **All Programs**, point to **Systems Management Server**, and then click **SMS Administrator Console**.

3. In the SMS Administrator console, expand **Site Database (001 – NWTraders)**, and then click **Software Updates**.

4. In the details pane, in the **Name** column, right-click **Flaw in NetBIOS Could Lead to Information Disclosure (824105)**, point to **All Tasks**, and then click **Distribute Software Updates**.

5. On the **Welcome to the Distribute Software Updates Wizard** page, click **Next**.

6. On the **Specify a Software Update Type** page, verify that **Select an update type** is selected and that the update type is **MBSA**, and then click **Next**.

7. On the **Create an SMS Package, or modify Packages and Updates** page, click **Next**.

8. On the **Identify the SMS Package** page, in the **Package name** box, type **NetBIOS Update**.

9. Click **Advanced**.

   Review the **Program Item Settings** dialog box. These settings are important because they enable you to import a custom authorization list.

10. Click **Cancel** to close the **Program Item Settings** dialog box.

11. Click **Next**.

12. On the **Customize the Organization** page, type **SMS administrator team** in the **Organization** box.

Note The **Import** button is used to import a file for client users to read when the notification appears to install the update.

---

13. Click **Next**.

14. On the **Select an Inventory Scanning Program** page, leave the default data in the **Inventory Scan Tool package** and **Program name** lists, and then click **Next**.

15. On the **Add and Remove Updates** page, in the **Name** column, select the **Flaw in NetBIOS Could Lead to Information Disclosure (824105)** check box, and then click **Next**.

16. On the **Specify a Source Directory for Files** page, in the **Package source directory** box, delete any existing directory file path, and then type **\\Dublin\C$\2596\Update**

17. Select **I will download the source files myself**, and then click **Next**.

18. In the **Distribute Software Updates Wizard** message box, click **No**.

19. On the **Software Updates Status** page, click **Properties**.

20. In the **Distribute Software Updates Wizard** dialog box, click **Import**.

21. In the **Open** dialog box, in the **Look in** box, browse to **C:\2596\Update**, click **WindowsXP-KB824105-x86-ENU.exe**, and then click **Open**.

22. In the **Parameters** box, type **/q /n** to configure the update distribution to run unattended, and then click **OK**.

23. On the **Software Updates Status** page, click **Next**.

24. On the **Update Distribution Points** page, select the **Dublin** check box, and then click **Next**.

25. On the **Configure Installation Agent Settings** page, select the **Collect client inventory immediately (may increase system activity)** check box.

26. In the **Postpone restarts for** list, select **Servers**.

27. Click **Next**.

28. On the next **Configure Installation Agent Settings** page, clear the **Perform unattended installation of software updates (recommended)** check box.

29. In the **After countdown** list, select **Install updates**.

Note   If you are performing an unattended installation, you can select the **Enforce start time and maximum installation time (Advanced Client only)** check box. Do not select this option unless you configure a mandatory advertisement.

---

30. Click **Next**.

31. On the next **Configure Installation Agent Settings** page, click **Require updates to be installed as soon as they are advertised**, and then click **Next**.

32. On the **Advertise Updates** page, select the **Advertise** check box, and then click **Browse**.

33. In the **Browse Collection** dialog box, click **All Windows XP Systems**, and then click **OK**.

34. Click **Next**.

35. On the **Completing the Distribute Software Updates Wizard** page, click **Finish**.

36. Close any open windows.

37. Leave the Glasgow, Dublin, and Bonn virtual machines running.

▶ **To force a policy update on the client**

1. On the Bonn virtual machine, click **Start**, and then click **Control Panel**.

2. Click **Performance and Maintenance**, and then click **Systems Management**.

3. In the **Systems Management Properties** dialog box, click the **Actions** tab.

4. Under **Actions**, click **Machine Policy Retrieval & Evaluation Cycle**, and then click **Initiate Action**.

5. In the **Machine Policy Retrieval & Evaluation Cycle** message box, click **OK**.

   This will force the policy to update on the client. It will take about two minutes to update.

6. Close the **Systems Management Properties** dialog box and **Control Panel**.

▶ **To run the software update installation on the client**

1. On the Bonn virtual machine, the **Software Updates Installation** icon should appear in the notification area of the taskbar, along with an update balloon. When the icon or the balloon appears, click it.

2. In the **Systems Management Server** dialog box, click **Show Detail**.

3. Click **Install Now**. After the update has finished installing, the Bonn virtual machine will automatically shut down and restart.

▶ **To verify the update**

1. On the Bonn virtual machine, in the **Windows Log On** dialog box, log the Bonn virtual machine on to the NWTRADERS domain with the user name **SMartinez** and the password **P@ssw0rd**.

2. Click **Start**, point to **All Programs**, point to **SMS 2003 Toolkit 1**, and then click **SMS Trace**.

3. On the **File** menu, click **Open**.

4. Verify that the current folder is **C:\Windows\System32\CCM\logs**.

5. Click **PatchInstall.log**.

6. Click **Open**.

7. Search the log for the following entries:

    - Title = Flaw in NetBIOS Could Lead to Information Disclosure (824105)

    - Success Code = (0) This entry means that the utility to scan for this update has been applied successfully.

8. Close the **SMS Trace** window.

▶ **To verify the update distribution by using a report**

1. On the Dublin virtual machine, click **Start**, point to **All Programs**, point to **Systems Management Server**, and then click **SMS Administrator Console**.

2. In the SMS Administrator console, expand **Site Database (001 – NWTraders)**, expand **Reporting**, and then click **Reports**.

3. In the details pane, right-click **Software updates for a specific computer**, point to **All Tasks**, point to **Run**, and then click **Dublin**.

4. In the **Computer Name** box, type **Bonn** and then click the **Display** icon.

5. In the report, view the **Distribution State** column to verify that the **Flaw in NetBIOS Could Lead to Information Disclosure (824105)** update installed.

6. Close any open windows.

7. On the Bonn virtual machine, on the **Action** menu, click **Close**.

8. Verify that **Save state and save changes** is selected in the list, and then click **OK**.

    The Bonn virtual machine begins to shut down.

9. Leave the Glasgow and Dublin virtual machines running.

Reflection questions

1. If the security and office inventory scans are for *software* updates, why must the Hardware Inventory Client Agent be enabled on the clients?

   _____

   _____

   _____

   _____

2. What is the implication of not having Internet access allowing automatic downloads for updates?

   _____

   _____

   _____

   _____

3. How should you configure the deployment of a critical software update that must be deployed immediately?

   _____

   _____

   _____

   _____

Discussion: Implementing SMS Software Update Tools and Managing Update Deployment

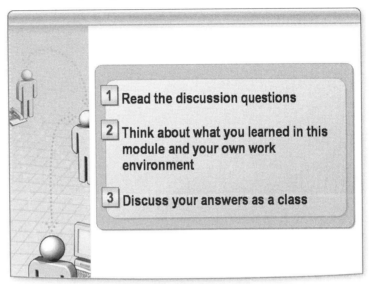

1. Think about your organization's IT requirements and policies. In your organization, what do you need to consider when deploying software updates to client computers? What do you need to consider when deploying software updates to file or application servers?

   _____

   _____

   _____

   _____

2. If your company does not have dedicated computers available for testing an update deployment, what is a good alternative?

   _____

   _____

   _____

   _____

Module 10: Using Remote Tools for Client Support

Contents

Overview

- Introduction to Remote Tools
- Configuring the Remote Tools Client Agent
- Using SMS Remote Tools in Troubleshooting

Introduction

Microsoft® Systems Management Server (SMS) 2003 Remote Tools is a suite of complementary applications that you can use to access any client in an SMS hierarchy that has the Remote Tools Client Agent components installed. By using Remote Tools, you can provide assistance and troubleshooting support from your computer to clients within your site. You can use Remote Tools to access and control clients that are using the Legacy Client or the Advanced Client.

You can use Remote Tools across a wide area network (WAN) or Microsoft Remote Access Service (RAS) links to assist clients at remote locations. Remote Tools supports RAS connections with a minimum speed of 28.8 kilobits per second (Kbps). You can also establish a connection to your organization and then access clients on your network.

In addition to SMS Remote Tools, SMS 2003 integrates Remote Assistance and Remote Desktop Connection into the SMS Administrator console for assisting applicable clients. You can also use the SMS Administrator console to manage and configure Remote Assistance settings for applicable clients throughout a site.

In this module, you will learn to configure and use Remote Tools to assist help desk personnel and to provide troubleshooting support to clients.

Objectives

After completing this module, you will be able to:

- Describe the tools available for remote control of SMS clients.
- Configure the Remote Tools Client Agent.
- Troubleshoot by using Remote Tools.

Lesson: Introduction to Remote Tools

* **What Is SMS Remote Tools?**
* **Tools in the SMS Remote Tools Suite**
* **How the Windows-Based Remote Support Tools Integrate with SMS**

Introduction

Remote client support extends your ability to improve and maintain the operating health of the hardware and software throughout an SMS site. SMS Remote Tools, along with the integration of the Microsoft Windows®–based Remote Assistance and Remote Desktop Connection tools, increase the affect that you can have in supporting clients and users that are separated from you by distance. By providing remote support to clients and users, you can perform a variety of activities to solve network operations and management problems.

In this lesson, you will learn to identify the main components of SMS Remote Tools. You will also learn about how SMS 2003 uses Remote Assistance and SMS Remote Tools.

Lesson objectives

After completing this lesson, you will be able to:

- Describe the purpose and use of SMS Remote Tools.
- Identify the tools in the SMS Remote Tools suite.
- Describe the Windows-based remote support tools that SMS uses.

What Is SMS Remote Tools?

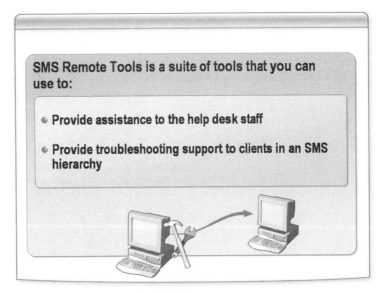

SMS Remote Tools is a suite of tools that you, as an administrator, can use to provide assistance to your help desk staff and to provide troubleshooting support to clients in an SMS hierarchy. With SMS Remote Tools, it is not necessary to physically be at the client's location to provide assistance. SMS Remote Tools gives you full control over the client computer and allows you to perform any operation as if you were physically at the client's location.

When you need to use a remote tool to provide assistance to a client, a connection must be established between the SMS Administrator console and the client. When the connection is established, you can use any tool in the SMS Remote Tools suite to provide assistance to clients. The SMS Remote Tools feature allows you to establish as many as four SMS Remote Tools connections so that you can provide assistance to up to four clients simultaneously from a single SMS Administrator console.

Because discovery data propagates from clients up the hierarchy, you can run SMS Remote Tools to access a client from any of the client's parent sites. From the central site, which has discovery data of all the clients of the hierarchy, you can run SMS Remote Tools to access any accessible client in the hierarchy.

Tools in the SMS Remote Tools Suite

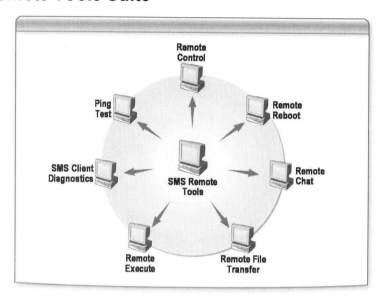

The SMS Remote Tools suite consists of the following tools:

- *Remote Control.* You can use Remote Control to operate a remote client. By establishing a Remote Control session, you can access the client desktop and files and perform mouse and keyboard functions as though you were physically at the client. You can also use Remote Control to troubleshoot hardware and software configuration problems on a client and to provide remote help desk support when access to the user's computer is necessary.

- *Remote Reboot.* You can use Remote Reboot to remotely shut down and restart a client. It might be necessary to restart a remote client to test a change to a startup procedure, to load a new configuration, or if a client is generating a hardware or software error.

- *Remote Chat.* You can use Remote Chat to communicate with the user at a remote client. When you initiate a chat session with the user, the SMS Remote Tools window becomes the chat window on your computer. On the remote client, a chat window also opens on the desktop. When either user types in his or her Local user box, that text also appears in the Remote user box on the other computer.

- *Remote File Transfer.* You can use Remote File Transfer to copy files between the computer on which you are running the SMS Administrator console and the connected client. For example, if you discover a corrupt or missing file on a client, you can use Remote File Transfer to transfer the required file from a local file directory to the client. You can also use Remote File Transfer to transfer files, such as log files, from the client to your computer for troubleshooting.

- *Remote Execute.* You can use Remote Execute to run executable files on a remote client. You can also run any command-line statement to complete tasks, such as running a virus checker on the client. This tool functions in the security context of the user logged on at the SMS administrator's computer, not the remote client.

■ *SMS Client Diagnostics.* You can use SMS to run diagnostics on all supported clients. You can then use the information that is gathered to troubleshoot client hardware or software problems.

- For clients running Microsoft Windows NT® 4.0 or later, you can use Windows Diagnostics in the SMS Administrator console.

- For clients running Windows 98, you can run diagnostics from the Remote Tools window after you have initiated a Remote Tools connection to the client.

■ *Ping Test.* You can use Ping Test to determine the reliability and speed of the SMS Remote Tools connection to a client on your network. You can access Ping Test from the Remote Tools window.

Uses for some of the SMS Remote Tools

By using one or a combination of the SMS Remote Tools, you can detect, diagnose, and successfully repair a wide range of problems with a client computer. You can assist users with hardware issues, software issues, and problems with the operating system. The following table describes some of the uses of a few of these tools.

SMS Remote Tool	Examples of Uses
Remote Control	• You can view the client while performing a problematic task and help identify errors.
	• You can use your keyboard and mouse to initiate keyboard and mouse strokes to the client computer to demonstrate the correct way to perform that task.
	• You can view error messages exactly as they appear on the client's screen, instead of depending on the user to paraphrase the error message.
	• You can examine a client that is working properly and compare registry settings to the registry settings on the client that is having troubles.
Remote File Transfer	• You can transfer a corrupted file from the client to the site server for investigation.
	• You can replace a corrupted file on a client by transferring an original version of the file from the SMS Administrator console computer.
Remote Reboot	• You can complete a software upgrade that requires a reboot.
	• You can see any restart-related problems that occur on the client.
	• You can restart a computer that has locked up because of a hardware or software malfunction.

How the Windows–Based Remote Support Tools Integrate with SMS

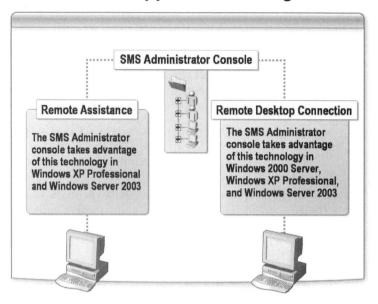

In addition to SMS Remote Tools, SMS 2003 integrates Remote Assistance and Remote Desktop Connection into the SMS Administrator console for assisting supported clients. You can also use the SMS Administrator console to remotely configure Remote Assistance settings for supported clients and then start Remote Assistance sessions.

What is Remote Assistance?

Remote Assistance is a technology in Windows XP Professional and Microsoft Windows Server™ 2003 that enables users to help each other over the network. With this tool, a support professional can view the desktop of a user, while the two people communicate through a chat box. With the user's permission, the support professional can even share control of the user's computer to resolve issues remotely. With Remote Assistance, a help desk can assist users on the network, which is known as the Offer Remote Assistance feature.

Remote Assistance also enables administrators and support personnel to offer assistance to their users without requiring the users to initiate the Remote Assistance session. This capability is called *Unsolicited Remote Assistance*. It is designed for use in enterprise corporations that are using domains. By default, this feature is turned off, and it can only be enabled by means of the Unattend.txt file, by using Group Policy, or by using SMS.

What is Remote Desktop Connection?

Remote Desktop Connection is a technology in Windows 2000 Server, Windows XP Professional, and Windows Server 2003 that is based on Terminal Services technology. Remote Desktop Connection provides system administrators with a rapid response tool. It lets you remotely access a server and see messages on the console, administer the computer remotely, or apply headless server control. Remote Desktop Connection works well even under low-bandwidth conditions because all your applications are hosted on the remote desktop. Only keyboard, mouse, and display information is transmitted over the network.

Note Remote Desktop Connection is the name used in Windows XP Professional and the Windows Server 2003 family for the technology previously called Terminal Services in earlier versions of Windows operating systems.

Differences between Remote Assistance and Remote Desktop Connection

Remote Assistance allows a support person to provide assistance to a user in a manner similar to SMS Remote Control. The support person sees the computer screen and communicates through a chat box. If the user gives permission, the support person can remotely control the computer to resolve a problem. Unlike Remote Desktop Connection, a user must always be present to grant remote control to the support person.

Remote Desktop Connection allows you to have access to a Windows session that is running on one computer when you are at another computer. It is similar to Terminal Services running in remote administration mode in Windows 2000 Server. It is useful for users who want to work from home and administrators who need to access a computer in another location. Unlike Remote Assistance, Remote Desktop is used for remote administration of a computer, not for controlling a user's session, as it logs off the user at the target computer.

The process: how these tools integrate with SMS

The Remote Assistance and Remote Desktop Connection features are integrated into the SMS 2003 Administrator console. This provides you with more options for remotely assisting clients from within the SMS Administrator console. You can also configure and apply site-wide Remote Assistance settings for applicable clients from within the SMS Administrator console. No status messages are generated by SMS when you use Remote Assistance and Remote Desktop Connection from within the SMS Administrator console.

The Remote Assistance and Remote Desktop Connection options are available only if both the client computer and the computer from which you are running the SMS Administrator console support them. If you install the SMS Administrator console on a computer, the Remote Desktop Client is also installed.

Important As a best practice, we recommend that you use the Remote Assistance and Remote Desktop Connection features of Windows XP Professional and Windows Server 2003, rather than SMS Remote Control, on computers running those platforms. Remote Assistance and Remote Desktop Connection are more secure technologies and, because they are built-in features of the operating system, they provide for better performance than SMS Remote Control.

Note For more information about Remote Assistance and Remote Desktop Connection, see Windows Help.

Practice: Identifying Remote Tools That Can Be Used to Troubleshoot Client Issues

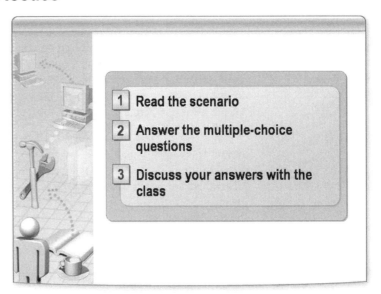

1 Read the scenario

2 Answer the multiple-choice questions

3 Discuss your answers with the class

Instructions

Read the scenario and then answer the multiple-choice questions that follow. In each problem, a user or client requires some form of remote assistance. Your task is to choose the best type of remote assistance or the best remote tool to resolve each issue. After you have completed the questions, discuss your answers with the class.

Scenario

You are a systems administrator for Northwind Traders. A few days ago, your team finished rolling out SMS 2003 to help manage the enterprise. The client base consists of Windows NT 4.0, Windows 2000 Server, and Windows XP clients deployed throughout the organization.

Questions

1. One of the remote Windows NT Server computers in the Northwind Traders enterprise is not performing well, and you need to get into the computer to view its log files. Which tool should you use? Circle the best answer.

   a. SMS Remote Tools

   b. Remote Assistance

   c. Remote Desktop Connection

   d. Ping Tool

2. A remote user on a Windows XP client calls and asks to be guided through a feature in Microsoft Word. Which tool should you use? Circle the best answer.

    a. SMS Remote Control

    b. Remote Assistance

    c. Remote Desktop Connection

    d. Remote Execute Tool

    _____

    _____

3. A remote user on a Windows XP client calls in for help. The client is on a slow 28.8 KB dial-up connection. To troubleshoot the issue, the user needs to be able to interact with you. Which tool should you use? Circle the best answer.

    a. SMS Remote Tools

    b. Remote Assistance

    c. Remote Desktop Connection

    d. Remote Chat Tool

    _____

    _____

4. What are your reasons for the answers that you chose?

    _____

    _____

    _____

    _____

Lesson: Configuring the Remote Tools Client Agent

* What Is the Remote Tools Client Agent?
* How to Enable the Remote Tools Client Agent
* Guidelines for Configuring General Properties of the Remote Tools Client Agent
* Guidelines for Configuring Security Options of the Remote Tools Client Agent
* Guidelines for Configuring Policy Options of the Remote Tools Client Agent
* Notification Options for the Remote Tools Client Agent
* Guidelines for Configuring the Advanced Options of the Remote Tools Client Agent

Introduction

In this lesson, you will learn to configure the basic settings for the Remote Tools Client Agent.

Lesson objectives

After completing this lesson, you will be able to:

- Describe the purpose of the Remote Tools Client Agent.
- Enable the Remote Tools Client Agent.
- Configure the general properties for the Remote Tools Client Agent.
- Configure the security options for the Remote Tools Client Agent.
- Configure the policy options for the Remote Tools Client Agent.
- Describe the notification options for the Remote Tools Client Agent.
- Configure the advanced options for the Remote Tools Client Agent.

What Is the Remote Tools Client Agent?

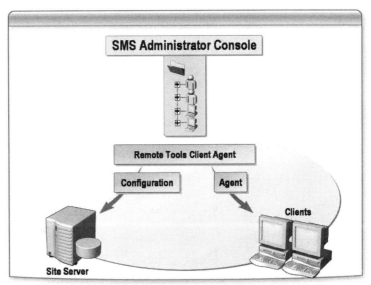

Before you can use SMS Remote Tools to connect to and support clients, you must configure the Remote Tools Client Agent settings for the site.

Remote Tools Client Agent is a component on the Legacy Client and the Advanced Client that determines whether and how you can access remote clients. When you configure the Remote Tools Client Agent, you can enable SMS Remote Tools, specify which administrators can initiate SMS Remote Tools sessions, and set system options such as policies, compression algorithms, and default protocols.

After you enable SMS Remote Tools on a site, the Remote Tools Client Agent components are automatically installed when new clients are installed to that site or when clients that are already installed update their site configuration.

How to Enable the Remote Tools Client Agent

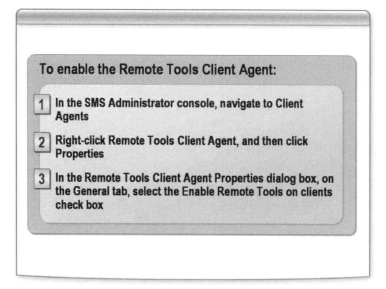

To enable the Remote Tools Client Agent:

1. In the SMS Administrator console, navigate to Client Agents

2. Right-click Remote Tools Client Agent, and then click Properties

3. In the Remote Tools Client Agent Properties dialog box, on the General tab, select the Enable Remote Tools on clients check box

You use the SMS Administrator console to enable and configure the Remote Tools Client Agent settings. The settings that you specify for each site apply to all the clients that are assigned to that site.

After you have installed the SMS primary site and have verified that all SMS services are running correctly, you can enable SMS Remote Tools on the site.

Procedure

To enable the Remote Tools Client Agent:

1. In the SMS Administrator console, navigate to Client Agents by expanding **Site Database**, **Site Hierarchy**, *site code – site name*, **Site Settings**, and then clicking **Client Agents**.

2. In the details pane, right-click **Remote Tools Client Agent**, and then click **Properties**.

3. In the **Remote Tools Client Agent Properties** dialog box, on the **General** tab, select the **Enable Remote Tools on clients** check box, and then click **OK**.

Important If you do not select this option, the Remote Tools Client Agent will not be installed on site clients, and you cannot use SMS for Remote Tools sessions.

How site settings are configured

You use the **Remote Tools Client Agent Properties** dialog box to configure your site settings. The tabs contain properties that you can set to customize SMS Remote Tools for the clients on your site. For example, you can specify whether end users must grant permission before an administrator can conduct a Remote Control session, the level of security, and protocol-related settings. These settings apply to all clients in your site.

You can also manage and configure Remote Assistance settings that apply to all applicable clients in your site. If you choose to manage Remote Assistance settings by using SMS, you can override user Remote Assistance settings and choose the level of Remote Assistance available to administrators.

The tabs included in this dialog box are:

- **General**

- **Security**

- **Policy**

- **Notification**

- **Advanced**

Guidelines for configuring the properties and options on these tabs are provided on the following pages.

Guidelines for Configuring General Properties of the Remote Tools Client Agent

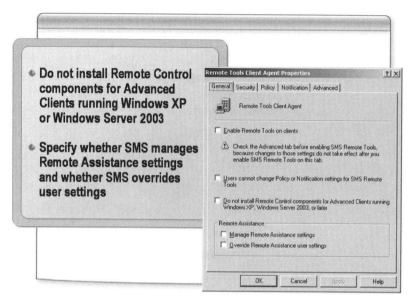

Where to configure general properties

The **General** tab contains settings that apply to both SMS Remote Tools and Remote Assistance. You can use this tab to:

- Enable SMS Remote Tools for all clients within the site.

- Prevent client users from changing **Policy** or **Notification** tab settings.

- Choose whether to manage Remote Assistance settings for applicable clients within the site and whether to override Remote Assistance user settings.

The purpose of the Policy or Notification settings check box

The **Users cannot change Policy or Notification settings for SMS Remote Tools** check box is cleared by default. If you select this check box, all clients in the site must use the settings that you specify for the site. Users cannot change the local SMS Remote Tools settings on clients. If you do not select this check box, users can change the following Remote Tools options:

- The SMS Remote Tools functions that an SMS administrator can perform remotely on the computer.

- Whether an SMS administrator must ask permission before an SMS Remote Tools session can be established.

- Whether visual or audio indicators indicate that a Remote Control session is taking place.

- Whether to display the SMS Remote Tools taskbar indicator in the notification area or as a high-security indicator on the client desktop.

Guidelines for specifying Remote Control components

Follow these guidelines when configuring the **General** tab settings:

- Select the option **Do not install Remote Control components for Advanced Clients running Windows XP, Windows Server 2003, or later** to prevent Remote Control from being installed on computers running those platforms.

  Use the Remote Assistance and Remote Desktop Connection features of Windows XP and Windows Server 2003 rather than SMS Remote Control on computers running those platforms. Remote Assistance and Remote Desktop Connection are more secure technologies and are built-in features of the operating system. SMS 2003 uses these tools for its Advanced Clients without installing the SMS Remote Tools.

- Specify whether SMS manages Remote Assistance settings and whether SMS overrides user settings. Both settings apply only to Windows XP and the Windows Server 2003 family clients.

  - Select **Manage Remote Assistance settings** to indicate that SMS controls clients' settings for Remote Assistance.

  - Select **Override Remote Assistance user settings** to indicate that Remote Assistance settings on clients are overridden by the SMS configuration.

Guidelines for Configuring Security Options of the Remote Tools Client Agent

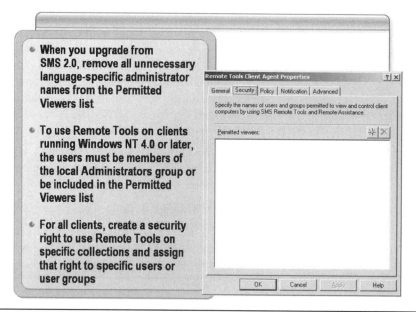

Where to configure security options

The **Security** tab contains settings that apply both to SMS Remote Tools and to Remote Assistance. You can use this tab to add non-administrator users and groups to the Permitted Viewers list. Permitted viewers are users and groups that can remotely access clients running Windows NT 4.0 or later. Members of the local Administrators group can access clients, regardless of whether they appear in the Permitted Viewers list.

Although the Permitted Viewers list appears to accept only user groups, you can also add user names to this list. It is more efficient to manage this list by using user groups, but the ability to specify a user name is available to those who need it.

Guidelines

Follow these guidelines when configuring security options:

- When you upgrade from SMS 2.0, remove all unnecessary language-specific administrator names from the Permitted Viewers list. Doing so enhances the performance of SMS Remote Tools by reducing the number of permitted viewers that are authenticated by the domain controller each time you initiate an SMS Remote Tools function. SMS 2003 Remote Tools automatically grants SMS Remote Tools access to the Administrators group. You do not need to add the Administrators group to the Permitted Viewers list.

- If you are going to use SMS Remote Tools on clients running Windows NT 4.0 or later, the users must be members of the local Administrators group or be included in the Permitted Viewers list.

- For all clients, you must also create a security right to use SMS Remote Tools on specific collections and assign that right to specific users or user.

Guidelines for Configuring Policy Options of the Remote Tools Client Agent

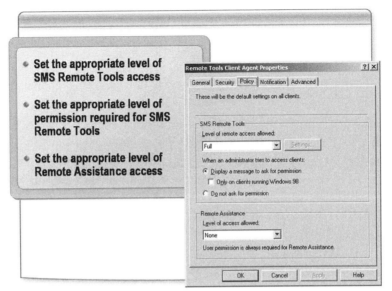

Where to configure policy options

The **Policy** tab contains settings that apply to both SMS Remote Tools and Remote Assistance. You can use this tab to:

- Specify the level of SMS Remote Tools access.
- Specify whether users must grant permission when an administrator tries to remotely access their client.
- Specify the level of Remote Assistance access.

Guidelines

Follow these guidelines when configuring policy options:

- Set the level of SMS Remote Tools access by selecting one of the following options:
  - *Full*. This option allows administrators to perform all SMS Remote Tools functions.
  - *Limited*. This option allows administrators to perform limited SMS Remote Tools functions, which you can then specify.
  - *None*. This option prevents administrators from performing any SMS Remote Tools functions.

- Set the level of permission required for SMS Remote Tools by choosing to allow administrators to perform SMS Remote Tools functions with or without client permission.

  When you select the **Do not ask permission** check box, using SMS Remote Tools on clients running Windows 98 is less secure than it is on clients running Windows NT 4.0 or later. Specifically, there is a greater risk of an unauthorized Remote Control session to a client running Windows 98. For this reason, it is recommended that you always display a message to ask for the user's permission on clients running Windows 98. You can do this in two ways:

  - Select the **Display a message to ask for permission** option. This displays a message on all clients.

  - Select the **Display a message to ask for permission** option, and then select the **Only on clients running Windows 98** check box. This displays a message only on clients running Windows 98.

- Set the level of Remote Assistance access by selecting one of the following options:

  - *Full control.* This option allows administrators to use Remote Assistance to fully control applicable clients.

  - *Remote viewing.* This option allows administrators to only remotely view applicable clients.

  - *None.* This option prevents administrators from using Remote Assistance to the target client using the SMS Administrator console.

  The level of control that you choose for this setting applies to all Remote Assistance sessions, whether you start them from within the SMS Administrator console or from the operating system.

  To enable all site-wide settings for Remote Assistance on the clients, SMS passes the settings to the clients and applies them by using local Group Policy. If you subsequently apply Group Policy settings at the site level, the domain level, or the organizational-unit level by using the Group Policy Microsoft Management Console (MMC) snap-in, the local Group Policy settings applied by SMS on clients are overwritten.

  If you select the **Users cannot change Policy or Notification settings for SMS Remote Tools** check box on the **General** tab, the user cannot override these settings on a client. User permission is always required when using Remote Assistance in the SMS Administrator console.

Notification Options for the Remote Tools Client Agent

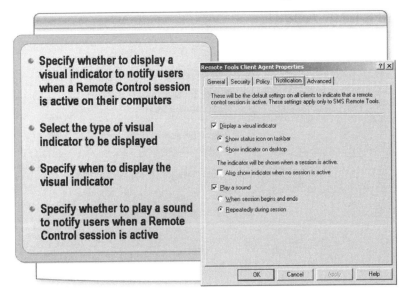

- Specify whether to display a visual indicator to notify users when a Remote Control session is active on their computers

- Select the type of visual indicator to be displayed

- Specify when to display the visual indicator

- Specify whether to play a sound to notify users when a Remote Control session is active

Where to configure notification options

You configure notification options on the **Notifications** tab. The settings on the **Notification** tab apply only to SMS Remote Tools, not to Remote Assistance. You can use this tab to:

- Specify whether to display a visual indicator to notify users when a Remote Control session is active on their computers. This visual indicator pertains to Remote Control only, not to other SMS Remote Tools functions.

- Select the type of visual indicator to be displayed. The visual indicators differ as to where they appear on the desktop and whether the indicator can be hidden from the user's view.

- Specify to display the visual indicator only when a Remote Control session is active or to display it regardless of whether a session is active.

- Specify whether to play a sound to notify users when a Remote Control session is active. You can specify that the sound should play only when a session begins and ends or that it play repeatedly during a session.

Types of visual indicators

There are two types of visual indicators:

- *Taskbar indicator.* The taskbar indicator appears in the notification area on the client's taskbar. The indicator changes its appearance when an SMS administrator initiates a Remote Control session with the client. You can configure the Remote Tools Client Agent to permit the user to hide this indicator.

- *High-security indicator.* The high-security indicator initially appears in the top right corner of the client's desktop. The user can move the icon but cannot hide it, which allows a user to always determine if and when a Remote Control session has been initiated. The indicator is displayed within the icon. The title bar of this indicator is gray until a Remote Control session is initiated, and then the title bar turns red.

Guidelines for Configuring the Advanced Options of the Remote Tools Client Agent

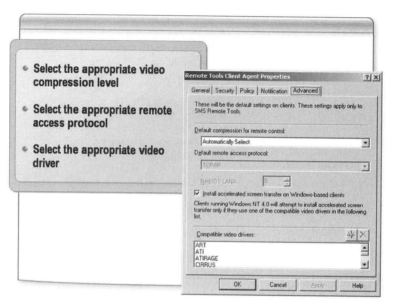

Where to configure advanced options

The **Advanced** tab contains hardware-related settings that apply only to SMS Remote Tools. For most installations, the default settings in this dialog box should not be changed. You can use this tab to:

- Select the default video compression level of remote screen captures during a Remote Control session.

- Select the default remote access protocol for all clients in the site.

- Enable video acceleration clients running Windows NT 4.0 or later and determine which video drivers can be accelerated for clients running Windows NT 4.0.

Important   If you change the settings on the **Advanced** tab after the Remote Tools Client Agent components have been installed on clients, the previously installed clients do not receive the new settings automatically. The revised **Advanced** tab settings are passed down to the clients during the next maintenance cycle of the Client Configuration Installation Manager (CCIM), but they are not implemented until you uninstall and reinstall the Remote Tools Client Agent components. This applies only to Legacy Clients.

Guidelines

Follow these guidelines for configuring advanced options:

- *Select the compression level according to your organization's needs.* SMS Remote Tools uses video compression to reduce the size of screen-capture data that is transmitted across the network during a Remote Control session. This minimizes the effect on network bandwidth.

  There are three video compression options in SMS:

  - *Low (RLE).* Low, Run Length Encoding (RLE) compression compresses screen data, but not as effectively as high compression. You should use RLE compression for clients running Windows NT 4.0.

- *High (LZ)*. High, Lempel-Ziv (LZ) compression provides greater data compression than low compression, but it is primarily for clients with high-speed processors above 150 megahertz (MHz). Clients running Windows 2000 or later achieve better compression with LZ compression. LZ compression should not be used for clients with slow processors below 150 MHz. LZ compression can be used only if video acceleration has been successfully loaded on the client, even if the client registry indicates that high compression should be used (compression = 1).

- *Automatically Select*. If you use the Automatically Select option, which is the default setting, SMS determines the best compression option to use based on the client type and CPU.

  - SMS selects high compression for Advanced Clients and Legacy Clients running Windows NT 4.0 and using Pentium CPUs that are above 150 MHz.

  - SMS selects low compression for Legacy Clients running Windows NT and using Pentium CPUs that are below 150 MHz and Legacy Clients running Windows 98.

■ *Adjust the remote access protocol*. If you are using the SMS 2003 Administrator console to configure an SMS 2.0 site, you can select Transmission Control Protocol/Internet Protocol (TCP/IP) or NetBIOS. For SMS 2003 sites, the only supported protocol is TCP/IP, and the default remote access protocol setting is not available.

■ *Add accelerated screen transfer drivers, as needed*:

  - On clients running Windows NT 4.0, video acceleration depends on the type of video driver on the client. These clients will install video acceleration only if they use one of the drivers that appear in the Compatible video drivers list, which is a list of drivers that have been tested by Microsoft and that can run with the screen transfer software (Idisntkm.dll) that SMS installs on the client when this option is enabled.

  - For clients running Windows NT 4.0 or later, video acceleration reduces the work that is associated with each client screen refresh during a Remote Control session, which significantly accelerates the session. To use video acceleration, you must enable this feature on the SMS site server.

  - On clients running Windows 2000 or later, video acceleration is not dependent on the type of video driver on the client. On these clients, video acceleration can activate and run with any client video driver.

Tip You can add drivers to the Compatible video drivers list by clicking the **New** button (the yellow star) on the **Advanced** tab. However, the screen transfer software works only with the video drivers listed and any other drivers compatible with those listed. If you add a driver to the list, be sure to test to ensure that the SMS Remote Tools session works properly.

Practice: Configuring the Remote Tools Client Agent

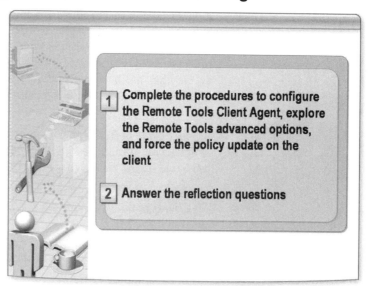

Instructions

Complete the procedures to configure the Remote Tools Client Agent, explore the Remote Tools advanced options, and force the policy update on the client. Then answer the reflection questions that follow.

In this practice, use the following values.

Variable	Value
Virtual machine—SMS Site 1	Dublin
Dublin\Administrator	JaePa (Jae Pak)
Virtual machine—domain controller	Glasgow
Domain administrator	Administrator
Virtual machine—SMS Advanced Client	Bonn
Bonn administrator	SMartinez (Sandra Martinez)

Procedures

▶ **To configure SMS Remote Tools**

1. Verify that the Glasgow virtual machine is running. If the Glasgow virtual machine is not running, log it on to the NWTRADERS domain with a user name of **Administrator** and a password of **P@ssw0rd**.

   After the Glasgow virtual machine opens, you can minimize it.

2. Verify that Dublin virtual machine is running. If the Dublin virtual machine is not running, log it on to the NWTRADERS domain with a user name of **JaePa** and a password of **P@ssw0rd**.

3. Log the Bonn virtual machine on to the NWTRADERS domain with a user name of **SMartinez** and a password of **P@ssw0rd**.

4. On the Dublin virtual machine, click **Start**, point to **All Programs**, point to **Systems Management Server**, and then click **SMS Administrator Console**.

5. In the SMS Administrator console, expand **Site Database (001 – NWTraders)**, expand **Site Hierarchy**, expand **001 - NWTraders**, expand **Site Settings**, and then click **Client Agents**.

6. Right-click **Remote Tools Client Agent**, and then click **Properties**.

7. In the **Remote Tools Client Agent Properties** dialog box, on the **General** tab, select the **Enable Remote Tools on clients** check box.

8. Select the **Do not install Remote Control components for Advanced Clients running Windows XP, Windows Server 2003, or later** check box.

9. On the **Policy** tab, click **Do not ask for permission**.

10. On the **Notification** tab, under **Play a Sound**, click **When session begins and ends**.

11. Click **Apply**.

▶ **To configure the advanced options for Remote Tools**

1. In the **Remote Tools Client Agent Properties** dialog box, click the **Advanced** tab.

Note Be aware that the default settings must be modified *before* installing the client agent. Any changes you make on the **Advanced** tab *after* the Remote Tools Client Agent has been enabled will have no effect. If you want to modify settings after the Remote Tools Client Agent has been installed, you must disable the agent, make the changes, and then re-enable the agent.

---

2. In the **Default compression for remote control** list, verify that **Automatically Select** is selected.

3. Click **OK**.

4. Close the SMS Administrator console.

▶ **To the force policy update on the client**

1. On the Bonn virtual machine, click **Start**, and then click **Control Panel**.

2. Click **Performance and Maintenance**, and then click **Systems Management**.

3. In the **Systems Management Properties** dialog box, click the **Actions** tab.

4. Under **Actions**, click **Machine Policy Retrieval & Evaluation Cycle**, and then click **Initiate Action**.

5. In the **Machine Policy Retrieval & Evaluation Cycle** message box, click **OK**.

    This will force the policy update on the client. Although you have forced the policy update, it will still take about two minutes to update.

6. Click **OK** to close the **Systems Management Properties** dialog box.

7. Close the Control Panel.

8. Leave the Glasgow, Dublin, and Bonn virtual machines running.

Reflection questions

1. Your site manages both Windows XP Professional and Windows 98 clients. The help desk staff must ask users for permission to connect, but once permission is granted they can have full control. How might you configure the Remote Tools Client Agent?

   _____

   _____

   _____

   _____

   _____

   _____

2. You receive a call from a one of your technical support professionals who describes the following problem while he was attempting to assist a remote user on a Windows XP client: After initiating the remote assistance session with the client, the support technician can view the remote user's computer, but can not make any changes.

   What is the likely cause for this issue and how can it be resolved?

   _____

   _____

   _____

   _____

   _____

   _____

Lesson: Using SMS Remote Tools in Troubleshooting

* The SMS Remote Tools Toolbar: Monitor and Control Components
* The SMS Remote Tools Toolbar: Diagnostics Components
* How SMS Remote Tools Are Installed on the Client Computer
* SMS Remote Tools Options on Clients
* Guidelines for Troubleshooting SMS Remote Tools

Introduction

In this lesson, you will learn how to use the SMS Remote Tools user interface. You will also learn how SMS Remote Tools are installed on the Legacy Client and on the Advanced Client, and how to troubleshoot various problems you might encounter with the operation of SMS Remote Tools on client computers.

Lesson objectives

After completing this lesson, you will be able to:

- Identify the monitor and control components of the SMS Remote Tools toolbar.
- Identify the diagnostics components of the SMS Remote Tools toolbar.
- Describe how SMS Remote Tools are installed on the client.
- Describe options that users can configure on clients.
- Troubleshoot SMS Remote Tools.

The SMS Remote Tools Toolbar: Monitor and Control Components

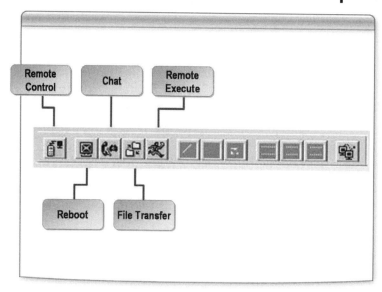

The five icons on the left side of the toolbar in the SMS Remote Tools window provide access to tools that you can use to directly control and monitor clients. The following table describes each of these tools.

SMS Remote tool	Description
Remote Control	You can use Remote Control to view the desktop of a remote client and to use your keyboard and mouse as if you were using the keyboard and mouse at the selected client.
	When you start the Remote Control tool, the Remote Control Client Viewer window opens. This window displays the client desktop to you, just as the user at the client sees it. When the Remote Control Client Viewer window is active, all your mouse actions and keystrokes are passed to the client and processed there.
Reboot	You can use Remote Reboot to restart a client. When you are providing support for a remote client, you might have to restart the client to test a change to a startup procedure, to load a new configuration, or to restart when a client has locked up because of a hardware or software malfunction.
Chat	You can use Remote Chat to communicate with a user at a selected client. When you start a chat session with a client, the Remote Tools window serves as the chat window in the SMS Administrator console, and a Remote Chat window opens on the client. When you or the user at the client types text in the Local User box, that text appears in the other computer's Remote User box.

(continued)

SMS Remote tool	Description
File Transfer	You can use File Transfer to transfer files between the SMS Administrator console computer and the selected client. When you discover a corrupt or missing file on the user's computer, you can use File Transfer to transfer files directly to a client's local drive or to transfer client files to your computer for troubleshooting. When a folder tree for both the client computer and the SMS Administrator console computer appears, you can create folders and copy and delete files on the client computer.
Remote Execute	The primary purpose of Remote Execute is to provide administrators with the ability to run applications in their own security context. By contrast, Remote Control launches applications in the logged-on user's security context at the target client.

You can use Remote Execute to run any command-line statement at the client. For example, you can perform tasks such as running a virus checker or defragmenting the local drive. |

The SMS Remote Tools Toolbar: Diagnostics Components

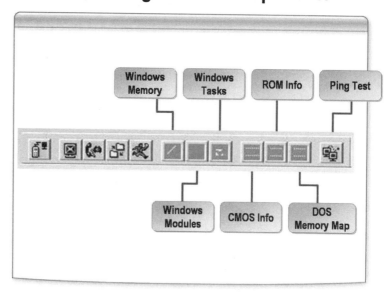

The seven icons on the right side of the toolbar in the SMS Remote Tools window provide access to tools that you can use to perform various remote diagnostics functions to help solve client hardware problems and troubleshoot other client problems. The first six of these icons represent tools that are only available for SMS 2003 Legacy Client computers running Windows 98 and for SMS 2.0 client computers running Windows 95 and Windows Millennium Edition. For computers running Windows NT 4.0, Windows 2000, Windows XP, and the Windows Server 2003 family, these tools are unavailable and their icons appear as they do in the screen shot on this slide.

The following table describes each of these tools.

Remote tool	Description
Windows Memory	You can use Windows Memory information to see how memory is allocated on a remote client.
Windows Modules	You can use Windows Modules to get information about selected system or program modules on a remote client. The list of modules includes drivers, dynamic-link libraries (DLLs), and any active applications.
Windows Tasks	You can use Windows Tasks to get information about Windows-based programs that appear on the Task List.
CMOS Information	You can use CMOS Information to display data that is stored in the selected client's complementary metal-oxide semiconductor (CMOS), which is a small amount of RAM powered by a battery. The CMOS contains information about the client's startup configuration. If the CMOS is corrupted, it can cause a client to start incorrectly or to fail to start.

(continued)

Remote tool	Description
ROM Information	You can use the ROM Information tool to view information about any ROM that is installed on the selected client. The list contains the name of each ROM (if available), the address of each ROM, and the size of each ROM in kilobytes. You can get more information about a ROM by selecting the ROM in the list.
DOS Memory Map	You can use the DOS Memory Map tool to see which programs are currently loaded into conventional and upper memory on the selected client.
	The list of programs running in conventional memory can be useful in diagnosing possible conflicts between terminate-and-stay-resident (TSR) programs and in evaluating whether there is enough available memory to run an application.
Ping Test	You can use Ping Test to test whether a client is connected to your network or to test connectivity before initiating a Remote Tools connection.
	Ping sends packets to the targeted computer by using your network's default protocol. Ping analyzes the number of packets returned in the elapsed time (four seconds) to determine the reliability and speed of the communications channel to the target.
	Ping Test is different from the standard TCP/IP ping utility. This ping tool can be used to test client connectivity regardless of the protocol being used.

How SMS Remote Tools Are Installed on the Client Computer

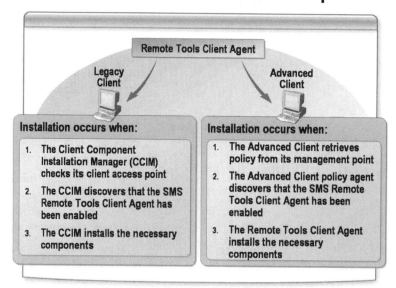

After you have enabled SMS Remote Tools on the site server, SMS automatically installs the Remote Tools Client Agent components on each client when that client is installed on the site. However, this component installation process for Legacy Clients differs from the process for Advanced Clients.

The process for Legacy Clients

The Remote Tools Client Agent components are automatically installed on each Legacy Client when the Client Component Installation Manager (CCIM):

1. Checks its client access point (CAP).

2. Discovers that the SMS Remote Tools Client Agent has been enabled.

3. Installs the necessary components.

The CCIM is an SMS client component that ensures that each Legacy Client is properly installed and assigned to the correct site. The CCIM also keeps the client data and the SMS site server data synchronized by creating Heartbeat Discovery data records, and it determines which optional components should be installed. This component runs as a thread of the SMS Client Service.

After the Remote Tools Client Agent components are installed on a Legacy Client, you have full SMS Remote Tools functionality, with the following exceptions:

- Clients running Windows NT 4.0 require a restart to load low-level drivers.

- Clients running Windows 98 require a restart to enable full-screen MS-DOS® sessions and some keyboard features.

The process for Advanced Clients

After you enable SMS Remote Tools on the site server, when Advanced Clients are installed on the site, the Remote Tools Client Agent components are automatically installed on each client. However, you can prevent the installation of the SMS Remote Tools component by selecting the **Do not install Remote Control components for Advanced Clients running Windows XP, Windows Server 2003, or later** check box.

The installation of the SMS Remote Tools component occurs when:

1. The Advanced Client retrieves policy from its management point.

2. The Advanced Client policy agent discovers that the SMS Remote Tools Client Agent has been enabled.

3. The Remote Tools Client Agent installs the necessary components.

When installing an Advanced Client, you have the option of installing the SMS Remote Tools components at the same time, instead of waiting for the site server to pass SMS Remote Tools policy down to the client. To do so, add SMSFULLREMOTETOOLS=1 to the Advanced Client installation properties.

However, before using this option, ensure that SMS Remote Tools is enabled for the site. Otherwise, the Remote Tools Client Agent components are disabled when the client contacts the management point.

What is the SMS Remote Control Agent?

The SMS Remote Control Agent, Wuser32.exe, is the key component for conducting all remote control operations and most other Remote Tools functions on clients. Wuser32.exe runs as a standard service in the context of LocalSystem on the client computer.

To determine whether the agent is started on clients running Windows NT 4.0 or later, you can use the **Processes** tab in Windows Task Manager. To determine whether the agent is started on clients running Windows 98, you can use the client's Control Panel.

SMS Remote Tools Options on Clients

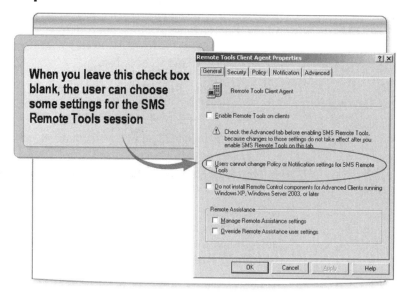

If the administrator has not enabled the **Users cannot change Policy or Notification settings for SMS Remote Tools** option on the **General** tab of the **Remote Tools Client Agent Properties** dialog box, the user at the client computer will be able to choose some site settings for the SMS Remote Tools session. For example, the user can specify:

- Which remote functions to enable.

- Whether permission for the SMS Remote Tools session must be granted first.

- How the SMS Remote Tools session will be announced on the client system.

The user can modify the remote control options on the client by double-clicking **Remote Control** in Control Panel. This icon is added to Control Panel when the Remote Tools Client Agent is installed.

Important   The client's remote control settings will take precedence over the site's default settings.

Guidelines for Troubleshooting SMS Remote Tools

- Check whether the client has changed its NetBIOS name

- Check whether the client is on a remote TCP/IP network

- Verify that the client has installed and started its Remote Control Agent

- Investigate the installation log file to confirm that the Remote Control Agent has been installed

- Investigate the Remote Control log file to further troubleshoot the problem

The main problem with using remote functions is establishing a connection with the client computer. If you are having trouble establishing a client connection, follow these guidelines to determine the cause:

- *Check to see whether the client has changed its NetBIOS name.* Two entries might exist in the inventory for one physical client.

- *Check whether the client is on a remote TCP/IP network.* Make sure that you are using Windows Internet Naming Service (WINS) or can resolve the client's NetBIOS name to its IP address by using the Lmhosts file.

- *Verify that the client has installed and started its Remote Control Agent.*

- *Investigate the installation log file to confirm that Remote Tools Client Agent has been installed.* The installation log file contains a list of the installation tasks that ran during the installation or removal of the Remote Tools Client Agent components, including registry key creation or removal.

To confirm that the Remote Tools Client Agent components have been installed on a client, verify that there is a *.log file on the client, as follows:

- Legacy Client: %SystemRoot%\MS\SMS\Clicomp\RemCtrl\Install.log

- Advanced Client, when Ccmsetup.exe is used to install the client: %SystemRoot%\System32\CCMSetup\Client.MSI.log

■ *Investigate the Remote Control log file to further troubleshoot the problem.*
The Remote Control log file is more detailed and records all significant
actions that the Remote Tools Client Agent performs. The Remctrl.log file
is essential for identifying Remote Tools functions after the Remote Tools
Client Agent components are installed and running. It is also essential for
identifying Hardware Munger and Security Munger actions on Legacy
Clients. The Remctrl.log file does not provide information about Remote
Control session functions.

The Remctrl.log file provides detailed information about:

- Operating system and local client language settings.

- Actions performed by the Hardware Munger and the Security Munger on
  the Legacy Client.

- Actions performed by the Remote Tools Client Agent on the Advanced
  Client.

- Installation and removal of the Remote Tools Client Agent components.

You can view the Remctrl.log file at the following directory on the client:

- Legacy Client: %SystemRoot%\MS\SMS\Logs

- Advanced Client: %SystemRoot%\System32\CCM\Logs

Practice: Using SMS to Initiate a Remote Desktop Session

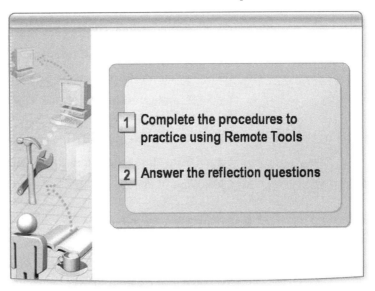

Instructions

Complete the procedures to practice using Remote Tools, and then answer the reflection questions that follow. In the procedures, you will enable Remote Desktop Connection on the Windows XP client, and then use the SMS Administrator console to initiate a Remote Desktop session with the Windows XP client. After the session is established, you will troubleshoot an issue for the client.

Important We recommend that, in your own organization, you use Remote Assistance to communicate with a Windows XP client. However, for the purposes of this practice, you will use Remote Desktop Connection.

In this practice, use the following values.

Variable	Value
Virtual machine—SMS Site 1	Dublin
Dublin\Administrator	JaePa (Jae Pak)
Virtual machine—domain controller	Glasgow
Domain administrator	Administrator
Virtual machine—SMS Advanced Client	Bonn
Bonn\Administrator	SMartinez (Sandra Martinez)

Procedures

▶ **To enable Remote Desktop on the Windows XP client**

1. Verify that the Glasgow, Dublin, and Bonn virtual machines are running.

2. On the Bonn virtual machine, click **Start**, and then click **Control Panel**.

3. Click **Performance and Maintenance**, and then click **System**.

4. In the **System Properties** dialog box, click the **Remote** tab.

5. Under **Remote Desktop**, select the **Allow users to remotely connect to this computer** check box.

6. Click **OK** in the **Remote Sessions** message box.

7. Click **OK** to close the **System Properties** dialog box.

8. Close Control Panel.

▶ **To use the SMS Administrator console to initiate a Remote Desktop session with the Windows XP client**

1. On the Dublin virtual machine, click **Start**, point to **All Programs**, point to **Systems Management Server**, and then click **SMS Administrator Console**.

2. In the SMS Administrator console, expand **Site Database (001 – NWTraders)**, expand **Site Hierarchy**, expand **Collections**, and then click **All Systems**.

3. In the detail pane, right-click **Bonn**, point to **All Tasks**, and then click **Start Remote Desktop Client**.

   The **Attempting to Connect with Bonn** dialog box will appear briefly while the connection to Bonn is established.

4. In the **Log On** dialog box, log on to the NWTRADERS domain with a user name of **JaePa** and a password of **P@ssw0rd**.

   Identify the reason why you cannot log on to Bonn, fix the problem, and try to log on again. Note: in addition to being able to log on to Bonn, you will also need to perform administrative verification and troubleshooting tasks on Bonn.

   _____

   _____

   _____

Tip For a comprehensive set of steps to complete this procedure, please refer to Appendix C: "Course 2596B, *Managing Microsoft Systems Management Server 2003 – Troubleshooting Practices Answer Key*" on your Student Materials compact disc. Also, you must fix this problem before proceeding.

▶ **To troubleshoot the Windows XP client**

1. On the Dublin virtual machine, right-click the task bar in the Bonn remote client's desktop, and then click **Task Manager**.

2. In the **Windows Task Manager** dialog box, click the **Processes** tab.

3. Verify that CcmExec.exe is running.

   This verifies that the SMS Advanced Client is running properly.

   Because Remote Desktop does not depend on the SMS client, it is an excellent tool for troubleshooting SMS client issues.

4. Close the **Windows Task Manager** dialog box.

5. On the Bonn remote client's desktop, click **Start**, and then click **Control Panel**.

6. Click **Performance and Maintenance**, and then click **Systems Management**.

7. In the **Systems Management Properties** dialog box, click the **Components** tab.

8. On the **Components** tab, verify that the **SMS Remote Tools Agent** component appears and that its status is **Enabled**.

Note   This component is installed by default regardless of whether the Remote Tools Client Agent is enabled for the site.

---

9. Click **OK** to close the **Systems Management Properties** dialog box.

10. In the Control Panel, click **Administrative Tools**, and then double-click **Services**.

11. In the **Services** detail pane, verify that the service **SMS Remote Control Agent** does not appear.

   This verifies that SMS has not installed the service for SMS Remote Tools.

12. Close the Services window and the Administrative Tools Control Panel window.

13. On the Bonn remote client's desktop, click **Start**, and then click **Disconnect**.

14. In the **Disconnect Windows** dialog box, click **Disconnect**.

   The Bonn remote client desktop closes, and then the SMS Administrator console appears again.

15. Close the SMS Administrator console.

16. On the Bonn virtual machine, on the **Action** menu, click **Close**.

17. Verify that **Save state and save changes** is selected, and then click **OK**.

   The Bonn virtual machine begins to shut down.

Important   The next time you log on to the Bonn virtual machine, be sure to change the user name back to **SMartinez**; otherwise, you will log on as **Administrator** again.

---

18. Leave the Glasgow and Dublin virtual machines running.

Reflection questions

1. What is the difference between SMS Remote Tools, Remote Assistance, and Remote Desktop?

   _____

   _____

   _____

   _____

   _____

2. If you want to control clients remotely and your computers are a mix of computers running Windows XP Professional and Windows NT 4.0, what is the best practice regarding the use of SMS Remote Tools, Remote Assistance, and Remote Desktop?

   _____

   _____

   _____

   _____

   _____

Discussion: Using SMS Remote Tools

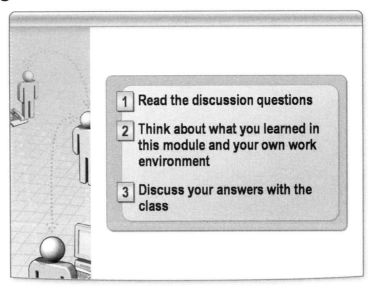

1. Why would you want to prevent the installation of the Remote Control components on Advanced Clients?

   _____

   _____

   _____

   _____

2. Why do you use compression levels?

   _____

   _____

   _____

   _____

3. What important fact should you be aware of regarding site-wide settings?
    How should you manage this potential issue?

    _____

    _____

    _____

    _____

Course Evaluation

Your evaluation of this course will help Microsoft understand the quality of your learning experience.

At a convenient time before the end of the course, please complete a course evaluation, which is available at http://www.CourseSurvey.com.

Microsoft will keep your evaluation strictly confidential and will use your responses to improve your future learning experience.

Module 11: Working with SMS Hierarchies

Contents

Overview

- Introduction to the SMS Site Hierarchy
- Configuring Site Communications
- Installing a Secondary Site Server
- Managing Roaming Clients in an SMS Hierarchy

Introduction

In this module, you will learn how to work within a Microsoft® Systems Management Server (SMS) site hierarchy. The sites in your organization can be connected together to create a single site hierarchy. Occasionally, site hierarchies must be modified and new sites must be created and added. The SMS secondary site is ideal for simplifying the installation and management of small branch offices. In this module, you will learn how to configure sites and work within a site hierarchy.

Objectives

After completing this module, you will be able to:

- Describe the site hierarchy architecture.
- Configure communication between SMS sites.
- Install an SMS secondary site server.
- Manage roaming clients in an SMS hierarchy.

Lesson: Introduction to the SMS Site Hierarchy

* The Two Types of Sites that SMS Provides
* The Function of Primary Sites in a Hierarchy
* The Function of Secondary Sites in a Hierarchy
* How Data Flows in a Site Hierarchy
* Guidelines for Managing Network Traffic

Introduction

To effectively administer an SMS site, you must understand how sites fit together in a hierarchy. All sites should eventually report to a central site. Secondary sites are useful for small locations that do not have local administrators, but they are not as flexible as primary sites.

Lesson objectives

After completing this lesson, you will be able to:

- Define the two types of sites.
- Describe the function of primary sites.
- Describe the function of secondary sites.
- Describe the flow of data in a site hierarchy.
- Describe how to manage network bandwidth in a site hierarchy.

The Two Types of Sites that SMS Provides

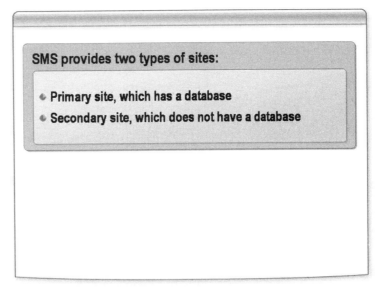

SMS provides two types of sites:

- A *primary site* is a site that has a database. It can have child sites, and it provides local administration.

- A *secondary site* is a site that does NOT have a database. It can only be a child site and never a parent site, and it has no ability to administer SMS locally.

The Function of Primary Sites in a Hierarchy

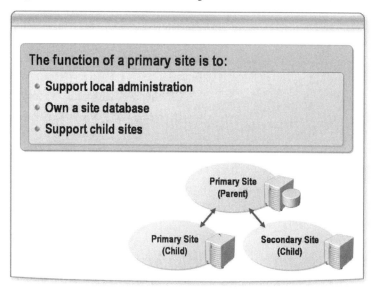

An SMS site consists of a site server, site systems, clients, and resources. SMS provides two types of sites: primary sites and secondary sites. The function of a *primary site* is to:

- Support local administration.
- Own a site database.
- Support child sites.

How primary sites support local administration

By default, the first SMS site you install is a primary site. Primary sites have administrative tools, such as the SMS Administrator console, that enable you to directly manage the site.

The primary site is especially useful if the computer management in your organization is decentralized. Depending on the scope of control, each IT management location is likely to require a primary site.

For example, after thorough planning, your IT department might create and document a high-level SMS site and client deployment plan. Central headquarters has three primary sites: one for the secondary sites to report to, another to assign local Advanced Clients to, and one to be the central site for reporting. This is only an example, not a recommendation.

The first site installed becomes the initial administrative site. It does not need to become your central site or remain your administrative site. You can continue to attach primary sites, install secondary sites, or do both until you have created the hierarchy. SMS Setup creates each primary site as a stand-alone site. Primary sites can have multiple secondary sites, which send data to the primary site.

Building a hierarchy involves choosing a primary site to serve as the central site and then making the central site the parent to other primary sites. This creates a hierarchy branch. The bottom of the branch is the lowest child site. The top of the branch extends to, and ends at, the central site. A site cannot have more than one parent, and a site cannot be its own parent or child.

How primary sites provide the database

A primary site stores SMS data for itself, and for all the sites beneath it, in the *SMS site database*.

The SMS site database at the central site acquires aggregate discovery inventory, software metering data, and status messages from the SMS hierarchy and collects details about any collections, packages, or advertisements created at the central site. At the central site, you can view and manage all sites and computers in the SMS hierarchy.

The Function of Secondary Sites in a Hierarchy

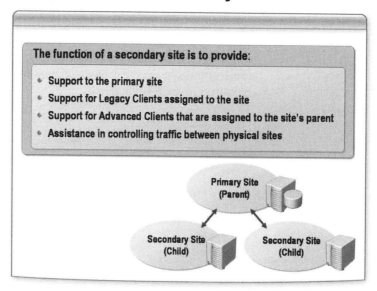

The function of a *secondary site* is to provide:

- Support to the primary site.

- Support for Legacy Clients assigned to the secondary site.

- Support for Advanced Clients that are assigned to the site's parent.

- Assistance in controlling traffic between locations.

A *secondary site* is used for smaller sites with 1,000 clients or less. A secondary site does not have a SQL database and therefore must rely on the primary site that it reports to in order to store information. That means less administrative overhead; therefore a secondary site is used when there is no local administrator available. The secondary sites have smaller hardware requirements and cannot handle the same load that a primary site can. Secondary sites must be administered from the primary site, so they are not good for locations that need to have greater configuration control or more SMS administrator oversight. The secondary site forwards the information it gathers from SMS clients, such as computer inventory data and SMS system status information, to the primary site where it is stored.

How the secondary site supports the primary site

Secondary sites reduce the primary site resource load, and they also reduce the network load. They reduce network load because they can be placed near clients that are not near a primary site. This enables clients to communicate with a closely located secondary site instead of a distant primary site.

How the secondary sites provide support for Legacy Clients

Secondary sites support Advanced and Legacy Clients differently. They allow administrators to define how they want Legacy Clients to be configured for clients at the secondary site location. Administrators also provide distribution points to install software for Legacy Clients at that site.

How the secondary sites provide limited support for Advanced Clients

Advanced Clients must be assigned to a primary site; however, they can use the secondary site management points for policy information, but the policies must be created at the primary site. The Advanced Client can also use secondary site distribution points for software distribution content.

Secondary sites do not provide configuration information for Advanced Clients. This information is set at the primary site to which the Advanced Client is assigned.

How Data Flows in a Site Hierarchy

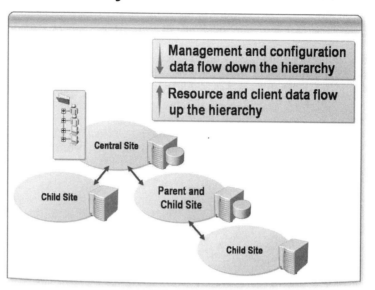

Management and configuration data flow

In general, management and configuration data moves down the hierarchy from higher-level sites. Resource and client data moves up the hierarchy from lower-level sites. More specifically, a parent site sends management instructions and data intended for client distribution down to its child sites. Child sites report their status up to their parent sites. This status includes the information they gather from SMS clients, such as computer inventory data and SMS system status information.

So why is this important? The structure of your hierarchy directly affects how SMS data flows, such as how sites report data to one another. Most data flow can be controlled between sites but not within sites.

For example, large numbers of advertised programs can increase the network traffic between the sites in your hierarchy. This traffic affects the network links that connect the sites in your hierarchy. If you carefully schedule SMS activities and spread the load by implementing multiple sites, you might be able to distribute the load more evenly on your network.

Resource and client data flow

Resource and client data flow up the hierarchy. Activities such as frequent hardware and software inventory updates will increase the network traffic between the sites in your hierarchy.

It is important to know who will access the data that SMS generates and which SMS sites should display discovery and inventory data. Because this data flows up the hierarchy, be aware of your business needs for data being gathered at particular levels or sites in the hierarchy.

Other examples of data that flow up the hierarchy include: client status messages (including advertisement status), server and site system status messages, and client data about metered applications.

Note .For more information, see Chapter 2, "Understanding SMS Sites," of *Microsoft Systems Management Server 2003 Concepts, Planning, and Deployment Guide* on the Additional Reading page of your Student Materials compact disc.

Guidelines for Managing Network Traffic

Network bandwidth guidelines for a site hierarchy:

- Spread the load on your network by implementing multiple sites
- Keep SMS clients from being remotely located from their SMS site systems
- Ensure that you do not have excessively large numbers of advertised programs or frequent hardware and software inventory intervals
- Install proxy management points

Managing network traffic is an important activity for an SMS Administrator. Four ways that you can help reduce network traffic are:

- Spread the load on your network by implementing multiple sites.

- Keep SMS clients from being remotely located from their SMS site systems.

- Ensure that you do not have excessively large numbers of advertised programs or frequent hardware and software inventory intervals. These settings can increase the network traffic between the sites in your hierarchy. This traffic affects the network links that connect the sites in your hierarchy.

- Install *proxy management points*. A management point at a secondary site is known as a proxy management point. It can be used for roaming Advanced Clients if the client is within the roaming boundaries of the secondary site. Installing a proxy management point can significantly reduce the effect on available network bandwidth created by Advanced Clients located within that site's roaming boundaries. Advanced Clients send inventory data, software metering data, and status data to the proxy management point. The data is then sent to the secondary site server which uses the site's sender functionality to transfer the data to the parent primary site. By using the sender's bandwidth control functionality, you can specify when the data is sent to the primary site.

Note   For further planning considerations of SMS 2003, see Course 2597 *Planning and Deploying Microsoft® Systems Management Server 2003*.

Practice: Applying SMS Hierarchy Principles to your Organization

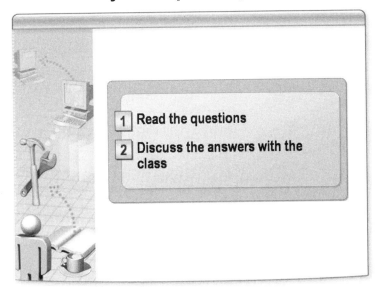

Instructions	Read the following questions and be prepared to discuss the answers with the rest of the class.
Discussion questions	1. In what situation or situations would it be beneficial to deploy a secondary site?

2. What are the implications of using secondary sites?

3. Can a primary site in standard security mode report to a central site in advanced mode?

_____

_____

_____

4. What is the recommended method for determining how many tiers to create in an SMS hierarchy?

_____

_____

_____

Lesson: Configuring Site Communications

- The Role of Senders in Site-to-Site Communications
- Types of Senders and the Connectivity They Support
- How Senders Work With Other SMS Components to Send and Receive Data
- What Is a Site Address?
- How to Attach a Child Primary Site to a Parent Primary Site
- How Collections, Packages, and Advertisements are Propagated in a Hierarchy
- Guidelines for Troubleshooting Site Attachment
- Guidelines for Troubleshooting Site-to-Site Communications
- Demonstration: How to Prepare a Primary Site for Secondary Site Installation

Introduction

The first step in configuring sites in an SMS site hierarchy is making sure the sites in the hierarchy can communicate. In this lesson, you will learn about senders on an SMS site and how they work with other SMS components to communicate with other sites. You will learn about site addresses, which provide communication information. The next part of the lesson introduces you to attaching sites to one another and explains the guidelines for troubleshooting site attachment.

Lesson objectives

After completing this lesson, you will be able to:

- Describe the role of senders in site-to-site communications.
- Describe the various types of senders.
- Describe how senders work with other SMS components to send and receive data.
- Describe the purpose of a site address.
- Attach a child primary site to a parent primary site.
- Describe how collections, packages, and advertisements are propagated in a hierarchy.
- Troubleshoot site attachment.
- Troubleshoot site-to-site communications.
- Prepare a primary site for secondary site installation.

The Role of Senders in Site-to-Site Communications

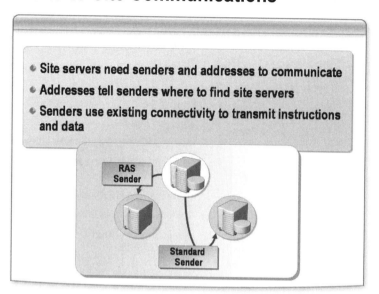

- Site servers need senders and addresses to communicate
- Addresses tell senders where to find site servers
- Senders use existing connectivity to transmit instructions and data

RAS Sender

Standard Sender

In an SMS hierarchy, a site needs to be able to communicate with its parent site, all its direct child sites, and remote sites within the SMS hierarchy. To provide reliable communication between sites servers, you must install and configure *senders* on each site and create *addresses* to the other sites that you want the site to communicate with.

Note Senders and addresses are required for communication between site servers. However, senders and addresses are not required for communication between other components of the site, such as site systems, clients, or the SMS Administrator console.

What are senders?

Senders are SMS components that use existing connectivity to transmit instructions and data from one site server to another site server in the hierarchy. For example, a child site will send inventory data and status information to its parent site by using a sender. A parent site will send information about required software updates to its child sites by using a sender.

SMS uses senders to control data flow and to provide reliable communication between sites. Senders do not provide a physical connection to another site. They use existing network connectivity to manage connections, ensure integrity of transferred data, recover from errors, and close connections when they are no longer necessary.

If a sender requires another communications service to connect to other sites, you must install that service on a computer at the site. For example, to use Asynchronous RAS Sender, you must install and configure Remote Access Service (RAS) on a computer running Microsoft Windows® 2000 Server or Microsoft Windows Server™ 2003.

What are addresses?

Administrators configure addresses to use senders to connect to a remote site. An address tells senders where to find the site servers of destination sites and the account to use to connect to the server.

Types of Senders and the Connectivity They Support

SMS supports three types of senders. Senders do not provide a physical connection to another site; they use existing network connectivity systems to manage connections, ensure integrity of transferred data, recover from errors, and close connections when they are no longer necessary. Choose your sender based on the existing connectivity system between your sites.

The following table describes the sender types and the connectivity that each one supports.

Sender type	Connectivity support
Standard Sender	Used to send data over reliable high-speed network connections, such as local area network (LAN) communications. Standard Sender is also used for wide area network (WAN) communications when routers are used to connect LAN segments. Standard Sender is installed by default.
RAS Sender	Used to operate over RAS connections. Select from one of four types of RAS senders: Asynchronous RAS, ISDN RAS, Systems Network Architecture (SNA) RAS, X25 RAS.
Courier Sender	Used to send and receive large volumes of SMS package data for software distribution through CDs, floppy disks, or tapes. Courier Sender is only used to send package source files to child sites, and is only used when available bandwidth is insufficient to transport the data.

How Senders Work with Other SMS Components to Send and Receive Data

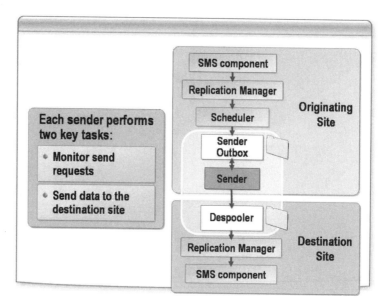

How data is sent to another site

The general method for sending data to another site begins with the following preparatory actions:

1. A component, such as Distribution Manager, creates a replication object and passes it to Replication Manager.

2. Replication Manager bundles data, providing a transaction ID if necessary, and creates a mini-job for the Scheduler.

3. The Scheduler initiates most data transfers by activating mini-jobs from the site database or its inbox.

4. The Scheduler prepares packages and instructions for sending and produces send requests. The send request file is placed in the appropriate sender outbox, as determined by the Scheduler.

The actual sending of the data involves the following action:

- Each sender monitors the outbox and transmits data as required.

How sites receive data from a sender

When the site receives the data from the sender it processes it in the following way:

1. The Despooler decompresses the data and sends it to Replication Manager.

2. Replication Manager passes the data to the appropriate component for processing.

Tasks that senders perform

Regardless of the sender type, each sender performs two key tasks:

- Monitoring send requests

  For each installed sender, except the Courier Sender, a sender dispatcher thread within the SMS_EXECUTIVE service monitors its outbox for send requests. The Scheduler places instructions and package files in Sms\Inboxes\Schedule.box\Tosend for the senders to process.

  Monitoring send requests consists of waiting for any file changes in the Sms\Inboxes\Schedule.box\Outboxes*sender* directory. If the sender is installed on a computer other than the site server, it might not be alerted by a Microsoft Windows NT® Changed Directory Event, so it will search every five minutes to look for send requests.

  When an .srq file is found in the sender's directory, another thread within the SMS_EXECUTIVE service is created to service the send request.

- Sending the data to the destination site

  Senders move data, such as a package and instruction files, to the destination site. The data is moved from the source site's Sms\Inboxes\Schedule.box\Tosend directory to the destination site's Sms\Inboxes\Despoolr.box\Receive directory. The Standard sender and remote access senders use standard file input/output (I/O) requests to move data to the destination site. No SMS components are required at the destination site to receive the data, because the Windows Server service receives the data and places it in the remote receive box.

  Data transferred by the senders is sent in blocks. The size of these blocks depends on the sender type. The Standard Sender, for example, transfers blocks of 256 kilobytes (KB). After each block is successfully sent, the send request status file is updated. If a send fails, the sender will retransmit the block starting after the last successfully sent block.

Note SMS 2003 SP1 allows the user to define the block sizes and the delay between block sends.

What Is a Site Address?

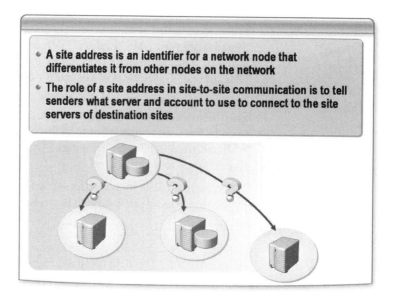

* A site address is an identifier for a network node that differentiates it from other nodes on the network
* The role of a site address in site-to-site communication is to tell senders what server and account to use to connect to the site servers of destination sites

Senders are of no use without addresses. A *site address* (also called just an *address*) is an identifier for a network node that differentiates it from other nodes on the network. Addresses tell senders what server and account to use to connect to the site servers of destination sites.

Addresses are sender-type specific, which means that the sending site needs both a different address for each destination site and a different address for each type of sender that is used. You configure multiple SMS addresses for each site to ensure that data is sent and received if the first address is not available.

For an SMS hierarchy to function properly, the sites in the hierarchy must communicate with each other. In particular, each site must communicate with its parent site and with its immediate child sites. Occasionally, a site might also need to communicate with other sites in the hierarchy. For example, you might need to send a package from a primary site to an indirect child site (a site below a direct child site).

For software distribution, SMS 2003 sites communicate by using package routing. During package routing, communications are passed down a hierarchy from site to site. This means that a site requires addresses for its parent site and child sites but not for other lower-level sites.

For senders to transmit data properly, you must also specify addresses, which are used by senders to locate sites. Your first step is to select the type of address that you want to create.

You can control certain aspects of how your sites communicate by configuring the properties of senders and addresses. For example, if one of the network connections in your SMS hierarchy is only available between 12 A.M. and 6 A.M. every day, you can set the sender's schedule to only communicate with the other site between those hours.

You can set the following address properties for the sender:

- The address priority order for multiple addresses.
- The schedule, including the time of day for SMS to use the connection for specific priority send requests.
- The percentage of available bandwidth that SMS can use during a site-to-site transfer.
- The destination SMS site.
- The destination site server name.
- The account to use to connect to the destination site server.

If a site loses its connection to other sites, the site continues to collect inventory and software metering data, distribute software, and maintain contact with and run scheduled instructions on its client computers. When the connection is restored, the site synchronizes its status and data with its parent-level sites.

Note For more information about choosing senders and planning for addresses, see Chapter 10, "Planning Your SMS Deployment and Configuration," of the *Microsoft Systems Management Server 2003 Concepts, Planning, and Deployment Guide* on the Additional Reading page of your Student materials compact disc.

How to Attach a Child Primary Site to a Parent Primary Site

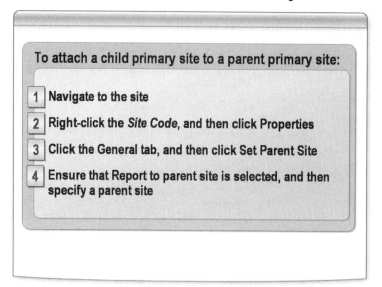

To attach a child primary site to a parent primary site:

1. Navigate to the site

2. Right-click the *Site Code*, and then click Properties

3. Click the General tab, and then click Set Parent Site

4. Ensure that Report to parent site is selected, and then specify a parent site

After you have added the required address information for a parent site, you can start to build your hierarchy by attaching to the site.

Preparation for attaching child site to a parent site

Before you attach a child site to a parent site:

- Ensure that you have Modify permissions for the site security object class or instance.

- Ensure that an address to the parent site is specified.

Procedure

Important   These steps are included for your information. Neither you nor your instructor should attempt to perform them in the classroom. If you perform these steps in the classroom environment, you might leave your computer in an incorrect state for upcoming practices.

To attach a child primary site to a parent primary site:

1. In the SMS Administrator console, navigate to the site. To do this, expand the following nodes, in order: **Site Database (*Site Code*) Site Hierarchy**, *Site Code*.

2. Right-click *Site Code*, and then click **Properties**.

3. In the **Site Properties** dialog box, on the **General** tab, click **Set Parent Site**.

4. In the **Set Parent Site** dialog box, ensure that **Report to parent site** is selected, and then specify a parent site.

Caution If the site being added to the hierarchy uses the same site code that was previously used in the hierarchy, and if software distribution objects were modified since the previous site detached, software distribution objects might be overwritten or corrupted. For instance, parent and child sites might have different definitions for the same package IDs. Carefully inspect any duplicates. After inspection, consider deleting packages that are no longer valid.

5. Click **OK** to close the **Set Parent Site** dialog box.

6. Click **OK** to close the **Site Properties** dialog box.

The process that occurs after a site attaches to a parent site

After the site is attached, data starts to flow between the child site and the parent site. If the child site already has several clients, normal Management Information Format (MIF) file processing at the parent site is delayed while the child site data is added to the parent's site database.

The following process occurs after a site attaches to a parent site:

1. The proposed configuration is written to the SMS database at the child site.

2. Hierarchy Manager at the child site reads the database and creates a site configuration file (a .ct2 file).

3. The child site creates a mini-job to send its site configuration information to the parent site.

4. The SMS Administrator console at the parent site displays the child site. It might be necessary to use the **Refresh** command to update the local site object in SMS Administrator console.

5. At the child site, additional mini-jobs are created to pass all the discovery and inventory data, in addition to status messages, to the parent site.

When the configuration has been completed at the parent site, an administrator at the parent site will see the new child site displayed under the local site in the console tree of the SMS Administrator console. After the child site's discovery data has been reported to the parent site, an administrator at the parent site will be able to view the resources in the child site and administer the child site server. Certain data will flow from the parent site to the child site as well. Such data includes collection definitions, packages, advertisements, and software metering rules.

How Collections, Packages, and Advertisements Are Propagated in a Hierarchy

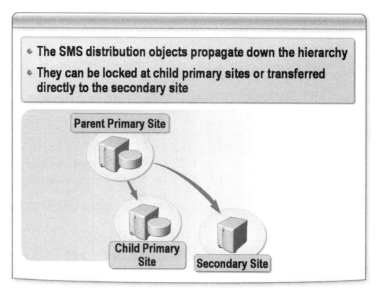

After you attach one site to another, data starts to flow from the child site to its parent site and from the parent site to its child site. With respect to collections, packages, and advertisements, the data flows from the parent site to the child site only.

The SMS software distribution objects (collections, packages, and advertisements), along with other objects, are replicated to the child site and can be used at the child site. However, those replicated objects are locked at the child site. The administrator at the child site cannot modify inherited objects.

Predefined objects, such as predefined collections that are inherited from a parent site, overwrite the corresponding objects at the child site.

The collection rules that are created on the parent are also sent to the child site, and they can be viewed in the SMS Administrator console for the child site. When refreshed, they show local site members that meet the collection rules.

Package information, in addition to programs and advertisements, is delivered to the child site. Delivering the package information and advertisements allows the child site administrator to distribute packages to appropriate distribution points.

SMS 2003 sends package changes to distribution points by using delta replication. Delta replication ensures that only the files on the package that have changed—not the entire package—are replicated to distribution points and child sites. This reduces network bandwidth between sites and between a site and its own distribution points.

Guidelines for Troubleshooting Site Attachment

> **Guidelines for troubleshooting site attachment:**
>
> - Verify the site attachment at the parent and/or child site
> - Verify that the name resolution is successful
> - Verify that the address to the parent site is correct
> - View the status messages at the parent site and/or child site
> - Check the logs at the parent site and/or child site

There are guidelines for troubleshooting site attachments. The following table provides guidelines for certain circumstances that require troubleshooting.

You are having difficulty communicating between the parent and child sites or you do not see the new child site displayed under the local site	<ul><li>Verify the site attachment at the parent site.</li><li>Verify the site attachment at the child site.</li><li>Verify that the name resolution is successful.</li><li>Verify the address to the parent site is correct.</li></ul>View the status message for the following components for both the parent and child sites:<ul><li>SMS_LAN_SENDER</li><li>SMS_SCHEDULER</li><li>SMS_DESPOOLER</li><li>SMS_REPLICATION_MANAGER</li><li>SMS_HIERARCHY_MANAGER</li></ul>
You need more information about a status message that reports failure	View the following log files for both the parent and child sites:<ul><li>Sender.log</li><li>Sched.log</li><li>Despool.log</li><li>Replmgr.log</li><li>Hman.log</li></ul>

Guidelines for Troubleshooting Site-to-Site Communications

Make sure that:

- The connectivity system software is installed and configured
- Each site has the appropriate senders installed and configured
- Each site has a site address for the other site
- The address is configured properly
- The site address account has been added as a member of the target site's SMS_SiteToSiteConnection_sitecode group

If you encounter problems when two sites are trying to communicate, ensure that the following criteria are met:

- The connectivity system software is installed and configured.
- Each site has the appropriate senders installed and configured.
- Each site has a site address for the other site.
- The address is configured properly.
- At each site, the site address account (standard security mode) or the site server computer account (advanced security mode) has been added as a member of the target site's SMS_SiteToSiteConnection_<sitecode> group.

Demonstration: How to Prepare a Primary Site for Secondary Site Installation

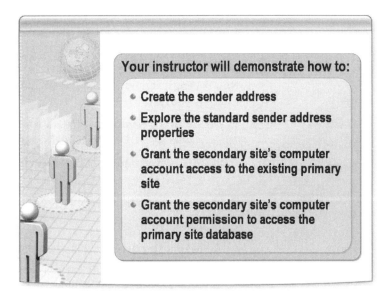

Your instructor will demonstrate how to:

- Create the sender address
- Explore the standard sender address properties
- Grant the secondary site's computer account access to the existing primary site
- Grant the secondary site's computer account permission to access the primary site database

In this demonstration, your instructor will show you how to create the sender address, grant the secondary site's computer account access to the existing primary site, and then install the secondary site.

Your instructor will use the following values in this demonstration.

Variable	Value
Virtual machine—SMS Site 1	Dublin
Dublin Administrator	JaePa (Jae Pak)
Virtual machine—domain controller	Glasgow
Domain administrator	Administrator
Virtual machine—SMS Site 2	Paris
Paris Administrator	DonHa (Don Hall)

Important These steps are included for your information. Do not attempt to perform them in the classroom. If you perform these steps in the classroom environment, you might leave your computer in an incorrect state for upcoming practices.

Demonstration steps performed by instructor only

▶ **To create the sender address**

1. Verify that the Glasgow virtual machine is running. If the Glasgow virtual machine is not running, log it on to the NWTRADERS domain with a user name of **Administrator** and a password of **P@ssw0rd**.

   After the Glasgow virtual machine opens, you can minimize it.

2. Verify that the Dublin virtual machine is running. If the Dublin virtual machine is not running, log it on to the NWTRADERS domain with a user name of **JaePa** and a password of **P@ssw0rd**.

3. Log the Paris virtual machine on to the NWTRADERS domain with a user name of **DonHa** and a password of **P@ssw0rd**.

4. On the Dublin virtual machine, click **Start**, point to **All Programs**, point to **Systems Management Server**, and then click **SMS Administrator Console**.

5. In the SMS Administrator console, expand **Site Database (001 – NWTraders)**, expand **Site Hierarchy**, expand **001 – NWTraders**, expand **Site Settings**, right-click **Addresses**, point to **New**, and then click **Standard Sender Address**.

6. In the **Standard Sender Address Properties** dialog box, on the **General** tab, type **002** in the **Destination site code** box.

7. In the **Site server name** box, type **Paris**.

▶ **To explore the standard sender address properties**

1. Click the **Schedule** tab.

   Use this tab to set the schedule of a sender address.

   The **Scheduled availability for selected time period** enables you to use the week chart, click to select an hour, or drag a rectangle of several hours over several days.

   The **Availability** options indicate the availability of this address during the selected time period. Following are the available options:

   - Open for all priorities

   - Allow medium and high priority

   - Allow high priority only

   - Closed

   SMS components usually determine the priority of various jobs; for example, site control files are high priority and collection properties are normal priority. However, you can specify the priorities of packages. If you specify a package as having high priority, the package is sent to child sites as high priority.

   The **Unavailable to substitute for inoperative addresses** option prevents this address from being used as a substitute for inoperative addresses during the selected time period.

2. Click the **Rate Limits** tab.

   Use this tab to set maximum data transfer rates, by hour, from the current site to this standard sender address.

   The **Unlimited when sending to this address** option sets the transfer rate to unlimited when the current site sends data to this address.

   The **Limited to specified maximum transfer rates by hour** option sets the hours of the day and the percentage of maximum transfer rate allowed for each hour. If no number appears beneath an hour, 100 percent of the maximum transfer rate is allowed for that hour.

The **Rate limit for selected time period** option specifies the maximum transfer rate for the selected time period.

Figure 11.1 Standard Sender Address Properties – Rate Limits tab

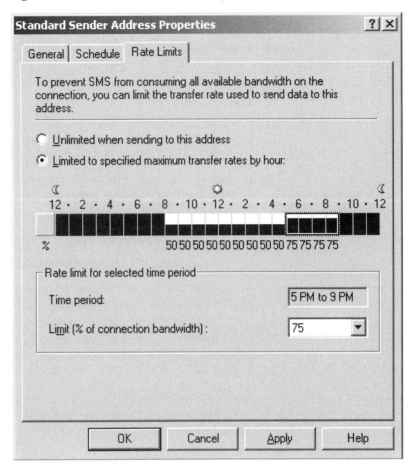

The **Time period** option enables you to choose the day chart as shown in the Figure 11.1 Standard Sender Address Properties – Rate Limits tab above.

The **Limit (% of connection bandwidth)** option enables you to set the percentage of the maximum transfer rate allowed for the selected time period. You can choose either a percentage or unlimited.

3. Click **OK**.

Note   In the details pane of the SMS Administrator console, notice that **002 – [Unknown]** now appears in the Name column. This is because the secondary site does not yet exist.

---

4. Close the SMS Administrator console.

► **To grant the computer account that will be used by the secondary site permission to access a primary site**

Note   To permit communication from the secondary site to the primary site, the secondary site's computer account needs to be added to the SMS_SiteToSiteConnection_*sitecode* group on the primary site server.

This group is created, as a local group on the site server, during primary site setup. Group members then have full-control access to the primary site's C:\SMS\inboxes\despoolr.box\receive folder.

---

1. On the Dublin virtual machine, click **Start**, point to **Control Panel**, point to **Administrative Tools**, and then click **Computer Management**.

2. In Computer Management, in the console tree, expand **Local Users and Groups**, and then click **Groups**.

3. Right-click **SMS_SiteToSiteConnection_001** and then click **Properties**.

4. In the **SMS_SiteToSiteConnection_001 Properties** dialog box, click **Add**.

5. In the **Select Users, Computers, or Groups** dialog box, click **Object Types**.

6. In the **Object Types** dialog box, select the **Computers** check box, clear the **Users** and **Groups** check boxes, and then click **OK**.

7. In the **Select Users, Computers, or Groups** dialog box, notice that the **Select this object type** box contains the word **Computers** and is unavailable.

8. Click **Advanced**.

9. In the advanced **Select Users, Computers, or Groups** dialog box, click **Find Now**.

10. In the **Search results** box, click **Paris**, and then click **OK**.

    Paris now appears in the **Enter the object names to select** box of the **Select Users, Computers, or Groups** dialog box.

11. In the **Select Users, Computers, or Groups** dialog box, click **OK**.

    NWTraders\PARIS appears in the **Members** box, of the **SMS_SiteToSiteConnection_001 Properties** dialog box.

12. In the **SMS_SiteToSiteConnection_001 Properties** dialog box, click **OK**.

▶ **To grant the computer account that will be used by the proxy management point permission to access a primary site database**

Note   To permit communication from the secondary site's proxy management point to the primary site's SQL database, the secondary site's computer account needs to be added to the SMS_SiteSystemToSQLConnection_*sitecode* group on the primary site server.

This group is created, as a local group on the site server, during primary site setup. Group members can then use integrated security to access the database.

---

1. On the Dublin virtual machine, in Computer Management, verify that **Groups** is expanded in the console tree, and that the local groups appear in the details pane.

2. Right-click **SMS_SiteSystemToSQLConnection_001** and then click **Properties**.

3. In the **SMS_SiteSystemToSQLConnection_001 Properties** dialog box, click **Add**.

4. In the **Select Users, Computers, or Groups** dialog box, click **Object Types**.

5. In the **Object Types** dialog box, select the **Computers** check box, clear the **Users** and **Groups** check boxes, and then click **OK**.

6. In the **Select Users, Computers, or Groups** dialog box, notice that the **Select this object type** box contains the word **Computers** and is unavailable.

7. Click **Advanced**.

8. In the advanced **Select Users, Computers, or Groups** dialog box, click **Find Now**.

9. In the **Search results** box, click **Paris**, and then click **OK**.

   Paris now appears in the **Enter the object names to select** box of the **Select Users, Computers, or Groups** dialog box.

10. In the **Select Users, Computers, or Groups** dialog box, click **OK**.

   NWTRADERS\PARIS appears in the **Members** box, of the **SMS_SiteSystemToSQLConnection_001 Properties** dialog box.

11. In the **SMS_SiteSystemToSQLConnection_001 Properties** dialog box, click **OK**.

12. Close Computer Management.

Practice: Configuring Site Communications

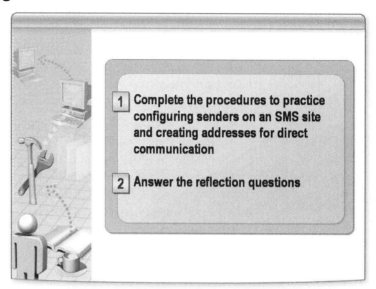

Instructions

Complete the procedures to practice configuring senders on an SMS site and creating addresses for direct communication, and then answer the reflection questions that follow.

In this practice, use the following values.

Variable	Value
Virtual machine—SMS Site 1	Dublin
Dublin Administrator	JaePa (Jae Pak)
Virtual machine—domain controller	Glasgow
Domain administrator	Administrator
Virtual machine—SMS Site 2	Paris
Paris Administrator	DonHa (Don Hall)

Procedures

▶ **To create the sender address**

1. Verify that the Glasgow virtual machine is running. If the Glasgow virtual machine is not running, log it on to the NWTRADERS domain with a user name of **Administrator** and a password of **P@ssw0rd**.

   After the Glasgow virtual machine opens, you can minimize it.

2. Verify that the Dublin virtual machine is running. If the Dublin virtual machine is not running, log it on to the NWTRADERS domain with a user name of **JaePa** and a password of **P@ssw0rd**.

3. Log the Paris virtual machine on to the NWTRADERS domain with a user name of **DonHa** and a password of **P@ssw0rd**.

4. On the Dublin virtual machine, click **Start**, point to **All Programs**, point to **Systems Management Server**, and then click **SMS Administrator Console**.

5. Expand **Site Database (001 – NWTraders)**, expand **Site Hierarchy**, expand **001 – NWTraders**, expand **Site Settings**, right-click **Addresses**, point to **New**, and then click **Standard Sender Address**.

6. In the **Standard Sender Address Properties** dialog box, on the **General** tab, type **002** in the **Destination site code** box.

7. In the **Site server name** box, type **Paris**

8. Click **OK**.

9. Close the SMS Administrator console.

▶ **To grant the computer account that will be used by the secondary site permission to access the primary site**

Note   To permit communication from the secondary site to the primary site, the secondary site's computer account needs to be added to the SMS_SiteToSiteConnection_*sitecode* group on the primary site server.

This group is created, as a local group on the site server, during primary site setup. Group members then have full-control access to the primary site's C:\SMS\inboxes\despoolr.box\receive folder.

---

1. On the Dublin virtual machine, click **Start**, point to **Control Panel**, point to **Administrative Tools**, and then click **Computer Management**.

2. In Computer Management, in the console tree, expand **Local Users and Groups**, and then click **Groups**.

3. Select **SMS_SiteToSiteConnection_001**. Right-click, and then click **Properties**.

4. In the **SMS_SiteToSiteConnection_001 Properties** dialog box, click **Add**.

5. In the **Select Users, Computers, or Groups** dialog box, click **Object Types**.

6. In the **Object Types** dialog box, select the **Computers** check box, clear the **Users** and **Groups** check boxes, and then click **OK**.

7. In the **Select Users, Computers, or Groups** dialog box, notice that the **Select this object type** box contains the word **Computers** and is unavailable.

8. Click **Advanced**.

9. In the advanced **Select Users, Computers, or Groups** dialog box, click **Find Now**.

10. In the **Search results** box, click **Paris**, and then click **OK**.

    Paris now appears in the **Enter the object names to select** box of the **Select Users, Computers, or Groups** dialog box.

11. In the **Select Users, Computers, or Groups** dialog box, click **OK**.

    NWTRADERS\PARIS appears in the **Members** box, of the **SMS_SiteToSiteConnection_001 Properties** dialog box.

12. In the **SMS_SiteToSiteConnection_001 Properties** dialog box, click **OK**.

▶ **To grant the computer account that will be used by the proxy management point permission to access the primary site database**

Note   To permit communication from the secondary site's Proxy management point to the primary site's SQL database, the secondary site's computer account needs to be added to the SMS_SiteSystemToSQLConnection_sitecode group on the primary site server.

This group is created, as a local group on the site server, during primary site setup. Group members can then use integrated security to access the database.

1. Select **SMS_SiteSystemToSQLConnection_001**. Right-click, and then select **Properties**.

2. In the **SMS_SiteSystemToSQLConnection_001 Properties** dialog box, click **Add**.

3. In the **Select Users, Computers, or Groups** dialog box, click **Object Types**.

4. In the **Object Types** dialog box, select the **Computers** check box, clear the **Users** and **Groups** check boxes, and then click **OK**.

5. In the **Select Users, Computers, or Groups** dialog box, notice that the **Select this object type** box contains the word **Computers** and is unavailable.

6. Click **Advanced**.

7. In the advanced **Select Users, Computers, or Groups** dialog box, click **Find Now**.

8. In the **Search results** box, click **Paris**, and then click **OK**.

   Paris now appears in the **Enter the object names to select** box of the **Select Users, Computers, or Groups** dialog box.

9. In the **Select Users, Computers, or Groups** dialog box, click **OK**.

   NWTRADERS\PARIS appears in the **Members** box, of the **SMS_SiteSystemToSQLConnection_001 Properties** dialog box.

10. In the **SMS_SiteSystemToSQLConnection_001 Properties** dialog box, click **OK**.

11. Close Computer Management.

Reflection question

What is the difference between a *sender* and a *sender address*?

_____

_____

_____

Lesson: Installing a Secondary Site Server

- Methods for Installing a Secondary Site
- Demonstration: How to Install a Secondary Site and Verify Installation

Introduction

In this lesson, you will learn the methods to install a secondary site server. The instructor will demonstrate how to install a secondary site and verify that the hierarchy is established, and then you will practice the procedure yourself.

Lesson objectives

After completing this lesson, you will be able to:

- Describe the methods of secondary site installation.
- Install a secondary site.

Methods for Installing a Secondary Site

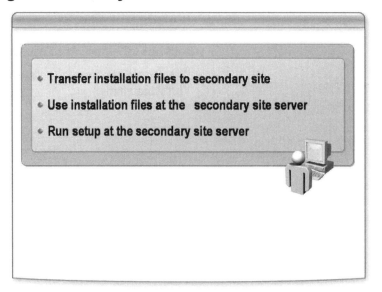

- Transfer installation files to secondary site
- Use installation files at the secondary site server
- Run setup at the secondary site server

There are several methods of installing a secondary site. The method you choose is dependent on the resources that are available to you at the location of the secondary site, available network bandwidth, and administrative privileges configured at your SMS site.

You can install a secondary site by using one of the following methods.

Transferring installation files to secondary site

One method of installation is to configure and initiate installation and transfer installation files to secondary site before installing by using the Secondary Site Creation Wizard from the SMS Administrator console at the primary site.

Using this method, you can have SMS transfer all required files from the primary site to the secondary site server during the installation process. Before you use this method, you must:

1. Install a parent primary site. The SMS Administrator console is not installed on a secondary site server.

2. Identify the site address to be used by the primary site to connect to the secondary site.

   - The site address account must be known to the destination site server. For SMS 2003 destination sites, the account should be added to the SMS_SiteToSiteConnection_<*site code*> group on the destination site server.

3. Have administrator privileges for the site address account on the secondary site server.

4. Identify the SMS Service account that will be used for the secondary site server (with advanced security, this is the computer account).

5. Ensure you have Create permission for the site security object class to perform the installation procedure.

Using Installation files at the secondary site server

Another method is to configure installation and access installation files already located at the secondary site server using the Secondary Site Creation Wizard from the SMS Administrator console at the primary site.

Using this method you can reduce network traffic during the installation by having SMS install the files locally from the secondary site server. Before you use this method, you must:

1. Install a parent primary site. The SMS Administrator console is not installed on a secondary site server.

2. Identify the site address to be used by the primary site to connect to the secondary site.

   • The site address account must be known to the destination site server. For SMS 2003 destination sites, the account should be added to the SMS_SiteToSiteConnection_<*site code*> group on the destination site server.

3. Identify the SMS Service account that will be used for the secondary site server (with advanced security, this is the computer account).

4. Ensure you have Create permission for the site security object class to perform the installation procedure.

5. Have administrator privileges for the site address account on the secondary site server.

6. Locate the files on the secondary server by accessing the SMS 2003 compact disc, the *local drive:*\SMSSetup folder, or the removable media drive.

Note Once the secondary site is installed, you can remove the Administrator privileges on the site address account.

Running setup at the secondary site server

The last method is to run SMS setup from an SMS 2003 compact disc at the secondary site server. Before you use this method, you must:

1. Identify the site address account to be used by the secondary site to connect to its primary parent site.

2. Identify the SMS Service account that will be used for the secondary site server (with advanced security, this is the computer account).

   • The site address account from the primary to the secondary site does not need Administrator rights.

   • The site address account must be known to the destination site server. For SMS 2003 destination sites, the account should be added to the SMS_SiteToSiteConnection_<*site code*> group on the destination site server.

3. Ensure that you have Create permission for the site security object class to perform the installation procedure.

Demonstration: How to Install a Secondary Site and Verify Installation

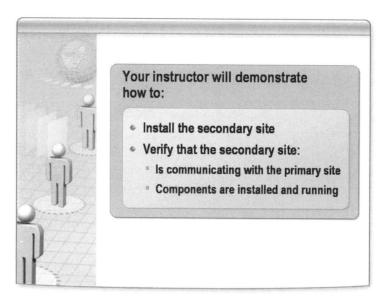

In this demonstration, your instructor will show you how to install a secondary site, verify that the secondary site has been successfully installed, verify that it is communicating with the primary site, and verify that its components are installed and running.

Your instructor will use the following values in this demonstration.

Variable	Value
Virtual machine—SMS Site 1	Dublin
Dublin Administrator	JaePa (Jae Pak)
Virtual machine—domain controller	Glasgow
Domain administrator	Administrator
Virtual machine—SMS Site 2	Paris
Paris Administrator	DonHa (Don Hall)

Important   These steps are included for your information. Do not attempt to perform them in the classroom. If you perform these steps in the classroom environment, you might leave your computer in an incorrect state for upcoming practices.

Demonstration steps performed by instructor only

▶ **To install a secondary site**

1. Verify that the Glasgow, Dublin, and Paris virtual machines are running.

2. On the Paris virtual machine, click **Start**, and then click **Windows Explorer**.

3. In the Windows Explorer tree hierarchy, expand **My Computer**, expand **Local Disk [C:]**, expand **2596**, and then click **SMS**.

4. Double-click **autorun.exe**.

5. In the **Systems Management Server 2003 Setup** dialog box, click the **SMS 2003** icon.

   The Systems Management Server Setup Wizard appears.

6. In the Systems Management Server Setup Wizard, click **Next**.

7. On the **System Configuration** page, click **Next**.

8. On the **Setup Options** page, click **Install an SMS secondary site**, and then click **Next**.

9. On the **Systems Management Server License Agreement** page, click **I Agree**, and then click **Next**.

10. In the **Product Registration** page, in the **Organization** box, type **Microsoft**, in the **CD Key** box, type **111 1111111**, and then click **Next**.

11. On the **SMS Site Information** page, in the **Site Code** box, type **002**, leave all the other settings at their default settings, and then click **Next**.

12. On the **SMS Security Information** page, verify that **Advanced security** is selected, and then click **Next**.

13. On the **Installation Options** page, in the **Options** box, verify that **Systems Management Server** is selected and dimmed, select the **Remote Tools** check box, and then click **Next**.

14. In the **Parent Site Information/Identification** page, in the **Parent site code** box, type **001**, in the **Parent site server name** box, type **Dublin**, leave the **Local Area Network** list at the default setting, verify that the **This computer and the parent site server are in the same Active Directory forest** check box is selected, and then click **Next**.

15. On the **Completing the Systems Management Server Setup Wizard** page, verify that all your previous options appear in the box, and then click **Finish**.

    A **Setup is evaluating your system** prompt appears briefly.

    The **SMS Setup** status dialog box appears and monitors the setup progress.

    Wait for the installation to complete. (This should take about five minutes.)

16. After the components install, the **Systems Management Server Setup Wizard** appears. Click **OK**.

17. Close all open windows.

▶ **To verify that the secondary site was successfully installed**

1. On the Dublin virtual machine, click **Start**, and then click **Windows Explorer**.

2. On the **Tools** menu, click **Map Network Drive**.

3. In the **Map Network Drive** dialog box, in the **Folder** box, type **\\PARIS\C$**, clear **Reconnect at logon**, and then click **Finish**.

   A new Windows Explorer window should open with the Paris local drive on C shown in the details pane.

   Note   If a new window does not open, use the current Windows Explorer window to navigate to the mapped drive, which should appear under My Computer as **c$ on 'Paris'**.

   ---

4. Double-click **SMSSetup.log**.

   SMSSetup.log opens in SMS Trace.

5. Verify that **SMS Setup completed successfully!** appears in the SMS Setup log.

6. Close the log and all open windows.

▶ **To verify that the secondary site is communicating with the primary site**

1. On the Dublin virtual machine, click **Start**, point to **All Programs**, point to **Systems Management Server**, and then click **SMS Administrator Console**.

2. In the console tree of the SMS Administrator console, expand **Site Database (001 – NWTRADERS)**, expand **Site Hierarchy**, click **001 – NWTRADERS**, and then press F5 to refresh the console tree.

3. In the details pane, verify that **002 – Microsoft** appears and that its state is active.

4. Leave the SMS Administrator console in its current expanded state.

▶ **To verify that the secondary site components are installed and running**

1. In the console tree, expand **Tools**, right-click **SMS Service Manager**, point to **All Tasks**, and then click **Start SMS Service Manager**.

2. In the SMS Service Manager window, on the **Site** menu, click **Connect**.

3. In the **Connect to Site** dialog box, in the **Site Server** box, type **Paris** and then click **OK**.

4. In console tree of the SMS Service Manager window, expand **002**, and then click **Components**

   The secondary site's components populate in the details pane.

5. In the details pane, right-click anywhere and then click **Select All**.

6. In the details pane, right-click anywhere and then click **Query**.

   An hourglass appears while SMS polls for the status of the components.

   Note   This process can take a minute or two.

   After the status is updated, a green arrow appears next to the components, indicating that they are active.

   All but three components will be active. The three stopped components include:

   - SMS_NETWORK_DISCOVERY
   - SMS_SITE_BACKUP
   - SMS_WINNT_SERVER_DISCOVERY_AGENT.

   It is normal for these components to be stopped at this time.

   Note   If SMS_WINNT_SERVER_DISCOVERY_AGENT is running, it will stop after the agent has completed discovery.

   ---

7. Close the SMS Service Manager window and the SMS Administrator console.

8. Leave the Glasgow, Dublin, and Paris virtual machines running because they will be used in subsequent practices.

Practice: Installing the Secondary Site

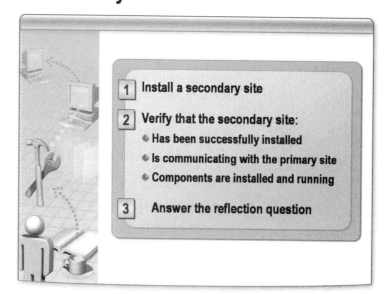

Instructions	Complete the procedures to practice installing the secondary site, and then answer the reflection questions that follow. As part of this practice, you will verify that the secondary site has been successfully installed, that it is communicating with the primary site, and that its components are installed and running.

In this practice, use the following values.

Variable	Value
Virtual machine—SMS Site 1	Dublin
Dublin Administrator	JaePa (Jae Pak)
Virtual machine—domain controller	Glasgow
Domain administrator	Administrator
Virtual machine—SMS Site 2	Paris
Paris Administrator	DonHa (Don Hall)

Procedures

▶ **To install a secondary site**

1. Verify that the Glasgow, Dublin, and Paris virtual machines are running.

2. On the Paris virtual machine, click **Start**, and then click **Windows Explorer**.

3. In the Windows Explorer tree hierarchy, expand **My Computer**, expand **Local Disk [C:]**, expand **2596**, and then click **SMS**.

4. In the details pane, double-click **autorun.exe**.

5. In the **Systems Management Server 2003 Setup** dialog box, click the **SMS 2003** icon.

   The Systems Management Server Setup Wizard appears.

6. In the Systems Management Server Setup Wizard, click **Next**.

7. On the **System Configuration** page, click **Next**.

8. In the **Setup Options** page, click **Install an SMS secondary site**, and then click **Next**.

9. On the **Systems Management Server License Agreement** page, click **I Agree**, and then click **Next**.

10. On the **Product Registration** page, in the **Organization** box, type **Microsoft**, in the **CD Key** box, type **111 1111111**, and then click **Next**.

11. On the **SMS Site Information** page, in the **Site Code** box, type **002**, leave all the other settings at the default settings, and then click **Next**.

12. On the **SMS Security Information** page, verify that **Advanced security** is selected, and then click **Next**.

13. On the **Installation Options** page, in the **Options** box, verify that **Systems Management Server** is selected and dimmed, select the **Remote Tools** check box, and then click **Next**.

14. On the **Parent Site Information/Identification** page, in the **Parent site code** box, type **001**, in the **Parent site server name** box, type **Dublin**, leave the **Local Area Network** list at the default setting, verify that the **This computer and the parent site server are in the same Active Directory forest** check box is selected, and then click **Next**.

15. On the **Completing the Systems Management Server Setup Wizard** page, verify that all your previous options appear in the box, and then click **Finish**.

    A **Setup is evaluating your system** prompt appears briefly.

16. The **SMS Setup** status dialog box appears and monitors the setup progress.

    Wait for the installation to complete. (This should take about five minutes.)

17. After the components install, the Systems Management Server Setup Wizard appears. Click **OK**.

    The Systems Management Server Setup Wizard closes, and Windows Explorer appears.

18. Close all open windows.

▶ **To verify that the secondary site has been successfully installed**

1. On the Dublin virtual machine, click **Start**, and then click **Windows Explorer**.

2. On the **Tools** menu, click **Map Network Drive**.

3. In the **Map Network Drive** dialog box, in the **Folder** box, type \\PARIS\C$, clear **Reconnect at logon**, and then click **Finish**.

   A new Windows Explorer window should open with the Paris local drive on C shown in the details pane.

   Note   If a new window does not open, use the current Windows Explorer window to navigate to the mapped drive, which should appear under My Computer as **c$ on 'Paris'**.

   ---

4. Double-click **SMSSetup.log**.

   SMSSetup.log opens in SMS Trace.

5. Verify that **SMS Setup completed successfully!** appears in the SMS Setup log.

6. Close the log and all open windows.

▶ **To verify that the secondary site is communicating with the primary site**

1. On the Dublin virtual machine, Click **Start**, point to **All Programs**, point to **Systems Management Server**, and then click **SMS Administrator Console**.

2. In the console tree of the SMS Administrator console, expand **Site Database (001 – NWTRADERS)**, expand **Site Hierarchy**, click **001 – NWTRADERS**, and then press F5 to refresh the console tree.

3. In the details pane, verify that **002 – Microsoft** appears and that its state is active.

4. Leave the SMS Administrator console open and in its current expanded state.

▶ **To verify that the secondary site components are installed and running**

1. In the console tree of the SMS Administrator console, expand **Tools**, right-click **SMS Service Manager**, point to **All Tasks**, and then click **Start SMS Service Manager**.

2. In the SMS Service Manager window, on the **Site** menu, click **Connect**.

3. In the **Connect to Site** dialog box, in the **Site Server** box, type **Paris** and then click **OK**.

4. In console tree of the SMS Service Manager window, expand **002**, and then click **Components**.

   The secondary site's components populate in the details pane.

5. In the details pane, right-click anywhere and then click **Select All**.

6. In the details pane, right-click anywhere and then click **Query**.

   An hourglass appears while SMS polls for the status of the components.

Note This process can take a minute or two.

After the status is updated, a green arrow appears next to the components, indicating that they are active.

All but three components will be active. The three stopped components include:

- SMS_NETWORK_DISCOVERY

- SMS_SITE_BACKUP

- SMS_WINNT_SERVER_DISCOVERY_AGENT.

It is normal for these components to be stopped at this time.

Note If SMS_WINNT_SERVER_DISCOVERY_AGENT is running, it will stop after the agent has completed discovery.

---

7. Close the SMS Service Manager window.

8. Leave the Glasgow, Dublin, and Paris virtual machines running because they will be used in subsequent practices.

Reflection questions

1. Can a secondary site in advanced security mode report to a primary site in standard security mode?

   _____

2. If a secondary site is installed in advanced security mode, does the secondary site become an Advanced Client by default?

   _____

3. You have just installed a secondary site with advanced security by using the Secondary Site Creation Wizard to install the site from a compact disc at the secondary site server. The senders have been defined at the parent and secondary sites to configure site-to-site communication. However, no data from the secondary site is arriving at the parent site. What are some likely reasons?

   _____

   _____

   _____

   _____

Lesson: Managing Roaming Clients in an SMS Hierarchy

- What Are Roaming Boundaries?
- The Difference Between Local Roaming Boundaries and Remote Roaming Boundaries
- The Difference Between Regional Roaming and Global Roaming
- What Is a Resident Management Point?
- What Is a Protected Distribution Point?
- Multimedia: Roaming in SMS 2003
- Demonstration: How to Configure Protected Distribution Points and Proxy Management Points

Introduction

In this lesson, you will learn about the types of roaming supported in an SMS hierarchy. You will also learn how the distribution of software depends on roaming boundaries and protected distribution points, if they are present.

Lesson objectives

After completing this lesson, you will be able to:

- Describe roaming boundaries.
- Distinguish between local roaming boundaries and remote roaming boundaries.
- Distinguish between regional roaming and global roaming.
- Describe resident management points.
- Describe protected distribution points.
- Describe roaming in SMS 2003 after watching a multimedia presentation.
- Configure protected distribution points and proxy management points.

What Are Roaming Boundaries?

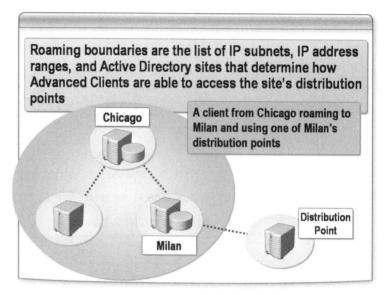

Roaming is the ability to move a computer running the SMS Advanced Client from one IP subnet or Active Directory site to another. Roaming always involves an IP address change on the client.

By using roaming boundaries, an SMS Advanced Client computer can move from one location to another in the organization and still be managed by SMS. Even when a client computer roams, it might need to receive software packages from SMS. Roaming boundaries enable SMS to provide software distribution to roaming Advanced Clients. Roaming boundaries are also used to configure protected distribution points. Access to a protected distribution point is restricted to only Advanced Clients that are in a specified set of boundaries configured by the SMS administrator.

Example

An example of roaming is when you remove a laptop computer from its network connection at work and plug it into a dial-up connection (or other Internet service provider connection) in your home or elsewhere.

Another example of roaming is when a user goes on a business trip to a different location in the organization, such as visiting a regional office.

Important Do not configure roaming boundaries to overlap in multiple SMS sites. If an Advanced Client is within the roaming boundaries of more than one SMS site, the client might not communicate with the correct site. If a client roams to a location that has no roaming boundaries defined, that client reverts to its assigned site's management point and distribution point. In this scenario, the client treats the distribution point as a remote distribution point.

How Advanced Clients are assigned to sites

Advanced Clients configured for auto-assignment are assigned to SMS sites based on the site's roaming boundary configuration. You can also manually assign the Advanced Client to an SMS site, regardless of boundaries.

The Difference Between Local Roaming Boundaries and Remote Roaming Boundaries

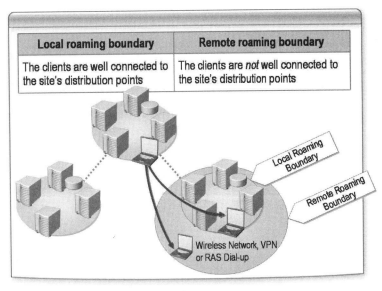

Local roaming boundary	Remote roaming boundary
The clients are well connected to the site's distribution points	The clients are *not* well connected to the site's distribution points

Local Roaming Boundary

Remote Roaming Boundary

Wireless Network, VPN or RAS Dial-up

Roaming boundaries are the list of IP subnets, IP address ranges, and Microsoft Active Directory® directory service sites that determine how roaming Advanced Clients access the site's distribution points. By default, SMS site boundaries are also configured as local roaming boundaries.

When configuring roaming boundaries, the SMS administrator specifies whether a roaming boundary is a local roaming boundary or a remote roaming boundary. This determines whether the Advanced Client treats distribution points in the site as being locally available for each roaming boundary that is configured. For example, you might want SMS clients in local roaming boundaries to run a package installation program over the network. In remote roaming boundaries, you might want SMS clients to download SMS packages before installing them.

The terms *local* and *remote* are designed to be used by the SMS administrator to label network segments as well-connected or not well-connected, respectively. If you define the roaming boundaries in this way, the following definitions apply.

What is a local roaming boundary?

A *local roaming boundary* is a roaming boundary in which the site distribution points are locally available to the Advanced Client and software packages are available to that client over a well-connected link. Advertisements sent to Advanced Clients specify whether the Advanced Client downloads the package source files from the locally available distribution point before running the program or runs the program directly from the distribution point.

What is a remote roaming boundary?

A *remote roaming boundary* is a roaming boundary in which the site distribution points are not well connected to the Advanced Client. Advertisements sent to Advanced Clients specify whether the client downloads the software program from a remote distribution point before running it, runs the package from a remote distribution point, or does nothing and waits until a distribution point becomes available locally.

Note   A distribution point in remote roaming boundaries is not considered to be locally available to the client. In other words, the distribution point is a remote distribution point. If you configure your remote roaming boundaries to include network segments that are not well connected to the SMS site, the distribution point is truly remote to the Advanced Client in physical proximity.

A client can roam to a nearby site and still be within the remote roaming boundaries of that site. In this case, the client treats the distribution points of that site as remote distribution points. Although the client is using the closest physically located distribution points, it does not treat them as locally available distribution points.

How roaming clients access distribution points

If Background Intelligent Transfer Service (BITS) is enabled on the distribution point, clients download programs in a throttled manner and use checkpoint restart to automatically recover from network communication errors. If BITS is not enabled on the distribution point, SMS clients download packages directly using server message block (SMB). Clients also use SMB to run programs directly from the distribution point.

If the Advanced Client is not located within any roaming boundaries, it connects to the default management point at its assigned site to retrieve Advanced Client policy. In this case, the client is still able to access package files, but it receives them from a remote distribution point, using BITS to download packages efficiently. Or, if the distribution points of the site are considered remote to the client's location, but a BITS-enabled distribution point cannot be located, the package files are downloaded using SMB.

The Difference Between Regional Roaming and Global Roaming

Global roaming	Regional roaming
The Advanced Client can roam to parent or sibling sites	The Advanced Client can only roam to child sites

What is regional roaming?

If Active Directory is not available, or if the Active Directory schema for SMS is not extended, Advanced Clients can roam only to the lower-level sites of their assigned site. This is called *regional roaming*. In regional roaming, the Advanced Client can roam to child sites and still receive software packages from distribution points from their assigned site or the roamed child site.

When an advertisement is sent to the Advanced Client, the client receives information about the advertised package location from its assigned management point if the SMS data was published in Active Directory. If the SMS data was not published in Active Directory, then the information concerning the advertised package is pulled from the assigned site. Or, if the client has roamed into a secondary site, it receives information about the advertised package location from a proxy management point, if one is available. The client then uses the distribution points of one of its assigned site's lower-level sites. Which distribution point it uses depends on which roaming boundary the client is in and whether the advertised package is available on the distribution point.

What is global roaming?

Global roaming allows the Advanced Client to roam to higher-level sites, sibling sites, and sites in other branches of the SMS hierarchy and potentially receive software packages from distribution points if the advertisement was created at a common higher-level site in the hierarchy. Global roaming requires Active Directory and the SMS Active Directory schema extensions. Global roaming cannot be performed across Active Directory forests.

What Is a Resident Management Point?

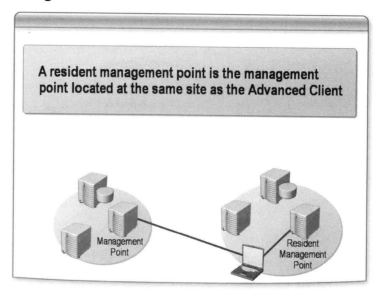

A resident management point is the management point located at the same site as the Advanced Client

A *resident management point* is the management point located at the site to which the Advanced Client roamed. It can be the assigned management point; that is, the management point of the site the client is assigned to when the client is at that location. Or, if the client has roamed to another location with a management point, the resident management point is the management point at the location that the client uses. Furthermore, it can be a management point at a primary site or a proxy management point, too, depending on what type of site the client has roamed to.

What Is a Protected Distribution Point?

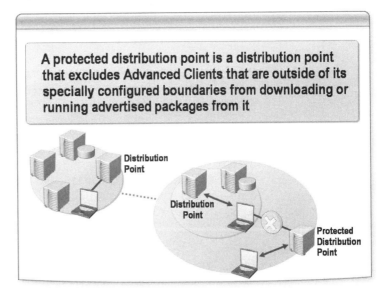

A protected distribution point is a distribution point that excludes Advanced Clients that are outside of its specially configured boundaries from downloading or running advertised packages from it

A *protected distribution point* is a distribution point that excludes Advanced Clients that are outside of its specially configured boundaries from downloading or running advertised packages from it.

If configured properly, protected distribution points ensure that Advanced Clients that are well connected to an SMS site do not access package source files from a distribution point located across a WAN link.

The protected distribution point provides bandwidth protection for package run and package download only. It does not prevent the Advanced Client from communicating with its assigned management point in the absence of a proxy management point for inventory data, status messages, and Advanced Client policy requests.

How Advanced Clients find distribution points

For local roaming only, Advanced Clients by default choose a distribution point from the list of available distribution points provided by the resident management point when making package source file requests. The Advanced Clients sort the list of distribution points returned by local IP subnet, then by the local AD site, then by the local SMS site. The Advanced Client then looks for a distribution point on the same subnet, then in the same Active Directory site, and lastly in the roamed SMS site. If there are multiple distribution points in the subnet, the Advanced Client randomly selects one. This is the same for both the Active Directory and the SMS site.

To restrict access to a distribution point that is across a slow or unreliable network link, enable it as a protected distribution point. By doing so, Advanced Clients that are outside of the protected distribution point's specially configured boundaries will not attempt to download or run software packages from the protected distribution point. This is beneficial at remote locations where a small number of SMS clients and a distribution point are connected to the primary site by a WAN.

How management points handle client requests

The client sends a package source file content location request, for example, to download or run a package program, to its resident management point. Depending on the client location the management point will handle the request in one of two ways.

IF	THEN
the client is **within** a set of boundaries that are configured for a protected distribution point,	the management point provides the client with a list of protected distribution point locations that contain the requested package source files

IF	THEN
the client is **outside** of the boundaries configured for a protected distribution point,	the management point does not provide the protected distribution point to the client as a content location

Multimedia: Roaming in SMS 2003

Roaming in SMS 2003

Instructions

This animation illustrates the concepts involved in roaming in SMS 2003:

1. Read the following questions before you watch the animation.

2. Watch the animation with the purpose of finding answers to the questions.

3. Discuss the answers to the questions with the class after the animation is complete.

Discussion questions

SMS Site and Roaming Boundaries

1. How are Advanced Clients assigned to an SMS site?

   _____

   _____

2. Why would an SMS administrator create roaming boundaries?

   _____

   _____

Advanced Clients and Management Points

1. How do SMS Advanced Clients interact with resident management points?

    _____

    _____

2. What is the difference between an assigned management point and a proxy management point and why would you configure a proxy management point?

    _____

    _____

3. How do SMS Advanced Clients interact with proxy management points?

    _____

    _____

Local Roaming Boundaries and Remote Roaming Boundaries

What is the difference between a local roaming boundary and a remote roaming boundary?

_____

_____

Advanced Clients, Advertisements, and Distribution Points

What are the ways that an advertisement can determine how the Advanced Clients download packages?

_____

_____

"BITS-Enabled"

What is the advantage of a BITS-enabled distribution point?

_____

_____

"Advertisement Properties"

1. How do SMS administrators configure advertisements to change package processing for Advanced Clients connected to remote roaming boundaries?

    _____

    _____

2. If an Advanced Client is located in a remote roaming boundary how does it receive packages?

    _____

    _____

Global and Regional Roaming

1. What is global roaming vs. regional roaming?

    _____

    _____

2. How does extending Active Directory schema affect Advanced Clients capability to roam in the site hierarchy?

    _____

    _____

Demonstration: How to Configure Protected Distribution Points and Proxy Management Points

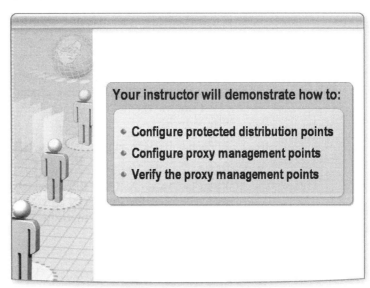

In this demonstration, your instructor will show you how to configure protected distribution points, configure proxy management points, and verify the proxy management points.

Your instructor will use the following values in this demonstration.

Variable	Value
Virtual machine—SMS Site 1	Dublin
Dublin Administrator	JaePa (Jae Pak)
Virtual machine—domain controller	Glasgow
Domain administrator	Administrator
Virtual machine—SMS Site 2	Paris
Paris Administrator	DonHa (Don Hall)

Important These steps are included for your information. Do not attempt to perform them in the classroom. If you perform these steps in the classroom environment, you might leave your computer in an incorrect state for upcoming practices.

Demonstration steps performed by instructor only

▶ **To configure protected distribution points from the SMS Administrator console**

1. Verify that the Glasgow, Dublin, and Paris virtual machines are running.

2. On the Dublin virtual machine, click **Start**, point to **All Programs**, point to **Systems Management Server**, and then click **SMS Administrator Console**.

3. In the console tree of the SMS Administrator console, expand **Site Database (001 – NWTraders)**, expand **Site Hierarchy**, expand **001 – NWTraders**, expand **002 – Microsoft**, expand **Site Settings**, and then click **Site Systems**.

4. In the details pane, right-click **\\PARIS**, and then click **Properties**.

5. In the **\\PARIS Site System Properties** dialog box, on the **Distribution Point** tab, verify that **Use this site system as a distribution point** is selected, select the **Enable as a protected distribution point** check box, and then click **Configure boundaries**.

6. In the **Boundaries** dialog box, click **New** ⁂ .

7. In the **New Boundaries** dialog box, in the ID column, verify that the default **IP Subnet** is selected, and then click **OK**.

8. In the **Boundaries** dialog box, click **OK**.

9. Leave the **\\PARIS Site System Properties** dialog box open.

▶ **To configure proxy management points**

1. In the **\\PARIS Site System Properties** dialog box, on the **Management Point** tab, select the **Use this site system as a management point** check box.

2. An **SMS Management Point** message appears to warn you that the SMS Administrator console might become unresponsive and might have to be closed and reopened. Click **OK**.

3. In the **Database** list, verify that **Use the parent site database** is selected.

4. Click **OK**.

5. In the **\\PARIS Site System** message box, click **Yes** to make this site system the default management point.

Practice: Configuring Roaming Boundaries to Allow an Advanced Client at a Secondary Site to Download Software

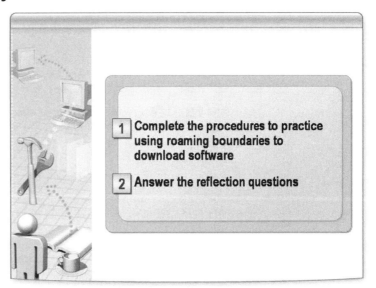

Instructions

Read the scenario, complete the procedures to practice using roaming boundaries to download software, and then answer the reflection questions that follow.

As part of this practice, you will reconfigure the site boundaries for the primary site and the secondary site and enable BITS. Next, you will add a secondary site as an available distribution point for an existing package and enable the Advertised Programs Client Agent to be installed in the secondary site. You will then install the Advanced Client on the secondary site and run the advertised program on the Advanced Client.

In this practice, use the following values.

Variable	Value
Virtual machine—SMS Site 1	Dublin
Dublin Administrator	JaePa (Jae Pak)
Virtual machine—domain controller	Glasgow
Domain administrator	Administrator
Virtual machine—SMS Site 2	Paris
Paris Administrator	DonHa (Don Hall)

Procedures

▶ **To reconfigure the site boundaries for the primary site**

1. Verify that the Glasgow, Dublin, and Paris virtual machines are running.

2. On the Dublin virtual machine, click **Start**, point to **All Programs**, point to **Systems Management Server**, and then click **SMS Administrator Console**.

3. In the console tree of the SMS Administrator console, expand **Site Database (001 – NWTraders)**, expand **Site Hierarchy**, right-click **001 – NWTraders**, and then click **Properties**.

4. In the **001 – NWTraders Site Properties** dialog box, on the **Roaming Boundaries** tab, clear the **Includes site boundaries within the local roaming boundaries of this site** check box.

5. To add a roaming boundary, click **New** .

6. In the **New Roaming Boundary** dialog box, in the **Boundary type** list, select **IP address range**.

7. In the **Starting IP address** box, type **192.168.0.1**

8. In the **Ending IP address** box, type **192.168.0.10**

9. Verify that **Designate this boundary as a local roaming boundary** is selected, then click **OK** twice.

10. Leave the SMS Administrator console open.

▶ **To reconfigure the site boundaries for the secondary site**

1. In the details pane of the SMS Administrator console, expand **Site Database (001 – NWTraders)**, expand **Site Hierarchy**, expand **001 – NWTraders**, right-click **002 – Microsoft**, and then click **Properties**.

2. In the **002 – Microsoft Site Properties** dialog box, click the **Roaming Boundaries** tab.

3. Clear the **Include site boundaries within the local roaming boundaries of this site** check box.

4. Click **New** .

5. In the **New Roaming Boundary** dialog box, in the **Boundary type** list, select **IP address range**.

6. In the **Starting IP address** box, type **192.168.0.11**

7. In the **Ending IP address** box, type **192.168.0.20**

8. Verify that **Designate this boundary as a local roaming boundary** is selected, and click **OK** twice.

9. Leave the SMS Administrator console open.

▶ **To configure proxy management points**

1. In the console tree, expand **Site Database (001 – NWTraders)**, expand **Site Hierarchy**, expand **001 – NWTraders**, expand **002 – Microsoft**, expand **Site Settings**, and then click **Site Systems**.

2. In the details pane, right-click **\\PARIS**, and then click **Properties**.

3. In the **\\PARIS Site System Properties** dialog box, on the **Management Point** tab, select the **Use this site system as a management point** check box.

4. An **SMS Management Point** message appears to warn you that the SMS Administrator console might become unresponsive and might have to be closed and reopened. Click **OK**.

5. In the **Database** list, verify **Use the parent site database** is selected.

6. Click **OK**.

7. In the **\\PARIS Site System** message, click **Yes** to make this site system the default management point.

8. Click **OK**.

9. Leave the SMS Administrator console open.

▶ **To enable BITS on the distribution point**

1. In the details pane, right-click **\\PARIS**, and then click **Properties**.

2. In the **\\PARIS Site System Properties** dialog box, on the **Distribution Point** tab, select the **Enable Background Intelligent Transfer Service [BITS]** check box, and then click **OK**.

3. Leave the SMS Administrator console open.

▶ **To add a secondary site as an available distribution point for an existing package**

1. In the console tree of the SMS Administrator console, expand **Site Database (001 – NWTraders)**, expand **Packages**, expand **Sales Computers PowerPoint 2003 Viewer**, right-click **Distribution Points**, point to **New**, and then click **Distribution Points**.

2. In the New Distribution Points Wizard, click **Next**.

3. On the **Copy Package** page, in the **Distribution points** box, select the **Paris** check box, and then click **Finish**.

4. Leave the SMS Administrator console open.

▶ **To install the Advanced Client on the secondary site server**

1. In the console tree of the SMS Administrator console, expand **Site Database (001 – NWTraders)**, expand **Collections**, and then click **All Systems**.

2. In the details pane, right-click **PARIS**, point to **All Tasks**, and then click **Install Client**.

3. In the Client Push Installation Wizard, click **Next**.

4. On the **Installation options** page, click **Advanced Client**, and then click **Next**.

5. On the **Client Installation Options** page, clear the **Include only clients assigned to this site** check box, and then click **Next**.

6. On the **Completing the Client Push Installation Wizard** page, review the installation details, and then click **Finish**.

7. Leave the SMS Administrator console open.

Important   Before continuing to the next procedure, wait for 5 to 10 minutes for the secondary site settings to take effect and for the Advanced Client installation to complete.

▶ **To verify that the client is a member of the All Systems collection**

1. In the console tree of the SMS Administrator console, expand **Site Database (001 – NWTraders)**, expand **Collections**, and then click **Sales Computers**.

2. Right-click **Sales Computers**, point to **All Tasks**, and then click **Update Collection Membership**.

3. In the **Sales Computers** warning box, click **OK**.

4. Press F5 to refresh the console tree.

5. In the details pane, verify that **PARIS** is a client and is assigned.

6. Close the SMS Administrator console.

▶ **To force policy retrieval from the client**

1. On the Paris virtual machine, click **Start**, point to **Control Panel**, and then click **Systems Management**.

2. On the **Actions** tab, click **Machine Policy Retrieval & Evaluation Cycle**, and then click **Initiate Action**.

3. On the **Machine Policy Retrieval & Evaluation Cycle** message box, click **OK**.

4. Click **OK** to close the **Systems Management Properties** window.

Note   You might need to wait a few minutes before proceeding to the next procedure.

▶ **To run the advertised program on the Advanced Client**

1. Verify that the Paris virtual machine is running.

2. On the Paris virtual machine, the **New Program Available** icon will automatically appear in the System Tray, along with the **New Program Available** update balloon.

3. Double-click the **New Program Available** icon or balloon.

    The **Add or Remove Programs** window will open.

4. Click the advertised program, and then click **Add**.

Note   If you receive a **Cannot Run Program** error because SMS is busy, wait a minute, and then try to **Add** the program again.

---

5. The **Program Download Required** window appears. Select the **Run program automatically when download completes** check box, and then click **Download**.

6. Follow the normal software installation procedures.

7. After the program installs successfully, close the **Add or Remove Programs** window.

8. On the Paris virtual machine, on the **Action** menu, click **Close**.

9. Verify that **Save state and save changes** is selected in the drop-down list, and then click **OK**.

   The Paris virtual machine begins to shut down.

10. Leave the Glasgow and Dublin virtual machines running.

Reflection questions

1. Why would an SMS administrator want to implement protected distribution points?

   _____

   _____

   _____

2. How does a proxy management point differ from an assigned management point?

   _____

   _____

   _____

Discussion: Working with SMS Hierarchies

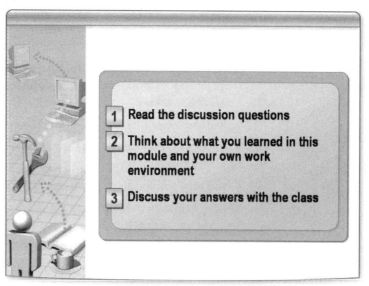

1. You have an SMS primary site, and you want to add a child site. However, the connection between the primary site location and the child site location is open only from midnight to 6 A.M., except for high-priority communication. How can you manage SMS site-to-site communication in this environment?

   _____

   _____

   _____

2. You suspect that a secondary site is not receiving data from its primary site. How can you verify this? What are the possible causes of the problem?

   _____

   _____

   _____

3. An SMS client has roamed to a secondary site that has a proxy management point and a distribution point. However, the client is not able to download a particular software distribution program. What are some possible causes of the problem?

_____

_____

_____

Module 12: Performing Site Maintenance, Backup, and Recovery Tasks

Contents

Overview

- Performing Site Maintenance
- Performing an SMS Site Backup
- Recovering an SMS Site

Introduction

In this module, you will learn how to perform site maintenance tasks and prepare for Microsoft® Systems Management Server (SMS) backup and recovery operations.

Planning is essential so that you can recover SMS sites and hierarchies quickly with the least possible amount of data loss.

Objectives

After completing this module, you will be able to:

- Perform site maintenance.
- Perform an SMS site backup.
- Recover an SMS site.

Lesson: Performing Site Maintenance

- **The Most Commonly Used Predefined Site Maintenance Tasks**
- **Predefined Maintenance Tasks Associated with Client Data**
- **How to Configure Predefined Site Maintenance Tasks**
- **How to Create a Customized SQL Command**

In this lesson, you will learn how to perform site maintenance tasks by using the SMS Administrator console.

Lesson objectives

After completing this lesson, you will be able to:

- Describe the most commonly used predefined site maintenance tasks.
- Describe the predefined maintenance tasks that are associated with client data.
- Describe how to configure predefined maintenance tasks.
- Create a customized SQL command.

The Most Commonly Used Predefined Site Maintenance Tasks

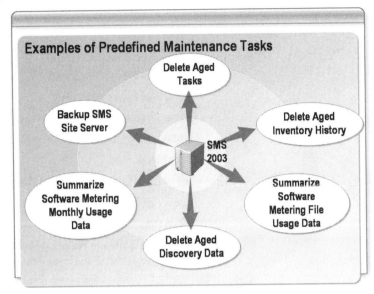

SMS 2003 has built-in or predefined maintenance tasks that target the SMS site database and help to maintain its performance. You schedule these tasks to continually remove orphaned and out-of-date data. Reducing the size of the database by removing unnecessary data improves the performance and the integrity of the database, increasing the efficiency of the site.

Common predefined tasks

Of the 13 predefined maintenance tasks, the most commonly used tasks are:

- Backup SMS Site Server
- Delete Aged Discovery Data
- Summarize Data on Software Metering File Usage
- Summarize Data on Monthly Usage of Software Metering
- Delete Aged Tasks
- Delete Aged Inventory History

Benefits of the Backup SMS Site Server task

The Backup SMS Site Server task is a vital maintenance tasks in SMS because it backs up an SMS site, including the SMS site database, SMS files, registry keys, and system configuration information. Backing up your site is essential for site recovery if your site fails. More information concerning backup of an SMS site will be discussed later in this module.

Note For more information about all the predefined maintenance tasks, see Chapter 13, "Maintaining and Monitoring SMS Systems," in *Microsoft Systems Management Server 2003 Operations Guide* on the Additional Reading page of your Student Materials compact disc.

Predefined Maintenance Tasks Associated with Client Data

Predefined Maintenance Tasks Relating to Client Data

- Delete Aged Inventory History
- Delete Aged Discovery Data
- Delete Aged Collected Files
- Delete Inactive Client Discovery Data
- Clear Install Flag
- Delete Aged Software Metering Data
- Delete Aged Software Metering Summary Data
- Summarize Software Metering File Usage Data
- Summarize Software Metering Monthly Usage Data

Nine of the13 predefined maintenance tasks relate to client data. These are important to know because client data, specifically software metering, constitutes the greatest amount of information stored on the site database. If these tasks are not configured and scheduled properly, your database might run out of disk space, unless you set it to autogrow. In that case, your database could grow to an extremely large size.

The maintenance tasks relating to client data are included in the following table.

Maintenance Task	Function
Delete Aged Inventory History	Deletes from the SMS site database all hardware inventory history data older than the number of days specified in the task properties dialog box.
Delete Aged Discovery Data	Deletes from the SMS site database all data associated with resources that are no longer considered part of the SMS hierarchy.
Delete Aged Collected Files	Use this task to remove orphaned software inventory records that are older than the number of days that have been specified, and to delete collected files that are older than the number of days specified in the task properties dialog box.
Delete Inactive Client Discovery Data	Deletes all client records that have not received heartbeat discovery records in a specified number of days.
Clear Install Flag	Use the Clear Install Flag task to flag uninstalled clients as uninstalled after a specified number of days, thus allowing them to be reinstalled by the Client Push Installation method.
Delete Aged Software Metering Data	Use this task to remove aged software metering data after a specified number of days, and to conserve space in the SMS site database.

(continued)

Maintenance Task	Function
Delete Aged Software Metering Summary Data	Use this task to remove aged software metering data after a specified number of days, and to conserve space in the SMS site database.
Summarize Software Metering File Usage Data	Use this task and other software metering maintenance tasks to summarize software metering data for reporting, and to conserve space in the SMS site database.
Summarize Software Metering Monthly Usage Data	Use this task and other software metering maintenance tasks to summarize software metering data for reporting, and to conserve space in the SMS site database.

How to Configure Predefined Site Maintenance Tasks

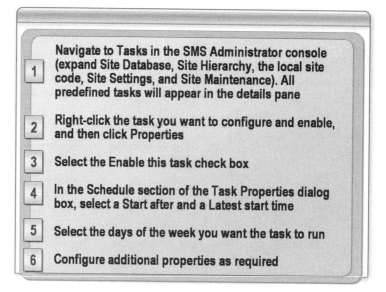

1 Navigate to Tasks in the SMS Administrator console (expand Site Database, Site Hierarchy, the local site code, Site Settings, and Site Maintenance). All predefined tasks will appear in the details pane

2 Right-click the task you want to configure and enable, and then click Properties

3 Select the Enable this task check box

4 In the Schedule section of the Task Properties dialog box, select a Start after and a Latest start time

5 Select the days of the week you want the task to run

6 Configure additional properties as required

Configuring the predefined site maintenance tasks is done from the SMS Administrator console.

Procedure

To configure a predefined site maintenance task:

1. Navigate to **Tasks** in the SMS Administrator console (expand **Site Database**, **Site Hierarchy**, the **local site code**, **Site Settings**, and **Site Maintenance**). All predefined tasks will appear in the details pane.

2. Right-click the task you want to configure and enable, and then click **Properties**.

3. Select the **Enable this task** check box.

4. In the **Schedule** section of the **Task Properties** dialog box, select a **Start after** and a **Latest start time**.

5. Select the days of the week you want the task to run.

6. Configure additional properties as required.

Note   Some tasks, such as Delete Aged Software Metering Data, have an additional property that you will need to configure. This property will be either **Delete data older than, Backup destination, or Client rediscovery period.**

How to Create a Customized SQL Command

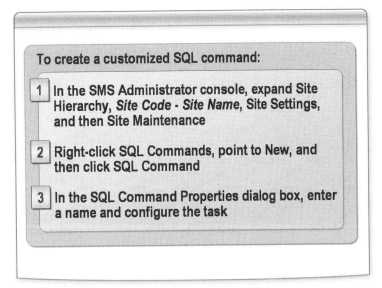

To create a customized SQL command:

1. In the SMS Administrator console, expand Site Hierarchy, *Site Code - Site Name*, Site Settings, and then Site Maintenance

2. Right-click SQL Commands, point to New, and then click SQL Command

3. In the SQL Command Properties dialog box, enter a name and configure the task

In addition to the predefined maintenance tasks, you can use SMS to create customized tasks by using SQL commands. If you are familiar with databases and SQL commands and want to run a maintenance task that is not in the list of predefined tasks, you can do so by writing a valid SQL command.

SQL commands run directly against the SMS site database. Any command that you can run in SQL Query Analyzer is a valid SQL command.

Important   Customized SQL commands are very powerful because they directly manipulate the SMS site database. Improper SQL commands can corrupt the SMS site database.

Procedure

To create a customized SQL command:

1. In the SMS Administrator console, navigate to **SQL Commands** by expanding **Site Hierarchy**, *Site Code - Site Name*, **Site Settings**, and then **Site Maintenance**.

2. Right-click **SQL Commands**, point to **New**, and then click **SQL Command**.

3. In the **SQL Command Properties** dialog box, enter a name and configure the task:

   • Specify an SQL command. You can specify either a single-line (255-character) SQL command or the name of a stored procedure that contains multiple SQL commands.

   • Specify a log file name if you want to review the results after the SQL command runs.

   • Specify a schedule for the SQL command.

Detailed steps about how to create a customized SQL command are included in the practice at the end of this lesson.

Note Before you schedule a customized SQL command, ensure that the SQL command is valid by testing it in SQL Query Analyzer.

Helpful SQL commands

The following table shows some SQL commands that might be helpful for customizing maintenance tasks.

SQL command	Function
DBCC (Database Consistency Checker)	Checks the integrity of the SMS site database
xp_sqlmaint	Runs database maintenance tasks
sp_who	Determines the number of Microsoft SQL Server™ connections currently in use by SMS or by other processes
sp_spaceused	Displays the number of rows, the disk space reserved, and the disk space used by a table in the current database, or displays disk space reserved and used by the entire database
sp_monitor	Displays SQL Server activities and statistics

Practice: Creating a Customized SQL Command

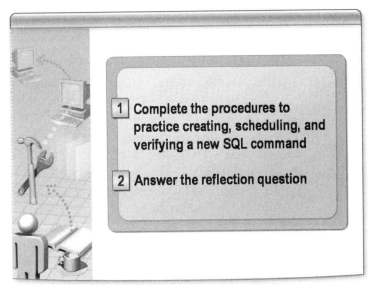

1 Complete the procedures to practice creating, scheduling, and verifying a new SQL command

2 Answer the reflection question

Instructions

Complete the procedures to practice creating, scheduling, and verifying a new SQL command, and then complete the reflection question that follows.

In this practice, use the following values.

Variable	Value
Virtual machine—SMS Site 1	Dublin
Dublin Administrator	JaePa (Jae Pak)
Virtual machine—domain controller	Glasgow
Domain administrator	Administrator

Procedures

▶ **To create a SQL command and schedule it**

1. Verify that the Glasgow virtual machine is running. If the Glasgow virtual machine is not running, log it on to the NWTRADERS domain with a user name of **Administrator** and a password of **P@ssw0rd**.

   After the Glasgow virtual machine opens, you can minimize it.

2. Verify that the Dublin virtual machine is running. If the Dublin virtual machine is not running, log it on to the NWTRADERS domain with a user name of **JaePa** and a password of **P@ssw0rd**.

3. On the Dublin virtual machine, click **Start**, point to **All Programs**, point to **Systems Management Server**, and then click **SMS Administrator Console**.

4. In the SMS Administrator console, expand **Site Database (001 – NWTraders)**, expand **Site Hierarchy**, expand **001 – NW Traders**, expand **Site Settings**, and then expand **Site Maintenance**.

5. Right-click **SQL Commands**, point to **New**, and then click **SQL Command**.

6. In the **SQL Command Properties** dialog box, in the **Name** box, type **Space Used**

7. In the **SQL command** box, type **sp_spaceused**

8. In the **Log Status To** dialog box, type **\\DUBLIN\SMS_001\Logs\SpaceUsed.log**

9. In the **Schedule** area, in the **Start after** box, enter a time that is three minutes past the current system time.

   For example, if the current system time is 2:00 P.M., set the **Start after** time to 2:03 P.M.

   Note   Refer to the system clock in the taskbar of the Dublin virtual machine to find the current system time.
   ---

10. In the **Latest start time** box, enter a time that is one hour after the **Start after** time.

    For example, if the **Start after** time is 2:03 P.M., set the **Latest start time** to 3:03 P.M.

11. Click **OK** to close the SQL Command Properties window.

12. Close the SMS Administrator console.

    Note   You might need to wait four minutes or more before you can continue with the following practice.

▶ **To verify the results of the SQL command**

1. On the Dublin virtual machine, click **Start**, point to **All Programs**, point to **SMS 2003 Toolkit 1**, and then click **SMS Trace**.

2. On the **File** menu, click **Open**.

3. In the **Open** dialog box, click **SpaceUsed.log**, and then click **Open**.

4. Click **Start**, point to **All Programs**, point to **Microsoft SQL Server**, and then click **Query Analyzer**.

5. In the **Connect to SQL Server** dialog box, in the **Connect using** box, click **Windows authentication**, and then click **OK**.

6. On the **Query** menu, click **Change Database**.

7. In the **Select Database of DUBLIN** dialog box, click **SMS_001**, and then click **OK**.

8. In the **Query** dialog box, type **exec sp_spaceused** and then, on the **Query** menu, click **Execute**.

9. In the **Query results** window, review the results of the query and compare them to those in the Spaceused.log.

10. Close the SQL Query Analyzer window.

11. A **SQL Query Analyzer** message will appear, asking whether you want to save the changes. Click **No**.

12. Close the SMS Trace window.

13. Leave the Glasgow and Dublin virtual machines running.

Reflection question

Why is the SQL command to execute the sp_spaceused stored procedure an important SMS administrative task?

_____

_____

_____

Lesson: Performing an SMS Site Backup

* How the SMS Backup Architecture Works
* Organizational Considerations for SMS Backup
* What Is the Backup Control File?
* How to Prepare for a Backup
* Demonstration: How to Review the Backup Control File
* What Is the Afterbackup.bat File?
* What Is the Backup SMS Site Server Task?
* Demonstration: How to Configure the Backup SMS Site Server Task
* Additional Tasks to Perform After a Site Backup

Introduction

In this lesson, you will learn to perform a backup of an SMS site. You will also learn about the criteria to consider when preparing for backup and recovery.

Lesson objectives

After completing this lesson, you will be able to:

- Explain how the SMS backup architecture works.
- Describe organizational considerations for SMS data backup.
- Explain the purpose of the Backup control file and how it is configured.
- Prepare for a Backup.
- Review the Backup Control file.
- Explain the purpose of the Afterbackup.bat file.
- Describe the purpose of the Backup SMS Site Server task.
- Configure the Backup SMS Site Server Task.
- Describe the additional tasks to perform after performing a site backup.

How the SMS Backup Architecture Works

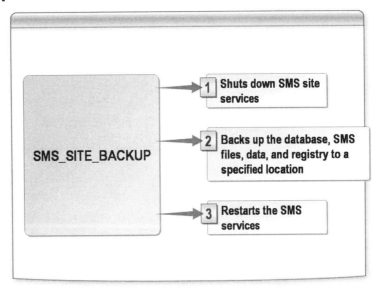

SMS backup operates in the context of the SMS_SITE_BACKUP service. All the tasks performed by the SMS_SITE_BACKUP service are specified in the Backup control file. You configure the backup control file to inform the SMS_SITE_BACKUP service what to back up and where it is to be stored.

The SMS_SITE_BACKUP service:

1. Shuts down the other site services.

2. Backs up the database, SMS files, data, and registry to a specified location.

3. Restarts the other SMS services after the backup is completed.

Organizational Considerations for SMS Backup

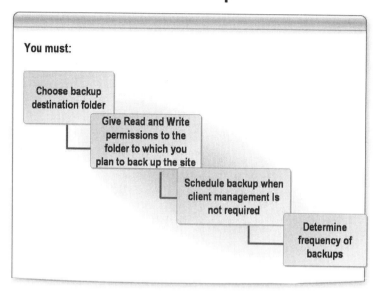

To ensure a smooth and accurate SMS backup that meets your organization's needs, you must take certain organizational needs into consideration before running the backup:

- *You must decide where to create the backup destination folder.* This can either be on the site server or on another computer. The backup operates significantly faster when the site, site database, and backup destination folder are on the same server.

- *You must give Read and Write permissions to the folder to which you plan to back up the site.* The SMS backup task runs under the SMS Service Account (in standard security) or the site server's computer account (in advanced security).

- *Because the site server is shut down, you should schedule backup to occur when the organization does not require client management.* On sites with large databases, the site might be down for a few hours. You must take into consideration the amount of time it will take to complete the backup.

- *You must decide the frequency of backups.* The more frequent your backups, the more recent the data that can be recovered if the site fails and must be recovered.

What Is the Backup Control File?

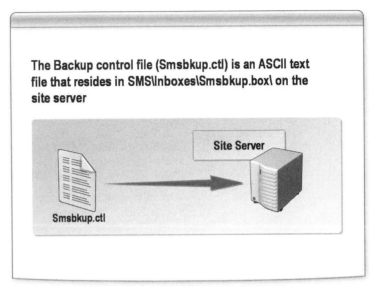

The *Backup control file*—Smsbkup.ctl—is an ASCII text file located on the site server at SMS\Inboxes\Smsbkup.box\. The Smsbkup.ctl file drives the Backup SMS Site Server task and determines what data is backed up from the site and where it is stored at the backup snapshot destination.

The Backup control file contains specific information that the backup task requires. This file contains the names of the files, registry keys, and site databases that need to be backed up. It also contains commands that run during the backup operation to gather configuration information. The Smsbkup.ctl file contains tokens that it uses during run time, such as the SITE_BACKUP_ DESTINATION token. When the backup task runs and uses the default Smsbkup.ctl file, it backs up all data necessary for recovery. You can customize this file to address specific backup needs of your site, such as to stop additional services prior to the backup and to restart them after the backup has completed.

How to Prepare for a Backup

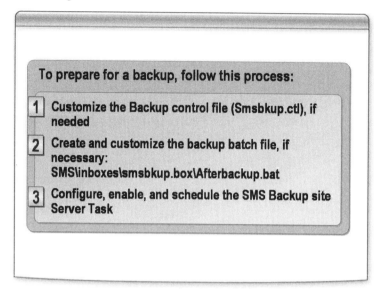

At its scheduled time, the SMS_SITE_BACKUP service starts a backup cycle. During the backup cycle, the service performs some initial steps and then backs up data from the site server. It then backs up data from the SMS site database server and from the provider server, if either is set up on a computer other than the site server.

Process

To prepare for a backup, perform the following tasks:

1. Customize the Backup control file (Smsbkup.ctl), if needed.

2. Create and customize the backup batch file (SMS\inboxes\smsbkup.box\Afterbackup.bat), if necessary.

3. Configure and schedule the SMS Backup site Server Task.

Demonstration: How to Review the Backup Control File

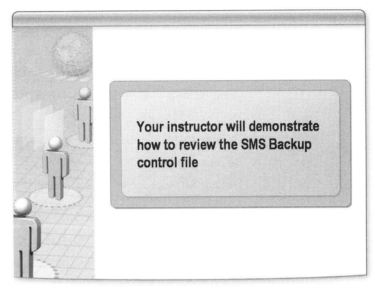

In this demonstration, your instructor will show you how to review the SMS Backup control file.

Your instructor will use the following values in this demonstration.

Variable	Value
Virtual machine—SMS Site 1	Dublin
Dublin Administrator	JaePa (Jae Pak)
Virtual machine—domain controller	Glasgow
Domain administrator	Administrator

Important These steps are included for your information. Do not attempt to perform them in the classroom. If you perform these steps in the classroom environment, you might leave your computer in an incorrect state for upcoming practices.

Demonstration steps performed by instructor only

▶ **To review the SMS Backup control file**

1. Verify that the Glasgow and Dublin virtual machines are running.

2. On the Dublin virtual machine, click **Start**, and then click **Windows Explorer**.

3. In Windows Explorer, browse to **C:\SMS\inboxes\smsbkup.box**.

4. Open the Smsbkup.ctl file in Notepad.

5. Review the Default Tokens section.

   Default Tokens define the folders where backup information is stored.

6. Review the Default Services section.

   Default Services shows the services that the Backup SMS Site server task stops by default. The Editing Allowed section enables you to customize the file to perform tasks after the SMS site services have been stopped.

7. Review the Default File backup tasks.

   Default File backup shows the files that the Backup SMS Site server task backs up by default. The Editing Allowed section enables you to add files to be backed up.

8. Review the Default Configuration backup tasks.

   Default Configuration backup tasks section shows the configuration that the Backup SMS Site server task backs up by default. The Editing Allowed section enables you to add configuration to be backed up.

9. Review the Default Registry backup tasks.

   Default Registry backup shows the registry keys that the Backup SMS Site server task backs up by default. The Editing Allowed section enables you to add registry keys to be backed up.

10. Review the Default SQL Data backup tasks.

    Default SQL Data backup shows the SQL Data that the Backup SMS Site server task backs up by default. The Editing Allowed section enables you to add SQL Data and custom commands to be backed up.

11. Close the Smsbkup.ctl file, and then close Microsoft Windows® Explorer.

12. Leave the Glasgow and Dublin virtual machines running.

What Is the Afterbackup.bat File?

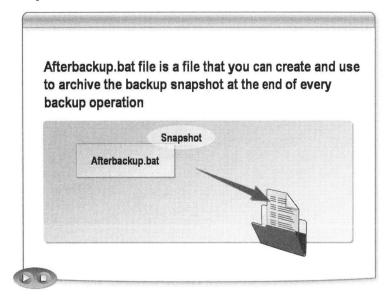

The *Afterbackup.bat* batch file is a file that you can create and use to archive the backup snapshot at the end of every backup operation. The Afterbackup.bat file does not exist by default, and therefore has no effect on the backup operation. You can create this file and add commands that run after the SMS backup task has finished.

You can use the Afterbackup.bat file to run a third-party tool that automatically archives the backup snapshot every time you back up your site. After successfully backing up the site, the SMS backup task runs the Afterbackup.bat batch file. The Afterbackup.bat file integrates the archive and the backup operations, thus ensuring that every new backup snapshot is archived.

What Is the Backup SMS Site Server Task?

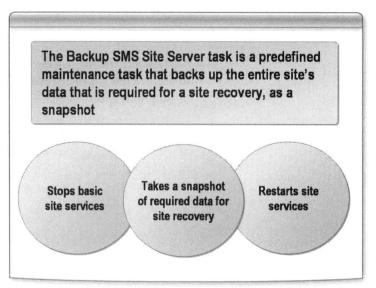

The *Backup SMS Site Server task* is one of the predefined maintenance tasks. The Backup SMS Site Server task backs up the entire site's data that is required for a site recovery, as a snapshot. This task is disabled by default. To use the task, you must configure it in the SMS Administrator console.

When the Backup SMS Site Server task backs up your site, it reads the configuration settings that you specified in the backup task properties dialog box. These values determine when and how often the task runs. The Backup SMS Site Server task also reads input from the Smsbkup.ctl control file. Another file that can be included in the backup cycle is the Afterbackup.bat batch file. You can edit these two files to customize the backup operation to fit your site backup needs.

The effect of the backup task

When the Backup SMS Site Server task runs, it interferes with regular site server activity. Most administrative functions will be unavailable, but clients will still function properly. To properly back up a site, the Backup SMS Site Server task stops the following basic site services:

- SMS_SITE_COMPONENT_MANAGER
- SMS_EXECUTIVE
- SMS_SQL_MONITOR

Without these services running on the site server, data arriving from clients is not processed. Also, you cannot perform some regular site operations. For example, you cannot:

- Troubleshoot client computers.
- Advertise new programs.
- Distribute new packages.
- Create new software metering rules.

Demonstration: How to Configure the Backup SMS Site Server Task

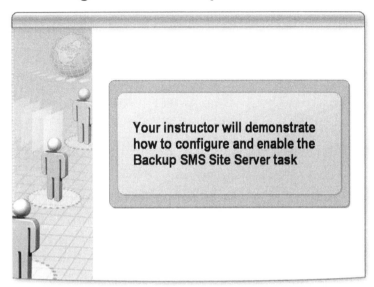

In this demonstration, your instructor will show you how to configure the Backup SMS Site Server task.

Your instructor will use the following values in this demonstration.

Variable	Value
Virtual machine—SMS Site 1	Dublin
Dublin Administrator	JaePa (Jae Pak)
Virtual machine—domain controller	Glasgow
Domain administrator	Administrator

Important These steps are included for your information. Do not attempt to perform them in the classroom. If you perform these steps in the classroom environment, you might leave your computer in an incorrect state for upcoming practices.

Demonstration steps performed by instructor only

▶ **To configure the Backup SMS Site Server task**

1. Verify that the Glasgow and Dublin virtual machines are running.

2. On the Dublin virtual machine, click **Start**, point to **All Programs**, point to **Systems Management Server**, and then click **SMS Administrator Console**.

3. In the console tree of the SMS Administrator console, expand **Site Database (001 – NWTraders)**, expand **Site Hierarchy**, expand **001 – NW Traders**, expand **Site Settings**, expand **Site Maintenance**, and then click **Tasks**.

4. In the details pane, right-click **Backup SMS Site Server**, and then click **Properties**.

5. In the **Backup SMS Site Server Task Properties** dialog box, select the **Enable this task** check box.

6. In the **Backup destination** box, type **C:\SMSSiteBackup**

7. In the **Schedule** area, in the **Start after** box, enter a time that is three minutes past the current system time.

   For example, if the current system time is 2:00 P.M., set the **Start after** time to 2:03 P.M.

   Note   Refer to the system clock on the taskbar of the Dublin virtual machine to find the current system time.

   ---

8. In the **Latest start time** box, enter a time that is one hour after the **Start after** time.

   For example, if the **Start after** time is 2:03 P.M., set the **Latest start time** to 3:03 P.M.

9. Select *today's day* as the day of week, and then click **OK**.

10. In the details pane, verify that the **Backup SMS Site Server** task is enabled.

11. Close the SMS Administrator console.

12. Leave the Glasgow and Dublin virtual machines running.

Additional Tasks to Perform After a Site Backup

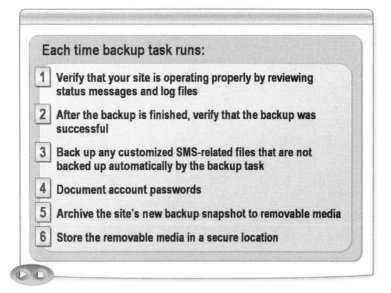

Each time the backup task runs, you should perform some additional tasks. These additional tasks are as follows:

1. Verify that the site backup started and completed successfully by reviewing status messages on the site server for components such as SMS_SQL_MONITOR and SMS_SITE_BACKUP. You can also view log files such as Smsdbmon.log or Smsbkup.log, to verify that the site backup started and completed successfully, or to troubleshoot any problems.

2. After the backup operation is finished, verify that the backup destination folder contains the backed up SMS database, registry, and inboxes.

3. Back up any customized SMS-related files that are not backed up automatically by the backup task.

4. Document account passwords.

5. Archive the site's new backup snapshot to removable media.

6. Store the removable media in a secure location.

Infrequently performed backup tasks

The following two tasks do not have to be performed each time the backup task runs, but they should be completed occasionally to ensure successful backups.

1. Perform a live recovery test by using the site's backup snapshot in a test environment.

2. Manually back up site data that the backup task does not back up.

   - Whenever there are changes to the passwords of accounts such as the Client Push Installation account, Site Address account, Site System Connection account, or Advanced Client Network Access account, you should note that change. This is important because you must be able to reenter these passwords during a site recovery operation.

   - If you use system tools to customize SMS site security, you need to back up the security data of the site.

Practice: Performing an SMS Site Backup

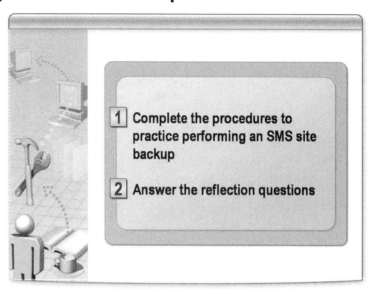

1 Complete the procedures to practice performing an SMS site backup

2 Answer the reflection questions

Instructions

Complete the procedures to practice performing an SMS site backup, and then answer the reflection question that follows. As part of this practice, you will:

- Modify the backup task to wait 15 seconds longer for SMS site services to shut down.

- Configure the Backup SMS Site Server maintenance task to back up the site and site database to a folder on the site server.

- Configure the Backup SMS Site Server task to start in three minutes.

- Monitor the backup process by viewing the Smsbkup.log and the delivery of material to the backup folder.

- Verify the results of the Backup control file modification in the backup log.

In this practice, use the following values.

Variable	Value
Virtual machine—SMS Site 1	Dublin
Dublin Administrator	JaePa (Jae Pak)
Virtual machine—domain controller	Glasgow
Domain administrator	Administrator

Procedures

▶ **To modify the backup task to wait 15 seconds longer for SMS site services to shut down**

1. Verify that the Glasgow and Dublin virtual machines are running.

2. On the Dublin virtual machine, click **Start**, and then click **Windows Explorer**.

3. In Windows Explorer, browse to **C:\SMS\inboxes\ smsbkup.box**.

4. Right-click the **smsbkup.ctl** file and then click **Open**.

   If a Windows dialog box appears that says "Windows cannot open this file: smsbkup.ctl," click **Select the program from a list**, and then click **OK**. In the **Open With** dialog box, select **Notepad**, and then click **OK**.

5. On the **Edit** menu, click **Find**.

6. In the **Find what** box, type **Add custom commands here:** and then click **Find Next**.

   Notepad finds the first instance of this text.

7. Click **Cancel** to close the **Find** dialog box.

8. Under **Add custom commands here**, review the statement **sleep 30**.

Note   Do not confuse the **sleep 30** statement with the # **sleep 30** (**Maximum 900 sec = 15 minutes**) comment.

---

9. Change the **sleep 30** statement to **sleep 45**.

10. On the **File** menu, click **Save**.

11. Close Smsbkup.ctl, and then close Windows Explorer.

▶ **To configure the Backup maintenance task to start in three minutes**

1. On the Dublin virtual machine, click **Start**, point to **All Programs**, point to **Systems Management Server**, and then click **SMS Administrator Console**.

2. In the console tree of the SMS Administrator console, expand **Site Database (001 – NWTraders)**, expand **Site Hierarchy**, expand **001 – NW Traders**, expand **Site Settings**, expand **Site Maintenance**, and then click **Tasks**.

3. In the details pane, right-click **Backup SMS Site Server**, and then click **Properties**.

4. In the **Backup SMS Site Serer Task Properties** dialog box, select the **Enable this task** check box.

5. In the **Backup destination** box, type **C:\SMSSiteBackup**

6. In the **Schedule** area, in the **Start after** box, enter a time that is three minutes past the current system time.

   For example, if the current system time is 2:00 P.M., set the **Start after** time to 2:03 P.M.

Note   Refer to the system clock in the taskbar of the Dublin virtual machine to find the current system time.

---

7. In the **Latest start time** box, enter a time that is one hour after the **Start after** time.

   For example, if the **Start after** time is 2:03 P.M., set the **Latest start time** to 3:03 P.M.

8. Select *today's date* as the day of the week.

9. Click **OK**.

10. In the details pane, verify that the **Backup SMS Site Server** task is enabled.

11. Close the SMS Administrator console.

Note   You might need to wait four minutes or more before you can successfully continue the practice. You are waiting for the SMS Site Backup service (Smsbkup.exe) to start, stop other SMS services, restart SMS services, and exit.

▶ **To monitor the backup process by viewing the Smsbkup.log and the delivery of material into the backup folder**

1. On the Dublin virtual machine, click **Start**, point to **All Programs**, point to **SMS 2003 Toolkit 1**, and then click **SMS Trace**.

2. On the **File** menu, click **Open**.

3. In the **Open** dialog box, select **smsbkup.log**, and then click **Open**.

4. Verify that the files and folders in C:\SMS\INBOXES were backed up.

Note   Be sure to note the backup destination folder for C:\SMS\INBOXES.

---

5. Verify that the \\DUBLIN\H_KEY_LOCAL_MACHINE\Software\ Microsoft\SMS registry key was backed up.

Note   Be sure to note the backup destination file for the registry key.

---

6. Verify that the site database SMS_001 was backed up.

Note   Be sure to note the backup destination file for the site database.

---

7. On the Dublin virtual machine, click **Start**, and then click **Windows Explorer**.

8. In the Windows Explorer tree hierarchy, expand **My Computer**, expand **Local Disk (C:)**, expand **SMSSiteBackup**, and then expand **001Backup**.

9. Verify that the SMS inboxes, SMS registry key, and SMS site database were backed up.

   Refer to the Smsbkup.log file for the backup destination folders and files.

10. Close Windows Explorer.

11. Leave SMS Trace open.

▶ **To verify results of the backup control file modification in the backup log**

1. On the Dublin virtual machine, in SMS Trace, click **Tools**, and then click **Highlight**.

2. In the **Highlight** dialog box, type **Slept for 45 seconds** and then click **OK**.

3. Verify that the text is highlighted in the log file.

4. Close SMS Trace.

▶ **To verify backup task status messages**

1. On the Dublin virtual machine, click **Start**, point to **All Programs**, point to **Systems Management Server**, and then click **SMS Administrator Console**.

2. In the console tree of the SMS Administrator console, expand **Site Database (001 – NWTraders)**, expand **System Status**, expand **Site Status**, expand **001 – NWTraders**, and then click **Component Status**.

Note   Since the Paris virtual machine is not running, SMS LAN_SENDER will report errors.

---

3. In the **Components** list, right-click **SMS_SITE_BACKUP**, point to **Show Messages**, and then click **All**.

4. In the SMS Status Message Viewer for <001> <NWTraders>, review the status messages to confirm that the site server and site database were successfully backed up. Of particular interest are the messages with IDs of 5009, 5011, 5013, and 5035.

5. Close the SMS Status Message Viewer and the SMS Administrator console.

6. Leave the Glasgow and Dublin virtual machines running.

Reflection question   You want to determine how long the SMS site is inoperable while the Backup SMS Site Server task is running. How can you do that?

_____

_____

_____

Lesson: Recovering an SMS Site

* The Process of Recovering an SMS Site
* Considerations for Preparing to Recover from Failure
* What Is the SMS Recovery Expert?
* Demonstration: How to Generate a Site Repair Plan
* What Is the SMS Site Repair Wizard?
* What the SMS Site Repair Wizard Does With Reference Sites
* Demonstration: How to Recover a Site from a Site Backup Snapshot
* The Role of Site Reset in the Recovery Process
* Demonstration: How to Reset an SMS Site

In this lesson, you will learn how to use the SMS Recovery Expert to document the steps that are necessary to restore an SMS site.

Lesson objectives

After completing this lesson, you will be able to:

■ Explain the process of recovering an SMS site.

■ Prepare for recovery from failure.

■ Describe the purpose of the SMS Recovery Expert.

■ Generate a site repair plan.

■ Describe the purpose of the SMS Site Repair Wizard in recovering an SMS site.

■ Recover from a site backup.

■ Explain the role of SMS site reset in the recovery process.

■ Reset an SMS site.

The Process of Recovering an SMS Site

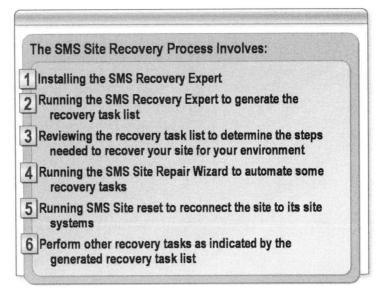

The process of recovering an SMS site involves using two recovery tools: the SMS Recovery Expert and the SMS Site Repair Wizard. The SMS Recovery expert helps identify what needs to be done to recover the site.

SMS Site Recovery involves the following tasks:

1. Installing the SMS Recovery Expert.

2. Running the SMS Recovery Expert to generate the recovery task list.

3. Reviewing the recovery task list to determine the steps needed to recover your site for your environment.

4. Running the SMS Site Repair Wizard to automate some recovery tasks.

5. Running SMS site reset to reconnect the site to its site systems.

6. Performing other recovery tasks as indicated by the generated recovery task list.

Considerations for Preparing to Recover from Failure

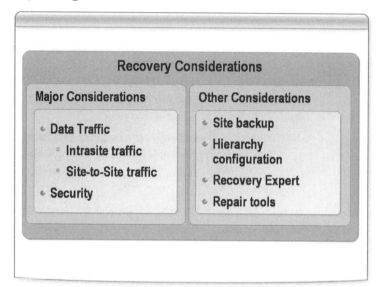

The two main things you should think about when preparing for a site recovery are data traffic and security issues.

Data traffic considerations

You must think about data traffic to ensure that data throughput issues are managed. The two types of data traffic that you must account for are:

- *Intrasite data traffic*. Clients continue to generate hardware and software inventory data, discovery data records, and status messages. This data is usually forwarded to client access points (CAPs) or management points, and then to the site server. Even while the site server is offline, clients forward this data to CAPs and management points.

- *Site-to-site traffic*. Sites will accumulate large amounts of data and transactions that need to be forwarded up and down the hierarchy, and then transmit when the inbound share becomes available to receive files. This traffic includes some client traffic, such as Discovery Data Records (DDRs) that are queued for transmission up the hierarchy.

Security considerations

Under certain conditions, security must be planned to prevent mismatched keys from preventing access to the site. There are some security issues involved in a recovery operation if all the following conditions exist:

- The site is part of a hierarchy.

- The site is configured with advanced security.

- The site cannot access the System Management container in the Active Directory® directory service.

- The site recovery involves reinstallation of the operating system.

When reinstalling the operating system, the site's original private and public keys are lost, and new keys are generated. The new public and private keys will no longer match the original public and private keys that the other sites have for the recovered site. In this situation, the site cannot access the System Management container to resynchronize the keys. The mismatched keys prevent communication between the recovered site and its parent, and between the recovered site and its child sites. To resynchronize the keys, use the Hierarchy Maintenance Utility (Preinst.exe). For information about using the Hierarchy Maintenance Utility, see SMS Administrator Help.

Other recovery preparations

There are other recovery preparations that need to be considered, and even though they do not have the same impact as traffic or security issues, they are still pertinent to your recovery operation. Additional considerations include:

- *Site backup*. If you have been regularly backing up the site, then ensure that:

  - You can access the most recent backup snapshot.

  - The log file of the most recent site backup operation indicates that the site was backed up successfully.

  - If any integrity tests were performed to ensure the integrity of the site's backup snapshot (such as a DBCC test), log files indicate that these tests have passed successfully.

  - The site backup task is not scheduled to run during the recovery operation.

- *Hierarchy configuration*. Gather information about your organization's hierarchy configuration.

- *Recovery Expert*. Ensure that the SMS Recovery Expert Web site is set up and that you can connect to that site and run the SMS Recovery Expert.

- *Repair tools*. Ensure that you can run the rest of the recovery and repair tools from the failing site, or from a remote server.

What Is the SMS Recovery Expert?

The SMS Recovery Expert is a Web-based recovery tool

Recovery scenarios:

- Rebuilding failed servers
- Restoring site data
- Repairing and re-synchronizing data
- Verifying the success of the recovery by testing the functionality of the recovered site

---

The *SMS Recovery Expert* is a Web-based recovery tool that guides you through a site recovery operation. Once installed locally, the SMS Recovery Expert Web site, found at http://<*servername*>/SMSRecoveryExpert/, is the Web site where you access the Recovery Expert. You can use it to help you recover from a site failure and to help develop a recovery plan before a site failure occurs.

When you run the SMS Recovery Expert, it scrolls through a series of Web pages that require responses to questions about the site failure scenario and the site configuration. The SMS Recovery Expert then evaluates your answers and presents a recovery task list. Perform these tasks, in the order that they are prescribed, to recover the failed site or the failed site system.

Note The SMS Recovery Expert can also be used to help recover sites and site systems in SMS 2.0.

Recovery activities

The SMS Recovery Expert Web pages provide assistance in the following activities:

- Rebuilding failed servers.
- Restoring site data.
- Repairing and re-synchronizing data.
- Verifying the success of the recovery by testing the functionality of the recovered site.

Demonstration: How to Generate a Site Repair Plan

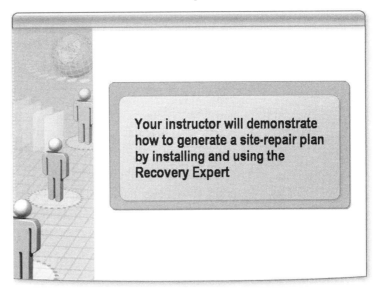

In this demonstration, your instructor will show you how to generate a site-repair plan by installing and using the Recovery Expert.

Your instructor will use the following values in this demonstration.

Variable	Value
Virtual machine—SMS Site 1	Dublin
Dublin Administrator	JaePa (Jae Pak)
Virtual machine—domain controller	Glasgow
Domain administrator	Administrator
Virtual machine—SMS Site 2	Paris
Paris Administrator	DonHa (Don Hall)

Important These steps are included for your information. Do not attempt to perform them in the classroom. If you perform these steps in the classroom environment, you might leave your computer in an incorrect state for upcoming practices.

Demonstration steps performed by instructor only

▶ **To install the Recovery Expert**

1. Verify that the Glasgow and Dublin virtual machines are running.

2. Log the Paris virtual machine on to the NWTRADERS domain with a user name of **DonHa** and a password of **P@ssw0rd**.

   After the Paris virtual machine opens, you can minimize it.

   Note   You will not actually be working on the Paris virtual machine; however, to complete this procedure you need to access Autorun.exe on the Paris virtual machine, and then run it from the Dublin virtual machine.
   ---

3. On the Dublin virtual machine, click **Start**, and then click **Run**.

4. In the **Run** dialog box, type **\\PARIS\C$\2596\SMS\AUTORUN.EXE** and then click **OK**.

5. In the **File Download** dialog box, click **Open**.

6. In the **Systems Management Server 2003 Setup** dialog box, click **Recovery Expert**.

7. In the **File Download** dialog box, click **Open**.

8. On the SMS Recovery Expert Web site Installation page, click **Next**.

9. On the **License Agreement** page, click **Next**.

10. On the **Select Destination Directory** page, click **Next**.

11. On the **Ready to Install** page, click **Next**.

12. On the **Installation Completed!** page, click **Finish**.

    The **Recovery Expert Entry** page appears.

▶ **To use the Recovery Expert to generate a site-repair plan**

1. On the Dublin virtual machine, on the **Recovery Expert Entry Page** page, click **Use The Recovery Expert**.

2. Under **Which version of SMS was installed on the site being recovered**, verify that **SMS 2003** is selected.

3. Under **Which system in your SMS Site failed?**, select the **SMS Site Server** check box, and then click **Submit**.

4. Under **Was the site being recovered a Primary or Secondary site?**, verify that **Primary Site** is selected.

5. Under **Was the site being recovered part of a hierarchy?**, select the **Was Part of a Hierarchy** check box.

6. Under **Did the site being recovered have a Parent or Child sites?**, select the **Had one or more Secondary Child sites** check box.

7. Click **Submit**.

8. Under **How was your site being recovered configured when it failed?**, select the following check boxes:

   - **Had an SMS Backup**

   - **Site was configured to use Advanced Security**

   - **Site used Advanced Client**

   - **Advertised Programs client agent was enabled**

   - **Hardware Inventory and/or Software Inventory agent was enabled**

9. Under **What is still accessible on the site being recovered?**, do not select any check boxes.

   You are leaving these options cleared because you want to generate a repair plan based on a site-failure scenario.

10. Click **Submit**.

11. Under **Will you use the Repair Wizard?**, select the **The Repair Wizard will be used** check box.

12. Click **Submit**.

    The Site Recovery Task List appears. Review the Prepare, Rebuild, Restore, Repair, and Troubleshooting tasks. You can then review the tasks that the SMS Site Repair Wizard will automatically perform.

13. Close the Site Recovery Task List.

14. In the **Systems Management Server Setup** dialog box, click **Exit**.

15. On the Paris virtual machine, on the **Action** menu, click **Close**.

16. Verify that **Save state and save changes** is selected in the drop-down list, and then click **OK**.

    The Paris virtual machine begins to shut down.

17. Leave the Glasgow and Dublin virtual machines running.

What Is the SMS Site Repair Wizard?

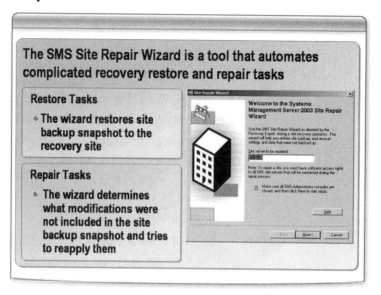

The *SMS Site Repair Wizard* is a tool that automates complicated recovery tasks. You can use the SMS Site Repair Wizard to simplify site recovery, increase the amount of data recovered, save time, and reduce the risks associated with recovery.

The SMS Site Repair Wizard is used in conjunction with the SMS Recovery Expert during a site-recovery operation. Using the SMS Site Repair Wizard during site recovery is strongly recommended. Each recovery task in the SMS Recovery Expert contains a note stating whether it can be automated by using the SMS Site Repair Wizard.

Stages of the SMS Site Repair Wizard

The following table shows what the SMS Site Repair Wizard does during the two main tasks of recovery and identifies which data is recovered in each.

Stage	Recovered data
Restore tasks	The wizard restores the site backup snapshot to the recovery site
Repair tasks	The wizard determines what modifications were not included in the site backup snapshot and tries to reapply them

What the SMS Site Repair Wizard Does with Reference Sites

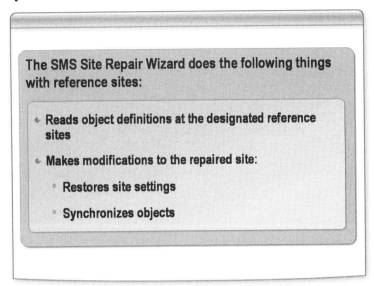

The SMS Site Repair Wizard does the following things with reference sites:

- Reads object definitions at the designated reference sites
- Makes modifications to the repaired site:
  - Restores site settings
  - Synchronizes objects

Reference sites are lower-level primary sites to which objects from a failing site were replicated. The SMS Site Repair Wizard reads object definitions at the designated reference sites and then uses those definitions to recreate the missing objects at the site being recovered.

The wizard can restore all SMS objects, such as collections, packages, programs, advertisements, and software metering rules, which were created before the last site backup. After restoring the site backup snapshot, the SMS Site Repair Wizard attempts to use reference child sites to restore, as much as possible, the data that was not backed up. From those reference sites, SMS can recover objects such as collections based on query rules, packages, programs, and advertisements, but it cannot restore data such as software metering rules, reports, custom queries, or direct membership rules in collections. The SMS Site Repair Wizard restores data by restoring site settings and synchronizing site objects with parent and child sites.

Modifications performed by the SMS Site Repair Wizard

The SMS Site Repair Wizard makes modifications to the repaired site to make sure that it operates well within its hierarchy. The modifications the SMS Site Repair Wizard makes are as follows:

- *Restores site settings*. The wizard prompts the user to input any changes to site settings that occurred after the most recent site backup. The SMS Site Repair Wizard then restores site settings according to the user input.

- *Synchronizes objects*. The SMS Site Repair Wizard restores control to collections based on query rules, packages, programs, and advertisements that were created on the failing site after the most recent backup and before the site failed. The wizard deletes objects at the recovering site that were inherited from upper-level sites but were then deleted at the originating site. Resynchronization helps prevent data corruption in the SQL database and site server registry by adjusting SMS object IDs and serial numbers.

Demonstration: How to Recover a Site from a Site-Backup Snapshot

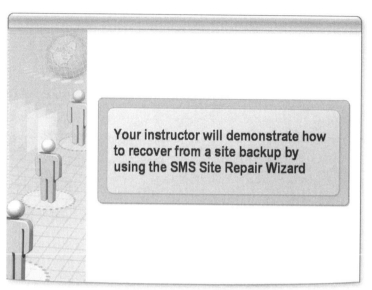

In this demonstration, your instructor will show you how to recover a site from a site-backup snapshot by running the SMS Site Repair Wizard. Your instructor will use the site backup created in the demonstration titled "How to Configure the Backup SMS Site Server Task," which appeared earlier in this module.

Your instructor will use the following values in this demonstration.

Variable	Value
Virtual machine—SMS Site 1	Dublin
Dublin Administrator	JaePa (Jae Pak)
Virtual machine—domain controller	Glasgow
Domain administrator	Administrator

Important   These steps are included for your information. Do not attempt to perform them in the classroom. If you perform these steps in the classroom environment, you might leave your computer in an incorrect state for upcoming practices.

Demonstration steps performed by instructor only

▶ **To recover a site from a site-backup snapshot by running the SMS Site Repair Wizard**

1. Verify that the Glasgow and Dublin virtual machines are running.

2. On the Dublin virtual machine, click **Start**, point to **All Programs**, point to **Systems Management Server**, and then click **SMS Site Repair Wizard**.

3. On the **Welcome to the Systems Management Server 2003 Site Repair Wizard** page, verify that Dublin appears in the **Site Server to be repaired** box, and then click **Next**.

4. On the **Access Rights and Permissions Required** page, click **Next**.

5. On the **Site Restore Steps** page, verify that **Restore from** is selected, type **C:\SMSSiteBackup** in the **Restore From** box, and then click **Next**.

6. On the **Restore Database** page, verify that **Restore the database from SMS backup** is selected, and then click **Next**.

   A site-repair process occurs. This will take a couple of minutes while services are stopped, data is restored, and files are copied.

7. On the **Site Backup and Failure Dates** page, click **Next**.

8. On the **Parent Site Setting** page, verify that **Central site** is selected, and then click **Next**.

9. On the **Verify Site Hierarchy** page, in the **Site hierarchy** list, verify that the primary and secondary sites are displayed, and then click **Next**.

10. On the **Objects Created After Backup** page, click **Next**.

11. On the **Package Recovery** page, click **Next**.

12. On the **Completing the Systems Management Server 2003 Site Repair Wizard** page, click **Finish**.

    A site repair process occurs. This will take a couple of minutes.

13. Close the SMS Site Repair Wizard.

14. Leave the Glasgow and Dublin and virtual machines running.

The Role of Site Reset in the Recovery Process

With SMS site reset, you can perform the following tasks:

• Repair a damaged site server

• Make account or password changed effective

• Force the site to use a different SQL Server database name, a different server running SQL Server, or a different SQL Server security mode

SMS site reset is used to do the following:

■ Repair a damaged site server.

■ Make account or password changes effective.

■ Force the site to use a different SQL Server database name, a different server running SQL Server, or a different SQL Server security mode.

SMS site reset stops the core SMS site services, removes them, and then reinstalls them. Site reset involves running the SMS Setup Wizard and selecting the **Modify or reset the current installation** option to initiate configuration changes in an SMS site. During site reset, changes specified while running the SMS Setup Wizard are written to the master site control file. SMS components and threads are removed from site servers and site systems and then reinstalled. Site reset is a required step in the site-recovery process because it allows the recovered site server to reconnect to its site systems.

Site reset automatically changes the passwords for some accounts if your site is running in standard security mode, such as the default SMS Client Connection Account and the SMS Remote Service Account, which is the account used by the service that runs on some site-system roles, such as CAPs, that are enabled on servers other than the site server.

You can use site reset to change passwords for the SMS Service Account if the site is running in standard security mode. You can also reset the account that the site uses to connect to the SQL Server site database.

Demonstration: How to Reset an SMS Site

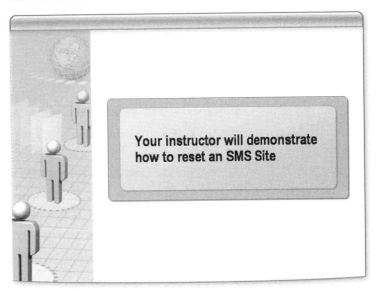

In this demonstration, your instructor will show you how to reset an SMS site.

Your instructor will use the following values in this demonstration.

Variable	Value
Virtual machine—SMS Site 1	Dublin
Dublin Administrator	JaePa (Jae Pak)
Virtual machine—domain controller	Glasgow
Domain administrator	Administrator

Important These steps are included for your information. Do not attempt to perform them in the classroom. If you perform these steps in the classroom environment, you might leave your computer in an incorrect state for upcoming practices.

Demonstration steps performed by instructor only

▶ **To reset an SMS site**

1. Verify that the Glasgow and Dublin virtual machines are running.

Note   On the Dublin virtual machine, verify that the SMS Administrator console is *closed*.

---

2. On the Dublin virtual machine, click **Start**, point to **All Programs**, point to **Systems Management Server**, and then click **SMS Setup**.

3. On the **Welcome to the Microsoft Systems Management Server Setup Wizard** page, click **Next**.

4. On the **System Configuration** page, click **Next**.

5. On the **Setup Options** page, click **Modify or reset the current installation**, and then click **Next**.

6. On the **SMS Security Information** page, click **Next**.

7. On the **Database Modification** page, click **Next**.

8. On the **Authentication mode for SMS Site Database** page, click **Next**.

9. On the **Completing the Systems Management Server Setup Wizard** page, click **Finish**.

10. In the **Warning** message box, click **Yes**.

11. After the site reset completes, the **System Management Server Setup Wizard** dialog box appears to confirm that the site was successfully reconfigured. Click **OK**.

12. Close all open windows.

13. Leave the Dublin and Glasgow virtual machines running for the course review.

Practice: Recovering an SMS Site

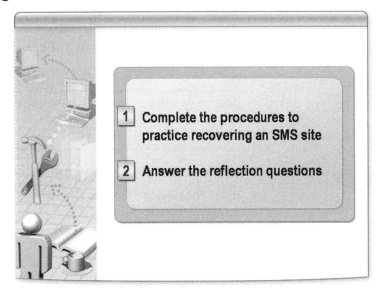

Instructions

Complete the procedures to practice recovering an SMS site, and then answer the reflection question that follows.

In this practice, use the following values.

Variable	Value
Virtual machine—SMS Site 1	Dublin
Dublin Administrator	JaePa (Jae Pak)
Virtual machine—domain controller	Glasgow
Domain administrator	Administrator
Virtual machine—SMS Site 2	Paris
Paris Administrator	DonHa (Don Hall)

Procedures

▶ **To install and use the SMS Recovery Expert**

1. Verify that the Glasgow and Dublin virtual machines are running.

2. Log the Paris virtual machine on to the NWTRADERS domain with a user name of DonHa and a password of **P@ssw0rd**.

   After the Paris virtual machine opens, you can minimize it.

Note   You will not actually be working on the Paris virtual machine; however, to complete this procedure you need to access Autorun.exe on this virtual machine, and then run it from the Dublin virtual machine.

---

3. On the Dublin virtual machine, click **Start**, and then click **Run**.

4. In the **Run** dialog box, type **\\PARIS\C$\2596\SMS\AUTORUN.EXE** and then click **OK**.

5. In the **File Download** dialog box, click **Open**.

6. In the **Systems Management Server 2003 Setup** dialog box, click **Recovery Expert**.

7. In the **File Download** dialog box, click **Open**.

8. On the SMS Recovery Expert Web site Installation page, click **Next**.

9. On the **License Agreement** page, click **Next**.

10. On the **Select Destination Directory** page, click **Next**.

11. On the **Ready to Install** page, click **Next**.

12. On the **Installation Completed!** page, click **Finish**.

    The **Recovery Expert Entry** page appears.

13. On the **Recovery Expert Entry Page** page, click **Use The Recovery Expert**.

14. Under **Which version of SMS was installed on the site being recovered?**, verify that **SMS 2003** is selected.

15. Under **Which system in your SMS Site failed?**, select the **SMS Site Server** check box, and then click **Submit**.

16. Under **Was the site being recovered a Primary or Secondary site?**, verify that **Primary Site** is selected.

17. Under **Was the site being recovered part of a hierarchy?**, select the **Was Part of a Hierarchy** check box.

18. Under **Did the site being recovered have a Parent or Child sites?**, select the **Had one or more Secondary Child sites** check box.

19. Click **Submit**.

20. Under **How was your site being recovered configured when it failed?**, select the following check boxes:

    - **Had an SMS Backup**

    - **Site was configured to use Advanced Security**

    - **Site used Advanced Client**

    - **Advertised Programs client agent was enabled**

    - **Hardware Inventory and/or Software Inventory agent was enabled**

21. Under **What is still accessible on the site being recovered?**, do not select any check boxes.

    You are leaving these options cleared because you want to generate a repair plan based on a site-failure scenario.

22. Click **Submit**.

23. Under **Will you use the Repair Wizard?**, select the **The Repair Wizard will be used** check box.

24. Click **Submit**.

    The Site Recovery Task List appears. Review the Prepare, Rebuild, Restore, Repair, and Troubleshooting tasks. You can then review the tasks that the SMS Site Repair Wizard will automatically perform.

25. Close the Site Recovery Task List.

26. In the **Systems Management Server Setup** dialog box, click **Exit**.

▶ **To use the SMS Site Repair Wizard**

1. On the Dublin virtual machine, click **Start**, point to **All Programs**, point to **Systems Management Server**, and then click **SMS Site Repair Wizard**.

2. On the **Welcome to the Systems Management Server 2003 Site Repair Wizard** page, verify that **Dublin** appears in the **Site Server to be repaired** box, and then click **Next**.

3. On the **Access Rights and Permissions Required** page, click **Next**.

4. On the **Site Restore Steps** page, verify that **Restore from** is selected, type **C:\SMSSiteBackup** in the **Restore From** box, and then click **Next**.

5. On the **Restore Database** page, verify that **Restore the database from SMS backup** is selected, and then click **Next**.

    A site-repair process occurs. This will take a couple of minutes while services are stopped, data is restored, and files are copied.

6. On the **Site Backup and Failure Dates** page, click **Next**.

7. On the **Parent Site Setting** page, verify that **Central site** is selected, and then click **Next**.

8. On the **Verify Site Hierarchy** page, in the **Site hierarchy** list, verify that the primary and secondary sites are displayed, and then click **Next**.

9. On the **Objects Created After Backup** page, click **Next**.

10. On the **Package Recovery** page, click **Next**.

11. On the **Completing the Systems Management Server 2003 Site Repair Wizard** page, click **Finish**.

    A site-repair process occurs. This will take a couple of minutes.

12. Close the SMS Site Repair Wizard.

▶ **To verify the results of the site repair**

1. On the Dublin virtual machine, click **Start**, point to **All Programs**, point to **SMS 2003 Toolkit 1**, and then click **SMS Trace**.

2. On the **File** menu, click **Open**.

3. Select **sms_srw.log**, and then click **Open**.

4. Verify that the site database and site files were successfully restored.

5. Close SMS Trace.

▶ **To simulate an error in the recovery process**

Note   You will run a script to simulate an error in the recovery process, and try to identify and fix the problem.

1. On the Dublin virtual machine, click **Start**, point to **All Programs**, point to **Accessories**, and then click **Windows Explorer**.

2. In Windows Explorer, browse to **C:\2596\Script**.

3. Double-click **Module12.vbs**.

4. Close Windows Explorer.

Note   Wait 15 seconds before proceeding to the next step.

5. Click **Start**, point to **All Programs**, point to **Systems Management Server**, and then click **SMS Administrator Console**.

Note   You will see an error in the SMS Administrator console. Identify and fix the problem. To begin resolving the error, consider which operating system component the SMS Administrator console uses to connect to the site database.

Note   For a comprehensive set of steps to complete this procedure, please refer to Appendix D: "Course 2596B, *Managing Microsoft Systems Management Server 2003* – Troubleshooting Practices Answer Key" on your Student Materials compact disc. Also, you must fix this problem before proceeding.

▶ **To reset the SMS site**

1. On the Dublin virtual machine, click **Start**, point to **All Programs**, point to **Systems Management Server**, and then click **SMS Setup**.

2. On the **Welcome to the Microsoft Systems Management Server Setup Wizard** page, click **Next**.

3. On the **System Configuration** page, click **Next**.

4. On the **Setup Options** page, click **Modify or reset the current installation**, and then click **Next**.

5. On the **SMS Security Information** page, click **Next**.

6. On the **Database Modification** page, click **Next**.

7. On the **Authentication mode for SMS Site Database** page, click **Next**.

8. On the **Completing the Systems Management Server Setup Wizard** page, click **Finish**.

9. On the **Warning** message box, click **Yes**.

10. After site reset completes, the **System Management Server Setup Wizard** dialog box appears to confirm that the site was successfully reconfigured. Click **OK**.

11. Close all open windows.

12. On the Paris virtual machine, on the **Action** menu, click **Close**.

13. Verify that **Save state and save changes** is selected in the drop-down list, and then click **OK**.

    The Paris virtual machine begins to shut down.

14. Leave the Dublin and Glasgow virtual machines running for the course review.

Reflection question   What are the advantages of restoring the SMS site database by using the SMS Site Repair Wizard instead of restoring it manually?

_____

_____

_____

_____

Discussion: Performing Site Maintenance, Backup, and Recovery Tasks

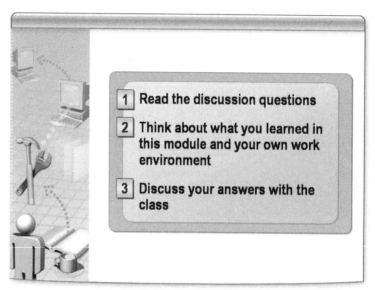

Clair Hector is the director of IT department for Northwind Traders. Jae Pak is the systems administrator in charge of managing the day-to-day operations of the network and server environment. To better understand what is needed to prepare for SMS site maintenance, backup, and recovery, Clair has asked Jae to gather information to help plan the Northwind Traders site maintenance, backup, and recovery strategy.

1. How do you determine the size of the backup database after the sp_spaceused SQL command has run?

_____

_____

_____

_____

2. Why is it important to back up an SMS site regularly, even if you do not make changes to the site?

   _____

   _____

   _____

   _____

3. Why is it important to use the SMS Recovery Expert before a site failure occurs?

   _____

   _____

   _____

   _____

4. An SMS primary site in your environment failed, and you need to recover it. The site used a management point installed on a different computer. How can you continue to use this management point after you have recovered the site?

   _____

   _____

   _____

   _____

Course Evaluation

Your evaluation of this course will help Microsoft understand the quality of your learning experience.

To complete a course evaluation, go to http://www.CourseSurvey.com.

Microsoft will keep your evaluation strictly confidential and will use your responses to improve your future learning experience.

Notes

Notes

Notes

Notes

Notes

Notes